A Guide to the
Library of Congress
Classification

Library and Information Science Text Series

A Guide to the Library of Congress Classification

Fifth Edition

Based on the Fourth Edition of
*Immroth's Guide to the
Library of Congress Classification*

Lois Mai Chan

1999
LIBRARIES UNLIMITED, INC.
Englewood, Colorado

LIBRARIES UNLIMITED, INC.
P.O. Box 6633
Englewood, CO 80155-6633
1-800-237-6124
www.lu.com

Library of Congress Cataloging-in-Publication Data

Chan, Lois Mai.
    A guide to the Library of Congress classification / by Lois Mai
Chan. -- 5th ed.
    xviii, 551 p. 17x25 cm. -- (Library and information science text series)
    "Based on the fourth edition of Immroth's Guide to the Library
of Congress classification."
    Includes bibliographical references and index.
    ISBN 1-56308-499-6 (cloth)
    ISBN 1-56308-500-3 (pbk.)
    1. Classification, Library of Congress.   I. Chan, Lois Mai.
Immroth's Guide to the Library of Congress classification. 4th ed.
II. Series.
    Z696.U4 C47 1999
    025.4'33--dc21   99-15279
                                                          CIP

In memory of
John Phillip Immroth,
who initiated this guide.

Contents

6—INDIVIDUAL CLASSES (*continued*)

Preface

A Guide to the Library of Congress Classification, initiated by John Phillip Immroth, first appeared in 1968. Since then, three revised editions have been published: the second edition (1971) by Immroth, and the third (1980) and fourth (1990) editions under the title *Immroth's Guide to the Library of Congress Classification* by Lois Mai Chan. This book is based on the fourth edition of *Immroth's Guide*. Its purpose is to continue to provide an exposition of the Library of Congress Classification and a tool for studying and for staff training in the use of the scheme.

Since 1990, several significant developments with regard to the Library of Congress Classification have taken place. With the publication of the *USMARC Classification Data*, the Library began to convert print schedules of the Classification into an electronic version based on the MARC format. In this format, all schedules and indexes that have been published in separate volumes were merged into one database. A resulting new product is a CD-ROM version called *Classification Plus*, which will eventually contain all schedules, tables, and indexes. In addition, it also contains the *Library of Congress Subject Headings* with links to the schedules where feasible. The electronic version facilitates the revision process and enables production of the print schedules from the MARC database. As a result, beginning in 1994, Library of Congress Classification print schedules have been issued in a new format with reformatting and renumbering of many of the tables used throughout the scheme. The Cataloging Policy and Support Office has also taken the opportunity to re-examine the content and structure of many of the classes and revise them where needed. In addition, the development of Class K, which has taken many years to accomplish, is now near completion.

The first chapter contains an introduction to the Library of Congress Classification and a brief history of its development. Chapters 2 to 4 set forth aspects and elements that are common throughout the scheme: chapter 2 introduces the reader to the general principles, structure, and format of the scheme; chapter 3 explains the notation; and chapter 4 discusses and illustrates the use of tables, organized by type of table according to the extent of their application in the Library of Congress Classification system, beginning with the most widely used tables. Chapter 5, on assigning Library of Congress call numbers in general, is a chapter new to this book. Chapters 6 and 7 continue the discussion of application with emphasis on individual classes and specific types of library materials.

Examples used throughout the book have been taken from recent Library of Congress MAchine-Readable Cataloging (LC MARC) records, most of which date from 1995 or later. The bibliography lists selected books and articles on the Library of Congress Classification. The appendixes contain tables that are used throughout the system and models for subarrangement of divisions and topics within disciplines.

This book is intended to be an introduction to the Library of Congress Classification. As such, it attempts to provide the reader with a basic understanding of the characteristics of the classification, the arrangement within the classes, the format of the schedules and tables, and Library of Congress policies with regard to the application of various features of the system. It is not a detailed treatment of each subclass and table. Nevertheless, the book contains sufficient details and many examples of application so that practicing classifiers may also find it useful.

The content of this book is based on the following sources: the *Outline* and schedules of the Library of Congress Classification; *Cataloging Service Bulletin*; *Subject Cataloging Manual: Classification*; *Subject Cataloging Manual: Shelflisting*; consultation with the staff of the Cataloging Policy and Support Office of the Library of Congress; LC MARC records; and books and articles on classification and subject analysis in general and on the Library of Congress Classification in particular.

In preparing this edition, I am indebted to many individuals for their assistance. I wish to acknowledge particularly Thompson A. Yee, Acting Chief, Cataloging Policy and Support Office, Library of Congress, and his staff for the many hours of consultation and invaluable comments and answers to endless questions. I wish to thank also Stella Cottam for bibliographical and research assistance. Special thanks go to Dr. Theodora Hodges for reading the entire manuscript and offering invaluable comments and suggestions. Dr. Hodges also prepared the index.

Lois Mai Chan
University of Kentucky
Lexington, Kentucky

Introduction

BACKGROUND AND EARLY DEVELOPMENT OF THE LIBRARY OF CONGRESS CLASSIFICATION

The Library of Congress (LC) Classification is the system by which the Library of Congress organizes its own collection. First articulated more than one hundred years ago, it has been updated continuously ever since. Although it was designed and developed to accommodate the Library's own extensive research collection, many other large American academic and research libraries have adopted the system for their own use; so have many general libraries. Many foreign libraries use the system as well.

There are many reasons for the system's popularity. Doubtless, one of the more important is that over the years the Library has made its cataloging data easily available to outsiders, first through printed cards and catalogs, and later—since the inception of its MARC (MAchine-Readable Cataloging) system in the late 1960s—by means of magnetic tapes and electronic distribution through networks such as OCLC Online Computer Library Center and RLIN (Research Libraries Information Network). Currently, LC MARC records are also accessible on the Internet through LOCIS (Library of Congress Information System). As a result, LC MARC records are now the backbone of most online library catalogs, including those that organize their collections by other classification systems. Furthermore, and significantly, they figure extensively in many other information retrieval systems as well.

Although in American libraries classification has been used primarily as a shelving device (offering limited subject access through shelf browsing), lately it has been proven a useful retrieval tool in online systems that offer sophisticated search options. With the wide availability of MARC records, LC classification information is increasingly being used for this purpose—in other words, the system has begun to play a new role in the overall information environment. It is therefore becoming important that all information professionals, not just those in the traditional library world, learn enough about the LC system to be able to make full and effective use of the retrieval potential inherent in LC class numbers.

The fact that all people using an information system need to know that system well to use it effectively is one of the premises that underlie this book. Another is that knowing how a system was conceived and how it developed are essential to understanding it fully. Therefore, in discussing the LC Classification—its application in bibliographical control, its potential for enhanced online retrieval—this book begins with the early history of the system and a brief account of how it has evolved to date.

Earliest Systems

The Library of Congress was established in 1800 when the American legislature was preparing to move from Philadelphia to the new capital city of Washington, D.C. Before that time, members of the U.S. Congress used libraries in New York and Philadelphia, namely, the New York Society Library and the Library Company of Philadelphia. Section five of "An Act to Make Further Provision for the Removal and Accommodation of the Government of the United States," signed by President John Adams on April 24, 1800, provided a sum of $5,000 "for the purchase of such books as may be necessary for the use of Congress and the said city of Washington, and for fitting up a suitable apartment for containing them."[1]

The first books, 740 in all, ordered from the London booksellers Cadell & Davies, reached Washington in May 1801. On January 26, 1802, "An Act Concerning the Library for the use of both Houses of Congress" was approved by Congress. It provided for a room for the Library of Congress, the establishment of suitable rules and regulations by the President of the Senate and the Speaker of the House, and the appointment of a librarian by the president. Three days later President Thomas Jefferson appointed John Beckley, the Clerk of the House, as the first Librarian of Congress.

Early on, the books were grouped by size and, within size groups, by accession number. The first catalog was issued by the Library in 1802, and the second, which shows the same arrangement, in 1804. The first recorded change in the arrangement of the collection appears in the Library's third catalog, issued in 1808, which shows added categories for special biblio-graphic forms such as plans, state laws, legislative and executive reports and papers, financial reports, and gazettes.[2]

Although book-arrangement schemes based on size and accession order were not uncommon in the early nineteenth century, subject classifica-tion schemes not only already existed but had had a long history; in fact, when Congress was housed in Philadelphia and used the collection of Benjamin Franklin's Library Company of Philadelphia, its members could approach wanted material through that library's subject classification scheme. The Philadelphia scheme, in use since 1789, had its basis in two considerably earlier schemes, Francis Bacon's system of classification and the system of classification of Jean le Rond d'Alembert.

Bacon's system, published in 1605 in his *Advancement of Learning*, was not designed as a library classification but as a way of categorizing knowledge, which Bacon divided into two broad categories: HUMAN KNOWLEDGE: "Information derived from the senses," and THEOLOGY: "Information derived from revelation." He subdivided Human Knowledge into History, Poesy, and Philosophy, based on three distinct faculties of the human mind—history coming from memory, poesy from imagination, and philosophy from reason. In 1751, when d'Alembert published his ideas on how Dénis Diderot's *Encyclopédie* might best be arranged—in short, his system for its classification—he cited his debt to Bacon.[3] However, d'Alembert made two major changes in Bacon's scheme: the first was to remove Theology from its separate location and to make it a subdivision of Philosophy; the second was to change Bacon's order of the three remaining main classes to History, Philosophy, and Poesy (or "Fine Arts" as he called Poesy).

The 1812 Library of Congress catalog showed by that time that the Library was organizing its collection on subject principles. The classifica-tion reflected in that catalog was based on the system used by the Library Company of Philadelphia; its eighteen categories were:

1. Sacred history;

2. Ecclesiastical history;

3. Civil history, including chronology, biography, antiquities, etc.;

4. Geography and topography; voyages and travels;

5. Law;

6. Ethics, or the moral system in general; theology and mythology;

7. Logic, rhetoric, and criticism;

8. Dictionaries, grammars and treatises on education;

9. General and local politics; political economy, etc.;

10. Trade and commerce;

11. Military and naval tactics;

12. Agriculture, rural economy, etc.;

13. Natural history; natural and experimental philosophy, etc.;

14. Medicine, surgery, and chemistry;

15. Poetry, and the drama; works on fiction, wit, etc.;

16. Arts and sciences, and miscellaneous literature;

17. Gazettes;

18. Maps, charts, and plans.[4]

Within classes, books were subdivided by size and arranged alphabetically.

Thomas Jefferson's System

During the War of 1812, on the night of August 24, 1814, British soldiers set fire to the Capitol, and most of the Library of Congress's collection was destroyed. Some time after, Thomas Jefferson offered to sell Congress his personal library; subsequently, in 1815, the Congress voted $23,950 to purchase Jefferson's 6,487-book library. These books were already classified by a system Jefferson had devised himself, and this classification was retained by the Library of Congress with some modifications until the end of the nineteenth century. Jefferson's system, which was also based on Bacon and d'Alembert, had forty-four main classes, or "chapters" as he called them, in three major groupings, History, Philosophy, and Fine Arts, with a final chapter for polygraphical works that could not be fitted into his other chapters. Jefferson's system is particularly interesting for his provision of subcategories, including some based on geography. Examples are:

Ch 2. Modern history, foreign, southern: General works, Italy, Rome, Florence, Naples, Venice, Spain, Portugal, France. Northern: General works, Lapland, Russia, Poland, Hungary, Sweden, Denmark, Prussia, Germany, Flanders, United Netherlands, Switzerland, Geneva, Turkey, Asia, Africa

Ch 3. Modern history, British, Scotland, Ireland

Ch 4. Modern history, American, Ante-Revolutionary: General, particular. Post-Revolutionary: General, particular. Newspapers

Ch 16. Philosophy, moral: Ethics, (1) moral philosophy, (2) law of nature and nations

Ch 19. Jurisprudence: Common law, bodies of law, statutes, courts, entries, conveyancing, criminal law, tracts, reports

Ch 24. Politics: General theories of government, special governments. Ancient. Modern. France: Monarchical, revolutionary, imperial, her colonies. England: Constitution, Parliament, dependencies. United States: Colonial, Revolutionary, reconstituted, States. Political economy: General, statistics, commerce, finance

Ch 43. Criticism. Languages, general: Polyglot, Oriental, Greek, Latin, Italian, Spanish, French, Northern, English, Welsh

Ch 44. Polygraphical.[5]

However, George Watterston, the Librarian of Congress at the time, did not use all of Jefferson's subdivisions. For example, in "Chapter 2. Modern history, foreign," Watterston arranged all the books into a single alphabet, ignoring Jefferson's geographic subdivisions.[6] Furthermore, each successive librarian made changes in the system, usually for practical reasons. Thus, although Jefferson's system provided the basic theoretical framework for what was done during the 1800s, changes and modifications during that time reflect an essentially pragmatic approach based on the needs of the collection.

Ainsworth Rand Spofford, Librarian of Congress from 1864 to 1897, made major adjustments in both classification and notation. His approach was to number shelves, grouping them by Jeffersonian chapter number and subarranging each group hierarchically. For example, 15/9456 might then mean chapter 15, Technology, shelf 9456, which was the shelf reserved for books on the subject of inter-ocean canals. Canal and river improvements in general might have an earlier number, say 15/9453. Thus, in chapter 15, Technology, shelf number 9453 would precede shelf 9456—allowing a linear display of subject matter from general to specific. In this way, Spofford's device allowed far more extensive subdivisions within each chapter than could be accommodated before. At first, his numbered shelves were fixed locations, not relative ones; however, as the collection of the Library grew and books on a given subject needed more than one shelf, the shelf number often came to denote a relative subject location rather than a physical space.[7]

THE NEW LIBRARY OF CONGRESS CLASSIFICATION

By the 1890s the Library's collection had grown from seven thousand books to nearly one million, and it became obvious that the Jeffersonian system was no longer adequate. The move to the new library building in 1897 made this fact painfully apparent. John Russell Young, Librarian of Congress at that time, instructed James C. M. Hanson, Head of the Catalogue Division, and Charles Martel, the newly appointed Chief Classifier, to study the possibilities of adopting a new classification system. In December 1897 Young gave the following advice:

> As an inflexible rule, no method of classification should be favored which would disintegrate the general collection. The Library of Congress must ultimately be the universal library of the Republic. To that end the most magnificent library edifice in the world has been erected and is destined to be, it is to be hoped, the home of America's literary and artistic genius, supplemented and strengthened by that of all lands and all time. And now, when the work of organization is in a plastic condition, before what is done hardens and consolidates and becomes difficult of undoing, no step should be taken without considering not alone what is most convenient today, but what will be most useful a hundred years from today.
>
> Therefore, in the work of classification, while each department maintains its respective character, the main purpose is the consolidation of the general library. What may be gone from its shelves to strengthen the medical or develop a law library, what may be contemplated in the way of a Congressional library of reference, can and should be replaced. But there must be no invasion of the general library's domain as one of universal reference.[8]

In tracing the initial development of the LC Classification system, Leo E. LaMontagne outlines the ideological possibilities existing at the time:

> Three main streams of thought were discernible: (1) the educational and philosophic system, which, originating in Greece, followed the development of Western thought and culminated in the French System of Jacques-Charles Brunet; (2) the seventeenth-century divisions of Francis Bacon

which, modified and adapted by d'Alembert and Jefferson, were transmitted to Melvil Dewey by Johnston and W. T. Harris; (3) the evolutionary order, in the nineteenth century, of Merlin and Lesley, which Cutter transmuted into his Expansive Classification.[9]

Two courses of action were open to the Library of Congress, LaMontagne continues: "to choose from the classification schemes already existing in printed form the one best suited to the needs of the Library; or, to build up an 'eclectic' system which would profit by the experience of other large reference libraries and utilize the best features of all existing classifications."[10]

Hanson and Martel investigated and evaluated three major published classification schemes: Melvil Dewey's *Decimal Classification*, then in its fifth edition;[11] the first six expansions of Charles Ammi Cutter's *Expansive Classification*;[12] and the *Halle Schema*[13] devised by Otto Hartwig. Some theoreticians of classification believe that it is perhaps regrettable that the Library of Congress could not adopt Dewey's *Decimal Classification* in 1898. One reason was Dewey's refusal to allow any major changes at that time; over one hundred libraries had adopted the *Decimal Classification*, and Dewey felt that it would be unfair to these libraries to allow the Library of Congress to make adjustments in his system. Furthermore, Martel criticized the *Decimal Classification* as a "system bound up in and made to fit the notation, and not the notation to fit the classification."[14] The *Halle Schema* was considered to be too strongly oriented in traditional German philosophical thought to be applicable to the Library of Congress. However, serious consideration was given to Cutter's *Expansive Classification*, perhaps in part because Cutter was quite helpful and willing to allow any necessary changes. In the end, Hanson and Martel concluded that the new classification should take Cutter's *Expansive Classification* as a guide to the order of classes but that considerable change was called for in notation.

Many years later, in 1929, Hanson recalled these early decisions:

> The situation as to classification was fully appreciated by men like Mr. Spofford and Mr. Hutcheson, and little or no opposition was made, therefore, when plans for a new system were submitted. . . . Cutter's *Expansive Classification* was selected as the chief guide, with, however, radical modifications in the notation. For instance, one, or at most two capital letters were to indicate classes, Arabic numerals in integral, not decimal sequence, with gaps (*Springende Nummer*) for subdivisions, and Cutter numbers for individual books. It was Spofford who insisted on the integral, not

decimal, sequence of numbers. Mr. Spofford was inexorably opposed to the decimal system, per se, and his opposition was shared in part by other members of the staff, including the chief of the Catalogue Division [Mr. Hanson himself], who felt that only by supplying a mixed notation and providing many radical changes would it have been possible for the Library of Congress to consider this system.[15]

Although Hanson and Martel worked intensively on a new classification, there was no immediate decision on accepting their work—probably in part due to the fact that Young's term as Librarian of Congress was coming to a close. In 1899, Herbert Putnam was appointed in his place. Putnam, then Librarian of the Boston Public Library, had been a witness at the 1896 congressional hearings on the "Condition of the Library of Congress" and his testimony at that time evidenced a strong interest in classification. Thus, at his appointment, the need for reclassifying the Library of Congress collection was again brought to the fore. In his 1899 annual report, Putnam stated:

> The present classification of the Library is but a slight expansion of that adopted by Thomas Jefferson in 1815 for his library of 6,700 volumes. It is meager, rigid, and inelastic, and unsuited to a library of a million volumes. The entire library must be reclassified.[16]

Hanson lost little time in presenting Putnam with his plans for reclassification and the development of a new classification scheme.[17] But although Putnam was strongly in favor of reclassification in general, he questioned whether the Library of Congress should develop its own system instead of adopting a nationally accepted scheme such as the *Dewey Decimal Classification*. Because of his doubts, reclassification was held up for two years. In the end, it was decided that a new system was needed, and that Hanson's proposal to develop a scheme along the lines of Cutter's *Expansive Classification* should be accepted. Reclassification continued in 1901.[18]

The Outlines of the New Classification

Before Hanson came to the Library of Congress, he had worked with Cutter's *Expansive Classification* at the University of Wisconsin Library. In developing the new classification for the Library of Congress, he was particularly influenced by two of the elements in Cutter's scheme: first, the outline (or order of classes) in its sixth expansion, and, second, the seventh expansion of his Class Z, Book Arts, which Martel used as the basis for the new Class Z, Bibliography and Library Science. For notation, Cutter used single letters for main subject classes, allowing for expansion through one or two additional letters. Instead, Hanson's outline used single letters expanded numerically. This resulted in the mixed notation of letters and numbers that was to be used for the LC Classification. The following comparison shows the parallels between Cutter's outline and Hanson's 1899 outline.

Cutter's Outline[19]		Hanson's First Outline (1899)[20]		
A	Reference and General Works	A	1-200	Polygraphy; Encyclo-pedias; General Periodi-cals; Societies &c.
B	Philosophy	A	201-3000	Philosophy
BR	Religion & Religions (except the Christian and Jewish)	A	3001-B9999	Religion; Theology; Church history
C	Christian and Jewish religions			
D	Ecclesiastical history			
E	Biography	C	1-9999	Biography; and studies auxiliary to history
F	History and subjects allied	D	1-9999	General history; periods; and local (except Amer-ica) with Geography
		E-F		America; history and geography
G	Geography and travels	G		Geography; general; and allied studies (e.g. Anthro-pology and Ethnology)
H	Social sciences	H	1-2000	Political science
		H	2001-9999	Law
I	Sociology	I	1-8000	Sociology

Outline continues on page 10.

Cutter's Outline		Hanson's First Outline (1899)		
J	Government, Politics			
K	Legislation. Law. Women. Societies	I	8001-9999	Women; Societies, clubs etc.
		J	1-2000	Sports; amusements
		J	2001-9999	Music
		K		Fine arts
		L-M		Philology & Literature
L	Science in general, and Physical sciences Includes Science and Arts (treated in the same book), Science (general works), Mathematics, Physics, Chemistry, Astronomy	N		Science; Mathematics; Astronomy; Physics; Chemistry
M	Natural history in general, Microscopy, Geology, Biology	O		Natural history; general; Geology
N	Botany	P		Zoology; Botany
O	Zoology			
Q	Medicine	Q		Medicine
R	Useful arts in general, Metric arts, Extractive and Productive arts, Chemical and Electrical arts, Domestic economy	R		Useful arts; Agriculture
S	Engineering & Building	S		Manufactures

Cutter's Outline		Hanson's First Outline (1899)	
T	Manufactures and Handicrafts	T	Engineering
U	Defensive and Preservative arts	U	Military, Naval science; light houses; life saving; fire extinction
V	Recreative arts: Sports, Theatre, Music	V-Y	Special collections
W	Fine Arts		
X	Language		
Y	Literature		
YF	Fiction		
Z	Book arts	Z	Bibliography (Book arts)

Cutter's outline demonstrates that the order of his main classes shows no direct relationship to the systems of Bacon or d'Alembert, but instead embodies the "evolutionary" order stated by Merlin and Lesley.[21] Of special interest in Cutter's ordering of classes is that he fully expanded Science to a main class, separating it from both Philosophy and History, and that he also brought Technology into close proximity to Science and Medicine. The outline also reveals that Cutter's notation was not consistently hierarchical; for example, Religion begins with the double letters BR, and the single letters C and D are used as divisions of BR. However, he did provide for subject subdivisions, and he also used numbers in a consistent pattern for form and place divisions.

Hanson followed Cutter's outline of classes to a large extent in his own outline; his major change in Cutter's order was to place the arts—fine arts, music, and literature—between the social sciences and the pure and applied sciences. It can be seen, however, that his innovations in notation were extensive and significant.

Hanson further perfected this outline in 1903, and brought it to its nearly final form the following year. One point of interest is the final expansion of Classes A and B. In Hanson's first outline, A1-200 was designed for

Polygraphic works, A201-3000 for Philosophy, and A3001-B9999 for Religion. In the 1903[22] outline Philosophy was reduced by 300 numbers—it started with A501 instead of A201. In the 1904 outline Polygraphy was allotted the entire Class A and Philosophy and Religion were combined in Class B. Also in this outline, double letters were used for the first time: B-BJ for Philosophy, BL-BX for Religion and Theology, H-HA for Social Sciences in general and for Statistics, HB-HJ for Economics, HM-HX for Sociology. The decision to move to double letters represents an important advance because their use greatly increased the expansion potential of the system.

The Development of Individual Schedules

It was noted earlier that the Library of Congress had appointed Charles Martel as Chief Classifier in 1897. Martel was heavily involved in the Library's reclassification efforts from the beginning, and, for the next two decades, he bore the major part of the double burden of the development of the new system and of reclassifying existing materials under that system. Martel drafted many of the early schedules, aided by staff classifiers—among whom was Clarence W. Perley, later to become Chief Classifier and to hold that position until 1937.[23]

Class Z, Bibliography and Library Science, was chosen as the first schedule to be developed because it covered the bibliographical works necessary for the reclassification project. The next two schedules to be tackled were E-F—American history and geography—because of their particular subject relevance.

Martel prepared the first version of Class Z in 1898, taking as his pattern a revision of the seventh expansion of Cutter's Class Z: Book Arts. His outline mirrored Cutter's quite closely, although he did not use Cutter's subclasses ZA Authorship, ZB Rhetoric, ZC Branches of literature, ZY Literary history, or ZZ Selection of reading; these were to be covered in subclass PN General literature and in Class P Language and Literature. And, as was the case in Hanson's outline for the whole LC Classification, Martel used numbers instead of double letters to represent subclasses in Class Z.

Each of the individual schedules was drafted by LC subject specialists who consulted bibliographies, treatises, comprehensive histories, and existing classification schemes in initially determining the scope and content of an individual class and its subclasses. Richard S. Angell, former Chief of the Subject Cataloging Division, described their approach in a 1969 article in *Law Library Journal*:

While in general outline and sequence of topics it [the LC Classification] has affinity with earlier systems, the Library's schedules basically represent a fresh start in the design of a system for its own particular purposes. The schedules were developed one by one, by specialists working under a central direction, but with considerable independence. They were built up for the most part inductively, that is, by taking account of the collections of the Library as they existed and as they were expected to develop because of the Library's needs for comprehensive collections in all fields of knowledge.

From these origins and impulses the Library of Congress classification has developed into a comprehensive practical system for the arrangement and management of collections of books. With one obvious exception [i.e., Class K, Law] it is a complete system, embracing all of the areas of human knowledge, the various components of this universe of knowledge having been allocated to the respective schedules. The objective in the partitioning of this universe is to secure well-defined areas corresponding to the concepts by which the separate fields are taught and expounded, and on which developmental research is based. Within each area the objective is to provide an orderly and apprehendable arrangement of the volumes in an array which will make direct access to the collections useful and meaningful to qualified students and scholars, and helpful to the staff in the control and servicing of items wanted for reference or circulation. To the extent that this partitioning is successful the classification as a whole becomes a seamless garment in that each of the parts exists basically for its place in the whole structure. At the same time the size and scope of the collections give each of the parts a considerable independence and self-sufficiency within its own field. This is particularly true of the manner in which certain common elements of a general classification scheme are treated in each of the parts of ours. Geographical and chronological arrangements, for example, are framed in accordance with the needs of each subject field; that is, they are not carried out by means of a single division table as is the case in certain other classifications. This feature of the schedules has been both criticized and praised; criticized for resulting in extremely detailed and bulky individual schedules, praised for the freedom allowed in each schedule for development according to its subject field's own intrinsic structure.[24]

One main unifying factor in all the classes is the notation, which consists of letters, cardinal numbers, and Cutter numbers. Initially, single letters were used to represent main classes, with double letters introduced later for subclasses. The schedule for subclass KF, first published in 1969, was the first schedule in which triple letters were used to indicate sub-subclasses. Currently, double letters are used for subclasses in all schedules except E-F, and triple letters also figure to some extent in Classes D and K.

The publication of the individual schedules began in 1901 with Class E-F, followed by Class Z in 1902. By June 1, 1904, the schedules for Classes D, E-F, M, Q, R, S, T, U, and Z had been completed, while Classes A, C, G, H, and V were still in process. By 1948, all schedules except those for Class K had been completed and published. The schedule for subclass KF, Law of the United States, the first schedule in Class K to be published, appeared in 1969. The remaining schedules for Class K were published as they were completed. With the publication of KZ Law of Nations, the development of Class K, with respect to comparative and uniform private and public international law on the global and regional level as well as domestic law on the jurisdictional level, is complete. The remaining subclasses to be developed are KB-KBZ for theocratic legal systems.

THE FOCUS OF THE LIBRARY OF CONGRESS CLASSIFICATION

The LC Classification was never intended as an embodiment of a pervasive philosophical system for classifying knowledge per se. Instead, it was originally designed and developed for a purely practical purpose, the effective organization of the Library's own collection—as it existed at the time and as it was expected to grow. Herbert Putnam emphasized the practical orientation of the Classification when he wrote in 1901:

> The system of classification thus far applied is one devised
> from a comparison of existing schemes (including the
> "decimal" and the "expansive"), and a consideration of the
> particular conditions in this Library, the character of its
> present and probable collections, and of its probable use. It
> is assumed that the departments of history, political and
> social science, and certain others will be unusually large. It
> is assumed that investigators will be more freely admitted
> to the shelves.

The system devised has not sought to follow strictly the scientific order of subjects. It has sought rather convenient sequence of the various groups, considering them as groups of *books*, not as groups of mere subjects.[25]

Furthermore, the system was not intended for use by any library other than the Library of Congress. This original intention was recalled by Martel in 1929:

After a careful study of available schemes and of the experience of other libraries, the decision was reached that the character of its collections and the conditions of their use called for the construction of a classification designed to satisfy the library's own requirements, with no direct deference to the possible use of it by other libraries.[26]

The same intention may be discerned in the following statement taken from the Library's 1916 annual *Report*:

In contrast with the card catalogue of the Library which, owing to the sale of the printed cards, is a matter of general concern to libraries, the classification of our collections was assumed to be of concern solely to ourselves—that is to the efficient administration of this Library within itself. Upon this assumption the scheme adopted has been devised with reference (1) to the character and probable development of our own collections, (2) to its operation by our own staff, (3) to the character and habits of our own readers, and (4) to the usages in vogue here, a distinguishing feature of which is the freedom of access to the shelves granted to serious investigators.

With these considerations the resultant scheme, while organic in the sense that certain fundamentals were the basis of each schedule, is unsymmetrical, since each schedule was devised with reference to its own utilities (as applied to that particular group of material) rather than with reference to its proportionate part in an integral whole.

There was therefore no expectation that the scheme would be adopted by other libraries; much less was there any profession that it would be suited to their needs. It is, moreover, still incomplete, and various schedules sufficiently advanced for our own use are yet unavailable in printed form.

Under the circumstances the number of other libraries
that are already adopting it in whole or in part is somewhat
surprising.[27]

Literary Warrant

A classification scheme, developed with reference to extant published materials rather than on a concept of the organization of knowledge
in the abstract, is said to be a classification based on *literary warrant*. A basis
in literary warrant means that the classification has been developed with
reference to the holdings of a particular library or to what is and has been
published; based, in other words, on what the actual literature of the time
warrants. And, for the Library of Congress, literary warrant for its new Classification derived from its own collections. Of course, most of the original
scheme was based on the literary warrant of the late nineteenth and early
twentieth centuries. But with the Library's policy of continuous revision,
current literary warrant is taken into account, so that new areas are developed as needed and obsolete elements are removed or revised as is appropriate.
As Charles Bead pointed out in 1966:

> The LC classification, being completely based on the Library's
> collections, is coextensive in scope with the book stock of
> the Library of Congress. Therefore, the LC classification is
> comprehensive but not truly universal at the present time.
> Expansion of the classification is governed by and depends
> upon the acquisition of new material.[28]

In addition to its focus on its own collections, the Classification also reflects
the demands of the Library of Congress's own special uses and services.
LaMontagne cites the Library's legislative reference service as one factor
that determined the order of the individual classes in the system:

> The primary purpose of the Library, that of legislative ref-
> erence, determined their order [i.e., order of the classes].
> The Classification, therefore, although universal in scope,
> is in its organization a special library classification.[29]

It can be concluded that many of the problems in the use of the LC Classification by other libraries result from its having been designed and developed
for a single library, one with somewhat specialized collections and with particular demands made upon those collections.

INCREASING USE OF THE CLASSIFICATION

Since its adoption, the LC Classification system has been directly sponsored and supported by a permanent national government organization, the United States Library of Congress. And from the beginning, it has been used and expanded daily by the Library's classifiers. Thus the system may now be considered as a government-supported organic classification system, one in which the results of its application, that is, LC call numbers, are available worldwide through the distribution of LC cataloging records.

Furthermore, in response to the wide adoption of its system by other libraries, the Library of Congress has demonstrated increasing awareness of the needs of outside users. This is evidenced in recent revisions and in the way the Classification is developing. One step in this direction was the establishment of the Cooperative Cataloging Council in the early 1990s, under which cooperating libraries began to contribute MARC records with assigned LC Classification numbers to the LC bibliographic database. Even more significantly, in 1996, the Library began accepting proposals for new numbers from cooperating libraries; once approved, the proposed numbers become part of the scheme. Thus, gradually, the Classification has become a more universal system than was originally projected.

The publication of the *Subject Cataloging Manual: Classification*[30] and *Subject Cataloging Manual: Shelflisting*[31] is yet another manifestation of the Library's efforts to communicate its policies and practice to the many outside users of the system.

Use of the Library of Congress Classification for Organizing Internet Resources

In the 1990s, with the rapid growth of the Internet and the enormous amount of electronic resources available, there is a growing need for effective devices to organize them. Increasingly, local online systems and search engines or Internet resource directories are using hierarchically structured or classification-based schemes to organize and navigate Internet resources. Traditional classification systems have been devised and used to organize library materials. Because classification was devised in the beginning as a response to the need for organizing a large amount of knowledge and information, it may have much to offer even in the electronic environment.[32] In an attempt to provide a structured approach to Internet resources, some libraries and Internet resource directories have adopted or adapted existing schemes, such as the *Dewey Decimal Classification*, the *Library of Congress Classification*, and the *Universal Decimal Classification*. Examples of using the LC Classification for such purposes include CyberStacks, the Scout Report Signpost, T. F. Mills Home Page, and the WWW Virtual Library. Two of these are described briefly below.

CyberStacks, whose address is http://www.public.iastate.edu/ ~CYBERSTACKS/, uses the LC Classification to organize selected Internet resources in science, technology, and related areas within the Iowa State University Library system. It uses the Classification as an organizational framework. Currently, it has made use of ten main classes: G (Geography, Anthropology and Recreation), H (Social Sciences), J (Political Science), K (Law), Q (Science), R (Medicine), S (Agriculture), T (Technology), U (Military Science), and V (Naval Science). Main classes, subclasses, and their subdivisions are displayed along with notation. On the second level are the subclasses, for example, SB, SD, SF, etc. Under each subclass, ranges of numbers, such as SD561-668 (Forest Policy & Administration), are given. Finally, under each span of numbers one finds lists of resources on the particular topic with hypertext links to them. Gerry McKiernan, the creator of CyberStacks, recalls the reason for choosing the LC Classification:

> The Library of Congress classification system is a well-established scheme that has been used for generations by libraries worldwide for organizing a variety of publications and media. Within its schedules, this classification system not only denotes subject coverage and content, but information format and conceptual relationships as well. It is believed that a classification system with the features found within the Library of Congress scheme offers appropriate context and structure that can facilitate identification of relevant WWW and other Internet resources.[33]

Another example is the Scout Report Signpost, whose address is http://www.signpost.org/signpost/index.html, an Internet resource discovery service and tool provided by the Internet Scout Project to "guide the U.S. higher education community to quality electronic resources." The resources selected and cataloged in Signpost are grouped into broad disciplinary areas according to the LC Classification. Two levels of the Classification, main classes and subclasses, are displayed.

In an article summarizing the development of Signpost, Aimée D. Glassel and Amy Tracy Wells describe the use of LC Classification:

> Disciplines are assigned one- to three-lettered class codes which represent different subject areas within the LC Classification system, to form a hierarchical tree or classification system. The Browse by Library of Congress Classification

section of Signpost lists the twenty-one broad disciplines of the LC Classification. Each broad discipline is then linked to a list of subdivisions for that subject area. For example, by choosing Social Sciences (LC Classification H-HX) from the Signpost home page, a user would link to a list of all sixteen subdivisions in Social Sciences, from HA-Statistics to HX-Socialism and Communism. . . . Each subdivision contains a hypertext link to a list of the resources assigned to the respective class code.[34]

In this project, three modifications are made to the LC Classification scheme. First, only the lettered class codes of the LC Classification, without class number extensions are assigned. Secondly, to facilitate access, many items have been assigned two different class codes when the topic belongs in more than one branch of the hierarchy. Thirdly, explanatory notes to selected LC Classification descriptions are added to assist the users. The same article goes on to give the reason for choosing the LC Classification for Signpost: "Since the Internet Scout Project assists the U.S. higher education and research community, this taxonomy was chosen because it presumably requires little to no learning curve to be used by its intended audience."[35]

THE NEW INTEGRATED SYSTEM AT THE LIBRARY OF CONGRESS

In 1998, the Library of Congress announced its decision to replace its automated system, an outdated system in use since the 1960s, with the integrated system Endeavor. Although it is too early to predict what effect the new system will have on LC Classification specifically, it is safe to assume that it will affect all aspects of bibliographic control at the Library of Congress, including its classification scheme.

NOTES

1.   John Y. Cole, ed., *The Library of Congress in Perspective: A Volume Based on the Reports of the 1976 Librarian's Task Force and Advisory Groups* (New York: R. R. Bowker, 1978), 5.

2.   Leo E. LaMontagne, *American Library Classification with Special Reference to the Library of Congress* (Hamden, CT: Shoe String Press, 1961), 44-45.

3. Ibid., 32.

4. William Dawson Johnston, *History of the Library of Congress, 1800-1864* (Washington, DC: Government Printing Office, 1904), 49 and plate 29.

5. Ibid., 145-46.

6. Ibid., 148.

7. LaMontagne, *American Library Classification*, 55-56.

8. David Chambers Mearns, *The Story Up to Now, The Library of Congress, 1800-1946* (Washington, DC: Government Printing Office, 1947), 162.

9. LaMontagne, *American Library Classification*, 218.

10. Ibid., 223.

11. Melvil Dewey, *Decimal Classification and Relativ Index for Libraries, Clippings, Notes, etc.*, 5th ed. (Boston: Library Bureau, 1894).

12. Charles Ammi Cutter, *Expansive Classification. Part 1: The First Six Classifications* (Boston: C. A. Cutter, 1891-1893).

13. Halle. Universität. Bibliothek, *Schema des Realkatalogs der königlichen Universitätsbibliothek zu Halle a.S.*, ed. Otto Hartwig. *Beihefte zum Zentralblatt für Bibliothekswesen*; v. 3. (Leipzig: O. Harrassowitz, 1888).

14. LaMontagne, *American Library Classification*, 224.

15. J. C. M. Hanson, "The Library of Congress and Its New Catalogue: Some Unwritten History," in *Essays Offered to Herbert Putnam by His Colleagues and Friends on His Thirtieth Anniversary as Librarian of Congress: 5 April 1929*, ed. William Warner Bishop and Andrew Keogh (New Haven, CT: Yale University Press, 1929), 186-87.

16. Library of Congress, *Report of the Librarian of Congress* (Washington, DC: Government Printing Office, 1899), 29.

17. LaMontagne, *American Library Classification*, 227.

18. Edith Scott, "J. C. M. Hanson and His Contribution to Twentieth Century Cataloging" (Ph.D. diss., University of Chicago, 1970), 177-228.

19. Charles Ammi Cutter, *Charles Ammi Cutter: Library Systematizer*, ed. Francis L. Miksa (Littleton, CO: Libraries Unlimited, 1977), 280-82.

20. LaMontagne, *American Library Classification*, 228-29.

21. Ibid., 218.

22. Ibid., 234-36.

23. "Historical Note on the Library of Congress Classification," in Library of Congress, Office for Subject Cataloging Policy, *Subject Cataloging Manual: Classification*, 1st ed. (Washington, DC: Cataloging Distribution Service, Library of Congress, 1992), 1.

24. Richard S. Angell, "Development of Class K at the Library of Congress," *Law Library Journal* 57 (November 1964):353-54.

25. Herbert Putnam, "Manual: Constitution, Organization, Methods, etc.," in *Report of the Librarian of Congress for the Fiscal Year Ending June 30, 1901* (Washington, DC: Government Printing Office, 1901), 234.

26. Charles Martel, "The Library of Congress Classification: Some Considerations Regarding the Relation of Book or Library Classification to the 'Order of the Sciences'," in *Essays Offered to Herbert Putnam*, 327.

27. Library of Congress, *Report of the Librarian of Congress and Report of the Superintendent of Library Grounds for the Fiscal Year Ending June 30, 1916* (Washington, DC: Government Printing Office, 1916), 103.

28. Charles C. Bead, "The Library of Congress Classification: Development, Characteristics, and Structure," in *The Use of the Library of Congress Classification: Proceedings of the Institute on the Use of the Library of Congress Classification*, ed. Richard H. Schimmelpfeng and C. Donald Cook (Chicago: American Library Association, 1968), 18.

29. LaMontagne, *American Library Classification*, 253.

30. Library of Congress, Office for Subject Cataloging Policy, *Subject Cataloging Manual: Classification*, 1st ed. (Washington, DC: Cataloging Distribution Service, Library of Congress, 1992).

31. Library of Congress, Cataloging Policy and Support Office, *Subject Cataloging Manual: Shelflisting*, 2nd ed. (Washington, DC: Library of Congress, 1995).

32. Lois Mai Chan, "Classification, Present and Future," *Cataloging & Classification Quarterly* 21, no. 2 (1995):5-17.

33. Gerry McKiernan, "The New/Old World Wide Web Order: The Application of 'Neo-Conventional' Functionality to Facilitate Access and Use of a WWW Database of Science and Technology Internet Resources," *Journal of Internet Cataloging* 1, no. 1 (1997):48.

34. Aimée D. Glassel and Amy Tracy Wells, "Scout Report Signpost: Design and Development for Access to Cataloged Internet Resources," *Journal of Internet Cataloging* 1, no. 3 (1997):38.

35. Ibid., 40.

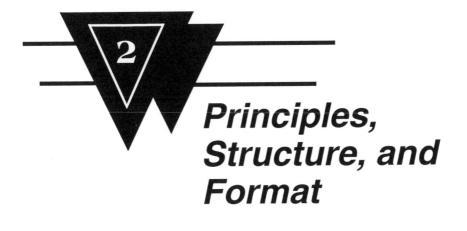

Principles, Structure, and Format

OUTLINE OF THE CLASSIFICATION

The basic outline of the Library of Congress (LC) Classification is typical of American classification systems originating in the nineteenth century. The entire field of knowledge is first divided into main classes that correspond largely to academic disciplines or areas of study. The main classes are then divided into subclasses representing branches of those disciplines. Finally, within each subclass, further subdivisions are provided to specify form, place, time, and subject (or topical) aspects. The progression is from general to specific, forming a hierarchical display of knowledge.

Certain assumptions underlay the development of the Classification. Leo LaMontagne stated its basic orientation:

> It was recognized that the classification should, in brief,
>
> 1. be oriented primarily toward the requirements of the Congress and secondarily to those of other government departments and agencies, scholars, and all other users;
>
> 2. provide for large amounts of diverse material, both scholarly and popular, for which no existing classification was adequate; and

3. afford a systematic approach to the Library's resources through the classed catalog and the arrangement of the books on the shelves.[1]

Based on these assumptions and using Cutter's *Expansive Classification* as a model, the structure of the Classification evolved to:

I.	A	General Works. Polygraphy
II.	B-P	Humanistic Disciplines and the Social Sciences
	B-BJ	Philosophy
	BL-BX	Religion
	C-F	History
	C	Auxiliary Sciences
	D	Universal and Old World
	E-F	America
	G	Geography. Anthropology. Folklore, etc.
	H-L	Social Sciences
	H	General
	HA	Statistics
	HB-HJ	Economics
	HM-HX	Sociology
	J	Political Science
	K	Law
	L	Education
	M	Music
	N	Fine Arts
	P	Language and Literature
III.	Q-V	Natural Sciences and Technology
	Q	General Science
	QA	Mathematics
	QB-QE	Physical Sciences
	QB	Astronomy
	QC	Physics
	QD	Chemistry
	QE	Geology
	QH-QR	Biological Sciences
	QH	Natural History. General Biology. Cytology
	QK	Botany
	QL	Zoology
	QM	Human Anatomy
	QP	Physiology

	QR	Bacteriology. Microbiology
	R	Medicine
	S	Agriculture
	T	Technology
	U	Military Science
	V	Naval Science
IV.	Z	Bibliography and Library Science

The rationale for the collocation of main classes and subclasses was articulated by Charles Martel:

> The concept underlying it may be stated as follows: (1. Class A) General works: Periodicals, Societies, Collections, Encyclopedic works, etc. (2. Class B) Theory, or theories, of man concerning the universe: Philosophy and Religion. (3.-6. Classes C-F) History and auxiliary sciences. (7. Class G) Geography and Anthropology: G, Descriptive and physical geography—man's abode and source of his means of subsistence; GF, Anthropogeography—man as affected by and affecting his physical milieu; GN, Physical anthropology and ethnology and Primitive or Prehistoric man; GR, Folklore, Tradition—mind and soul of man in transition from primitive to advanced culture; GT, Manners and customs; and GV, Amusements, sports, etc., related to GR; as a class, G may be therefore regarded as supplementary to History and leading to groups (8.-9. Classes H-J) Economic and Social evolution of man, (10. Class K) Law, (11. Class L) Education, and (12. Class M), (13. Class N), and (14. Class P) Fine arts and Letters—the esthetic and intellectual development and state of man. Together, classes B-P form the group of the Philosophico-historical and philological sciences. The second group embraces the Mathematico-physical, Natural, and Applied Sciences: (15. Class Q) Science, (16. Class R) Medicine, (17. Class S) Agriculture, (18. Class T) Technology, (19. Class U) Military science, and (20. Class V) Naval science. Bibliography, which in many libraries is distributed through the different classes, is kept together in the Library of Congress and forms together with Library science (21. Class Z).[2]

NOTATION

Notation for the LC Classification is a mixed system using letters in the Roman alphabet and Arabic numerals. Main classes are denoted by single capital letters with double or triple capital letters used for subclasses. Because it was assumed from the beginning that the library serving the United States Congress would possess an extensive collection in history and the social sciences, the classes in history (C through G) and in the social sciences (H through L) are given a larger amount of space within the notational structure than are the classes for natural sciences and technology (Q through V).

Within each main class or subclass, the integers 1-9999 are used for subdivisions, with many breaks (unused numbers) left for future needs. It was first decided not to use decimal numbers, but that decision was rescinded later, and decimal extensions of numbers are used where there are no available integers for new subjects.

After the first set of letter(s) and numerals in any given class number, another set follows. The latter is called a *Cutter number* and is based on the alphanumeric book numbering system devised by Charles Ammi Cutter. The Cutter number is always preceded by a period (or full stop); this denotes the fact that the numerical part of a Cutter number is treated decimally and filed accordingly, that is, .C52, .C6, .C74, .C8, etc. In the LC system, the Cutter number may be used as an extension of the class number or as an item number.

Details concerning the notation will be presented in chapters 3 and 4.

ENUMERATIVE DISPLAY

The LC Classification is essentially enumerative; that is, aspects of a subject are explicitly provided for in the schedules, as are many compound subjects. Furthermore, common subdivisions and even many form divisions are listed explicitly under each subject. In common with many other classification schemes, the LC system includes many auxiliary tables that allow for increased specificity. These are mainly used for pinpointing specific numbers within ranges of numbers provided in the schedules themselves. Such an approach differs from that followed in many other systems, for example, the *Dewey Decimal Classification*, the *Bliss Bibliographic Classification*, and the *Colon Classification*, all of which provide additional notational segments to be **attached to** a main number in order to render it more specific. Thus, there is relatively little notational synthesis in the LC system and as a result its schedules are more voluminous than those of most other systems.

GENERAL CHARACTERISTICS AND COMMON FEATURES

Because the individual schedules of the Classification have been developed separately by different groups of persons working more or less independently, the system has been called a "series of special classifications."[3] Nonetheless, there are certain unifying characteristics common to all the schedules, namely, physical format, internal arrangement of classes and subclasses, notation, and auxiliary tables. These are discussed in detail below.

Physical Format

Until 1993, the Classification was available only in a series of printed volumes. In 1993, under the supervision of Rebecca Guenther of the Network Development and MARC Standards Office, the Library of Congress began converting its classification data to machine-readable form using the USMARC Classification Format for such data.[4] Computer programs were developed so that the schedules could be produced directly from MARC classification records. As a result, the Classification is now available in several formats.

Electronic Version

The machine-readable version of the Classification is available in the Minaret software for internal use by the LC staff.

CD-ROM Version

For users outside of the Library, the machine-readable classification data have been incorporated into a desktop cataloger's workstation called *Classification Plus*,[5] which is a full-text, Windows-based CD-ROM product that is updated quarterly. *Classification Plus* also includes the full text of *Library of Congress Subject Headings*, with links between the two where appropriate. *Classification Plus* was first issued before all schedules had been converted to machine-readable form; however, more and more schedules are being added to the desktop as conversion progresses.

Classification Plus is produced with the Folio software. It can be used as a stand-alone or as part of a networked environment. It allows searching by key words, using Boolean combinations, wildcard characters, proximity, and truncation. Several files can be displayed simultaneously, allowing a user to compare data from different class schedules. It also allows browsing class numbers up and down the hierarchy.

Print Version

Until the schedules were converted to machine-readable form, they were available only in print. Printed schedules, now produced from electronic data, continue to be published.

Individual Schedules

The printed schedules of the Classification published so far comprise nearly fifty individual volumes for the main classes, subclasses, and tables. A full set of schedules contains more than ten thousand pages. The individual schedules are as follows:

A	General works
B-BJ	Philosophy. Psychology
BL,BM,BP,BQ	Religion: Religions, Hinduism, Judaism, Islam, Buddhism
BR-BV	Religion: Christianity, Bible
BX	Religion: Christian Denominations
C	Auxiliary Sciences of History
D-DJ	History (General), History of Europe, Part 1
DJK-DK	History of Eastern Europe (General). Soviet Union, Poland
DL-DR	History of Europe, Part 2
DS-DX	History of Asia, Africa, Australia, New Zealand, etc.
E-F	History: America
G	Geography. Maps. Anthropology. Recreation
H	Social Sciences
J	Political Science
K	Law (General)
KD	Law of the United Kingdom and Ireland
KDZ,KG-KH	Law of the Americas, Latin America and the West Indies

KE	Law of Canada
KF	Law of the United States
KJ-KKZ	Law of Europe
KJV-KJW	Law of France
KK-KKC	Law of Germany
KL-KWX	Law of Asia and Eurasia, Africa, Pacific Area and Antarctica
KZ	Law of Nations
K	Tables
L	Education
M	Music and Books on Music
N	Fine Arts
P-PA	Philology, Linguistics, Classical Philology, Classical Literature
PB-PH	Modern European Languages
PG	Russian Literature
PJ-PK	Oriental Philology and Literature, Indo-Iranian Philology and Literature
PL-PM	Languages of Eastern Asia, Africa, Oceania, Hyperborean, Indian, and Artificial Languages
P-PM	Supplement: Index to Languages and Dialects
PN	General Literature
PR,PS,PZ	English and American Literature, Juvenile Belles Lettres
PQ	French, Italian, Spanish, and Portuguese Literatures
PT, Part 1	German Literature
PT, Part 2	Dutch and Scandinavian Literatures
P-PZ	Language and Literature Tables
Q	Science
R	Medicine
S	Agriculture
T	Technology
U-V	Military Science. Naval Science
Z	Bibliography and Library Science

Besides these schedules, there is an outline for the entire system.

Format of Each Schedule

Because the schedules were published over the course of many decades, their formats vary depending on when they were issued. Before the print schedules were produced electronically, they had similar if not identical formats. With the electronically produced print schedules, the format was revised. Almost every schedule now includes the following sections: (1) a preface; (2) a broad outline, displaying the subclasses; (3) a detailed outline displaying a two- or three-level hierarchical structure of the classes or subclasses covered in the schedule; (4) the schedule itself, in other words the main classification; (5) any necessary auxiliary tables; and (6) a detailed index.

The following is an example of a broad outline taken from the schedule for B-BJ Philosophy. Psychology:

OUTLINE

B	PHILOSOPHY (GENERAL)
BC	LOGIC
BD	SPECULATIVE PHILOSOPHY
BF	PSYCHOLOGY. PARAPSYCHOLOGY. OCCULT SCIENCES
BH	AESTHETICS
BJ	ETHICS. SOCIAL USAGES. ETIQUETTE

The outline for each of the classes in the LC Classification is included in chapter 6 of this guide.

A small portion of the detailed outline from Class B is given below to demonstrate the greater detail represented in the outline. An outline to a schedule can be most useful to the beginning classifier, particularly because it displays whatever logical or hierarchical order is inherent in the schedule in question.

OUTLINE

B	1-5802	Philosophy (General)
	69-99	General works
	108-5802	By period
		Including individual philosophers and schools of philosophy
	108-708	Ancient
	720-765	Medieval
	770-785	Renaissance
	790-5802	Modern
	808-849	Special topics and schools of philosophy
	850-5739	By region or country
	5800-5802	By religion

BC	1-199	Logic
	11-39	History
	25-39	By period
	60-99	General works
	171-199	Special topics

BD	10-701	Speculative philosophy
	10-41	General philosophical works
	95-131	Metaphysics
	143-237	Epistemology. Theory of knowledge
	240-260	Methodology
	300-450	Ontology
		Including being, the soul, life, death
	493-701	Cosmology
		Including teleology, space and time, structure of matter, plurality of worlds

BF	1-990	Psychology
	38-64	Philosophy. Relation to other topics
	173-175.5	Psychoanalysis
	176-176.5	Psychological tests and testing
	180-198.7	Experimental psychology
	203	Gestalt psychology
	207-209	Psychotropic drugs and other substances
	231-299	Sensation. Aesthesiology
	309-499	Consciousness. Cognition
		Including learning, attention, comprehension, memory, imagination, genius, intelligence, thought and thinking, psycholinguistics, mental fatigue

The main portion of the schedule, listing the class numbers and captions, appears next. The following example contains a section of the first page of the schedule for B-BJ. It can be seen from this excerpt that a general philosophy periodical in the German language would be assigned the basic notation of "B3." A general conference on philosophy would be classed in "B20."

B	PHILOSOPHY (GENERAL)	B

Philosophy (General)
    For general philosophical treatises and introductions to philosophy, see BD1+
    Periodicals.   Serials

1.A1-A3	Polyglot
1.A4-Z	English and American
2	French and Belgian
3	German
4	Italian
5	Spanish and Portuguese
6	Russian and other Slavic
8.A-Z	Other. By language, A-Z
	Societies
11	English and American
12	French and Belgian
13	German
14	Italian
15	Spanish and Portuguese
18.A-Z	Other. By language, A-Z
20	Congresses
	Collected works (nonserial)
20.6	Several languages
20.8	Latin
21	English and American
22	French and Belgian
23	German
24	Italian
25	Spanish and Portuguese
26	Russian and other Slavic
28.A-Z	Other. By language, A-Z
29	Addresses, essays, lectures
	Class here works by several authors or individual authors
31	Yearbooks
35	Directories
	Dictionaries
40	International (Polyglot)
41	English and American
42	French and Belgian
43	German

44	Italian
45	Spanish and Portuguese
48.A-Z	Other. By language, A-Z
	Terminology. Nomenclature
49	General works
50	Special topics, A-Z
51	Encyclopedias
	Historiography
51.4	General works
51.6.A-Z	Biography of historians
51.6.A2	Collective
51.6.A3-Z	Individual, A-Z
51.8	Pictorial works

The next example shows a partial section of one of the tables in schedule B-BJ. The use of tables is discussed in chapters 4 and 6.

B-BJ8	TABLE FOR LATIN AMERICAN PHILOSOPHY B-BJ8
	(COUNTRIES ENDING 5-9)
5	Collected works (nonserial)
6	General works, biography (Collective), etc.
7	General special
8.A-Z	Special topics, A-Z
8.F54	Finalism
8.G3	German philosophy
8.O5	Ontology
8.P48	Phenomenology
8.P6	Positivism
8.R3	Rationalism
9.A-Z	Individual philosophers, A-Z

In the printed schedules, there is a detailed index that follows the main classification section and the auxiliary tables. There are some references from one schedule to another in some of the indexes, but in most cases the indexes refer only to the individual schedules of which they are a part. The following example is taken from Class B.

INDEX

A

A priori (Epistemology):
BD181.3
Abbagnano, Nicola: B3611.A23
Abbot, Francis Ellingwood:
B945.A26
Abbt, Thomas: B2632
Abduction
Logic: BC199.A26
Abelard (Pierre Abailard):
B765.A2
Abhinavagupta, Rajanaka:
B133.A35
Ability
Child psychology: BF723.A25
Infant psychology: BF720.A24
Ability testing: BF431+
Abnormalities of the will:
BF635
Abraham ben David, ha-Levi:
B759.A2
Absent-mindedness
Psychology: BF323.A27
Absolute, The
Ontology: BD416
Philosophy
German philosophy
Fichte: B2849.A2
Hegel: B2949.A28
Schelling: B2899.A23
Scottish philosophy
Hamilton: B1428.A25
Abstraction
Epistemology: BD235
Philosophy
English philosophy
Berkeley: B1349.A2
Philosophy
Greek philosophy
Plato: B398.A25
Psychology: BF443+
Testing of
Psychology: BF443.4+
Absurd, The
Philosophy: B105.A3
Abū al-Barakāt Hibat Allāh
ibn 'Alī: B748.A2
Academic achievement and
personality: BF698.9.A3
Academy, The (Greek
philosophy):   B338

Accident
Philosophy
Greek philosophy
Aristotle: B491.A24
Accidents
Astrology: BF1729.A25
Achievement
Child psychology: BF723.P365
Achievement motivation
Child psychology: BF723.M56
Acintyabhedābheda: B132.A27
Ackley, H.A. (Spirit
messages):   BF1311.A2
Acosta, Uriel: B3899.A3
Acri, Francesco: B3611.A3
Act
Logic: BC199.A28
Philosophy: B105.A35
German philosophy
Hegel: B2949.A3
Kant: B2799.A28
Greek philosophy
Aristotle: B491.A27
Active intellect
Philosophy
Medieval philosophy: B738.S68
Active vs. meditative life
(Ethics):   BJ1493
Adaptability
Child psychology: BF723.A28
Adelard of Bath: B765.A25
Adjective Check List:
BF698.8.A32
Adjective generation
technique: BF698.8.A34
Adjustment
Adolescent psychology:
BF724.3.A32
Psychic research: BF1045.A34
Psychology: BF335+
Adler, Mortimer: B945.A286
Adlerian psychology
Psychoanalysis: BF175.5.A33
Adolescence
Developmental psychology: BF724
Adolescents
Graphology: BF905.A3
Adopted child
Child psychology: BF723.A3
Adorno, Theodor W.:   B3199.A3
Adult-child relations
Child psychology: BF723.A33

In the electronic version, with different classes collected into one database, indexes to individual classes have also been merged into a combined index. In order to expedite the conversion process, little editorial work was done to harmonize or reconcile index entries derived from individual schedules. This is one area the Library intends to pursue after its new integrated system, to be implemented in 1999, is in place.

Divisions

Initially, the arrangement of divisions within a class, subclass, or subject followed a general pattern, often called "Martel's seven points."[6] In developing the earlier schedules, the subject specialists made use of these seven points or appropriate parts of them:

(1) General form divisions: Periodicals, Societies, Collections, Dictionaries, etc.

(2) Theory. Philosophy

(3) History

(4) Treatises. General works

(5) Law, Regulation. State Relations
[Since the development of the K schedules, legal topics relating to specific subjects have been moved to Class K.]

(6) Study and teaching

(7) Special subjects and subdivisions of subjects progressing from the more general to the specific and as far as possible in logical order.

In recently revised schedules, classifiers at the Library of Congress follow the guidelines below:[7]

(1) Preliminary section: forms of publication and special aspects of the discipline as a whole. These include:
(a) General form subdivisions
(b) Philosophy
(c) History
(d) Biography
(e) General works
(f) Study and teaching
Under each, geographic subdivisions may be provided.

(2) Logical breakdown of the discipline into subtopics. Based on these general principles, models for subarrangement within disciplines have been established for Classes D, H, Q, and R (see appendix B).

The following is a discussion of the general types of division with examples.

Preliminary Section

General Form Divisions. In addition to periodicals, societies, collections, and dictionaries, general form divisions may contain congresses, exhibitions, museums, documents, or any other general form division peculiar to a specific class or subclass. The following extract from the beginning of subclass RD serves as an example:

RD	SURGERY
1	Periodicals. Societies. Serials
	Hospitals, clinics, etc., *see* RA960+
9	Yearbooks
9.2	Congresses
	Directories of surgeons
10.A1	General
10.A3-Z	By region or country, A-Z
	Collected works (nonserial)
11	Several authors
14	Individual authors
16	Nomenclature. Terminology. Abbreviations
	Cf. RB115, Pathology
17	Dictionaries and encyclopedias

Unlike other classification systems, which usually have a standard set of form subdivisions applicable to all subjects, form divisions in the LC Classification are developed individually under each subject and are based largely on literary warrant. Generally, broader subjects on which there is a larger amount of library material are provided with more form divisions, while many narrow subjects do not have any form divisions at all. In Class K, Law, a set of common form subdivisions has been established that apply to the schedules for laws of individual jurisdictions, except the common law schedules KF, KD, and KE.

Although general form divisions usually precede all other divisions, this is not an absolute rule. For instance, in Class CN, Epigraphy (the study of inscriptions), "CN70 Dictionaries. Encyclopedias" is separated from the other general form divisions by the elements "CN40-42 Philosophy. Theory," "CN44-46 Methodology. Technique," "CN50 Study and teaching," "CN55 History of epigraphy (General)," and "CN61-62 Biography of epigraphists" as may be seen in the following excerpt:

CN	EPIGRAPHY
1	Periodicals. Societies. Serials
15	Congresses
	Collected works (nonserial)
20	Several authors
20.5	Individual authors
25.A-Z	Museums, libraries, and other institutions. By place, A-Z
30.A-Z	Private collections. By collector, A-Z
	Philosophy. Theory
40	General works
41	Relation to archaeology, history, etc.
	Relation to architectural decoration, *see* NA4050.I5
42	Relation to religion
	Methodology. Technique
44	General works
46	Photographic methods
50	Study and teaching
55	History of epigraphy (General)
	Biography of epigraphists
61	Collective
62.A-Z	Individual, A-Z
70	Dictionaries. Encyclopedias

Philosophy. This element of the general principle of arrangement is used primarily in the main classes and subclasses. It is often only a single number. However, this element, like all the other elements, may be expanded to many numbers in some instances. The theory and philosophy of literature, for example, receives thirteen numbers, PN45-57. This particular element may be compared to the standard subdivision "01" in the *Dewey Decimal Classification*.

PN	LITERATURE (GENERAL)
	Theory. Philosophy. Esthetics
45	General works. Ideals, content, etc. Plots, motives
45.5	Forms of literature
	Relation to and treatment of special elements, problems, and subjects
46	Inspiration
47	Life
48	Nature
49	Philosophy, ethics, religion, etc.
50	Relation to history
51	Relation to sociology, economics, political science, etc. (social ideas, forces, etc., in literature)
52	Relation to education
53	Relation to art
54	Relation to language
55	Relation to science
	Other special
56.A-Z	Topics, A-Z
56.A23	Abjection
56.A24	Absurdity
56.A3	Adventure
56.A4	Aeronautics
	. . . . . .
56.3.A-Z	Countries, cities, ethnic groups, and races, A-Z
56.3.A43	Algeria
56.3.A45	America
56.3.A9	Australia
56.3.B3	Basques. Basque provinces
56.3.B4	Berlin
	. . . . . .
	Characters
56.4	General works
56.5.A-Z	Special classes of people, A-Z
	. . . . . .
57.A-Z	Individual characters, A-Z

History. The history element of a class or subject is most commonly divided chronologically. This may be seen in subclass HG231-256 for the history of money.

HG	FINANCE
	Money
	History
231	General works
	Primitive, see GN450+
237	Ancient
	Medieval
241	Contemporary works
243	Modern works
	16th-18th centuries
248	Contemporary works
249	Modern works
253	19th century
	20th century
255	General works
256	1971-

When a topic is subdivided by several time periods, each period is closed before a new period is added. The closing date of one span is identical with the opening date of the next span, for example,[8]

1945-1958

1958-1971

1971-

A span such as 1958-1971 is interpreted to mean from 1958 up to, but not including, 1971.

The caption **Through [*date*]** is used when the earliest period does not have a definable beginning date. Time periods established earlier sometimes carry the caption **To [*date*]**, which is interpreted to mean *up to but not including* the date.

Frequently, the history division is combined in some manner with a provision for individual regions and countries.

In some cases, a topic may be subdivided by dates of publication, for example,

Through 1800

1801-1859

1860-1900

1901-

Note that in these cases, the ending date of a span does not overlap the beginning date of the following span.

Biography. Under subclasses, disciplines, and broad subjects, special numbers for biography are generally provided. Typically, separate numbers for collective and individual biography are enumerated, for example:

T	TECHNOLOGY (GENERAL)

	Biography
	Including inventors
39	Collective
40.A-Z	Individual, A-Z
	Class preferably with special subject in
	classes TA-TT

TK	ELECTRICAL ENGINEERING. ELECTRONICS. NUCLEAR ENGINEERING

	Biography
139	Collective
140.A-Z	Individual, A-Z

General Works. This element is used for comprehensive works covering a particular class, subclass, or subject. The caption used with this element may be "Treatises," "General works," or "General." The caption "General works" is established when there is any other subtopic under a topic,[9] for example:

SF	ANIMAL CULTURE

Pets
   Rabbits and hares

451	Periodicals. Societies. Serials
453	General works
453.2	Juvenile works

SH	AQUACULTURE. FISHERIES. ANGLING

Angling
  Methods of angling
   Lure fishing

445.8	General works
	Fly fishing
456	General works
456.2	Saltwater fly fishing
456.3	Plug fishing

In earlier schedules, the provision for "General" or "General works" sometimes appears in sequence with the provision for "General special" or "Special aspects of the subject as a whole," which means special aspects relating to the subject as a whole and does not include any hierarchical divisions or branches of the subject.

GN	ANTHROPOLOGY

General works, treatises, and textbooks

23	Early through 1870
24	1871-1974
25	1975-
27	General special (Special aspects of the subject as a whole)
29	Addresses, essays, lectures

In recent editions of schedules, no new numbers of this type are established.

Under many subclasses and disciplines, there are provisions in the sequence of general works and treatises for "Popular works," "Juvenile works," "Addresses, essays, lectures," and occasionally "Elementary textbooks." "Addresses, essays, lectures" is a category no longer represented in subject headings subdivisions but still used here and there in the classification schedules for works that consist of collected papers, miscellaneous articles, anthologies of readings, and so on.[10]

Often, the element "General works" is subdivided chronologically. For example:

TL   MOTOR VEHICLES.   AERONAUTICS. ASTRONAUTICS

          Aeronautics.   Aeronautical engineering
          General works
544   Early to 1900
545   1900-
546   Textbooks

In chronological arrangements of this type, placement is determined by the imprint date of the work being classified. Under some subjects, however, there may be provision for two sorts of chronological division, by period covered and by date of publication. For example:

RG   GYNECOLOGY AND OBSTETRICS

          Obstetrics
          History
511   General works
512   Primitive
513   Ancient
514   Medieval
515   Modern through 1800
516   19th-20th centuries
518.A-Z   By region or country, A-Z
519   Anatomical descriptions
520   Atlases.   Pictorial works
          General works
             For works before 1800, *see* RG81+
521   1800-1900
522   1901-1930
524   1931-
525   Popular works
525.5   Juvenile works
526   General special

<u>Study and Teaching</u>. This element often occurs as a single number, as it does in "CN50, Study and teaching" of epigraphy. Just as in the case of "Philosophy," "Study and teaching" may be said to parallel a standard subdivision in the *Dewey Decimal Classification*, "-07." Occasionally, "Study and Teaching" is given more than a single number as in the case of "PR31-55, Study and teaching of English literature," in which the whole number PR55 is devoted solely to individual biographies.

PR	ENGLISH LITERATURE
	Literary history and criticism
	Study and teaching
31	Periodicals. Societies. Serials
33	General works. Treatises, etc.
	Outlines, syllabi, etc. *see* PR87
35	General special
37	Addresses, essays, lectures
	By period
41	Middle ages to 1600
43	17th-18th centuries
45	19th century
47	20th century
51.A-Z	By region or country, A-Z
53.A-Z	By school, A-Z
	Biography of teachers, critics, and historians
54	Collective
55.A-Z	Individual, A-Z

In one instance, "MT1-960, Musical Instruction and Study," an entire subclass is devoted to this element.

Topics and Subdivisions of Topics

Topics and subdivisions of topics constitute the bulk of the individual developments or expansions of classes and subclasses. The specialists responsible for each discipline develop each schedule often independently for each class, subclass, and discipline. Where appropriate, models of development established for certain subject areas are followed; and, insofar as possible, a logical order is employed.

"JN2916-2988," the numbers for political rights and participation in France, serve as an example here. The logical subdivisions of this particular subject are Citizenship, Suffrage, and Elections and Electoral system. Obviously, one subdivision naturally or logically precedes the other. For example, Suffrage precedes Elections, because one cannot have elections without suffrage.

JN	CONSTITUTIONAL HISTORY AND PUBLIC ADMINISTRATION
	Europe
	France
	Political rights. Political participation
2916	General works
2919	Citizenship.
	Suffrage. Right to vote
2941	General works
2954	Woman suffrage. Women's right to vote
	Elections. Electoral systems. Voting
2959	General works
2960.A-Z	Local, A-Z
2988	Political corruption

Geographic Division

Geographic division in LC Classification follows one of two general patterns. Continents and countries are arranged either alphabetically or in a preferred order. Alphabetical geographic division is used when one class number is designated for geographic division, for example, "By region or country, A-Z." (For details, see chapter 4.)

When a span of numbers is used for geographic subdivision, the arrangement follows a classified pattern as shown below:

America
   North America
      United States
      British North America.   Canada
      Mexico
   Central America
   West Indies
   South America

    Europe
        Great Britain
        Continental Countries
    Asia
    Africa
    Australia and New Zealand
    Pacific Islands
    Arctic regions
    Antarctic regions

Within each region further subdivision is made either naturally or alphabetically.

The use of geographic division by a classified rather than alphabetical order allows a particular geographic area to have its own specific and even unique subject subdivisions, an option that is often particularly advantageous in the social sciences.

Topical Division Under Country

Often in the Classification, especially in the social sciences, the citation order for topics involving place is topic under place instead of the usual place under topic. Thus, a class or subclass may be divided geographically and then be further divided by topic. This is most obvious in Classes C through G (History and Geography) and in Class K, in which the laws of individual nations are classed first by jurisdiction, then by topic and form. Another example of such division is "Political Institutions and Public Administration" in Class J (Political Science), where subdivision by countries occurs before further subdivisions by topic in subclasses JK, United States; JL, Canada, Latin America; JN, Europe; and JQ, Asia, Africa, Australia, Pacific Area, etc. The advantage of topic-under-place citation order is that it allows more specific enumeration under each country of topics appropriate to that country.

Example of Subdivisions

The types of division discussed above may appear under topics in the schedules in various combinations and order, and many types of divisions may appear in a particular schedule. As a step toward achieving consistency among related disciplines, the Library of Congress has developed models for subarrangement within disciplines for four classes: D, H, Q, and R. These are included in appendix B.

The following development for Nuclear and particle physics from subclass QC serves as an example of the patterns of general divisions.

QC	PHYSICS	QC

Nuclear and particle physics.   Atomic energy.
Radioactivity
Cf. QC170+, Constitution of matter.   Atomic
physics
Cf. QD601+, Radiochemistry
Cf. TK9001+, Nuclear engineering
Cf. UG1282.A8, Atomic bombs

770	Periodicals, societies, congresses, serial collections, yearbooks
771	Collected works (nonserial)
772	Dictionaries and encyclopedias
	Communication of information
772.2	General works
772.4	Information services
	History
773.A1	Development and projects leading to production of first atomic bombs
773.A2-Z	General works
773.3.A-Z	By region or country, A-Z
	Biography
774.A2	Collective
774.A3-Z	Individual, A-Z
774.2	Directories
776	General works, treatises, and advanced textbooks
777	Elementary textbooks
778	Popular works
778.5	Juvenile works
780	Addresses, essays, lectures
782	Special aspects of the subject as a whole
782.5.A-Z	Special topics, A-Z
782.5.P4	Photography
	Cf. QC787.N78, Nuclear emulsions
783	Handbooks, tables, formulas, etc.
	Data processing
783.3	General works, treatises, and textbooks
783.4	Laboratory manuals
783.5	Pictorial works and atlases
	Study and teaching
783.8	General works

783.85	Problems, exercises, examinations
784	Laboratory manuals
784.5	Atomic and nuclear measurements
	Including atomic units
	Instruments and apparatus
785.5	Periodicals, societies, congresses, serial
	collections, yearbooks
785.7	Collected works (nonserial)
786	General works, treatises, and textbooks
786.2	Addresses, essays, lectures
	Nuclear reactors for research. Reactor physics
	Cf. TK9202+, Nuclear reactor engineering
786.4	Periodicals, societies, congresses, serial
	collections, yearbooks

As illustrated in this example, the first form division under a discipline or major topic is usually "Periodicals, societies, etc.," followed by nonserial "Collected works" and "Dictionaries and encyclopedias." The division for "Communication of information" is relatively new and appears in recently developed schedules or revisions of older schedules. Following history and biography, which usually appear together, are further form divisions including general works and special aspects of the subject as a whole (called "General special" in many of the older schedules). Subject or topical divisions, in this case beginning with "Atomic and nuclear measurements," normally follow other types of divisions. This schedule also illustrates the fact that each level of the hierarchy may have its own development of detailed divisions, depending on literary warrant. For instance, the topic "Instruments and apparatus," a subdivision under "Nuclear and particle physics," has its own form divisions; so does "Nuclear reactors for research," which, in turn, is a further subdivision under "Instruments and apparatus."

Notes in Classification Schedules

In the schedules, class numbers and captions (that is, headings and subheadings) are often accompanied by notes. The notes generally fall into one of the following categories.

Scope Notes

Scope notes are used to explain what goes under a particular caption. In most cases, a scope note is used to explain how the Library of Congress separates material when the topic in question is similar in nature to a topic located in another area, for example,

> QD   CHEMISTRY
>
>   Inorganic chemistry
> 181.A-Z   Special elements. By chemical symbol, A-Z (Table Q1)
>   Class here works on the origin, properties,
>   preparation, reactions, isotopes, and
>   analytical chemistry of individual elements and
>   their inorganic compounds.
>   For the determination of atomic and molecular
>   weights, *see* QD464.A+

Explanatory *See* Notes

The second note in the example above, when used alone, is called an *explanatory see note*.

> SB   PLANT CULTURE
>
>   Propagation
>   For works limited to special plants, *see* the plant,
>   e.g., SB406.7-83, Flowers; SB419, House plants
> 119   General works

Such a note is used to identify certain concepts which, although logically covered by the caption immediately above the note, are to be classed elsewhere under a different number. In the past, "prefer notes" (which have been discontinued) were used for the same purpose.

In notes, a span of numbers is indicated by the initial number with a plus sign, for example:

> RJ   PEDIATRICS
>
> 240   Immunization of children (General)
>   For immunization against specific diseases, *see*
>   RA644.A+

Confer Notes

A *confer note* informs the user that information related to the topic in question is also found under another number or other numbers in the scheme, or that (going down hierarchically) the list of subtopics under the caption in question is not complete and additional subtopics are found under another class number. The note consists of a class number with a statement of what the class number represents.

SB	PLANT CULTURE
112.5	Physiology
	Cf. SB130, Postharvest physiology

See Notes

A *see* note is used most often in cases where a decision has been made to relocate a topic in the scheme. The existing class number is removed or parenthesized with a *see* reference added at the end of the caption.

TK	ELECTRICAL ENGINEERING. ELECTRONICS. NUCLEAR ENGINEERING
	Digital video
(6683)	Underwater television
	see TK6679.5

SB	PLANT CULTURE
112	Irrigation farming
(113)	Nursery catalogs, etc.
	see SB115

Z	SUBJECT BIBLIOGRAPHY
7295	Roads. Highways
	Rubber, *see* Z6297
7335	Salt

Including Notes

Including notes are used to indicate by example the kinds of topics subsumed under the caption, for example:

RM	THERAPEUTICS. PHARMACOLOGY
138	Drug prescribing
	Including dosage

LA	HISTORY OF EDUCATION
	By region or country
	South America
540-544	General (Table L2)
	Including Latin America in general

Frequently, they help identify concepts the reader would not ordinarily assume to be included within the scope of the caption.

Divided Like Notes

Divided like notes, which refer from a range of numbers to another range of numbers, are used to save space in the printed schedules. For example:

BX	CHRISTIAN DENOMINATIONS
5410-5595	Church of Ireland
	Divided like BX5210-5395

AG	DICTIONARIES AND OTHER GENERAL REFERENCE BOOKS
	Dictionaries. Minor encyclopedias
1	International. Polyglot
5-90	Other
	Divided like AE5-89.9
	e.g., AG5.M4, Mee, the book of knowledge

In recently revised schedules, *divided like* notes are often replaced by enumeration or by instructions to use tables.

Parenthesized Numbers

Within the schedules, certain numbers are enclosed in parentheses. The parentheses indicate that the number enclosed is not used by the Library of Congress. In some cases, a number is placed in parentheses when the Library of Congress cancels the number but wishes to leave it in the schedule for keeping track of previous practices or for use by other libraries that may prefer the older number. An example is shown below:

BX   CHRISTIAN DENOMINATIONS

	Protestantism
	By region or country
(4830)	America, *see* BR500+
(4831)	United States, *see* BR513+
(4832)	Canada, *see* BR570+
4832.5	Latin America
4833	Mexico

Alternate Class Numbers

On many LC cataloging records, one or more alternate class numbers are provided in addition to the regular LC call number.[11] Alternate class numbers indicate that there are other appropriate class placements than the one the Library of Congress has chosen for its own use. Alternate class numbers are generally provided for incunabula, for subject bibliographies regularly classed in Z, and for analytics in series or sets classed as a whole. Also, on cataloging records for works in medicine produced through the cataloging program shared between the National Library of Medicine and the Library of Congress, alternate class numbers based on the National Library of Medicine Classification scheme are given in addition to the LC call numbers. Details of alternate class numbers appear in chapters 6 and 7.

SUPPLEMENTARY AIDS TO THE USE OF THE CLASSIFICATION

A General Index to the Schedules

Although most of the individual classification schedules include detailed indexes, the Library of Congress has never issued a general index to the entire series of printed schedules. When the electronic version of the Classification is completed and all classes are included in one file, a general index resulting from collating the individual indexes will emerge. However, because each of the indexes was compiled individually without regard to the others, the merged index will contain many inconsistencies and much incompatible vocabulary. It will be a service to the profession if addressing this problem remains a high priority for the Library of Congress after its new integrated system has been installed.

Manuals for the Classification

For many years, there was no official manual explaining the Classification. The dearth was filled to some extent in 1987, when the Library published its *Subject Cataloging Manual: Shelflisting*[12] to explain its shelflisting (i.e., cuttering) policies and procedures. A second edition appeared in 1995. Even more helpful was the publication of another manual, *Subject Cataloging Manual: Classification,*[13] in 1992. This manual sets forth the Library's policies on developing the schedules and assigning class numbers. Together, these two manuals contain the most detailed information regarding the application of the LC Classification.

Other Aids to Using the Classification

Leo LaMontagne's *American Library Classification with Special Reference to the Library of Congress*[14] is a detailed treatment of the history, theory, and use of the Classification. This book is particularly valuable as it contains many citations from material available only in Library of Congress departmental reports or in other internal sources. Although it was published in 1963, it is still a highly useful guide.

Another useful aid is the publication *Library of Congress Classes JZ and KZ: Historical Notes and Introduction to Application,*[15] which was prepared by Jolande E. Goldberg of the Library of Congress, who is responsible for developing and maintaining the Class K schedules. Because subclasses JZ and KZ for international treaties and international law have only recently been developed, this book is especially useful to classifiers who work with materials in those areas.

Mary Lynette Larsgaard's *Map Librarianship: An Introduction,*[16] now in its third edition, is particularly helpful in the classification of cartographic materials.

USE OF LC CATALOGING RECORDS

One major reason why many libraries are now using the LC Classification has been the presence of complete call numbers on the LC cataloging records that serve as cataloging copy for most of the cataloging agencies and libraries in this country. The great advantage of using cataloging copy is increased productivity. One disadvantage is the problem of assigning compatible Cutter numbers to those works for which LC records are not available. Other disadvantages include undetected errors in LC records and the fact that the Library's classification placement may not always be optimal or even suitable for local needs. Nevertheless, such disadvantages seem to be outweighed by the benefits of quick access, on the Internet and through bibliographic utilities, to almost the entire range of current LC MARC records.

REVISIONS AND EXPANSIONS

There are two ways individual schedules are kept current: (1) *LC Classification, Additions and Changes*, which is published quarterly by the Library of Congress; and, (2) periodic new editions of the individual schedules. Over the years, more than 270 issues of *LC Classification, Additions and Changes* have been published. Because the publication is not cumulative, it may be a time-consuming effort to go through back issues to find a new number or to verify an existing one. The availability of the electronic schedules not only makes consultation easier for those who have access to them but facilitates greatly the production of printed schedules. Thus, new print editions incorporating the latest revisions have appeared more frequently in recent years, supplying classifiers who depend on printed schedules with tools that are relatively up-to-date and much easier to use.

Publication of Print Schedules

The printed schedules have been issued in three types of editions:
1. New schedules. A new schedule contains a class or subclass that has never been published before. In recent years, while no main classes have been added to the scheme, several new subclasses have been developed. Examples include subclasses JZ International relations, KZ Law of Nations, and ZA Information resources.

2.   Cumulative editions. A cumulative edition is simply the cumulation of an existing edition with its subsequent additions and changes. Its preparation, including reformatting, compiling new indexes, and updating terminology, is fairly mechanical and efficient because relatively little revamping or rethinking of the classification is involved. Most recently issued editions are of this type. In some cases, large classes have been divided into parts that are then cumulated and published separately, for example, Classes B, D, K, and P. Currently, the Library hopes to produce new cumulative editions of at least two schedules each year.[17]

3.   Revised editions. Some schedules undergo considerable revamping in a process that involves reviewing and rethinking the entire schedule. Many numbers are changed, form and chronological subarrangements are standardized, notes are added to clarify usage, and terminology is updated and made compatible with Library of Congress Subject Headings wherever feasible. The preparation of such an edition involves not only individual catalogers but also the Cataloging Policy and Support Office, and it requires a great deal more time and effort than the production of a cumulative edition. In some cases, only some (perhaps one or two) of the subclasses in a schedule undergo intellectual revamping, with the rest of the schedule receiving only routine revision. An example is the thorough revision of subclass HJ, Public finance.

It should be pointed out that there is no fixed time schedule for revision. Each classification schedule is revised as feasible, depending on the urgency of the need for revision and on whether the needed personnel and time are available. Class Q has gone through at least seven editions, while some classes have only gone through two or three or are even still in the first edition. Since 1994, when the print schedules were first generated from machine-readable files, the Library of Congress has discontinued the practice of numbering revised editions. New editions are now designated as 1995 edition, 1996 edition, etc.

SuperLCCS

In 1989, the publishing company Gale began publication of *Library of Congress Classification Schedules Combined with Additions and Changes through 1988*,[18] the title of which was later changed to *SuperLCCS*. This publication consists of a series of print schedules published annually, each of which integrates the latest edition of a given schedule with all the pertinent changes that appeared in *LC Classification, Additions and Changes* during the previous year.

In general, except for schedules for which the Library of Congress has issued new editions in the past year, Gale issues completely updated volumes annually for schedules that have undergone changes in the previous year.[19] *SuperLCCS* are also available in electronic form issued quarterly as a CD-ROM product.

Procedure for Revision and Expansion

Revisions and changes in the Classification occur continuously through adding new numbers or revising existing ones, and are the responsibility of the Cataloging Policy and Support Office of the Library of Congress. Proposals for changes originate with LC catalogers, who in the process of classifying become aware of anomalies among existing numbers and of new topics that have no LC numbers. A proposed change normally consists of the proposed number, its caption, its anchor point (i.e., the exact location in the schedules where the new number would be inserted), a previously existing pattern (if any) on which the proposed number is based, other numbers that would be affected by the change, and the cataloger's explanation (if any). Many class number proposals are based on analogous situations in other portions of the same schedule.

Each week, the editorial staff collects the new proposals, assesses the wording of anchor points, annotations, instructions, and index entries. New proposals are reviewed at the weekly editorial meeting[20] attended by the Chief and the Assistant Chief of the Cataloging Policy and Support Office, a subject cataloging policy specialist, the Editor of Classification Schedules, an assistant editor, and a subject cataloger serving as secretary. If approved, new numbers and related changes are put into effect immediately: they are entered into the machine-readable file and published in the quarterly *LC Classification, Additions and Changes*; eventually they are incorporated into new editions of the schedules. Revisions and changes to existing numbers or notes follow a similar procedure.

Methods for Expansion

There are five methods for the possible expansion of the Classification:

1. By using the unused letters I, O, W, X, and Y. (It should be noted that the letter W has been used by the National Library of Medicine for its own classification schedule for medicine, which may be used by libraries adopting the LC system if they prefer it to Class R.)

2.   By adding a third capital letter or even a fourth to the existing double letters, for example, DJK, KJW, etc. Triple letters for subclasses are presently being used in Classes D and K. (This use is discussed in chapter 6.)

3.   By assigning unused numbers and double letters in existing schedules.

4.   By extending existing numbers decimally.

5.   By making further use of Cutter numbers, including extending some existing ones.

To date, the Library of Congress has not used the first method. Obviously, its use would cause major reclassification within the schedules and would destroy the long-lasting relative stability of the Classification. The Library has, however, made some use of the other four.

NOTES

1.   Leo E. LaMontagne, *American Library Classification with Special Reference to the Library of Congress* (Hamden, CT: Shoe String Press, 1961), 253.

2.   Ibid., 254.

3.   Arthur Maltby, *Sayers' Manual of Classification for Librarians*, 5th ed. (London: Andre Deutsch, 1975), 175; also J. Mills, *A Modern Outline of Library Classification* (London: Chapman & Hall, 1967), 89.

4.   Rebecca S. Guenther, "Automating the Library of Congress Classification Scheme: Implementation of the USMARC Format for Classification Data," *Cataloging & Classification Quarterly* 21, nos. 3-4 (1996):177-203.

5.   "Classification Plus," *Cataloging Service Bulletin* 71 (Winter 1996):74; 73 (Summer 1996):50.

6.   Charles Martel, "Classification: A Brief Conspectus of Present Day Library Practice," *Library Journal* 36 (August 1911):415; reprinted in *Theory of Subject Analysis: A Sourcebook*, ed. Lois Mai Chan, Phyllis A. Richmond, and Elaine Svenonius (Littleton, CO: Libraries Unlimited, 1985), 74.

7.   "Subarrangement Within Disciplines," Library of Congress, Office for Subject Cataloging Policy, *Subject Cataloging Manual: Classification*, 1st ed. (Washington, DC: Cataloging Distribution Service, Library of Congress, 1992), F195.

8.   "Classification and Time Periods," Library of Congress, *Subject Cataloging Manual: Classification*, F320.

9.   "General Works," Library of Congress, *Subject Cataloging Manual: Classification*, F280.

10.   "Addresses, Essays, Lectures," Library of Congress, *Subject Cataloging Manual: Classification*, F300.

11.   Lois Mai Chan, "Library of Congress Classification: Alternative Provisions," *Cataloging & Classification Quarterly* 19, nos. 3-4 (1995):67-87.

12.   Library of Congress, Subject Cataloging Division, *Subject Cataloging Manual: Shelflisting* (Washington, DC: Library of Congress, 1987); and Library of Congress, Cataloging Policy and Support Office, *Subject Cataloging Manual: Shelflisting*, 2nd ed. (Washington, DC: Library of Congress, 1995).

13.   Library of Congress, Office for Subject Cataloging Policy, *Subject Cataloging Manual: Classification*, 1st ed. (Washington, DC: Cataloging Distribution Service, Library of Congress, 1992).

14.   LaMontagne, *American Library Classification*.

15.   Jolande E. Goldberg, *Library of Congress Classes JZ and KZ: Historical Notes and Introduction to Application* (Washington, DC: Cataloging Distribution Service, Library of Congress, 1997).

16.   Mary Lynette Larsgaard, *Map Librarianship: An Introduction*, 3rd ed. (Englewood, CO: Libraries Unlimited, 1998).

17.   "Historical Note on the Library of Congress Classification," Library of Congress, *Subject Cataloging Manual: Classification*, 1.

18.   Rita Runchock and Kathleen Droste, eds., *Library of Congress Classification Schedules Combined with Additions and Changes through 1988* (Detroit, MI: Gale Research, 1989).

19.   Ibid., v.

20.   "Historical Note on the Library of Congress Classification," Library of Congress, *Subject Cataloging Manual: Classification*, 1.

Notation

GENERAL FEATURES OF THE NOTATION

Call numbers in the Library of Congress (LC) Classification, like those in most other classification systems used for shelving purposes, consist of two principal elements: a class number that is taken or derived from the schedules, and an item number that distinguishes among items classed under the same class number. As indicated in the outline reproduced in chapter 2, class numbers in the LC system are alphanumeric: one, two, or three capital letters are followed by integral (or whole) numbers from 1 through 9999, with possible decimal or other extensions for further topical breakdown. Item number notation usually begins with a Cutter number (a single capital letter preceded by a decimal point, plus Arabic numbers that are read in decimal sequence—so that .A52 or .A5999 precedes .A6). Usually, other distinguishing information, including publication date, follows the Cutter number.

The notation is not hierarchical. In choosing a notational system, early LC classifiers decided on one that would be hospitable but would not entail long class numbers. (A classification is said to be hospitable if it can easily accommodate new topics or finer divisions of existing topics.) On these points, Charles Martel remarked:

> The practically unlimited flexibility and expansibility of
> the Library of Congress classification, the variety of notation
> devices for subdividing subjects by form, local, or subject
> subdivisions without resorting to excessively long and
> complicated marks or symbols, permit not only the addition
> and incorporation of new subjects in the schedules wherever
> desired but would make it possible with a three-letter class

symbol to substitute gradually class by class an entirely new set of schedules.[1]

In the following sections, varying patterns in LC call numbers are presented, followed by more detailed discussions of both class numbers and item numbers. The final section of chapter 3 is a brief account of the display of LC call numbers on physical items and MARC records.

Call Numbers

Call numbers—class numbers plus item numbers—do not all follow quite the same pattern. The two most common patterns are shown below; they differ in the fact that the second class number includes a topical extension expressed by a Cutter number.

Class number:
   One, two, or three capital letters
   Whole number 1 through 9999
   Possible decimal extension
Item number
   Cutter number based on main entry
   Year of publication, as required

Class number:
   One, two, or three capital letters
   Whole number 1 through 9999
   Possible decimal extension
   First Cutter number based on term for topic, place,
      or form
Item number
   Second Cutter number based on main entry
   Year of publication, as required

The following examples illustrate these patterns. The first is based on Erich Fromm's *Social character in a Mexican village* (HN113.5 .F74 1996); the second on William Gerdts's *Complementary visions of Louisiana art* (N6530.L8 G47 1996).

CALL NUMBER	*EXAMPLE*	*SIGNIFICATION*
Class number:		
Capital letters	HN	Social history and conditions
Whole number	113	Mexico
Decimal extension	.5	1945-
Item number (Cutter number)	.F74	Fromm (main entry)
Year of publication	1996	
Class number:		
Capital letter	N	Visual arts
Whole number	6530	Art in U.S.
First Cutter number	.L8	Louisiana
Item number (second Cutter number)	G47	Gerdts (main entry)
Year of publication	1996	

In the call number for the Fromm book, the class number includes a decimal extension to indicate subarrangement by period, and the item number is a Cutter number based on the main entry. In the call number for the Gerdts book, the class number includes a topical Cutter number to indicate subarrangement by place; a second Cutter number, this one based on the main entry, is then needed as the item number.

In addition to these typical patterns, there are others that occur less frequently. Occasionally, a class number is followed by a date but not an item number. Furthermore, in many cases, notation in a given class reflects conditions particular to that class: for example, call numbers in subclass G for maps and atlases often contain what appear to be triple Cutter numbers, and in Class M, many call numbers for musical works contain opus numbers or thematic index numbers. (Chapter 6 discusses unusual patterns of call numbers, in detail and with examples.)

The following example shows how the system's notational design meets Martel's goal of avoiding long numbers. Andrew Trout's *City on the Seine : Paris in the time of Richelieu and Louis XIV*, published in 1996, has the following call numbers in the LC and Dewey systems, respectively.

	Library of Congress Classification	Dewey Decimal Classification
Class number	DC729	944.361033
Item number	.T76	T758c
Publication date	1996	

In this example, both the LC class number DC729 and the Dewey class number 944.361033 stand for history of Paris in 17th-18th centuries. ".T76" is the item number in the LC system and is based on the LC Cutter table, while T758c is the item number under the Dewey system and is based on the three-figure Cutter table used with that system. Elaborated with schedule captions, the LC elements in the above comparison become:

DC   Subclass: History of France
729   Paris in 17th-18th centuries
.T76   The Cutter number for the main entry, Trout
1996   The date of publication added to a monograph

DC729 comes from the schedule for Class D-DJ, History (General) History of Europe, Part 1. Although there are further directions for topical cuttering at some points in the schedules, there are none at DC729; the .T76 (a Cutter number based on the main entry, the author's surname) is the item number. This is an example of a simple LC call number in which the class number and the item number are easily separable.

Class Numbers

As noted above, classes and subclasses in the LC system are designated by one, two, or three capital letters. A single letter denotes a main class, and most subclasses are designated by double letters. Classes E and F, however, do not use double letters, and so far, triple-letter combinations have been used only for some subclasses in D and K. An interesting feature of the LC classification is that the single letter is used both for the class as a whole and for its first subclass (usually general works pertaining to the whole class, but, sometimes, its most prominent subdiscipline). Examples of the latter usage are:

> Class P: Language and literature
> > Subclass P: Philology and linguistics (General)
> Class N: Fine arts
> > Subclass N: Visual arts (General)

Thus, depending on the context, a single letter may stand either for a main class or for its first subclass.

Each of the integral numbers in the arrays under each subclass, division, or subdivision may be topically extended decimally or through the use of Cutter numbers that represent terms for the topics in question. Occasionally, two Cutter numbers are used in a single call number.

The partial outline from Class S shown below illustrates many aspects of how class numbers are arrayed to make up a schedule. Notice particularly the sequence breaks between runs of numbers, the alphabetical gaps between SB, SD, and SF, and the occasional use of decimal numbers. All three are hospitality features, allowing easy interpolation of new or expanded subjects and/or their subdivisions. Subject expansion by Cutter number, mentioned above, is another hospitality provision; this use of Cutter numbers is treated in detail in the latter part of this chapter.

S
1-(972)	Agriculture (General)
21-400.5	Documents and other collections
403	Agricultural missions, voyages, etc.
419-482	History
530-559	Agricultural education
560-571.5	Farm economics. Farm management. Agricultural mathematics
583-587.73	Agricultural chemistry. Agricultural chemicals
588.4-589.6	Agricultural physics
589.7	Agricultural ecology (General)
589.75-589.76	Agriculture and the environment
589.8-589.87	Plant growing media. Potting soils
590-599.9	Soils. Soil science
600-600.7	Agricultural meteorology. Crops and climate
602.5-604.37	Methods and systems of culture. Cropping systems
604.5-604.64	Agricultural conservation

List continues on page 64.

604.8-621.5	Melioration: Improvement, reclamation, fertilization, irrigation, etc., of lands
622-627	Soil conservation and protection
631-667	Fertilizers and improvement of the soil
671-760.5	Farm machinery and farm engineering
770-790.3	Agricultural structures. Farm buildings
900-(972)	Conservation of natural resources

SB

1-1110	Plant culture
39	Horticultural voyages, etc.
71-87	History
107-109	Economic botany
109.7-111	Methods for special areas
112	Irrigation farming
113.2-118.46	Seeds. Seed technology
118.48-118.75	Nurseries. Nursery industry
119-124	Propagation
125	Training and pruning
126	Artificial light gardening
126.5-126.57	Hydroponics. Soilless agriculture
127	Forcing
128	Growth regulators
129-130	Harvesting, curing, storage
169-172.5	Tree crops
175-177	Food crops
183-317	Field crops
317.5-319.864	Horticulture. Horticultural crops
320-353.5	Vegetables
354-402	Fruit and fruit culture
403-450.87	Flowers and flower culture. Ornamental plants
450.9-467.8	Gardens and gardening
469-(476.4)	Landscape gardening. Landscape architecture
481-486	Parks and public reservations
599-990.5	Pests and diseases
992-998	Economic zoology applied to crops

SD
1-669.5	Forestry
11-115	Documents
119	Voyages, etc.
131-247.5	History of forestry. Forest conditions
250-363.3	Forestry education
388	Forestry machinery and engineering
388.5	Tools and implements
389	Forest roads
390-390.43	Forest soils
390.5-390.7	Forest meteorology. Forest microclimatology
391-410.9	Sylviculture
411-428	Conservation and protection
430-(559)	Exploitation and utilization
561-669.5	Administration. Policy

SF
1-1100	Animal culture
41-55	History
84-84.64	Economic zoology
84.82-85.6	Rangelands. Range management. Grazing
87	Acclimatization
89	Transportation
91	Housing and environmental control
92	Equipment and supplies
94.5-99	Feeds and feeding. Animal nutrition
101-103.5	Brands and branding, and other means of identifying
105-109	Breeding and breeds
111-113	Cost, yield, and profit. Accounting
114-121	Exhibitions
170-180	Working animals
191-275	Cattle
277-360.4	Horses
361-361.73	Donkeys
362	Mules
371-379	Sheep. Wool
380-388	Goats
391-397.83	Swine
402-405	Fur-bearing animals
405.5-407	Laboratory animals

List continues on page 66.

408-408.6	Zoo animals
409	Small animal culture
411-459	Pets
461-473	Birds. Cage birds
481-507	Poultry. Eggs
508-(510.6)	Game birds
511-511.5	Ostrich
512-513	Ornamental birds
515-515.5	Reptiles
518	Insect rearing
521-539.8	Bee culture
541-560	Sericulture. Silk culture
561	Lac-insects
600-1100	Veterinary medicine

Item Numbers

In a call number, the item number follows the class number; its purpose is to bring about an orderly array of whatever material has been classed under a given number. Most item numbers begin with a Cutter number, which may be followed by other elements needed to make further item-specific distinctions. These might include a work letter, a volume or issue number, "Suppl." (for a supplement), "Index" (for an index to an individual work), a publication date, and a copy number. (It should be noted that the copy number appears on the physical item only and not in the bibliographic record.) With respect to publication or imprint dates, under current LC policy established in 1982, an imprint date is routinely added to item numbers for all monographs, including first editions.

There are some cases in which the usual way of distinguishing among works under a given class number is not followed. For instance, whenever there are two Cutter numbers in a class number, a third may not be added as an item number because it is current LC policy that no call number may contain more than two Cutter numbers. Also, in some cases the first division for material under a class number is by date, for example, CD1055 1991, CD1055 1992, and CD1055 1994; here, it would be redundant to include the publication date in the item number. Such exceptions are discussed later in this chapter, with instructions and examples.

At the Library of Congress, Cutter numbers are drawn from a simplified version of the Cutter tables used with some other classification systems. Once the determination of the first one or two digits of an item number has been made, the cataloger must check the shelflist to see if the number will fit without duplication into the existing sequence of Cutter numbers already assigned under the particular class number in question; if not, it must be adjusted to do so. At the Library of Congress, the process of assigning item numbers is called *shelflisting* and is carried out by shelflisters rather than by the professional catalogers who assign class numbers. In local cataloging agencies, it is usually the same individual who selects both class number and item number.

Constructing Call Numbers

Many factors come into play as a classifier tries to decide where a given item might best be placed in the topical array reflected in a classification system. For the Library of Congress system, the general principles guiding a classification decision are treated in chapter 5 of this book, with special factors relating to the different classes and to different types of material discussed in subsequent chapters. The main concern here is what a classifier may have to do once a general placement decision is made, and the classifier has located the place in the schedules where the topic of the item in hand is best accommodated. Once that is found, it may be that a suitable number may be listed explicitly—this is often true even in the case of Cutter extensions to class numbers. For some areas of the schedules, however, one must use an auxiliary table to arrive at the basic class number. For others, one must use the Cutter table and perhaps other directives in the schedules to derive the Cutter extension. And in all cases, the Cutter table and sometimes other devices must be used to construct item numbers, often a matter of some complexity because they must be fitted into the existing sequence of Cutter numbers already assigned under the particular class number in question. Accordingly, the rest of this chapter focuses on LC Cutter numbers. Chapter 4 deals with tables.

LIBRARY OF CONGRESS CUTTER NUMBERS

The purpose of Cutter numbers is to maintain alphabetization whenever such an array is desired. Cutter numbers may be based on personal names, corporate names, geographic names, words for topics, or on titles. An LC Cutter number is a combination of a capital letter with one or two Arabic numerals; longer numbers are needed in some circumstances. How one constructs Cutter numbers depends in part on their purpose—primarily, whether they are part of the class number itself or whether they serve as item numbers. There are special provisions for developing many of the Cutter numbers used in the schedules, and extensions are often needed in item numbers. The following discussion explains various aspects of the use and construction of the Cutter numbers in call numbers for materials classed under the LC system.[2] The selection of Cutter numbers for specific classes and for special types of materials is discussed in chapters 6 and 7.

Cutter Table

As noted above, in the shelflist and on the shelf, a Cutter number as an item number is the means by which an alphabetical arrangement of books and other documents is achieved, with the Cutter number usually reflecting the main entry of the work. This alphabetical arrangement is based on the LC filing rules[3] with certain modification and on the table titled "Preferred Shelflist Order - Individual Authors" (see page 84). The general principle is to file elements in an entry, e.g., a personal name, in exactly the form and order in which they appear on the bibliographic record. Filing is first word-by-word, and then character-by-character.[4]

The LC Cutter table is simple and easy to use; the table itself, with examples, can be accommodated on one page and is reproduced in its entirety on the next page.[5]

A letter not included in the table is assigned the next higher or lower number adjusted as required by previous assignments in the particular class.

Initial articles in the nominative case, for example, a, an, das, la, les, the, etc., that appear at the beginning of a main entry are disregarded in assigning Cutter numbers.

For Roman or Arabic numerals, the Cutter numbers .A12-.A19 are used, unless under the particular class number, these Cutter numbers have been reserved for special purposes. In such cases, the Cutter numbers for numerals follow the reserved Cutter numbers.[6]

Cutter Table

After initial vowels

for the second letter:	b	d	l-m	n	p	r	s-t	u-y
use number:	2	3	4	5	6	7	8	9

After initial letter S

for the second letter:	a	ch	e	h-i	m-p	t	u	w-z
use number:	2	3	4	5	6	7	8	9

After initial letters Qu

for the second letter:	a	e	i	o	r	t	y
use number:	3	4	5	6	7	8	9

For initial letters Qa-Qt
use numbers: 2-29

After other initial consonants

for the second letter:	a	e	i	o	r	u	y
use number:	3	4	5	6	7	8	9

For expansion

for the letter:	a-d	e-h	i-l	m-o	p-s	t-v	w-z
use number:	3	4	5	6	7	8	9

The following examples show Cutters that would be used if entries already shelflisted conform to the table above. In most cases, Cutters must be adjusted to file an entry correctly and to allow room for later entries.

Vowels		*S*		*Q*		*Consonants*	
IBM	.I26	Sadron	.S23	*Qadduri	.Q23	Campbell	.C36
Idaho	.I33	*Scanlon	.S29	*Qiao	.Q27	Ceccaldi	.C43
*Ilardo	.I4	Schreiber	.S37	Quade	.Q33	*Chertok	.C48
*Import	.I48	*Shillingburg	.S53	Queiroz	.Q45	*Clark	.C58
Inman	.I56	*Singer	.S57	Quinn	.Q56	Cobblestone	.C63
Ipswich	.I67	Stinson	.S75	Quorum	.Q67	Cryer	.C79
*Ito	.I87	Suryani	.S87	Qutub	.Q88	Cuellar	.C84
*Ivy	.I94	*Symposium	.S96	*Qvortrup	.Q97	Cymbal	.C96

*These Cutters reflect the adjustments made to allow for a range of letters on the table, e.g., **l-m,** or for letters not explicitly stated, e.g., **h** after an initial consonant.

Note: Do not end a Cutter with the numeral 1 or 0.

In assigning Cutter numbers based on numerals, the following filing rule is observed:

> Arrange numerals after a decimal point digit by digit, one place at a time. Arrange decimal numerals that are not combined with a whole numeral (e.g., .45) before the numeral 1. Arrange decimal numerals that are combined with a whole numeral after all entries with the same whole numeral alone. Examples:
> .303 -inch machine gun and small armies
> 1 2 3 for Christmas
> 1,2, buckle my shoe
> 1/4 famba y 19 cuentos mas
> 1a [i.e. Prima] Mostra Toscenta/scultura
> 2 1/2 minute talk treasury
> 3/4 for 3
> 3 died variously
> IV [i.e. Cuarto] Concurso El Poeta Joven del Peru
> 838 ways to amuse a child
> 1984
> A is for anatomy
> Aa, Abraham[7]

Because the Cutter table provides a general framework for the assignment of Cutter numbers, the symbol for a particular name or work is constant only under a single class number. Each entry must be added to the existing entries in the shelflist in such a way as to preserve alphabetical order in accordance with LC filing rules. This is relatively easy to do because Cutter numbers are treated decimally and not ordinally and so may be expanded decimally as far as necessary. However, for several reasons, classifiers are advised not to end a Cutter number with the numeral "1" or "0" except in special situations designated in the schedules or tables.

Single Cutter Number

When there is no specific instruction in the schedule for using a Cutter number to represent part of the subject, a single Cutter number based on the main entry of the work is used as the item number under the class number. Most LC call numbers contain a single Cutter number.

O'Dell, Cecil. *Pioneers of old Frederick County, Virginia.* 1995

F	Subclass: Local history of the United States
225	Collective biography of people from Virginia
.O34	The Cutter number for the main entry, O'Dell
1995	The date of publication

Levine, Stephen. *Paper trails : a guide to public records in California.* 1996

CD	Subclass: Diplomatics, Archives, Seals
3111	General history and statistics of California archives
.L48	The Cutter number for the main entry, Levine
1996	The date of publication

Double Cutter Numbers

The term *double Cutter numbers* refers to the use of two Cutter numbers within a call number for a particular work or subject. In double Cutter numbers, for example .F5S45, the first is used to extend the class number to bring out an aspect (form, period, place, or subtopic) of the main subject, and the second is usually but not necessarily the item number. The second Cutter number, when used as an item number, usually stands for the main entry, which is often the author's name. In some cases, both Cutter numbers may be used to express parts of the subject. The examples that follow illustrate both types of double Cutter numbers. The first portion of each example is a schedule excerpt, while the second shows the application.

Class number extension; item number:
The simpler case is when the schedule calls for a one-stage extension by Cutter number.

QC	PHYSICS
	Nuclear and particle physics. Atomic energy. Radioactivity
	Elementary particle physics
793.3	Special topics, A-Z
793.3.A4	Algebra of currents
793.3.A5	Angular momentum

★ ★ ★ ★ ★

793.3.E93	Exotic nuclei
793.3.F5	Field theories

Selected topics in field theory, high energy, and astroparticle physics : 22 May-7 June, 1994 / editors, J. Pati, Q. Shafi.   1996

QC	Subclass: Physics
793.3	Elementary particle physics - Special topics, A-Z
.F5	The first Cutter number representing the topic, Field theories
S45	The second Cutter number for the main entry under the title, *Selected topics . . .*
1996	The date of publication

In this case, the class number continues through the first Cutter number .F5, and the item number does not begin until S45. The full call number is thus QC793.3.F5 S45 1996. Note that with double Cutter numbers only one decimal point is used.

Class number extension; further subdivision of subject

The case of double Cutter numbers in the schedules themselves is somewhat different, because each has topical significance. The use of two topical Cutter numbers is indicated by specific instructions in the schedules, usually in the form of "A-Z." Such use of double Cutter numbers is illustrated by the following examples:

DS	HISTORY OF ASIA
	Israel (Palestine). The Jews
	Special topics.
	Jews outside of Palestine.
135.A-Z	By region or country, A-Z.

★ ★ ★ ★ ★

	Sweden
135.S87	General works.
135.S88A-Z	Local, A-Z.

Mantel, Hanah. *Lidingo : memories of the small Swedish haven which 200 girls called 'home' after the Holocaust.*   1998

DS	Subclass: History of Asia
135	Special topics relating to Jews outside of Palestine, by country, A-Z
.S88	The first Cutter number for local subdivisions of Sweden, A-Z

L53613   The second Cutter number (L536) for the local subdivision, Lidingo, and the successive element (13) for an English translation
1998   The date of publication

Further examples:

Analysis of impediments to fair housing choice in Washington.   [1996]
HD   Subclass: Economic history and conditions
7288.76   Open housing, by region or country, A-Z
.U52   The first Cutter number for states in the United States
W23   The second Cutter number for the state of Washington
1996   The date of publication

Piwonka, Ruth.   *A visible heritage, Columbia County, New York : a history in art and architecture.*   1996
N   Subclass: Visual arts
6530   History in the states of the United States, according to table N5
.N72   The first Cutter number (N7) for the state of New York with the successive element (2) meaning a local subdivision other than cities
C646   The second Cutter number for Columbia County
1996   The date of publication

Vasso, Madame.   *Fergie : the very private life of the Duchess of York.* 1996
DA   Subclass: History of Great Britain
591   Biography and memoirs of contemporaries of Queen Elizabeth II
.A45   The first Cutter number for royal family members
Y6786   The second Cutter number for the biographee, York, Sarah Mountbatten-Windsor, Duchess of (form of authorized personal heading)
1996   The date of publication

In cases like these, no further item number is assigned because, in the LC system, with the exception of call numbers for maps in class G, call numbers contain no more than two Cutter numbers. If more than one work on the same subject exists, it would be necessary to add a distinguishing feature (e.g., an additional digit) to the second Cutter number to differentiate between them, as shown in the following example.

York, Sarah Mountbatten-Windsor, Duchess of. *My story.* 1996

DA	Subclass: History of Great Britain
591	Biography and memoirs of contemporaries of Queen Elizabeth II
.A45	The first Cutter number for royal family members
Y6788	The second Cutter number for the biographee, York, adjusted to distinguish different works about York
1996	The date of publication

This use of double Cutter numbers may confuse those accustomed to *Dewey Decimal Classification* class numbers and Cutter-Sanborn author numbers with work marks. When both Cutter numbers are used as further subdivisions of the subject, the shelflisting of LC numbers becomes a process more closely related to classification than to the shelflisting process in the *Dewey Decimal Classification*.

Topical Cutter Numbers

The use of Cutter numbers to bring out subtopics under a subject results in an alphabetical arrangement of these subtopics. Ordinarily, concepts in a classification scheme should be arranged logically, not alphabetically. Therefore, wherever possible, subtopics of a discipline in the LC Classification are designated by class numbers rather than Cutter numbers. However, where a systematic sequence of coordinate subdivisions is not feasible or cannot be accommodated due to a shortage of integers or decimal numbers or when "a series of topics does not lend itself to a logical or hierarchical order,"[8] the classification schedules frequently provide for an alphabetical order through the use of Cutter numbers to designate individual topics, for example:

QP	PHYSIOLOGY
	Heart
	Study and teaching. Research
	Research techniques.
112.4	General works
112.5.A-Z	Special, A-Z
112.5.C3	Cardiography
112.5.E4	Electrocardiography
112.5.E46	Electrophysiology

112.5.M33	Magnetocardiography
112.5.N83	Nuclear magnetic resonance
112.5.R6	Radiography

The device of "By topic, A-Z," "Special, A-Z," or "Special topics, A-Z" is generally not used to present a breakdown of a discipline into its component parts unless the area in the notation allotted for the topic is tight and there is no room available for expansion by other means. In some cases, limited hierarchical breakdown is attempted within the alphabetical arrangement, for example:

QL	ZOOLOGY
	Chordates. Vertebrates
	Mammals
737	Systematic divisions. By order and family, A-Z
	Cetacea
737.C4	General works
	Mysticeti (Whalebone whales)
737.C42	General works
737.C423	Balaenidae (Right whales)
737.C424	Balaenopteridae (Rorquals)
737.C425	Eschrichtiidae (Gray whales)
	Odontoceti (Toothed whales)
737.C43	General works
737.C432	Delphinidae (Dolphins)
737.C433	Monodontidae (Belugas; narwhales)

This results in an alphabetico-classed arrangement.

Previously, under a given number that is divided alphabetically, only representative or sample Cutter numbers were enumerated in the schedules. This practice has been discontinued; currently all topical Cutter numbers are established and printed in the schedules.

Wherever possible, captions used with topical Cutter numbers match comparable Library of Congress subject headings.

Unlike topical Cutter numbers, Cutter numbers for personal, corporate, and geographic names, names of languages, and titles of individual works (except for literary works from early periods up to 1500) are not enumerated in the schedules. Only representative samples are listed under each given number.

Subdivisions that lend themselves particularly to alphabetical arrangement are personal or corporate names that are part of the subject. Typical cases are individual biographies and works about individual corporate bodies, for example:

QA	MATHEMATICS
	Biography
28	Collective
29	Individual, A-Z
	e.g.
29.G3	Gauss
29.J2	Jacobi
29.N2	Napier

AS	ACADEMIES AND LEARNED SOCIETIES
	British North America. Canada
40	General works
42	Individual societies and institutions, A-Z

Since 1981, the alphabetical arrangement of topics or names represented by Cutter numbers has followed the provisions of the *Library of Congress Filing Rules*.[9]

When *Anglo-American Cataloguing Rules*, second edition, 1988 revision[10] (*AACR2R*) was implemented in 1989, personal or corporate names that were changed as a result of following *AACR2R* continued to be assigned previously established Cutter numbers. *See* references are made from the new forms of the names.

Cutter Numbers As Geographic Subdivisions

Geographic subdivisions[11] are frequently represented by Cutter numbers following the class number that designates the subject. The caption used in the schedules is normally one of the following:

By region or country, A-Z

By region or state, A-Z

By region or province, A-Z

By individual island or group of islands, A-Z

By place, A-Z

By city, A-Z

The caption "By country, A-Z," found in many places in older schedules, is now obsolete and should be interpreted to mean "By region or country, A-Z" unless specific provisions in the particular schedule indicate otherwise. The obsolete form is being replaced gradually during the course of major revisions or at the time an entire schedule is issued in a new edition.

Geographic Cutter numbers are based on the latest forms of place names unless different provisions are noted in the schedules.

Because geographic Cutter numbers are used throughout the system, a set of tables for cuttering regions and countries has been developed in order to achieve consistency. These tables appear in appendix A, and their use is discussed in chapter 4 (see pages 93-97).

"A" and "Z" Cutter Numbers

Frequently, under a class number, a span of Cutter numbers at the beginning ("A" Cutter numbers) or at the end ("Z" Cutter numbers) of the alphabetical sequence is set aside for special purposes. The "A" Cutter numbers are used most frequently for form divisions such as periodicals or official publications, and the "Z" Cutter numbers are often assigned to special divisions of the subject: for biography and criticism of a literary author, for instance, or for corporate bodies associated with the field.

RA	PUBLIC ASPECTS OF MEDICINE
	Medical centers. Hospitals. Dispensaries. Clinics
	Nursing homes. Long-term care facilities
	By region or country
	General and United States
997.A1	Periodicals. Societies. Serials
997.A15	Congresses
997.A2	Directories
997.A3-Z	General works

In the example above, the Cutter numbers ".A1, .A15, and .A2" have been assigned special meanings. General works on nursing homes in the United States are not assigned any Cutter number in the range ".A1-.A2." In other words, a treatise on this subject by an author named Abell, which normally would be cuttered ".A2," will receive a Cutter number greater than ".A3." Following ".A1" and ".A2" a second Cutter number (i.e., item number) based on the main entry is added, for example, RA997.A1 J68. This is different from ".A3-Z," which indicates the range to be used as the first Cutter number or item number, for example, RA997 .R6 (*not* RA997.A3 R6). ".A3-Z" means all Cutter numbers except .A1 and .A2.

In the past, the Library of Congress used "A" Cutter numbers for government or official publications and periodicals under many class numbers even when there were no explicit instructions in the schedules to do so. The use of these unprinted "A" Cutter numbers has been discontinued. Now, the "A" Cutter numbers are used only when there are specific instructions in the schedules for their use.

The following example shows instructions on the use of "A" and "Z" Cutter numbers as given in the schedule:

UA	ARMIES: ORGANIZATION, DISTRIBUTION, MILITARY SITUATION
	By region or country
	Europe
	France
	Army
	Artillery
705.A1-A5	Documents
705.A6-Z4	General works
705.Z5A-Z	Bataillons d'artillerie à pied
705.Z6	Regiments. By number and author

In the tables in Class P, the "Z" Cutter numbers are used frequently for works of criticism of individual authors.

Successive Cutter Numbers

The term *successive Cutter numbers* refers to a series of Cutter numbers (e.g., .C5, .C6, .C7, etc.) or, more typically, decimal extensions of a Cutter number (e.g., .B4, B42, B43, etc.) in an established succession or order. Successive Cutter numbers are generally used for logical subarrangement of materials classed in the same number. In the past, the use of successive Cutter numbers was often announced in the schedules in the manner shown in the following example from the third edition of the R schedule:

RA	PUBLIC ASPECTS OF MEDICINE
	Medical centers. Hospitals. Dispensaries. Clinics
	By country.
984	Other American countries, A-Z
	Under each (using successive Cutter numbers):
	(1) General works
	(2) Government hospitals
	(3) States, provinces, etc., A-Z
	(4) Cities, etc., A-Z
	e.g. Mexico
	.M3 General works
	.M4 Government hospitals
	.M5 States, A-Z
	.M6 Cities, A-Z

In this case, the successive Cutter numbers are indicated by (1), (2), (3), and (4) which become .M3, .M4, .M5, and .M6 when applied to Mexico. Both this method of announcing successive Cutter numbers and the use of single-digit Cutter number sequence (except those already established in the shelflist) are now obsolete.

Successive Cutter numbers are now announced in the manner shown below from the 1995 edition of the R schedule:

RA   PUBLIC ASPECTS OF MEDICINE
        Medical centers.   Hospitals.   Dispensaries.   Clinics
      By region or country
        America
984   Other American regions or countries, A-Z
               Under each country:
               .x   General works
               .x2   Government hospitals.   By author
               .x3   By state, province, etc., A-Z
               .x4   By city, A-Z

In this case, the successive Cutter numbers are represented by .x, .x2, .x3, and .x4. In such an instruction, .x stands for the Cutter number assigned to the topic, place, person, or corporate body in question. For example, when the successive Cutter numbers in the table above are applied to China, they become .C6, .C62, .C63, and .C64. Note that the Cutter number .x1 is not used because the use of a Cutter number ending in 1 is generally avoided.

Successive Cutter numbers are frequently used in tables. For further discussion and examples, see chapter 4.

DATE IN LC CALL NUMBERS

Date As Part of Class Number

Occasionally, the date is used as a subdivision of the class number and precedes the item number. In cases of monographs where a year of publication has been added, the call number may contain two dates, one as part of the class number and the other for the date of publication, for example:

Sherrow, Victoria.   *Hardship and hope : America and the Great Depression.*   1997

HB   Subclass: Economic theory
3717   History of crises

1929	The date of the crisis
.S54	The Cutter number for the main entry, Sherrow
1997	The date of publication

In the following example, the date is brought out in the form of a decimal extension of the class number:

Chou, B. Ralph.   *Your complete guide to the solar eclipse of May 10, 1994.*   1993

QB	Subclass: Astronomy
544	The subdivision meaning solar eclipses from 1900 to 1999
.94	The decimal number bringing out the year of the eclipse, 1994
.C48	The Cutter number for the main entry, Chou
1993	The date of publication

In Class P, Literature, the date of edition or publication is often represented by a date letter consisting of a letter followed by two digits. For example, in the call number PR4470.F37, the ".F37" means 1937, and this Cutter-like date letter takes the place of the Cutter number. For a detailed discussion and example, see chapter 6, page 365.

In the classification of maps in Class G, the date of map situation is included as part of the class number. In this case, the date precedes the item number. For example:

Color-Art, Inc.   *California-Nevada.*   1996

G	Subclass: Geography (General), atlases, maps
4361	A subject map of the State of California
.P2	The subject-letter number meaning Roads
1996	The date of map situation
.C6	The Cutter number for the main entry, Color-Art, Inc.

Date of Imprint As Part of Class Number

If the schedule indicates that works classed in a number are to be subarranged by "imprint date" or "by date," the year of publication follows the class number immediately without further Cutter numbers or date,[12] for example:

CD1055	CD1055	CD1055	CD1055
1990	1991	1992	1994

Treasury Board papers, 1772-1775 (T1/498-511). 1994

CD	Subclass: Diplomatics, Archives, Seals
1055	General calendars of the Treasury of Great Britain, by date (cf. Table C4)
1994	The date of publication

A letter ("b" or higher) is added to the date to differentiate documents with the same date.

Date of Period, Policy, etc., As Part of Class Number

If the date of period, policy, etc., forms part of the class number, this date usually remains the same for each edition. Then it is possible to keep the editions together by using the same Cutter number, and the imprint dates are then added to differentiate the editions. For example, the following call numbers have been assigned to various editions of John Kenneth Galbraith's *The great crash*:

HB	HB	HB	HB
3717	3717	3717	3717
1929	1929	1929	1929
.G32	.G32	.G32	.G32
1979	1988	1988b	1997

Date of Publication

The date of imprint or copyright is added to the Cutter number(s) for all monographic publications and to later editions of serials except in the following cases where the date is not included in the call number:[13] (1) loose-leaf materials that are continuously kept up to date; and (2) legal publications in Class K where the final Cutter number is based on dates. The procedure for assigning the date of publication is discussed below.

Selecting the Appropriate Date

The Library of Congress has provided the following guidelines for selecting the appropriate date of publication for inclusion in the call number.[14] The decision is based on the imprint or copyright date given in the "publication, distribution, etc. area" in the bibliographic record. The date found in this area is used rather than those appearing in the note area or the uniform title area. The following table shows forms of the date element in the call number. Note the use of "z" after an uncertain date.

Date in bibliographic record	Date in call number
1976?	use 1976
ca. 1976	use 1976
1981, c1980	use 1981
1971, c1972	use 1972
1979 [i.e.1978]	use 1978
1962 or 1963	use 1962
1969 (1973 printing)	use 1969
1980 printing, c1957	use 1957
1979 [distributed] 1980	use 1979
1979-1981	use 1979
between 1977 and 1980	use 1977
1978/79 [i.e. 1978 or 1979]	use 1978
1977 (cover 1978)	use 1978
197-	use 1970z [if corporate body, use 1970]
197-?	use 1970z [if corporate body, use 1970]
19--	use 1900z [if corporate body, use 1900]
19--?	use 1900z [if corporate body, use 1900]

Following are examples of using the letter "z" to represent uncertain dates:

Ruiz, Yuyo.   *The Bambino visits Cuba, 1920 : unedited notes regarding the visit of Babe Ruth to Cuba in 1920.*   [19--?]

GV	Subclass: Recreation, Leisure
865	Individual biography of people in baseball, A-Z
.R8	First Cutter number for the biographee, Ruth
R787	Second Cutter number for the main entry, Ruiz
1900z	The date of publication

AiSH, Assured Income for the Severely Handicapped : a guide. Alberta Family and Social Services, [199-?]

HD	Subclass: Economic history and conditions
7105.25	Disability insurance, by region or country, A-Z
.C2	First Cutter number for Canada
A37	Second Cutter number for the main entry under the title, *AiSH* . . .
1990z	The date of publication

For a photocopy or facsimile reprint, the work letter "a" is added to the date of the original work, for example:

.U54 1952

.U54 1952a

.U54 1952aa

.U54 1952ab

etc.

If there are two or more editions of a title published in the same year, the same imprint date is used, followed by a letter ("b" or higher) in order of receipt, for example:

.R67 1998

.R67 1998b

.R67 1998c

.R67 1998d

etc.

DISTINGUISHING WORKS BY THE SAME AUTHOR

Work marks (also called *work letters*), based on the titles of the works used for the purpose of distinguishing different works by the same author on the same subject, such as those used with the *Dewey Decimal Classification*, are not used in the LC Classification, except in the classification of juvenile belles lettres (see chapter 7). Works by the same author on the same subject (i.e., with the same class number) are differentiated by adjusting the item numbers. For example, the following works on the *Universal Decimal Classification* by the same author receive the same class number but different item numbers.

> Benito, Miguel. *Kompendium i UDK : en introduktion till Universella Decimalklassifikationssystemet.* 1995
> LC CALL NUMBER: Z696.U87 B46 1995
> Benito, Miguel. *El sistema de clasificacion decimal universal CDU : manual de aprendizaje.* 1996
> LC CALL NUMBER: Z696.U87 B464 1996

The Library of Congress has provided the following guidelines for assigning Cutter numbers to works by an individual author.[15] Unless there are specific instructions in the particular schedule indicating otherwise, the works of an individual author classed in a particular class number are arranged by category of publication, using a series of successive Cutter numbers, as indicated in the table below.

Preferred Shelflist Order - Individual Authors

When the works of an individual author are filed in a single class number, they are arranged in the following order:

		Example
Collected works	By date	.L54 1966
Translations	By date	.L5412-5419 1986
Selected works	By date	.L542 1986
Translations	By date	.L54212-54219 1986
Separate works	By title	
Original work	Cutter and date	.L55 1952
Facsimile or photocopy of original work	Cutter and date with *a*	.L55 1952a (.L55 1952aa, ab, etc.)
Edition or reprint	Cutter and date	.L55 1967
Facsimile or photocopy of edition	Cutter and date of edition with *a*	.L55 1967a (.L55 1967aa, ab, etc.)

Translation	Cutter expanded by 12 - 19 and date	.L5513 1963 *[English translation]*
Selection, abridgement, or condensed version	Cutter expanded by 2 and date	.L552 1981 .S6L552 1981
Translation of selection, abridgement, or condensed version	Cutter expanded by 212 - 219 and date	.L55213 1982 *[English translation]*
Adaptations	By adapter, A-Z *[used only for works cataloged prior to AACR 2. Adaptations are now classed with works of adapter]*	
Criticism	Cutter expanded by 3 or 3 - 39 and date	.L553T5 1976 .S6L5537 1976
Biography and criticism	By author, A-Z	.L56B78 1986

The table shown above is applied only when it does not conflict with any specific instructions or provisions in the schedule being used. Often only a portion of the table is applicable to a particular number. For example, if a biography in connection with a particular topic has been given a separate number in the schedule, the biography provision of the table above should be ignored. In the subclasses in Class P the table above is not used because there are special tables there for arranging the works of individual literary authors.

Distinguishing Editions of a Work

The term *edition*, when used in relation to books, pamphlets, and other print materials, is defined in *AACR2R* as follows:

> All copies produced from essentially the same type image (whether by direct contact or by photographic or other methods) and issued by the same entity.[16]

Various manifestations of editions of a particular work are assigned Cutter numbers and dates according to the table "Preferred Shelflist Order - Individual Authors" shown above. For a discussion and examples of classifying different editions of a work, see chapter 5.

Translations

Translations[17] of a work that are classed in the same number as the original work normally follow the original text in an alphabetical arrangement by language. This is achieved by using successive Cutter numbers. The numeral 1 is inserted in order to avoid interference with other titles by the same author. The following table provides a general guide for arranging translations of works (except autobiographies or correspondence) by personal authors when a uniform title with designation of language(s) is given in the bibliographic record.

TRANSLATION TABLE

.x	Cutter number for original work
.x12	Polyglot
.x13	English translation
.x14	French translation
.x15	German translation
.x16	Italian translation
.x17	Russian translation
.x18	Spanish translation

This table is *not* used in the following cases:

1. when the main entry is under a corporate body or conference heading, or when there are specific provisions for translations in the schedules;

2. when the caption for the class number is "By language, A-Z"; in such cases, a Cutter number based on the name of the language is used, e.g., E5 for English, G4 for German, etc.; and,

3. when the work involved is assigned a number in Class M, Music, for which the Music Translation Table (see appendix A) is used.

If the language of the work being cataloged is not found in the Translation Table, a number which would place the language in the proper alphabetical position in the table and/or the shelflist is used. For example, if a Bulgarian, Chinese, or Czech translation is to be inserted, the Cutter number .x12 may be used; if a Hebrew translation, .x15 or .x16; a Portuguese translation, .x16 or .x17, depending on what has already been used.

If two languages are named in the uniform title, the Cutter number is based on the first language listed. In the past, the numeral 1 was frequently omitted from the Cutter number representing the translation, for example, .B3, original work; .B33, English translation; .B34, French translation; etc.

This practice has been discontinued except in cases in which the pattern has already been established in the shelflist or when there are specific instructions in the schedules.

DISPLAY OF THE NOTATION

There are many different ways an LC call number can be displayed on a physical item. Examples of call numbers on the spines of books at the Library of Congress are shown below:

B	BJ	BJ	BJ
162	466	455	455
.6	.S7	.B3S6	.B3S6
.S5	1986	1986	1986
1987	Copy 2	vol.3	Suppl.
		Copy 2	Copy 3

The letter or letters representing the subclass and the integral number appear on separate lines. (On work sheets, on the other hand, the class letter or letters with the integral number appear on the first line.[18]) Any decimal extension of the integral number would follow on a separate line to avoid the possibility of confusion should the decimal point be accidentally dropped. The next line is introduced by the decimal point for the Cutter number or numbers, which usually fill only one line even if there are two Cutter numbers. The use of the decimal point before the first element of the Cutter number may be traced to Charles A. Cutter's own use of Cutter numbers. Following the item number on a separate line is the date of publication, which in turn may be followed by "Suppl." (for a supplement), a volume number, and/or a copy number when applicable.

Many libraries do not follow this pattern of representation of the notation. For example, some libraries do not use the introductory decimal point for the Cutter numbers, and many prefer having the decimal extension on the same line as the main class number.

MARC CODES FOR LC CALL NUMBERS

In a bibliographic record, LC call numbers are tagged according to USMARC formats as follows:

In a MARC record, the LC call number appears in field 050. Two indicators and three subfield codes are used:[19]

Indicators

First   Existence in LC collection
ƀ   No information provided
0   Item is in LC
1   Item is not in LC

Second   Source of call number
0   Assigned by LC
4   Assigned by agency other than LC

Subfield Codes
$a   Classification number
$b   Item number
$3   Materials specified (used with archival-type materials to indicate the part of the described material to which the field applies)

For example,

00$a HD8391 $b .B374 1997
00$a E457.99 $b .L495 1997
00$a QP552.C24 $b G85 1996
00$a G1899.Z8 $b P5 1996
00$a G5404.R6E635 1996 $b .W4   {call number for a map}

The first indicator shows whether the book is in LC (0) or not in LC (1), and the second indicator is for the source of the call number, showing whether the call number is assigned by LC (0) or by an agency other than LC (4). Subfield code $a precedes the class number including the date or first Cutter number that forms part of it, and subfield code $b precedes the item number and date. If an alternate class number is provided, it appears in the same field, separated from the first class number by subfield code $a, for example,

00 $a Z5815.R6 $b V55 1997 $a LA972

In its own collections, in certain situations, the Library of Congress uses call numbers that are different from those provided in the current schedules. Such cases include incunabula, sound recordings, and items bearing obsolete numbers that have not been revised for lack of resources. In many cases of this nature, it is considered desirable to also provide current class numbers. When this is the case, multiple 050 (Library of Congress call number) fields are assigned. The first 050 field contains a current class number with indicator 1 set to "1" (not in LC under this number), and a second 050 field contains the number under which the item is shelved at the Library of Congress with indicator 1 set to "0" (in LC under this number).[20]

Classification authority records are coded according to *USMARC Format for Classification Data*.[21]

NOTES

1.   Charles Martel, "The Library of Congress Classification: Some Considerations Regarding the Relation of Book or Library Classification to the 'Order of the Sciences'," in *Essays Offered to Herbert Putnam by His Colleagues and Friends on His Thirtieth Anniversary As Librarian of Congress: 5 April 1929*, ed. William Warner Bishop and Andrew Keogh (New Haven, CT: Yale University Press, 1929), 330-31.

2.   "Call Numbers," Library of Congress, Cataloging Policy and Support Office, *Subject Cataloging Manual: Shelflisting*, 2nd ed. (Washington, DC: Library of Congress, 1995), G60.

3.   Library of Congress, *Library of Congress Filing Rules* (Washington, DC: Library of Congress, 1980).

4.   "Filing Rules," Library of Congress, *Subject Cataloging Manual: Shelflisting*, G100.

5.   "Call Numbers," Library of Congress, *Subject Cataloging Manual: Shelflisting*, G60, p. 14-15.

6.   Ibid., 15.

7.   Ibid., G100, p. 10.

8.   "Cutter Numbers: Topical Cutters," in Library of Congress, Office for Subject Cataloging Policy, *Subject Cataloging Manual: Classification*, 1st ed. (Washington, DC: Cataloging Distribution Service, Library of Congress, 1992), F350, p. 1.

9.   Library of Congress, *Library of Congress Filing Rules*.

10.   *Anglo-American Cataloguing Rules*, 2nd ed., 1988 revision, prepared under the direction of the Joint Steering Committee for Revision of AACR, a committee of: the American Library Association, the Australian Committee on Cataloguing, the British Library, the Canadian Committee on Cataloguing, the Library Association, the Library of Congress; ed. Michael Gorman and Paul W. Winkler (Chicago: American Library Association, 1988).

11.   "Regions and Countries Table," Library of Congress, *Subject Cataloging Manual: Shelflisting*, G300.

12.   "Dates," Library of Congress, *Subject Cataloging Manual: Shelflisting*, G140, p. 4.

13. Ibid., 5.

14. Ibid., 1.

15. "Call Numbers," Library of Congress, *Subject Cataloging Manual: Shelflisting*, G60, p. 13.

16. *Anglo-American Cataloguing Rules*, 617.

17. "Translations," Library of Congress, *Subject Cataloging Manual: Shelflisting*, G150.

18. "Basic Shelflisting Procedures," Library of Congress, *Subject Cataloging Manual: Shelflisting*, G50, p. 12.

19. *USMARC Format for Bibliographic Data, Including Guidelines for Content Designation*, prepared by Network Development and MARC Standards Office, 1994 ed. (Washington, DC: Cataloging Distribution Service, Library of Congress, 1994-), 050, p. 1.

20. "Current Classification Number/Shelf Number," *Cataloging Service Bulletin* 75 (Winter 1997):48.

21. *USMARC Format for Classification Data, Including Guidelines for Content Designation*, prepared by Network Development and MARC Standards Office (Washington, DC: Cataloging Distribution Service, Library of Congress, 1991).

Tables

INTRODUCTION

The Library of Congress (LC) Classification makes heavy use of tables, which provide a way to represent the sorts of subject subdivisions that occur over and over in the schedules. The use of such tables is an economical way of achieving specificity in class numbers without inflating the size of individual schedules. A table that represents a pattern of subdivision unique to a specific subject and that is only applicable to a specific span of numbers often appears at the beginning or the end of the span of numbers involved; such internal tables may vary in length from two to three lines to several pages. Tables that are called for at various points throughout an entire class or subclass normally appear at the end of a schedule immediately before the index. A number of tables are used throughout the whole system and may be called *free-floating tables*. Previously, in spite of their general application, these tables were reproduced in only a few schedules; now they also appear in *Subject Cataloging Manual: Shelflisting*.[1]

In general, the tables represent different patterns of subdivision: some by form, some by geographic area, some by time period, and some by topic. In classes B, M, N, and P, tables are also used to subarrange works by and about individual authors and artists.

Notations in tables are generally of two types: Cutter numbers and Arabic numbers. A Cutter number taken from a table, such as .U6 for United States, is attached to a class number or to another Cutter number as an extension. The numbers in a table of Arabic numbers indicate the order of subdivisions as they appear within a span of class numbers. To obtain the correct class number for a subtopic, the appropriate number from a table is *added* to a base number and *not attached* to the class number as an additional segment. This is a main difference between the numerical tables in the *Library of Congress Classification* and the auxiliary tables in the *Dewey Decimal Classification*.

The following section contains a discussion and demonstration of the use of various types of tables in the Library of Congress system. The tables covered range from those that are most widely applicable to those that are used only with limited spans of numbers. The order of treatment is

  (I) Tables of general application
  (II) Tables of limited application
    (1) Tables applicable to an entire class or subclass
    (2) Tables for internal subarrangement

Most of the examples in this chapter illustrate tables that occur in more than one class or one schedule. Detailed presentations and examples of tables unique to a specific class or schedule may be found in chapter 6, where each of the schedules is discussed in turn.

TABLES OF GENERAL APPLICATION

A number of tables that were initially used with a limited number of schedules have now been made applicable to all classes. These include certain geographic tables based on Cutter numbers, the Biography Table, and the Translation Table.

Geographic Division in Alphabetical Arrangement

This type of table represents geographic division in an alphabetical order by means of Cutter numbers. Examples are "Regions and Countries Table" and "Canadian Provinces." Applicable to numbers scattered throughout the system, these tables were originally printed in only a few schedules. They have since been included in the *Subject Cataloging Manual: Shelflisting*. The following discussion presents these commonly used tables, with examples. For specific details, see appendix A.

Regions and Countries Table

Used whenever the instruction "By region or country, A-Z" (or its equivalent, such as "By country, A-Z") is given in the schedules, this table appears in the *Subject Cataloging Manual: Shelflisting*[2] and in appendix A.

The table provides general guidance to assigning Cutter numbers for regions and countries. However, if the name of a country or region has already been established in either the shelflist or the classification schedule with a Cutter number different from that indicated in the table, the established number is used and the Cutter numbers for all new entries are then adjusted accordingly.

Normally, the table is applied in the following manner whenever the schedules call for its use.

Countries. The numbers listed in the table are used for countries as appropriate. For any area falling within the current boundaries of a country (defined as a sovereign nation), the Cutter number for the country is assigned if the caption in the schedule reads "By region or country, A-Z," even in a case where the subject heading assigned to the work is subdivided by the specific locality.[3] For example:

By region or country, A-Z

United States	.U6
Maryland	.U6 (area within the United States)
Great Britain	.G7
Scotland	.G7 (area within Great Britain)

If a region formerly belonged to another country, the Cutter number designated for the country to which it currently belongs is assigned, regardless of the period treated in the work.

Regions. When the subject is treated with reference to a region that either is larger than a country or crosses national boundaries and the class number covers all geographic areas with the designation: "By region or country, A-Z," a Cutter number based on the name of the region is used, for example:

By region or country, A-Z

Africa, North	.A355 (encompasses several countries)
Baltic States	.B29
Persian Gulf Region	.P35

If the class number is limited to a country or a continent and the work being classified treats a region within a country or a region within a continent and the name of the region contains the name of the country or continent, a Cutter number based on the name of the region in its natural order is assigned, for example:

Brazil, local A-Z

Brazil, North	.N6
Brazil, Central West	.C4

Regions or countries of Africa, A-Z

Africa, North	.N7

However, if the class number represents an area larger than the country and the region in question is located within a country, the same Cutter number assigned to the country is used for all the regions within it, for example:

South America, by region or country, A-Z

Brazil	.B6
Brazil, North	.B6
Brazil, Central West	.B6

Historical Jurisdictions/Entities. Historical countries and entities whose territories are not encompassed by any current country are cuttered according to their established forms of headings, for example:

Islamic Empire	.I742

Islands. If an island or group of islands is near the country to which it belongs, it is cuttered under the name of the country.

Jutland	.D4	[Cutter number for Denmark]
Sicily	.I8	[Cutter number for Italy]

If it is isolated from the parent country, it is cuttered under its own name, for example:

Falkland Islands	.F3
Puerto Rico	.P9

Subarrangement

In many cases, further subdivision by local place is provided under countries in the schedules. The local Cutter number then appears as the second Cutter number in a call number. For example:

By region or country, A-Z
Under each (local numbers used under country only);
.x   General works [x = Cutter number for country]
.x2   Local, A-Z

By region or country, A-Z
Under each (local numbers used under country only);
.x   Periodicals. Societies. Serials
.x2   General works
.x25   Local, A-Z
.x3   By company, A-Z

This subarrangement is used for localities under individual countries only, not under regions.

The following examples show the application of the Regions and Countries Table:

Greenprint : conservation in New Zealand.   1996

S	Subclass: Agriculture (General)
934	Conservation of natural resources in regions or countries
.N45	The first Cutter number (based on the Regions and Countries Table) for New Zealand
G74	The second Cutter number for the main entry under the title, *Greenprint* . . .
1996	The date of publication

American culture in the Netherlands   1996

E	Subclass: History: America
183	Political history of the United States
.8	Relations with individual countries, A-Z
.N4	The first Cutter number (based on the Regions and Countries Table) for the Netherlands
A44	The second Cutter number for the main entry under the title, *American* . . .
1996	The date of publication

United States

This table, listing Cutter numbers for individual states in the United States, is used when the instruction is "By state, A-Z" or "By region or state, A-Z," and when there is no conflict in the shelflist. It is included in the *Subject Cataloging Manual: Shelflisting*[4] and in appendix A. In case of conflict, the pattern of Cutter numbers established in the shelflist continues to be used.

A report of a survey on educating and training the work force [in Arkansas. 1996]

LC	Subclass: Special aspects of education
1046	Vocational education in the United States, by region or state, A-Z
.A8	The first Cutter number (based on the table, United States) for Arkansas
R47	The second Cutter number for the main entry under the title, *report* . . .
1996	The date of publication

New Hampshire forest resources plan.   1996

SD	Subclass: Forestry
144	Forest conditions in the United States, by region or state, A-W
.N4	The first Cutter number (based on the table, United States) for New Hampshire
N49	The second Cutter number for the main entry under the title, *New Hampshire* . . .
1996	The date of publication

Provinces in Canada

This table is used when the instruction "By province, A-Z" or "By region or province, A-Z" is given under a class number for Canada and when there is no conflict in the shelflist. It appears in the *Subject Cataloging Manual: Shelflisting*[5] and in appendix A. In case of conflict, the pattern of Cutter numbers established in the shelflist continues to be used.

Binkley, Marian Elizabeth.   *Risks, dangers, and rewards in the Nova Scotia offshore fishery.*   1995

SH	Subclass: Aquaculture. Fisheries. Angling
224	Fisheries in Canadian provinces
.N8	The first Cutter number (based on the table, Canadian Provinces) for Nova Scotia
B56	The second Cutter number for the main entry, Binkley
1995	The date of publication

Name Changes

For a jurisdiction that has undergone name changes, a Cutter number is normally assigned for the latest form of the name, regardless of the name used within the work. Similarly, unless there is provision to the contrary in the schedule, if a locality in question was formerly located within the territorial boundaries of another country, the Cutter number for the country in which it is presently situated is used, even if the work in hand describes conditions applicable to its earlier status. For example, a work relating to Persia, now Iran, is cuttered .I7 for Iran even though the work covers only the period when the locality was Persia.

Nasr, Seyyed Hossein.   *The Islamic intellectual tradition in Persia.* 1996

B	Subclass: Philosophy (General)
743	Medieval Islamic philosophers. By region, A-Z
.I7	The first Cutter number (based on the Regions and Countries Table) for Iran
N37	The second Cutter number for the main entry, Nasr
1996	The date of publication

Many geographic headings now have forms different from those used prior to 1981, when *AACR2* was implemented. If the new form of a geographic name varies slightly from the old (e.g., the variation is in the qualifier or in spelling that does not affect the filing position), the former Cutter number continues to be used. However, if the *AACR2R* form of the heading is significantly different from the pre-*AACR2R* form, a new Cutter number is established under the new form of the heading unless the obsolete number is already established in the shelflist under the class number in question. At the Library of Congress, previously assigned Cutter numbers are updated only when records are reprinted or revised for other reasons.

Biography Table

For subarrangement of works about a person, including biographies and autobiographical writings such as letters, diaries, and interviews, the Biography Table showing extensions of the Cutter number assigned to the person is used except when special provisions are given in the schedules. This table appears in *Subject Cataloging Manual: Shelflisting*[6] and is reproduced below:

BIOGRAPHY TABLE

.x	Cutter for the biographee
.xA2	Collected works. By date
.xA25	Selected works. Selections. By date
	Including quotations
.xA3	Autobiography, diaries, etc. By date
.xA4	Letters. By date
.xA5	Speeches, essays, and lectures. By date
	Including interviews
.xA6-Z	Individual biography, interviews, and criticism. By main entry
	Including criticism of selected works, autobiography, quotations, letters, speeches, interviews, etc.

The notation "x" in the table represents the first Cutter number assigned to the biographee. In the following example, the notation ".xA4" in the table is replaced by the Cutter numbers .M643A4:

Morris, May. *On poetry, painting, and politics : the letters of May Morris and John Quinn.*   1997

CT	Subclass: Biography
788	Individual biography of a person from Great Britain or England
.M643	The first Cutter number for the biographee, Morris
A4	The second Cutter number based on the Biography Table, meaning Letters
1997	The date of publication

For further discussion and examples of biographies, see chapter 7, pages 446–57.

Translation Table

The Translation Table is used throughout the system for arrangement of translations of a work. It appears in the *Shelflisting* manual[7] and in appendix A of this book. For details of this table and a discussion of its application, as well as limitations to its use, see chapter 3, pages 86-87.

TABLES OF LIMITED APPLICATION

Tables Applicable to an Individual Class or Subclass

Many of the tables appearing in individual schedules apply to an entire class or subclass. Examples are the author tables used throughout the schedules for Class P, Language and Literature; the form tables used in the schedules of Class K, Law; and the geographic tables in Class H, Social Sciences, and Class S, Agriculture. Following is a discussion of the application of these tables with examples. The discussion of individual classes in chapter 6 provides further examples illustrating their use.

Tables that apply to an individual schedule or to a group of schedules may be in the form of numerical tables, Cutter tables, or a combination of both.

In applying numerical tables, these steps should be followed:

1. Determine the range of numbers in the schedule within which the subject being represented falls.

2. Choose the appropriate table to be applied to the specific range of numbers.

3. Select the number in the table that represents the subject and fit the number (normally by simple substitution or addition of the table number to the base number) into the range of numbers from the schedule.

Author Tables

Author tables for subarranging works by and about individual writers are found in Class B, for philosophers, and in Class P, for literary authors. A given author may have been allotted a span of numbers, or one number, or a Cutter number or numbers. The allocations for philosophers in subclass B, Philosophy (General), are 50, 9, 5, 4, 1 (whole numbers), or a range of 5 Cutter numbers. The allocations for authors in Class P are 49, 19, 9, 5, 1 (whole numbers), or a Cutter number. In Class P, there are also tables for subarranging different manifestations (such as editions, translations, and criticism) of a particular work. The following examples illustrate the use of author tables, and further details and examples are found in chapter 6.

Authors with Fifty Numbers. The classification of works by and about the German philosopher Immanuel Kant illustrates the use of a table for an author with fifty numbers. In subclass B, Philosophy (General), Kant is assigned the range B2750-2799. Table B-BJ1, located before the index in the schedule for B-BJ, is used for philosophers with 50 numbers. The table is shown on following pages.

B-BJ1	TABLE OF SUBDIVISIONS (PHILOSOPHERS WITH 50 NUMBERS)	B-BJ1
	Use 0-49 or 50-99	
0	Periodicals. Societies. Serials	
1	Dictionaries	
	Collected works	
3	Original (vernacular) texts. By date	
4	Editions with commentary. By editor	
5	Partial editions, selections, etc. By editor or date	
	Translations	
	Including translations with original texts	
	Subarrange by translator or date	
6	Greek	
7	Latin	
8	English	
9	French	
10	German	
11	Italian	
12	Spanish and Portuguese	
13.A-Z	Other languages, A-Z	
15-44	Separate works	
	Alphabetically. By title (if not otherwise provided for)	
	Subarranged:	
	Works with 5 numbers:	
	0 or 5 *Original texts. By date*	
	1 or 6 *Editions with commentary. By editor*	
	2 or 7 *Selections, paraphrases, etc. By date*	
	3 or 8 *Translations (with or without*	

	notes). By language and translator or date *Assign two cutters, the first for language, the second for translator*
4 or 9	*Commentaries, interpretation, and criticism (with or without translations)*

Works with 3 numbers:

1	*Original texts. By date*
2	*Translations (with or without notes). By language and translator or date* *Assign two cutters, the first for language, the second for translator*
3	*Commentaries, interpretation and criticism (with or without translations)*

Works with 1 number:

.A3	*Original texts. By date*
.A4-.Z5	*Translations (with or without notes). By language and translator or date* *Assign two cutters, the first for language, the second for translator*
.Z7	*Commentaries, interpretation and criticism (with or without translations)*

Works with Cutter numbers:

.x	*Original texts. By date*
.x15	*Selections, paraphrases, etc. by date*
.x2	*Translations. By language, A-Z, and date*
.x3	*Commentaries, interpretations and criticism (with or without translations)*

Table continues on page 102.

45	Spurious and apocryphal works
46	Indexes, outlines, paraphrases, etc.
47	Biography and memoirs

       Subarrange:

.A1-.A19	*Periodicals. Societies. Serials*
.A3	*Autobiography. By date*
.A4	*Letters. By date*
.A5	*Speeches. By date*
.A6-.Z	*General works*
48	Criticism and interpretation
49	Special topics, A-Z

       For examples of topics, see B398, B491

The table indicates that the number 8 represents an English translation of collections of an author. An English translation of Kant's works, then, is classed in B2758. Note that the last digit in this class number matches the number given in the table.

Kant, Immanuel. *Kant's Latin writings : translations, commentaries, and notes* / Lewis White Beck ... [et al.]. 1996

B	Subclass: Philosophy (General)
2758	An English translation of Kant's works
.B356	The Cutter number for the translator, Beck
1996	The date of publication

Kant, Immanuel. *Practical philosophy.* [Translated and edited by Mary J. Gregor]. 1996

B	Subclass: Philosophy (General)
2758	An English translation of Kant's works
.G74	The Cutter number for the translator, Gregor
1996	The date of publication

As can be seen in the schedule, the more important of Kant's individual works are assigned a whole number or a range of numbers each, as enumerated in the schedule. Lesser works are classed together in one number, B2794, subarranged by Cutter numbers. His separate works fall in the range of numbers B2765-2794, which corresponds to the numbers 15-44 in Table B-BJ1 for separate works by a philosopher with 50 numbers.

Individual works of a philosopher may be assigned a range of 5 or 3 numbers, a whole number, or a Cutter number. Kant's *Kritik der reinen Vernunft* has been assigned a range of 5 numbers, B2775-2779. Various manifestations of this work are subarranged according to the instruction given under "Separate works" with 5 numbers in Table B-BJ1. For example, a translation of *Kritik der reinen Vernunft* is classed in the fourth number (i.e., 3 in the range of 0-4 or 8 in the range 5-9 in Table B-BJ1), B2778.

Kant, Immanuel. *Critique of pure reason* / translated and edited by Paul Guyer, Allen W. Wood. 1998

B	Subclass: Philosophy (General)
2778	Translation of Kant's *Kritik der reinen Vernunft*
.E5	English
G89	Cutter number for the translator, Guyer
1998	The date of publication

A commentary on the same work is represented by the number 4 or 9 in the table and is therefore assigned the number B2779 in this case.

Hinske, Norbert. *Die Kritik der reinen Vernunft und der Freiraum des Glaubens.* 1995

B	Subclass: Philosophy (General)
2779	Commentary on Kant's *Kritik der reinen Vernunft*
.H55	Cutter number for the main entry, Hinske
1995	The date of publication

Schultz, Johann. *Exposition of Kant's Critique of pure reason.* 1995.

B	Subclass: Philosophy (General)
2779	Commentary on Kant's *Kritik der reinen Vernunft*
.S3213	Cutter number (.S32) for the main entry, Schultz, and the successive element (13 from the Translation Table) for an English translation of the criticism
1995	The date of publication

Minor works by Kant are classed in the number B2794 with each work receiving a Cutter number. The tables again give instructions on subarranging editions of the work and works about it, as shown in the following example:

> Kant, Immanuel. *Lectures on ethics.* [Uniform title: *Essays. English. Selections*] 1996
>
> | | |
> |---|---|
> | B | Subclass: Philosophy (General) |
> | 2794 | Works by Kant other than those assigned their own class numbers |
> | .E892 | The first Cutter number (.E89) assigned to the uniform title *Essays* and the successive element (2) meaning a translation |
> | E5 | The second Cutter number meaning an English translation |
> | 1996 | The date of publication |

In the example above, the first Cutter number (.E892) is derived by first assigning a Cutter number (.E89) for the uniform title, *Essays* and then going to Table B-BJ1 for instructions for subarrangement under a work with a Cutter number. Under "Works with Cutter numbers" in Table B-BJ, the successive element (.x2) represents a translation, with the instruction for further subarrangement by language in alphabetical order. An English translation is, therefore, represented by the Cutter number E5.

The number 48 in Table B-BJ1 represents criticism and interpretation of a philosopher's works. Criticism of Kant's works in general is therefore classed in B2798.

> Renaut, Alain. *Kant aujourd'hui.* c1997
>
> | | |
> |---|---|
> | B | Subclass: Philosophy (General) |
> | 2798 | Criticism and interpretation of Immanuel Kant's works (48 in Table B-BJ1) |
> | .R425 | The Cutter number for the main entry, Renaut |
> | 1997 | The date of publication |

> Strathern, Paul. *Kant in 90 minutes.* 1996
>
> | | |
> |---|---|
> | B | Subclass: Philosophy (General) |
> | 2798 | Criticism and interpretation of Immanuel Kant's works (48 in Table B-BJ1) |
> | .S87 | The Cutter number for the main entry, Strathern |
> | 1996 | The date of publication |

Authors with Nineteen or Nine Numbers. The application of the literature tables in Class P for authors is quite similar to that for the tables for philosophers illustrated above. The literature tables are published in a separate volume: *P-PZ Language and Literature Tables* (1998 edition). Table

P-PZ32 is for nineteen-number authors, and Table P-PZ33 is for nine-number authors.

Jane Austen is an example of a nine-number author in subclass PR, English literature; she has been assigned the range of numbers PR4030-4038 in the schedule with the instruction to use Table P-PZ33. The following examples illustrate the use of this table.

Austen, Jane. *The complete novels.* [1995?]

PR	Subclass: English literature
4030	Collected works of Jane Austen
1995	The date of publication

Because, in Table P-PZ33, collected works of an author are arranged by date and the author's name is already implied in the class number, no Cutter number is assigned.

In the literature tables, collected works and selected works are sometimes given different numbers. Therefore, the classifier must determine the scope of the work being classified in order to assign the appropriate number. For subarrangement of selected works, Table P-PZ33 indicates "By editor, if given, or date."

Austen, Jane. *Sanditon and other stories* / edited and introduced by Peter Washington. 1996

PR	Subclass: English literature
4032	Selected works of Jane Austen
.W37	The Cutter number for the editor, Washington
1996	The date of publication

A work about Austen is classed in PR4037 as shown below:

Critical essays on Jane Austen. c1998

PR	Subclass: English literature
4037	A general criticism of Jane Austen
.C75	The Cutter number for the main entry under the title, *Critical . . .*
1998	The date of publication

In classifying individual works of literary authors, it is often necessary to use two tables in combination, one for subarranging works by and about the author and the other for subarranging editions and criticism of a particular work. Individual works of Austen are classed in PR4034, a number corresponding to the number (4) in Table P-PZ33 for separate works. Each individual work is assigned a Cutter number, as shown in the examples below.

> Austen, Jane. *Pride and prejudice.* 1996
>
> | PR | Subclass: English literature |
> |------|------------------------------|
> | 4034 | Separate works of Jane Austen |
> | .P7 | The Cutter number for the title, *Pride* . . . |
> | 1996 | The date of publication |
>
> Austen, Jane. *Emma.* 1996
>
> | PR | Subclass: English literature |
> |------|------------------------------|
> | 4034 | Separate works of Jane Austen |
> | .E5 | The Cutter number for the title, *Emma* |
> | 1996 | The date of publication |

For editions and criticism of an individual work, Table P-PZ43, Separate Works with Successive Cutter Numbers, is used. Table P-PZ43 uses three successive Cutter numbers to subarrange editions and criticism of an individual work. As the note in the table indicates, the numbers (1), (2), and (3) represent successive Cutter numbers. In the case of *Emma*, the successive Cutter numbers are .E5, .E52, and .E53. The Cutter number .E5 instead of .E51 is used because Cutter numbers ending in the digit 1 are generally avoided. The following example illustrates the use of the third successive Cutter number for a criticism of this work.

> Gay, Penny. *Jane Austen's Emma.* 1995
>
> | PR | Subclass: English literature |
> |------|------------------------------|
> | 4034 | Separate works of Jane Austen |
> | .E53 | The first Cutter number (.E5) for the title, *Emma*, with the successive element (3) meaning a work about it |
> | G38 | The second Cutter number for the main entry, Gay |
> | 1995 | The date of publication |

Authors with One Number or a Cutter Number. Authors with only one number or a Cutter number require a table using "A" and "Z" Cutter numbers to achieve differentiation. Tables P-PZ37 and P-PZ39 in Class P are designed for authors with one number. Tables P-PZ38 and P-PZ40 are for authors with only a Cutter number. Tables P-PZ37 and P-PZ38 are intended for authors, such as Richard Crashaw (PR3386) or Kate O'Flaherty Chopin

(PS1294.C63), who wrote very few works but who have had a good deal of material written about them. Therefore, only a small range of numbers is assigned to separate works with the majority of numbers devoted to biography and criticism. On the other hand, Tables P-PZ39 and P-PZ40 contain larger ranges of numbers assigned to individual works and use the "Z" Cutter numbers for biography and criticism, as shown in the tables reproduced below.

P-PZ39	TABLE FOR AUTHORS (1 NO.)	P-PZ39
	Collected works	
0.A1	By date	
0.A11-A13	By editor, if given	
0.A14	Collected prose works. By date	
0.A15	Collected fiction. By date	
0.A16	Collected essays. By date	
0.A17	Collected poems. By date	
0.A19	Collected plays. By date	
	Translations (Collected or selected)	
	Where the original language is English, French or German, omit numbers for original language in P-PZ39 0.A2-0.A49	
0.A199	Modern versions of early authors in the same language. By date	
0.A1995	Polyglot. By date	
0.A2-A29	English. By translator, if given, or date	
0.A3-A39	French. By translator, if given, or date	
0.A4-A49	German. By translator, if given, or date	
0.A5-A59	Other. By language	
0.A6	Selected works. Selections. By date	
0.A61-Z48	Separate works. By title	
	Subarrange each work by Table P-PZ43	
	Biography and criticism	
0.Z481-Z489	Periodicals. Societies. Serials	
0.Z49	Dictionaries, indexes, etc. By date	
0.Z5A3-Z5A39	Autobiography, journals, memoirs. By title	
0.Z5A4	Letters (Collections). By date	
0.Z5A41-Z5A49	Letters to and from particular individuals. By correspondent (Alphabetically)	
0.Z5A5-Z5Z	General works	

P-PZ40	TABLE FOR AUTHORS (CUTTER NO.)	P-PZ40
	Collected works	
.x	By date	
.xA11-.xA13	By editor, if given	
.xA14	Collected prose works. By date	
.xA15	Collected fiction. By date	
.xA16	Collected essays. By date	
.xA17	Collected poems. By date	
.xA19	Collected plays. By date	
	Translations (Collected or selected)	
	Where the original language is English, French or German, omit numbers for original language in P-PZ40 .xA2-.xA49	
.xA199	Modern versions of early authors in the same language. By date	
.xA1995	Polyglot. By date	
.xA2-.xA29	English. By translator, if given, or date	
.xA3-.xA39	French. By translator, if given, or date	
.xA4-.xA49	German. By translator, if given, or date	
.xA5-.xA59	Other. By language	
.xA6	Selected works. Selections. By date	
.xA61-.Z458	Separate works. By title	
	Biography and criticism	
.xZ4581-.xZ4589	Periodicals. Societies. Serials	
.xZ459	Dictionaries, indexes, etc. By date	
.xZ46-.xZ479	Autobiography, journals, memoirs. By title	
.xZ48	Letters (Collections). By date	
.xZ481-.xZ499	Letters to and from particular individuals. By correspondent (alphabetically)	
.xZ5-.xZ999	General works	

In Table P-PZ40, for example, the majority of the range of Cutter numbers, A-Z, is given to separate works, .xA61-Z458. Biography and criticism have only the range .xZ4581-999. It should be observed that this is a single alphabetical range of A-Z, with many "A" and "Z" Cutter numbers.

The following examples illustrate the use of Table P-PZ40. Ernest Hemingway, an American novelist, is an example of a Cutter-number author. Works by and about Hemingway are classed in PS3515.E37. "PS" means American literature; PS3515 is the number within American literature for modern authors whose last name begins with "H"; and E37 is the Cutter number for Hemingway based on the "-emingway" part of the name, as the "H" has already been designated in the number 3515. Unless indicated otherwise in the schedule, Table P-PZ40 is used for authors with Cutter numbers. The following examples illustrate how this table is used for works by and about Hemingway.

The Complete Short Stories of Ernest Hemingway. 1987

PS	Subclass: American literature
3515	Modern American authors whose last names begin with the letter "H"
.E37	The first Cutter number for Hemingway
A15	The second Cutter number derived from Table P-PZ40 meaning collected fiction
1987	The date of publication

Hemingway, Ernest. *The short stories.* 1997

PS	Subclass: American literature
3515	Modern American authors whose last names begin with the letter "H"
.E37	The first Cutter number for Hemingway
A6	The second Cutter number derived from Table P-PZ40 meaning Selected works
1997	The date of publication

Hemingway, Ernest. *Across the river and into the trees.* 1998

PS	Subclass: American literature
3515	Modern American authors whose last names begin with the letter "H"
.E37	The first Cutter number for Hemingway
A7	The second Cutter number based on the title of the separate work, *Across . . .*
1998	The date of publication

The reason that the second Cutter number for the title, *Across the River and into the Trees*, in the example above is A7 rather than A2 as it should be if assigned according to the Cutter Table is that all separate works by Hemingway are classed between the Cutter numbers .xA61-Z458 as shown in Table P-PZ40 (where .x stands for the author's Cutter number). Any number for an individual work must be greater than A61 and smaller than Z458.

Hemingway, Ernest.   *The old man and the sea.*   1995

PS	Subclass: American literature
3515	Modern American authors whose last names begin with the letter "H"
.E37	The first Cutter number for Hemingway
O4	The second Cutter number based on the title of the separate work, *old . . .*
1995	The date of publication

As general works of criticism are represented by the numbers .xZ5-999 in Table P-PZ40, all such works about Hemingway are classed in PS3515.E37Z5 through PS3515.E37Z999, subarranged alphabetically by main entry. An example is shown below.

Tessitore, John.   *The hunt and the feast : a life of Ernest Hemingway.* 1996

PS	Subclass: American literature
3515	Modern American authors whose last names begin with the letter "H"
.E37	The Cutter number for Hemingway
Z8918	The second Cutter number for the main entry, Tessitore, a number within the range of .Z5-.999 according to Table P-PZ40
1996	The date of publication

The "Z8918" represents the Cutter number for the main entry, Tessitore. "8918" was chosen to place this work nearer the end of the alphabet, to reflect the relative position of the letter "T" in the alphabet. Of course, "8918" does not normally represent "Tessitore"; it does so only in this particular case. Because all critical works and biographies of Hemingway are classed in a small range of Cutter numbers, the item numbers can be quite long in some cases.

Readings on Ernest Hemingway.   1997

PS	Subclass: American literature
3515	Modern American authors whose last names begin with the letter "H"
.E37	The Cutter number for Hemingway

Z75455   The second Cutter number for the main entry under the title, *Readings. . .* , a number within the range of .Z5-.Z999 according to Table P-PZ40

1997   The date of publication

Burrill, William.   *Hemingway : the Toronto years.*   1994

PS   Subclass: American literature

3515   Modern American authors whose last names begin with the letter "H"

.E37   The Cutter number for Hemingway

Z5841615   The second Cutter number for the main entry, Burrill, a number within the range of .Z5-.Z999 according to Table P-PZ40

1994   The date of publication

A work about an individual work is assigned a number based on that of the original work, so that a work and the works about it stand together on the shelves.

Ernest Hemingway's The old man and the sea.   1996

PS   Subclass: American literature

3515   Modern American authors whose last names begin with the letter "H"

.E37   The first Cutter number for Hemingway

O52   The second Cutter number for a work about *The old man and the sea*

1996b   The date of publication

In this case, the Cutter numbers .O4 for the original work and .O52 for the commentary are successive Cutter numbers. Another commentary on *The old man and the sea* entitled *Hemingway's debt to baseball in The old man and the sea* has been assigned PS3515.E37 O5224 1992.

Form Tables

A form table provides a pattern of subarrangement of materials on a particular subject by physical or bibliographic form. These tables are usually used when geographic or chronological division is not needed or has already been extensively provided in the schedules. There are many such "form tables" in the schedules for Class K (Law). An example is the use of Table K12 (formerly Table IV) for form divisions in schedule KJV-KJW, Law of France. The new Table K12 appears in *K Tables: Form Division Tables for Law* (1999).

K12	TABLE FOR COUNTRIES, STATES, PROVINCES, ETC. (CUTTER NO.)	K12

.xA15-.xA199	Periodicals Including official gazettes, yearbooks, bulletins, etc.
.xA2	Legislative documents. Working documents. Official reports. By date Treaties. Statutes. Statutory orders (Collective or individual). Rules
.xA29-.xA299	Serials
.xA3	Monographs. By date Cases. Decisions (Collective or individual). Measures. Opinions
.xA5-.xA519	Serials
.xA52	Monographs. By date
.xA7-.xZ9	General works. Treatises

The following examples illustrate the application of this table.

Guide juridique du salarie. 1993

KJV	Subclass: Law of France
3475	Labor law for particular industries or occupations
.S24	The first Cutter number for salaried employees
G58	The second Cutter number (within the range of .xA7-.xZ9 in Table K12) for a general work entered under the title, *Guide . . .*
1993	The date of publication

The schedule also indicates that Table K12 is to be used with KJV4207, Equality of particular groups before the law. In this table, general works are assigned the Cutter numbers .xA7-.xZ9, where x equals the Cutter number for the particular group and A7-Z9 is the range of Cutter numbers assigned to general works.

Weisberg, Richard H.   *Vichy law and the Holocaust in France.*   1996

KJV	Subclass: Law of France
4207	Equality of particular groups before the law
.J49	The first Cutter number for the group, Jews
W45	The second Cutter number (within the range of .xA7-.xZ9 in Table K12) for a general work with the main entry, Weisberg
1996	The date of publication

For further examples of the use of form tables in Class K, see the discussion in chapter 6, pages 301–306.

Geographic Tables

The LC Classification provides for two types of geographic division. One is in alphabetical order by jurisdictional or place name, accomplished through using Cutter numbers; this arrangement was discussed earlier in this chapter. The second is a classified arrangement, with geographic areas given numbers in a classified order. The numbers used in classed tables vary from case to case, depending on the ranges of numbers assigned to specific topics in a given schedule. An example is "S2 Geographical Distribution Tables" found in Class S. This two-column table is shown on pages 114-15.

63-64	Soviet Union
65-66	Spain
67-68	Sweden
69-70	Switzerland
71-72	Turkey
73.A-Z	Other regions or countries, A-Z
75	Asia
77-78	China
79-80	India
81-82	Japan
83-84	Iran
85-86	Philippine Islands
87-88	Soviet Union in Asia. Siberia
89-90	Turkey in Asia
91.A-Z	Other regions or countries, A-Z
	e.g.
91.T3	Taiwan
93	Africa
95-96	Egypt
98.A-Z	Other regions or countries, A-Z
	Indian Ocean islands
98.5	General works
98.6.A-Z	By island or group of islands, A-Z
99-100	Australia
100.2	New Zealand
100.8	Pacific Area
	Pacific islands. Oceania
100.9	General works
101.A-Z	By island or group of islands, A-Z

The application of this table is shown in the following examples.

Dargavel, John.	*Fashioning Australia's forests*. 1995
SD	Subclass: Forestry
243	The number (base number 144 + table number 99) meaning a history of forestry in Australia
.D37	The Cutter number for the main entry, Dargavel
1995	The date of publication

The class number 243 is arrived at by following the instructions in the schedule and the procedure outlined above for the use of tables. In the schedule, the numbers SD145-246 have been assigned to the history of forestry subdivided by country according to Table S2, with the instruction: "Add number in the table to SD144." In Table S2 reproduced above, the numbers 99-100 are assigned to Australia, the first being used for a general work, meaning a work about the country as a whole. Adding 99 to the base number 144 results in the desired number 243.

A work about forest conditions in a local subdivision of Australia is classed in SD244, the second number assigned to Australia.

Taylor, Peter.	*Growing up : forestry in Queensland.* 1994
SD	Subclass: Forestry
244	The number (base number 144 + table number 100) meaning a history of forestry in a local subdivision of Australia
.Q8	The first Cutter number for Queensland
T38	The second Cutter number for the main entry, Taylor
1994	The date of publication

The Tables of Geographical Divisions in Classes H and N are much more complex than those in Class S, but they are applied in much the same way. For examples of using these tables, see chapter 6, pages 243–51.

Tables for Internal Subarrangement

The most common tables in the LC system are those used for subarrangement of the ranges of numbers assigned to specific topics or places within the schedules. Some of these represent a combination of form, period, geographic, and subject elements. They range from a few lines of instructions to several pages. In older schedules, they typically appear just before or after the spans of numbers involved. In recent editions produced from electronic data, many tables that previously appeared within a schedule have been moved to its end, where they are printed just before the index. This was done to facilitate machine manipulation of tables in the electronic version of the schedules. An example is the set of tables used with the span of numbers HC94-1085.2. These tables, previously appearing just before those numbers, have been converted to Tables H15-17 and placed before the index. Whether these internal tables appear at the end of the schedules or within them, the procedure for their application is similar.

**Tables for Internal Subarrangement
Appearing at the End of Schedules**

Internal tables appear in various formats in different schedules. An example of a table for internal arrangement appearing at the end of the schedule is Table Z7 in Class Z.

Z7	BOOK SELLING AND PUBLISHING
	Add the appropriate number from this table to the first number of the classification number span to which the table applies
0	General works
	Including topics and forms not otherwise provided for
1	Bibliography
2	History. Biography
	Including histories of individual firms
	Subarrange individual biographies or histories of individual firms by assigning two Cutters, the first for the person or firm and the second for the author
	For catalogs, *see* Publishers' catalogs in national bibliography, e.g. Z1217, United States publishers' catalogs
3	Special lines of business (not A-Z)
4	Directories
5	Handbooks, manuals, etc.
6	Periodicals. Societies. Congresses
7	Collections
	Local
7.3.A-Z	By state or region, A-Z
7.6.A-Z	By city, A-Z

Table Z7 is designed for use with countries that have been assigned eight numbers, 0-7; for example, the span of numbers Z323-330 is allotted to bookselling and publishing in Great Britain. The history of a publisher in Britain is, therefore, assigned the number Z325, resulting from matching the table number to the schedule numbers or by adding the number 2 from Table Z7 to the first number (Z323) in the range Z323-330.

Bower, Tom.   *Maxwell : the final verdict.*   1995.

Z	Subclass: Book industries and trade
325	The third number (2 in Table Z7) in the range Z323-330 for a history of an individual firm in Great Britain
.M394	The first Cutter number for the name of the firm, Maxwell
B68	The second Cutter number for the main entry, Bower
1995	The date of publication

Table Z9 is designed for use with countries that have been assigned a Cutter number.

Z9	BOOK SELLING AND PUBLISHING
.x	General works
	Including topics and forms not otherwise provided for
.x2	Bibliography
.x3	History. Biography
	Including histories of individual firms
	Subarrange individual biographies or histories of individual firms by assigning two Cutters, the first for the person or firm and the second for the author
	For catalogs, *see* Publishers' catalogs in national bibliography, e.g. Z1217, United States publishers' catalogs
.x4	Special lines of business (not A-Z)
.x5	Directories
.x6	Handbooks, manuals, etc.
.x7	Periodicals. Societies. Congresses
.x8	Collections
	Local
.x83A-Z	By state or region, A-Z
.x86A-Z	By city, A-Z

The following example illustrates the use of this table:

Ferns, Martin. *National Seminar on Primary Textbook Publishing in Zambia : report of an EMU/SIDA Seminar : Lusaka, 31 May and 1 June 1993.* [1993?]

Z	Subclass: Book industries and trade
470	Countries in Africa
.Z334	The first Cutter number .Z33 for Zambia from the Regions and Countries Table and the element 4 from Table Z9 above meaning special lines of business, in this case primary textbook publishing
F47	The second Cutter number for the main entry, Ferns
1993	The date of publication

The table shown below is one of the tables designed for use with the range of numbers, HC94-1085, Economic history and conditions by region or country.

H15	TABLE OF ECONOMIC SUBDIVISIONS	H15
	(10 NOS.)	

	Documents
1.A1-A3	Serial documents
	Separate documents
1.A4	Administrative documents. By date
	Other documents, see 3
1.A5-Z	Periodicals. Societies. Serials
2	Dictionaries. Encyclopedias
2.2	Directories
	For export-import or foreign trade directories, see HF3221-HF4040.7
	Biography
	For particular industries, see HD
2.5.A2	Collective
2.5.A3-Z	Individual, A-Z
3	General works
3.5	Natural resources
	By period
	Period divisions vary for different countries
4	Early
	Including Medieval

Table continues on page 120.

5	Later
	Local
	Used under countries only
7.A-Z	By state, etc., A-Z
8.A-Z	By city, A-Z
	For local annual reviews of "Commerce," "Finance," "Trade," etc., see HF3163 and HF3221-HF4040.7, subdivision (10) under each country; general, HC14
9	Colonies
	Including exploitation and economic conditions. For colonial administration and policy, see JV.
10.A-Z	Special topics (not otherwise provided for), A-Z
	For list of topics, see HC79
	For special topics in areas within a country, see subdivisions 7 and 8, Local

The tables found in subclass HC are typical of internal tables printed in recently published schedules. In the schedule, the economic conditions of Canada receive a range of numbers, HC111-120, with an instruction to use Table H15. A work on the economic conditions of British Columbia is classed in HC117.B8, that is, the seventh number in the range according to Table H15, with the addition of the Cutter number ".B8" for the province.

High technology industries in British Columbia : the agenda for growth : a discussion paper. 1995

HC	Subclass: Economic history and conditions
117	Economic conditions of Canada subdivided by province, A-Z, based on Table H15
.B8	The first Cutter number for British Columbia
H54	The second Cutter number for the main entry under the title, *High technology . . .*
1995	The date of publication

**Tables for Internal Subarrangement
Appearing Within Schedules**

Many tables for subarrangement appear within the schedules, immediately preceding the range of numbers to which they apply. Most of them are relatively short, containing a few numbers only. Following is an example of a simple internal table:

HC	ECONOMIC HISTORY AND CONDITIONS
	By region or country
	America. Western Hemisphere
	North America
	United States
107.A2-W	Individual states, A-W

Under each state:

.x	*General works*
.x2A-Z	*By region, country, parish, A-Z*
.x3A-Z	*Special topics, A-Z*
	For list of topics, see HC79

Illegal dumping : assessment of impacts on county governments in the Texas-Mexico border region, 1996. [1997]

HC	Subclass: Economic history and conditions
107	Regions and states in the United States
.T43	The first Cutter number (.T4) for Texas from the States Table with the successive element (3) from the internal table shown above for a special topic
P555	The second Cutter number (.P55) for Pollution (as listed under HC79) and the additional successive element (5) to differentiate works on the same topic
1997	The date of publication

Some of the internal tables can be rather long. An example is Table CD3070/1, which is used with the span of numbers CD3070-3615, state archives in the United States. The table appears within the schedule in the following form.

CD   DIPLOMATICS.   ARCHIVES.   SEALS
        Archives
          History and statistics
            By region or country
              America
                North America
                  United States

3070-3615   By state
                      Under each:
                      TABLE CD3070/1
                        Table for archives, etc. by state

0	*Periodicals. Societies. Serials*
1	*General history and statistics*
4	*State archives*
6.A-Z	*State departments, A-Z*
	e.g.
6.S8	*State department*
6.5	*Legislative Branch (Table C4)*
	Counties
7.A1	*General works*
7.A2-Z	*By county, A-Z*
	Municipal
8.A1	*General works*
8.A2-Z	*By municipality, A-Z*
	Parish registers
8.5	*Collective*
8.6.A-Z	*By diocese, parish, or other division, A-Z*
9.A-Z	*Religious and academic institutions. By place, A-Z*

In the schedule, archives of California are assigned the range of numbers CD3110-3119. Based on the table, a general work about archives in California is classed in CD3111, the number matching the second number (1) in the internal table.

Levine, Stephen. *Paper trails : a guide to public records in California.* 1996

CD	Subclass: Diplomatics, Archives, Seals
3111	A general work about public papers in California
.L48	The Cutter number for the main entry, Levine
1996	The date of publication

Similarly,

> *Guide to archives and historical collections in the Washington metropolitan area.* 1995
>
> CD   Subclass: Diplomatics, Archives, Seals
>
> 3161   A general work about archives in the District of Columbia
>
> .G85   The Cutter number for the main entry under the title, *Guide . . .*
>
> 1995   The date of publication

> Massachusetts Archives.   *Subject guide to records in the Massachusetts Archives.* [1996]
>
> CD   Subclass: Diplomatics, Archives, Seals
>
> 3294   State archives (4 in Table CD3070/1) of Massachusetts
>
> .M38   The Cutter number for the main entry, Massachusetts Archives
>
> 1996   The date of publication

For the public finance of individual states in the United States, the following table is used to indicate the assignment of the three numbers allotted to each state:

HJ   PUBLIC FINANCE
      Local finance
        By region or country
          United States
9191-9343   States
                Under each:
                  Table for local finance by state (United States)
          1   *General works*
          2   *Revenue.   Taxation*
                        Including revenue sharing by a state with its local jurisdictions
          2.4   *Public debts*
          2.7   *Administration*
          3.A-Z   *Local, A-Z*

The numbers HJ9191-9343 are designated for public finance of states in the United States. The third number assigned to each state is used for local subdivision within the state. The state of Maryland is assigned the numbers HJ9251-9253. The following examples illustrate the use of the internal table shown above.

Maryland. General Assembly. Dept. of Fiscal Services. *General Assembly study of state mandates on local governments in general government.* 1997

HJ	Subclass: Public Finance
9251	The first number (according to the internal table) designated for Maryland for a general work
.M37	The Cutter number for the main entry, Maryland
1997	The date of publication

Tax capacity and effort of local governments in Maryland : FY1993-FY1994. [1997]

HJ	Subclass: Public Finance
9252	The second number (according to the internal table) designated for Maryland for a work about taxation
.T39	The Cutter number for the main entry under the title, *Tax . . .*
1997	The date of publication

Bilanin, Jeanne E. *The fiscal impact of annexation on the City of Mount Rainier.* [1996]

HJ	Subclass: Public Finance
9253	The third number (according to the internal table) designated for Maryland for a work about local finance
.M68	The first Cutter number for the city of Mount Rainier
B55	The second Cutter number for the main entry, Bilanin
1996	The date of publication

It should be noted that the table numbers are ordinals that indicate the order of the numbers to be assigned. In other words, "1" means the first number in the span for the state. For example, the numbers designated for California are HJ9203-9205. In this case, a work about taxation in California would be assigned the number HJ9204, the second number in the range. If the addition method is used, the base number to which the table number is added is the first number in the range minus one, that is, HJ9202.

In many cases, the classifier must use more than one table to arrive at a particular call number. As seen in the examples above, many auxiliary tables and internal tables contain instructions for local subdivision A-Z, calling for the use of the general tables for geographic subdivision. The Biography and Translation Tables, particularly, are often used in combination with other tables. Frequently, an internal table or an auxiliary table applicable to an entire class or subclass is used in conjunction with another internal table or a free-floating table for building the call number. The following example from Class N illustrates the use of multiple tables.

Drawing, Design, and Illustration in specific countries are classed in NC101-377 with the use of Table N3 in Class N. In this table each country is assigned three numbers, one number, a decimal number, or a Cutter number. Three internal tables are provided in the schedule to give instruction on how to subarrange the numbers allotted to each country. For example, according to Table N3, French drawing is represented by the number 146. The fact that the next number in the table (assigned to German, Austrian, and Swiss [Collectively]) is 148.6 indicates that France is a three-number country: 146-148. These numbers, when added to the base number 100 given under NC101-377 in the schedule, become NC246-248, the actual numbers to be used for French drawing. An internal table given under NC101-377 indicates how the three numbers are used:

Under each (three-number countries):	
1	*General works*
2.A-2.Z	*Local, A-Z*
3.A-3.Z	*Special artists, A-Z*

According to this table, the first number for each country is used for general works on drawing, that is, NC246 for French drawing in the following example:

Fogg Art Museum. *David to Corot : French drawings in the Fogg Art Museum.* 1996

NC	Subclass: Drawing, Design, Illustration
246	A general work (the first number according to the internal table) on French drawing
.F64	The Cutter number for the main entry, Fogg Art Museum
1996	The date of publication

The third number is used for special artists.

Fouladvind, Hamid. *Aragon : anti-portrait.* [1997]

NC	Subclass: Drawing, Design, Illustration
248	French drawing: special artists (the third number according to the internal table)
.A62	The first Cutter number for the artist, Aragon
.F68	The second Cutter number for the main entry, Fouladvind
1997	The date of publication

Chapter 6, which treats individual classes one by one, provides further discussion and examples of the use of tables.

NOTES

1. Library of Congress, Cataloging Policy and Support Office, *Subject Cataloging Manual: Shelflisting*, 2nd ed. (Washington, DC: Library of Congress, 1995).

2. "Regions and Countries Table," Library of Congress, *Subject Cataloging Manual: Shelflisting*, G300, pp. 4-9.

3. Ibid., 1.

4. "American States and Canadian Provinces," Library of Congress, *Subject Cataloging Manual: Shelflisting*, G302, pp. 1-2.

5. Ibid., 2.

6. "Biography," Library of Congress, *Subject Cataloging Manual: Shelflisting*, G320, p. 5.

7. "Translations," Library of Congress, *Subject Cataloging Manual: Shelflisting*, G150, p. 1.

Assigning Class Numbers

INTRODUCTION

Chapters 1 through 4 of this book present the general principles upon which the Library of Congress (LC) Classification was conceived and developed, and describe the classificational structure that was built as a result. The remaining chapters deal with the practical aspects of assigning class numbers and constructing call numbers. This chapter sets forth general policies and guidelines affecting the choice of class numbers. Chapter 6 details the particularities of individual classes, and chapter 7 treats the classification of special types of materials.

The discussions in these concluding chapters are based on three sources of information: (1) the LC publications, *Subject Cataloging Manual: Classification*,[1] *Subject Cataloging Manual: Shelflisting*,[2] and *Cataloging Service Bulletin*;[3] (2) consultation with the staff of the Cataloging Policy and Support Office of the Library of Congress; and (3) examination of LC MARC records.

For a classifier, putting an item in its appropriate place in any given classificational array requires not only strong subject knowledge in the area to which the item belongs but also an intimate knowledge of the schedules being used. It requires familiarity with the collection at hand and with the practices and policies of the agency in which the classifier works. For libraries using LC MARC records as cataloging copy, it is, of course, also important to be familiar with LC classification policies.

GENERAL POLICY

The general policy of assigning call numbers, as stated in *Subject Cataloging Manual: Classification*,[4] is to class a work according to its subject matter in the most specific number available that covers the content of the work. When a co-extensive number is not available, the Library may establish it when feasible. Otherwise, a broader number is assigned, normally one that is one level up in the hierarchy.

The second principle is to class a work in hand with similar works (that is, on the same subject treated from the same perspective) that are already in the collection. Ways to ascertain where works on the same subject have been classed previously include: (1) consulting existing records in the catalog by searching under the subject or the author, (2) consulting class numbers listed under appropriate subject headings in *Library of Congress Subject Headings*, and (3) consulting the outline to the whole classification to locate possibly appropriate individual schedules and then studying their outlines and indexes.

Because the Classification is organized by discipline, the first step in formulating a call number is to select the appropriate main class and subclass. As implied in the previous paragraph, this can best be accomplished by consulting the overall schedule outline. Once an appropriate schedule is chosen, the second step is to locate the most suitable placement within it. In doing so, one must pay particular attention to indentions of topics since they indicate the hierarchical position of a topic in the overall classification. After the class number has been determined, an item number and the date, if required, are added to complete the call number. The completed call number must then be checked in the shelflist to ascertain whether other works on the same subject have been assigned that number. If so, the item number must be adjusted to ensure that the call number is unique.

Works on a Single Topic

For a work on a single topic, the most specific class number that represents the overall content of the work is assigned. Ideally, the meaning of the number is co-extensive with, that is, as specific as, the content of the work being classified. When there is no co-extensive number—either pre-existing or newly established—then the next appropriate broader number is chosen. The following two examples show cases where a co-extensive number could be found; the third shows an item classed under a broader number:

Overview of school health services : school nurse review.   c1993

RJ	Subclass: Pediatrics
247	School nursing
.O94	The Cutter number for the main entry under the title, *Overview* . . .
1993	The date of publication

Sprinthall, Richard C.   *Educational psychology : a developmental approach.*   c1998

LB	Subclass: Theory and practice of education
1051	Educational psychology
.S6459	The Cutter number for the main entry, Sprinthall
1998	The date of publication

Willan, Anne.   *Perfect chocolate desserts.*   1997

TX	Subclass: Home economics
767	Recipes for special food products
.C5	The first Cutter number for Chocolate
W56	The Cutter number for the main entry, Willan
1997	The date of publication

Works on a Single Topic with Respect to One or More Facets

Many works treat a topic with respect to one or more facets, that is, aspects such as form, place, or period. A class number covering the topic as well as the facet or facets, if available, is chosen.

Onsager, Lars.   *The collected works of Lars Onsager : with commentary.*   1996

QD	Subclass: Chemistry
3	Collected works (nonserial)
.O56	The Cutter number for the main entry, Onsager
1996	The date of publication

If a class number covering the topic as well as the facet or facets is not available, the "general works" number for the specific topic is chosen.

General Works

Under most class numbers with subdivisions, a number is designated for "general works"; such numbers are used for works on the topic in general. The examples below show excerpts from the schedules, followed by classification data for items classed under the general works provision.

Schedule excerpt

RJ	PEDIATRICS
	Nursing of children. Pediatric nursing
245	General works
247	School nursing

Example

Wong, Donna L.   *Whaley & Wong's essentials of pediatric nursing.* c1997

RJ	Subclass: Pediatrics
245	General works on Pediatric nursing
.W46	The Cutter number for the main entry, Wong
1997	The date of publication

Schedule excerpt

PN	DRAMA
	Motion pictures
1994.A52-Z	General works
1995	Juvenile literature

Example

Giannetti, Louis D.   *Understanding movies.*   c1999

PN	Subclass: Drama
1994	General works on motion pictures
.G47	The Cutter number for the main entry, Giannetti
1999	The date of publication

General Special

Under certain topics and following "General works" numbers, there are numbers that are designated "General special" or "Special aspects of the subject as a whole."[5] Although the practice of establishing new "General special" numbers has been discontinued, those already established have not been deleted and continue to be used. Such numbers are used in the following circumstances: (1) "amorphous" works with undefinable concepts; and (2) works on subjects so new that their proper placements in the classification hierarchy cannot be established immediately. For example:

Segesvary, Victor. *Inter-civilizational relations and the destiny of the West : dialogue or confrontation?*   c1998

CB	Subclass: History of civilization
151	General special, including special aspects and relations of the history of civilization
.S38	The Cutter number for the main entry, Segesvary
1998	The date of publication

Ochoa, George. *The Wilson chronology of ideas.*   1998

CB	Subclass: History of civilization
151	General special, including special aspects and relations of the history of civilization
.O37	The Cutter number for the main entry, Ochoa
1998	The date of publication

Carroll, Noel (Noel E.) *Interpreting the moving image.*   1998

PN	Subclass: Drama
1995	"General special" works on motion pictures, including criticism, aesthetics, etc.
.C3547	The Cutter number for the main entry, Carroll
1998	The date of publication

In the eye of the beholder : critical perspectives in popular film and television. c1997

PN	Subclass: Drama
1995	"General special" works on motion pictures, including criticism, aesthetics, etc.
.I565	The Cutter number for the main entry under the title, *In*...
1997	The date of publication

Form

For a work treating a topic with regard to a particular form, the number that represents both the topic and the form, if available, is chosen.

A dictionary of computing.   1997

QA	Subclass: Mathematics
76.15	Dictionaries and encyclopedias of electronic computers
.D526	The Cutter number for the main entry under the title, *dictionary* . . .
1997	The date of publication

Sotomayor, Gladys G.   *Art directory : galleries, alternative spaces, and resources in P.R.*   c1996

N	Subclass: Visual arts
55	Directories in places outside of the United States, A-Z
.P9	The first Cutter number for Puerto Rico
S67	The second Cutter number for the main entry, Sotomayor
1996	The date of publication

When the schedules provide for a specific topic but special numbers for form subdivisions are not provided under that topic, the "General works" number for the specific topic rather than the form number under a broader topic is chosen.

Miermont, Jacques. *A dictionary of family therapy.*   English ed. 1995

RC	Subclass: Internal medicine
488.5	Family psychotherapy: General works
.M5313	The Cutter number .M53 for the main entry, Miermont, with the successive element (13 from the Translation Table) for an English translation
1995	The date of publication

In the example above, the class number RC488.5 (for general works on family psychotherapy) is chosen over the number RC475.7, Dictionaries and encyclopedias of psychotherapy, a number which would bring out the form but would place the work some distance away from others on its specific topic. Other examples:

> *The Blackwell dictionary of neuropsychology.* 1996
>
> QP   Subclass: Physiology
>
> 360   Neuropsychology: general works
>
> .B577   The Cutter number for the main entry under the title, *Blackwell* . . .
>
> 1996   The date of publication

> International Workshop on ERS Applications (2nd : 1995 : London, England) *Proceedings of the Second International Workshop on ERS Applications : London, 6-8 December 1995.* c1996
>
> QE   Subclass: Geology
>
> 33.2   Special topics
>
> .A7   The first Cutter number for the topic, Artificial satellites in geology
>
> I58   The second Cutter number for the main entry, International . . .
>
> 1995   The date of the conference

In the last example, the class number QE33.2.A7 is chosen rather than the number QE1, Periodicals, societies, congresses, serial collections, yearbooks of Geology.

Place

For a work treating a topic with regard to a particular locality, the number that brings out both the topic and the place, if available, is chosen.

> *Mozambique national mine survey.* [1994]-
>
> TN   Subclass: Mining engineering
>
> 119   Divisions of Africa, A-Z, according to Table T1
>
> .M85   The first Cutter number for Mozambique
>
> M69   The second Cutter number for the main entry under the title, *Mozambique* . . .
>
> 1994   The date of publication

If a work treats a topic with respect to two or three localities, the number representing the place emphasized is chosen. If emphasis is equal, the number for the first place is assigned.

> New York (State). Office of the State Comptroller. Division of Management Audit. *The Port Authority of New York and New Jersey : productivity of toll collection operations.* [1996]

HE	Subclass: Transportation and communications
554	Ports in North America: By place, A-Z
.N7	The first Cutter number for New York
N393	The second Cutter number for the main entry, New York (State) . . .
1996	The date of publication

> Gillett, R. D. *The market for Pacific Island fish jerky in Honolulu, Seattle and Southern California : a report prepared for the South Pacific Commission.* c1997

HD	Subclass: Economic history and conditions
9469	Fishery product industry: special products
.D743	The first Cutter number .D74 for the special product, dried fish, with the successive element (3 from Table H21) for local subdivision
O254	The second Cutter number for the place, Oahu
1997	The date of publication

If there are no geographic provisions under the specific topic, the number for the topic is preferred, unless there are instructions in the schedules or precedents in the shelflist to the contrary. Such instructions often appear in the following forms:

> *Under the caption for the topical number:*
> Class works limited to a specific geographic area in [. . .]

> *Under the caption for the geographic number:*
> Including specific topics

In the following example, since there were no contrary instructions, placement is under the specific topic; and the place, Montana, is not reflected in the class number:

Rolfe, William A.   *A history of Herefords in Montana*.   c1995

SF	Subclass: Animal culture
199	Cattle: Breeds
.H4	The first Cutter number for the breed, Hereford
R65	The second Cutter number for the main entry, Rolfe
1995	The date of publication

For the example below, the geographic provision under the specific topic is broader than the area covered in the item. Because placement under topic is preferred, in this case, the number HD8396 (based on 16 from the internal table under HD8101-8942.5) for the Chartists movement in Great Britain (specific topic with broader geographic division) is chosen instead of the number HD8397.M3x (based on 17.A-Z in the internal table) for Labor in politics in the city of Manchester (broader topic with specific geographic division).

Pickering, Paul A.   *Chartism and the chartists in Manchester and Salford*.
1995

HD	Subclass: Economic history and conditions
8396	The number (HD8100 + 280 [Table H8] + 16 [internal table under HD8101-8942.5]) meaning Labor in politics: Chartists movement in Great Britain
.P52	The Cutter number for the main entry, Pickering
1995	The date of publication

Period

For a work treating a topic with regard to a particular period, the number that brings out both the topic and the period, if available, is chosen.

Fleury, Michel.   *Naissance de Paris*.   1997

DC	Subclass: History of France
725	Early history (to 1515) of Paris
.F54	The Cutter number for the main entry, Fleury
1997	The date of publication

When period divisions are provided under a topic and the work being classified covers several of the time spans listed in different numbers, the class number corresponding to the earliest period on which the work focuses is selected, unless the earlier period or periods are covered only briefly or are used to introduce the principal time period(s) being discussed.[6]

Liu, Bea Exner. *Remembering China, 1935-1945 : a memoir.* 1996
DS	Subclass: History of Asia
777.488	China, 1928-1937
.L567	The first Cutter number for the biographee, Liu
A3	The second Cutter number for an autobiography
1996	The date of publication

In the example above, the choice is between the numbers representing two different periods in the history of modern China: DS777.488 (1928-1937) and DS777.5195 (1937-1945).

Multi-Faceted Works

Many works treat a topic with respect to more than one facet. A class number representing all facets covered in the item, if available, is chosen.

Kriz, Kay Dian. *The idea of the English landscape painter : genius as alibi in the early nineteenth century.* c1997
ND	Subclass: Painting
1354.5	Landscape painting in Great Britain in the nineteenth century
.K75	The Cutter number for the main entry, Kriz
1997	The date of publication

If a number covering all facets is not available, the number representing the facet emphasized in the work or the one considered to be more prominent is chosen. In each of the three examples that follow, the place is represented in the number, while the period is ignored:

Tyomkin, Edward. *The Hindu pantheon : an introduction illustrated with 19th century Indian miniatures from the St. Petersburg collection.* 1994
ND	Subclass: Painting
1337	History of miniature painting: Special regions or countries, A-Z
.I5	The first Cutter number for India
T96	The second Cutter number for the main entry, Tyomkin
1994	The date of publication

Jehin, Philippe. *Les hommes contre la forêt : l'exploitation des forêts dans le Val d'Orbey au XVIIIe siècle.* 1993

SD	Subclass: Forestry
194	The number (SD144 + 50) meaning history of forestry in provinces in France, A-Z
.O73	The first Cutter number for the place, d'Orbey
J44	The second Cutter number for the main entry, Jehin
1993	The date of publication

Gomez Rodriguez, Ma. Soledad (Maria Soledad) *El Hospital de la Misericordia de Toledo en el siglo XIX.* 1995

RA	Subclass: Public aspects of medicine
989	Medical centers or hospitals in Europe, regions or countries, A-Z
.S74	The first Cutter number (.S7) for Spain with the successive element (4) meaning subdivision by city, A-Z
T7354	The second Cutter number for the city, Toledo
1995	The date of publication

In the following example, the place facet is represented in the number, but not the form, directories:

NLG-SEA (Organization) *NLG-SEA directory : telex, fax & e-mail directory of libraries and information centres in Southeast Asia.* 1995

Z	Subclass: Libraries
845	Asia, by region, state, or place, A-Z
.S6	The first Cutter number for the place, Southeast Asia
N57	The second Cutter number for the main entry, NLG-SEA
1995	The date of publication

Multi-Topical Works

When the content of the work covers more than one topic and there is no available number that covers all topics treated in the work, a choice often must be made between two or more numbers, each of which covers part or parts of the content of the work. In such cases, the choice is made according to policies discussed below.

The class number for a work treating two or more topics is chosen according to instructions, if any, printed in the schedules. If no specific instructions are given, the number for the dominant subject in the work, if one can be determined, is chosen.

> Matlak, Richard E. *The poetry of relationship : the Wordsworths and Coleridge, 1797-1800.* 1997

PR	Subclass: English literature
5883	19th-century author Wordsworth's relations to contemporaries (according to Table P-PZ31)
.M34	The Cutter number for the main entry, Matlak
1997	The date of publication

> Cadieux, Charles L. *Great RV trips : a guide to the best RV trips in the United States, Canada, and Mexico.* 1994

F	Subclass: United States local history
590.3	Guidebooks to West (United States)
.C33	The Cutter number for the main entry, Cadieux
1994	The date of publication

If no subject is dominant, the number is chosen according to the following guidelines.

Works on Two or Three Topics

For a work on two or three topics, if emphasis on the topics is equal, the number for the topic treated first is assigned.

> Brown, Jules. *Hong Kong and Macau : the rough guide.* 1996

DS	Subclass: History of Asia
796	Cities in China
.H73	The first Cutter number (H7) for Hong Kong with the successive element (3 according to Table DS-DX4) for guidebooks
B75	The second Cutter number for the main entry, Brown
1996	The date of publication

Dasgupta, Sanjukta. *The novels of Huxley and Hemingway : a study in two planes of reality.* 1996

PR	Subclass: English literature
6015	Modern authors (1900-1960) whose names begin with the letter "H"
.U9	The first Cutter number for Huxley
Z5965	The second Cutter number for criticism, adjusted for the main entry, Dasgupta
1996	The date of publication

Chemistry of arsenic, antimony, and bismuth. 1998

QD	Subclass: Chemistry
181	Special elements, A-Z
.A7	The first Cutter number for Arsenic according to Table Q1
C48	The second Cutter number for the main entry under the title, *Chemistry* . . .
1998	The date of publication

Zimmerman, Elena Irish. *Sevierville, Gatlinburg, and Maryville : a postcard tour.* 1996

F	Subclass: United States local history
444	Cities in Tennessee, A-Z
.S38	The first Cutter number for the city Sevierville
Z56	Second Cutter number for the main entry, Zimmerman
1996	The date of publication

The number for a broader subject is chosen if the work deals with several subjects that, taken together, constitute the total content of the broader subject or a major part of it.

Coleridge, Keats and Shelley. 1996

PR	Subclass: English literature
590	19th century, including Romanticism, Lake School, and the Age of Wordsworth
.C57	Cutter number for the main entry under the title, *Coleridge* . . .
1996	The date of publication

Classical closure : reading the end in Greek and Latin literature. 1997

PA	Subclass: Classical languages and literature
3009	Relation of classical literature to history, civilization, culture, etc.
.C53	Cutter number for the main entry under the title, *Classical*...
1997	The date of publication

In the last example, the number PA3009 is chosen over PA3069 Relation of Greek literature to history, civilization, culture, etc., or PA6019 Relation of Latin literature to history, civilization, culture, etc.

Works on Four or More Topics

For a work treating four or more topics, a general number that encompasses all the topics is chosen.

Dabney, Betty Page. *The silver sextant : four men of the Enlightenment.* 1993

CT	Subclass: Biography
781	National biography of Great Britain: 17th-18th centuries
.D33	Cutter number for the main entry, Dabney
1993	The date of publication

Melford, Michael. *Big sky country : a view of paradise : the best of Montana, North Dakota, Wyoming, and Idaho.* 1996

F	Subclass: United States local history
590.7	Historic monuments: Illustrative material on the West
.M45	The Cutter number for the main entry, Melford
1996	The date of publication

High Hoch Times Zeiten : Thomas Baumann, Malachi Farrell, Seamus Farrell, Filippo di Giovanni, Fernando Palma de Rodriguez. c1996

NC	Subclass: Drawing, Design, Illustration
95	20th century
.H53	The Cutter number for the main entry under the title, *High*...
1996	The date of publication

Phase Relations

A work that treats the relationship between or among two or more topics is classed in the most specific number covering the relationship, if available.

Lewis, Charles A.   *Green nature/human nature : the meaning of plants in our lives.*   c1996

QK	Subclass: Botany
46.5	Special topics, A-Z
.H85	The first Cutter number for the topic, Human-plant relationships
L48	The second Cutter number for the main entry, Lewis
1996	The date of publication

When a work deals with the influence of one subject on another, the number for the subject being influenced is chosen.

Wladika, Michael.   *Kant in Hegels "Wissenschaft der Logik".*   c1995

B	Subclass: Philosophy
2942	The individual work, *Wissenschaft der Logik*, by the modern German philosopher, Georg Wilhelm Friedrich Hegel
.Z7	The first Cutter number for commentaries, interpretation, and criticism, according to Table B-BJ1
W53	The second Cutter number for the main entry, Wladika
1995	The date of publication

The influence of economic and development policies on science and technology in Africa : proceedings of a training seminar on the integration of science and technology, economic, and development policies in Africa : Kampala, May, 1993.   [1994]

Q	Subclass: Science
127	History, by region or country, A-Z
.A4	The first Cutter number for Africa
I54	The second Cutter number for the main entry under the title, *influence . . .*
1994	The date of publication

A work treating the application of a topic to another is classed with the topic being acted on.

> *Computers and the history of art.*   1990- Vol. 1, pt. 1-
>
> N   Subclass: Visual arts
> 380   Study of the history of art
> .C663   The Cutter number for the main entry under the title,
>   *Computers . . .*

In cases where two or more numbers appear equally satisfactory, the number is chosen on the basis of the author's intent or on useful collocation.

SPECIAL CONSIDERATIONS

Classifying Different Editions of the Same Work

In classifying other editions of the same work, the same class number is used, as long as the time period covered in each edition remains essentially the same. On the other hand, if the new edition focuses first on a later period for which there is a number in the schedules, the number for that period is assigned. In such cases, the new edition will not stand with the old on the shelves.

The Library of Congress prepares a new record for each new edition of a work, including editions published simultaneously in different countries or languages. The word *edition* refers to issues and reprints as well as to revised or updated editions (but not adaptations) for which separate bibliographic records have been prepared. Normally, as long as the new edition has the same author and its contents do not vary significantly from the original, the class number and Cutter number assigned to the original edition are used, with the date of the later edition added.[7] If the main entry changes (e.g., from author to title) from one edition to another but the contents remain basically the same, the same class and Cutter numbers as those assigned to the earlier edition, but with the date of the later edition, are used. If the main entry has changed from the edition cataloged before *AACR2R*, but the contents remain basically the same, the same class number is assigned to the new edition with a new Cutter number based on the new form of the name. If the later edition of a work entered under the title has a new title, the Cutter number is based on the new title.

Furthermore, a new edition of a work cataloged in accordance with *AACR2R* is assigned the appropriate class number without regard to where the edition cataloged before *AACR2R* was classed. If the new edition has a main entry that is different from the pre-*AACR2R* edition, a new author Cutter number is assigned, and the two editions will not stand together on the shelves. This exception does not apply if both the old and the new edition have been cataloged in accordance with *AACR2R*.

For simultaneously published editions, the Library of Congress uses the following guidelines to determine the *original edition*. The edition published in the United States, if there is one, is treated as the original edition. For editions published simultaneously in different languages, the original edition is designated in the following order of preference: English, French, German, Spanish, Russian. If none of the languages listed above applies, the first item cataloged is designated as the original edition.

City Regions and Metropolitan Areas

Under a particular topic, if local subdivisions by city are provided through the use of Cutter numbers, the Cutter number assigned to a particular city is used also for works pertaining to the corresponding city region or metropolitan area,[8] for example,

John A. Volpe National Transportation Systems Center (U.S.) *Enhanced planning review of the Washington, D.C. metropolitan area.* [1996]

HE	Subclass: Transportation and communications
310	Cities or metropolitan areas in the United States, A-Z
.W3	The first Cutter number for Washington
J65	The second Cutter number for the main entry, John . . .
1996	The date of publication

The New York City region in the 1990s : a look at economic performance compared to the nation's largest cities. [1997]

HC	Subclass: Economic history and conditions
108	Cities in the United States, A-Z
.N7	The first Cutter number for New York City
N325	The second Cutter number for the main entry under the title, *New . . .*
1997	The date of publication

Textbooks

Textbooks covering several subjects are classed in subclass LT. Textbooks on a particular subject are classed with the subject in Classes B-K and M-Z under a particular subject, a textbook is classed in the "Textbooks" number if one exists.[9]

Samuelson, Paul Anthony. *Economics.* c1998

HB	Subclass: Economic theory
171.5	A recent English text.book
.S25	The Cutter number for the main entry, Samuelson
1998	The date of publication

Shipman, James T. *An introduction to physical science.* c1997

Q	Subclass: Science (General)
161.2	Elementary textbooks, 1970-
.S44	The Cutter number for the main entry, Shipman
1997	The date of publication

Clarkson, Sandra Pryor. *Introduction to algebra.* c1994

QA	Subclass: Mathematics
152.2	Elementary textbooks, 1971-
.C57	The Cutter number for the main entry, Clarkson
1994	The date of publication

If a textbook number is not available, the work is placed in "General works" "Juvenile works," or in the only number designated for the topic.

Chan, Lois Mai. *Cataloging and classification : an introduction.* 1994

Z	Subclass: Libraries
693.5	Cataloging, by region or country, A-Z
.U6	The first Cutter number for the United States
C48	The second Cutter number for the main entry, Chan
1994	The date of publication

In some cases, general works, treatises, and textbooks are designated by the same number.

Hodel, Richard E. *An introduction to mathematical logic.* c1995

QA	Subclass: Mathematics
9	General works, treatises, and textbooks on mathematical logic, A5-Z
.H547	The Cutter number for the main entry, Hodel
1995	The date of publication

Samuelson, Paul Anthony. *Microeconomics.* c1998

HB	Subclass: Economic theory, Demography
172	Recent general works, treatises, and textbooks in English on microeconomics
.S155	The Cutter number for the main entry, Samuelson
1998	The date of publication

For further examples of textbooks, see the discussion in chapter 7.

NOTES

1. Library of Congress, Office for Subject Cataloging Policy, *Subject Cataloging Manual: Classification*, 1st ed. (Washington, DC: Cataloging Distribution Service, Library of Congress, 1992).

2. Library of Congress, Cataloging Policy and Support Office, *Subject Cataloging Manual: Shelflisting*, 2nd ed. (Washington, DC: Library of Congress, 1995).

3. *Cataloging Service Bulletin* 1- , Summer 1978- (Washington, DC: Processing Services, Library of Congress).

4. "General Principles of Classification," Library of Congress, *Subject Cataloging Manual: Classification*, F10.

5. "General Special," Library of Congress, *Subject Cataloging Manual: Classification*, F290.

6. "Classification and Time Periods," Library of Congress, *Subject Cataloging Manual: Classification*, F320.

7. "Editions," Library of Congress, *Subject Cataloging Manual: Shelflisting*, G740.

8. "City Regions and Metropolitan Areas," Library of Congress, *Subject Cataloging Manual: Classification*, F550.

9. "Juvenile materials," Library of Congress, *Subject Cataloging Manual: Classification*, F615.

Individual Classes

INTRODUCTION

This chapter contains an introduction to the individual classes of the Library of Congress (LC) Classification. Each unit begins with a synopsis of the class as found in the official *LC Classification Outline*[1], in the online version available at the Library's web site, or in the schedules; the synopsis is intended to orient the reader to the scope of the individual class. Next, a brief history traces the development of the schedule or schedules making up each class. The sequence within each class and subclass is discussed, and the order of subdivisions, that is, order in array, is illustrated by numerous examples. Additional tables or extensions of important schedules that are found only in *LC Classification, Additions and Changes* or accessible through the Internet are mentioned. Significant problems in the use of each class schedule are discussed, including the inclusiveness and exclusiveness of its scope and problems of internal terminology and typography. Typical problems in the use of tables are presented and explained with examples of LC call numbers in the same fashion as in chapters 4 and 5. Any unusual elements that may occur in the notation of each class are explained, for example, the use of triple letters in Class D and Class K, the use of subject letter-numbers in Class G, etc.

147

The chapter should serve to orient classifiers to individual schedules. Each unit is designed to provide an introductory rather than a definitive treatment. Examples are used to illustrate typical tables or tables that were not previously analyzed, to examine an important or confusing variation in the use of notation, or to clarify directions provided within the schedule or tables. Treatment is confined to the parts of schedules or tables that pose special difficulties; consequently, many subclasses are not fully analyzed. Readers will benefit by studying the schedule or schedules for each class in conjunction with the examples and tables presented in the individual chapter units. In addition, readers may wish to check their libraries' online catalogs and the LC MARC databases, now available on the Internet, for additional examples of each problem. The most effective way to use this chapter is to go through the following steps:

1. read the introductory and explanatory material in each unit carefully;

2. study the examples provided in the text;

3. consult the LC Classification schedules for the class under discussion.

All examples appearing in the chapter are taken from recent LC MARC records; class numbers reflect those shown in the latest edition of, and later additions and changes for, the particular class at the time of this writing.

CLASS A—GENERAL WORKS

AC	
1-199	Collections. Series. Collected works
1-195	Collections of monographs, essays, etc.
1-8	American and English
9-195	Other languages
200	Collections of Jewish readers
801-895	Inaugural and program dissertations
901-995	Pamphlet collections
999	Scrapbooks
AE	
1-(90)	Encyclopedias
5-(90)	By language
AG	
2-600	Dictionaries and other general reference books
AI	
1-21	Indexes
21	Indexes to individual newspapers
AM	
1-(501)	Museums. Collectors and collecting
10-100	By country
111-160	Museology. Museum methods, technique, etc.
200-(501)	Collectors and collecting
AN	
	Newspapers
	For history and description of individual newspapers, see PN4899-PN5650
AP	
1-(271)	Periodicals
101-115	Humorous periodicals
200-203	Juvenile periodicals
(250)-(265)	Periodicals for women
(270)-(271)	Periodicals for Blacks
AS	
1-945	Academies and learned societies
2.5-4	International associations, congresses, conferences, etc.
11-785	By region or country

Class A continues on page 150.

AY
10-2001	Yearbooks. Almanacs. Directories
10-29	Annuals
30-1730	Almanacs
2001	Directories

AZ
(20)-999	History of scholarship and learning. The humanities
101-(181)	Philosophy. Theory
191-193	Evaluation
200-361	History
200-361	By region or country
999	Popular errors and delusions

Class A—General Works is the generalia class in the Library of Congress (LC) Classification. The outline of the class was developed in 1906 and first published in 1911. Subsequent editions were published in 1915 (2nd edition), 1947 (3rd edition), and 1973 (4th edition). Beginning with the 1998 edition, the schedule has been produced using the new automated system.

Class A is designed for works too general or comprehensive to be classed with any particular subject; it is a default class, not used for works that can possibly be classed in a special subject. As shown in the outline, there are ten subclasses in Class A: AC for collections, series, and collected works that cannot be classed by subject or in subclass AS for collections published under the auspices of learned bodies; AE for general encyclopedias; AG for dictionaries and other general reference works including minor general encyclopedias, juvenile encyclopedias, question and answer books, notes and queries, and clipping bureaus; AI for general indexes which are not classed by subject or in Class Z; AM for general museums and collectors and collecting; AN for newspapers (a subclass not yet fully developed in the classification scheme); AP for general periodicals, arranged first by language and then grouped geographically, with separate ranges of numbers for humorous periodicals and juvenile periodicals; AS for academies and learned societies of a general character; AY for general yearbooks, almanacs, and directories; and AZ for the history of scholarship and learning and for writings on the humanities. It may be observed that two common subjects for a generalia class are not included in Class A: both bibliography and library science are located in Class Z.

Individual subclasses are arranged in alphabetical order. All the subclass labels except AZ have mnemonic force: AC, Collections; AE, Encyclopedias; AM, Museums, etc. Class A is one of the few places in the LC Classification where mnemonics play a role. The most common forms of division in the subclasses are language and place. Each country or other geographic area is assigned a range of numbers, one number, or a Cutter number; many simple tables for internal subarrangement are used.

This schedule should not present any major problems in application. Nineteen tables, numbered A1-A19, are used for subarrangement of topics or places. The following examples demonstrate the classification of materials of a general nature in Class A.

Works About Museums

Museums of a general nature are classed in subclass AM. The numbers AM10-100 are designated for description and history of museums, and the number AM101 is assigned to the description and history of individual museums. Description and history of museums are divided first by country, then by state, province, etc., and finally by city. Each country is assigned three, two, one, or a Cutter number. Four tables, A14-A17, are used for subarrangement within each country, for example:

A15	TABLE FOR MUSEUMS (2 NOS.)
1.A1	Periodicals. Societies
1.A2	General works
1.A3-Z	Provinces, etc., A-Z
2.A-Z	Cities, towns, etc. A-Z
A16	TABLE FOR MUSEUMS (1 NO.)
0.A2	General works
0.A3A-Z	States, provinces, etc., A-Z
0.A4-Z	Cities, towns, etc. A-Z

Italy has been assigned two numbers: AM54-55. Therefore, the Cutter numbers for the following work were constructed according to the table above, using the provision for a two-number country:

Il museo come azienda culturale : ricerca sui musei di Verona. 1996

AM	Subclass: Museums
55	The second number assigned to museums in Italy, subdivided by cities (according to Table A15 for two-number countries)
.V47	The first Cutter number for the city, Verona
M87	The second Cutter number for the main entry under the title, *museo* . . .
1996	The date of publication

Belgium has been assigned one number: AM56. Therefore, the Cutter numbers for the following work were constructed according to Table A16, following the instructions for a one-number country:

Huet, Leen. *Belgisch museumboek : reis langs 21 musea.* 1996

AM	Subclass: Museums
56	Museums in Belgium
.A2	The first Cutter number meaning General works (based on Table A16 for a one-number country)
H84	The second Cutter number for the main entry, Huet
1996	The date of publication

Material issued by or written about an individual museum is classed at AM101, subdivided by place. Certain older and larger museums have been subarranged by Table A1, Table for Individual Museums, which is now obsolete. Nevertheless, these museums (specified in the LC shelflist) continue to be subarranged according to this obsolete table. The British Museum example below illustrates the use of Table A1:

British Museum. *The Collections of the British Museum.* 1989

AM	Subclass: Museums
101	The integral number meaning individual museums
.B85	The first Cutter number .B8 for the British Museum and the successive element (5) from Table A1 meaning guidebooks and catalogs
1989	The date of publication

Museums not subarranged according to Table A1 are subarranged first by place and then by the main entry, as shown in the following examples:

Casa Real de la Moneda (Potosi, Bolivia) *La Casa de la Moneda : museum guide.* 1997

AM	Subclass: Museums
101	Individual museums
.P7482	The first Cutter number for the place, Potosi, Bolivia
C384	The second Cutter number for the main entry, Casa Real . . .
1997	The date of publication

Smith, Murphy D. *A museum : the history of the cabinet of curiosities of the American Philosophical Society.* 1996

AM	Subclass: Museums
101	Individual museums
.P496	The first Cutter number for the place, Philadelphia
S65	The second Cutter number for the main entry, Smith
1996	The date of publication

Itinerario del Museo Nacional de Colombia, 1823-1994. 1995

AM	Subclass: Museums
101	Individual museums
.B6	The first Cutter number for the place, Bogota, Colombia
I85	The second Cutter number for the main entry under the title, *Itinerario* . . .
1995	The date of publication

Buttlar, Gertrud. *Stadtmuseum Wiener Neustadt : Katalog.* c1995

AM	Subclass: Museums
101	Individual museums
.W54	The first Cutter number for the place, Wien, Austria
B88	The second Cutter number for the main entry, Buttlar
1995	The date of publication

Academies and Learned Societies

In subclass AS, Academies and learned societies (including societies of a general character), international associations, congresses, conferences, etc., are classed in AS2.5 for General works and AS4 for Individual associations, etc., with a unique Cutter number assigned to each association, etc. Works by and about a particular association are subarranged by means of successive Cutter numbers. An example showing the subarrangement of publications by and about UNESCO is given in the schedule:

AS	ACADEMIES AND LEARNED SOCIETIES
	United Nations Educational, Scientific and
	Cultural Organization (UNESCO)
	Official documents
4.U8A1-.U8A5	Serials
4.U8A6-.U8Z	Monographs. By title
4.U82A-Z	Committees, etc. By name, A-Z
4.U825A-Z	Reports of national delegations. By country, A-Z
4.U83A-Z	Individual authors, A-Z
	Including official publications of
	preliminary conferences

The following examples illustrate the application of this range of numbers:

Medium-term strategy, 1996-2001 : draft.   1995 [published by UNESCO]

AS	Subclass: Academies and learned societies
4	Individual international associations, etc.
.U8	The first Cutter number for an official monograph about UNESCO
M43	The second Cutter number for the main entry under the title, *Medium-term . . .*
1995	The date of publication

Unesco General Conference.   1996-   *Manual of the General Conference.*   1996 ed.-

AS	Subclass: Academies and learned societies
4	Individual international associations, etc.
.U82	The first Cutter number for UNESCO (.U8) and the successive element (2) meaning Committees, etc., by name, A-Z

G46   The second Cutter number for General Conference

a   Letter indicating a serial publication

News from the Australian National Commission for Unesco. [1996-]
June 1996-   Irregular

AS   Subclass: Academies and learned societies

4   Individual international associations, etc.

.U825   The first Cutter number for UNESCO (.U8) and the
             successive element (25) meaning Reports of national
             delegations, by country, A-Z

A857   The second Cutter number for Australia

Spaulding, Seth. *Historical dictionary of the United Nations Educational, Scientific and Cultural Organization (UNESCO).* 1997

AS   Subclass: Academies and learned societies

4   Individual international associations, etc.

.U83   The first Cutter number for UNESCO (.U8) and the
             successive element (3) meaning works by individual
             authors, A-Z

S69   The second Cutter number for the main entry, Spaulding

1997   The date of publication

Tables Used with Society Publications

Five tables, A2-A4 and A18-19, are used for subarranging publications by or about individual regional, national, and local societies, associations, institutions, etc. Tables A2-A4 are used for societies, etc. in the United States. Table A4 is preferred unless Tables A2 or A3 has already been applied to a specific body. For societies in other countries, Tables A18 and A19 are used when specified in the schedule. Table A4, which is similar to the *Societies Table* included in *Subject Cataloging Manual: Shelflisting,*[2] is shown below:

A4   SOCIETIES TABLE
                    Official serials.   By title
.xA1-.xA29   Titles beginning A-H
.xA3-.xA39   Titles beginning I-Q
.xA4-.xA49   Titles beginning R-Z
.xA5-.xA7   Official monographs.   By title
.xA8-.xZ   Nonofficial publications

Application of Table A4 is shown in the following examples:

Minnesota Humanities Commission. *Report to the state of Minnesota.* [1990?-] July 1, 1989 to June 30, 1990- Annual

AS	Subclass: Academies and learned societies
36	Individual societies and institutions in the United States, by city, A-Z
.S37	St. Paul, Minnesota
A15	Official serials (between .xA1-.xA29 according to Table A4) based on the earlier title, *Annual report*

Kinard, Agnes Dodds. *Celebrating the first 100 years of The Carnegie in Pittsburgh, 1895-1995.* c1995

AS	Subclass: Academies and learned societies
36	Individual societies and institutions in the United States, by city, A-Z
.P79	Pittsburgh, Pennsylvania
K54	The Cutter number (between .xA8-.xZ for a nonofficial publication according to Table A4) for the main entry, Kinard
1995	The date of publication

Tables in Subclass AY

Two tables, A5-A6, are used for subarranging almanacs published in countries other than the United States classed in AY410-1730. Table A5 is used for almanacs of countries to which ten or eleven numbers have been designated, and Table A6 is for countries with two numbers. Examples include:

Gartenlaube Kalender für das Jahr . . . Annual

AY	Subclass: Almanacs
856	The number, ending in 6 (according to Table A5) in the range AY850-860 for literary and magazine almanacs published in Germany
.G3	The Cutter number for the main entry under the title, *Gartenlaube . . .*

The Book of Australia. 1990-   Almanac 1991-92-

AY	Subclass: Almanacs
1604	The number, ending in 4 (according to Table A5) in the range AY1600-1609 for general almanacs published in Australia
.B65	The Cutter number for the main entry under the title, *Book* ...

Tables in Subclass AZ

Six tables, A7-A12, are designed to be used with AZ 501-908, History of scholarship and learning by region or country, to provide for appropriate subarrangement under region or country. Table A7 for ten-number countries is shown below:

A7	TABLE FOR SCHOLARSHIP AND LEARNING (10 NO. COUNTRIES)
0	Collections
	General works. History
1	General works
2	Early. Origins
3	Middle Ages
4	Modern
6	General special. Relations, aspects, etc.
7	Addresses, essays, lectures. Pamphlets
8.A-Z	States, regions, provinces, etc., A-Z
(9)	Cities
	see Subclasses DA-DU and Classes E-F

Many countries are assigned ten numbers, for example, Germany, AZ660-669. The following work, a history of the humanities in Prussia, Germany, illustrates the use of Table A7:

Pisanski, Georg Christoph.   *Entwurf einer preussischen Literärgeschichte in vier Büchern : mit einer Notiz über den Autor und sein Buch.*   1994

AZ	Subclass: History of scholarship and learning
668	The number (based on Table A7) meaning a work about the humanities in a region or province of Germany
.P82	The Cutter number .P8 for Prussia with the successive element (2, based on Table A7) for an early history
P52	The second Cutter number for the main entry, Pisanski
1994	The date of publication

A variation is Great Britain, which is assigned eight numbers, AZ610-617, with special numbers for its regions: England—Local, AZ620-623; Scotland, AZ625-628; Ireland, AZ630-633; and Wales, AZ635-638. Table A7 is used for Great Britain in general, and Table A9 is used for the regions.

The United States is assigned nine numbers, which are enumerated in the schedule. Therefore, no table is required. For example, a work on the humanities in Kentucky is assigned the number AZ513 from the schedule for Class A:

> Kentucky. Education, Arts, and Humanities Cabinet. *Kentucky Education, Arts, and Humanities Cabinet report to the Commonwealth.* 1993

AZ	Subclass: History of scholarship and learning
513	The humanities in the United States, by region or state, A-Z
.K4	The first Cutter number for Kentucky
K46	The second Cutter number for the main entry, Kentucky. Education, . . .
1993	The date of publication

Although Tables A8 and A10 specify five numbers and three numbers respectively, the actual number assigned to a country in these categories is either four or two. This should not create any problem as the last number in each of the tables is optional and is not used by the Library of Congress.

There were no indexes in previous editions of Class A. This deficiency was rectified in the fourth edition.

CLASS B—PHILOSOPHY. PSYCHOLOGY. RELIGION

B
1-5802   Philosophy (General)
69-99   General works
108-5802   By period
                        Including individual philosophers and
                            schools of philosophy
108-708   Ancient
720-765   Medieval
770-785   Renaissance
790-5802   Modern
808-849   Special topics and schools of philosophy
850-5739   By region or country
5800-5802   By religion

BC
1-199   Logic
11-39   History
25-39   By period
60-99   General works
171-199   Special topics

BD
10-701   Speculative philosophy
10-41   General philosophical works
95-131   Metaphysics
143-237   Epistemology.   Theory of knowledge
240-260   Methodology
300-450   Ontology
                        Including being, the soul, life, death
493-701   Cosmology
                        Including teleology, space and time,
                            structure of matter, plurality of
                            worlds
BF
1-990   Psychology
38-64   Philosophy.   Relation to other topics
173-175.5   Psychoanalysis
176-176.5   Psychological tests and testing
180-198.7   Experimental psychology
203   Gestalt psychology
207-209   Psychotropic drugs and other substances
231-299   Sensation.   Aesthesiology
309-499   Consciousness.   Cognition

Class B continues on page 160.

	Including learning, attention, comprehension, memory, imagination, genius, intelligence, thought and thinking, psycholinguistics, mental fatigue
501-505	Motivation
511-593	Affection. Feeling. Emotion
608-635	Will. Volition. Choice. Control
636-637	Applied psychology
638-648	New thought. Menticulture, etc.
660-685	Comparative psychology. Animal and human psychology
692-692.5	Psychology of sex. Sexual behavior
697-697.5	Differential psychology. Individuality. Self
698-698.9	Personality
699-711	Genetic psychology
712-724.85	Developmental psychology
	Including infant psychology, child psychology, adolescence, adulthood
725-727	Class psychology
795-839	Temperament. Character
839.5-885	Physiognomy. Phrenology
889-905	Graphology. Study of handwriting
908-940	The hand. Palmistry

1001-1389	Parapsychology
1001-1045	Psychic research. Psychology of the conscious
1048-1108	Hallucinations. Sleep. Dreaming. Visions
1111-1156	Hypnotism. Suggestion. Mesmerism. Subliminal projection
1161-1171	Telepathy. Mind reading. Thought transference
1228-1389	Spiritualism
	Including mediumship. spirit messages, clairvoyance

1404-1999	Occult sciences
1444-1486	Ghosts. Apparitions. Hauntings
1501-1562	Demonology. Satanism. Possession
1562.5-1584	Witchcraft
1585-1623	Magic. Hermetics. Necromancy
1651-1729	Astrology
1745-1779	Oracles. Sibyls. Divinations
1783-1815	Seers. Prophets. Prophecies
1845-1891	Fortune-telling

BH

1-301	Aesthetics
81-208	History
301	Special topics

BJ
1-1725	Ethics
71-1185	History and general works
	Including individual ethical philosophers
1188-1295	Religious ethics
1298-1335	Evolutionary and genetic ethics
1365-1385	Positivist ethics
1388	Socialist ethics
1390-1390.5	Communist ethics
1392	Totalitarian ethics
1395	Feminist ethics
1518-1697	Individual ethics. Character. Virtue
	Including practical and applied ethics, conduct of life, vices, success, ethics for children
1725	Ethics of social groups, classes, etc.
	Professional ethics
1801-2195	Social usages. Etiquette
2021-2078	Etiquette of entertaining
2139-2156	Etiquette of travel
2195	Telephone etiquette

Religion

BL
1-2790	Religions. Mythology. Rationalism
74-98	Religions of the world
175-290	Natural theology
300-325	The myth. Comparative mythology
425-490	Religious doctrines (General)
500-547	Eschatology
550-619	Worship. Cultus
624-627	Religious life
660-2670	History and principles of religions
690-980	European. Occidental
1100-1295	Hinduism
1300-1380	Jainism
1600-1695	Semitic
2400-2490	African
2700-2790	Rationalism

BM
1-990	Judaism
150-449	History
480-488.5	Pre-Talmudic Jewish literature
487-488.5	Dead Sea scrolls

Class B continues on page 162.

495-532	Sources of Jewish religion. Rabbinical literature
600-645	Dogmatic Judaism
650-747	Practical Judaism
750-755	Biography
900-990	Samaritans

BP
1-610	Islam. Bahaism. Theosophy, etc.
1-253	Islam
50-68	History
70-80	Biography
75-77.75	Muhammad, d. 632
87-89	Islamic literature
100-137.5	Sacred books
100-134	Koran
166-166.94	Theology (Kalam)
174-190	The practice of Islam
191-253	Branches, sects, and modifications
300-395	Bahaism
500-585	Theosophy
595-597	Anthroposophy
600-610	Other beliefs and movements

BQ
1-9800	Buddhism
251-799	History
840-999	Biography
860-939	Gautama Buddha
1001-1045	Buddhist literature
1100-3340	Tripitaka (Canonical literature)
4061-4570	Doctrinal and systematic Buddhism
4620-4890	Buddhist pantheon
4911-5720	Practice of Buddhism. Forms of worship
5851-5899	Benevolent work. Social work
5901-5975	Missionary work
6001-6388	Monasticism
7001-9800	Modifications, schools, etc.

BR
	Christianity
1-1725	Christianity
60-67	Early Christian literature. Fathers of the Church, etc.
140-1500	History
1690-1725	Biography

BS
1-2970	The Bible
410-680	Works about the Bible
701-1830	Old Testament
1901-2970	New Testament

BT
10-1480	Doctrinal theology
19-30	Doctrine and dogma
98-180	God
119-123	Holy Spirit. The Paraclete
198-590	Christology
595-685	Mary, Mother of Jesus Christ. Mariology
695-748	Creation
750-810.2	Salvation
819-891	Eschatology
899-950	Future life
1095-1255	Apologetics. Evidences of Christianity
1313-1480	History of specific doctrines and movements

BV
1-5099	Practical theology
5-530	Worship (Public and private) Including the church year, Christian symbols, liturgy, prayer, hymnology
590-1652	Ecclesiastical theology Including the Church, church and state, church management, ministry, sacraments, religious societies, religious education
2000-3705	Missions
3750-3799	Evangelism. Revivals
4000-4470	Pastoral theology
4485-5099	Practical religion. The Christian life

BX
1-9999	Christian denominations
1-9.5	Church unity. Ecumenical movement
100-189	Eastern churches. Oriental churches
200-754	Orthodox Eastern Church
800-4795	Roman Catholic Church
4800-9999	Protestantism

Class B—Philosophy. Psychology. Religion was originally published in two volumes, *Part I, B-BJ: Philosophy.   Psychology* (1910) and *Part II, BL-BX: Religion* (1927). Because of the increasing size of Part II, it was decided later to divide the schedule into four separately published schedules—*B-BJ: Philosophy. Psychology*; *BL, BM, BP, BQ: Religion: Religions, Hinduism, Judaism, Islam, Buddhism*; *BR-BV: Religion: Christianity, Bible*; and *BX: Religion: Christian Denominations*.

The individual schedules of Class B are discussed below.

Subclasses B-BJ

The first edition of *B-BJ: Philosophy. Psychology* was developed under the direction of Charles Martel and published in 1910. A second edition followed in 1950, and the third edition in 1979. A new edition, produced from the MARC-based system, was issued in 1996.

This schedule covers philosophy and psychology. Psychology and parapsychology are sandwiched between speculative philosophy and aesthetics. Geographic and language divisions are regularly employed in these subclasses, and there are nine tables specific to B through BJ.

Subclass B includes serials and collections in general philosophy, the history of philosophy and philosophical systems, and, with some exceptions, works by and about individual philosophers. As in other classification systems, classification of works by individual philosophers presents a special problem. Subclass B provides numbers (B108-5802) for individual philosophers based on nationality and period; while numbers based on philosophical topics (logic, metaphysics, epistemology, ontology, cosmology, aesthetics, ethics, and so on) are provided in subclasses BC, BD, BH, and BJ. This dual provision of what Jean M. Perreault[3] calls "national-philosophy classes" and subject classes results in typical instances of cross classification. Works by individual philosophers may be classed in subclass B with the author numbers or in other subclasses with the topical numbers. For example, although Bertrand Russell, a philosopher, is given a specific number, B1649.R9 in subclass B, some of his works on specific philosophical topics are not classed there. His work *Authority and the individual* is classed in HM136 .R8, a number in subclass HM Sociology meaning Individualism. This problem is even more apparent when the philosopher in question is also a theologian. The works of theologians, particularly modern theologians, may be scattered throughout the entire Class B.

Numbers for classical philosophy exist in both B and PA schedules. The numbers in PA are used for original Greek and Latin texts, Latin translations of Greek texts, and texts with textual criticism. Translations of Greek (except translations into Latin) and Roman philosophical works, with or without original text, are classed in B.

The philosophers who are classed in subclass B each must be carefully verified with LC practice. This can be done by checking the numbers assigned to the works by and about the philosopher in LC MARC records.

In subclass B there are nine tables numbered B-BJ1 to B-BJ9 (cf. the current schedule for subclasses B-BJ and a discussion with examples in chapter 4, pages 100-104) used for subarrangement of works by and about individual philosophers. Tables B-BJ1 to B-BJ5 are similar to the author tables discussed in chapter 4, and are designed for philosophers who have been assigned fifty numbers; nine numbers; four or five numbers; one number; or five Cutter numbers. The remaining tables are Table B-BJ6, Language Subdivisions; Table B-BJ7, Table for Separate Works by Plato and Aristotle; and Tables B-BJ8 and B-BJ9, Tables for Latin American Philosophy.

The general pattern of subarrangement of a philosopher's works is:

1. Collected works

2. Separate works

3. Biography, criticism, etc.

The French philosopher Jean Paul Sartre's works may be used as examples of classifying a philosopher's works in subclass B. Sartre has been given the class number B2430.S3, and the instruction in the schedule indicates that Table B-BJ5, Table of Subdivisions (Philosophers with 5 Cutter numbers), is to be used for subarranging works by and about him. The numbers that have been assigned by the Library of Congress to existing cataloging records indicate that five successive Cutter numbers have been developed for Sartre as follows:

Table numbers	*Numbers assigned to Sartre*	
		Collected works.
.x	.S3	Original texts. By date.
.x1	.S31	Partial editions, selections, etc. By editor or date.
.x2A-Z	.S32A-Z	Translations. By language, A-Z, and date.
.x3A-.x3Z7	.S33A-Z7	Separate works, A-Z.
		Biography, autobiography, criticism, etc.
.x3Z8-.x3Z99	.S33Z8-Z99	Dictionaries, indexes, concordances, etc.
.x4A1-.x4A19	.S34A1-A19	Periodicals. Societies. Serials
.x4A3	.S34A3	Autobiography, diaries, etc. By date
.x4A4	.S34A4	Letters. By date
.x4A5	.S34A5	Speeches. By date
.x4A6-.x4Z	.S34A6-Z	General works

The subarrangement with five Cutter numbers set forth in Table B-BJ5 is, therefore, used to class works by and about Sartre. The Cutter number .S33 is used for Sartre's separate works, with a second Cutter number within the range of A-Z7 based on the individual titles. The following examples illustrate the treatment of a philosopher's individual works:

Sartre, Jean-Paul. *Being and nothingness.* 1994

B	Subclass: Philosophy (general)
2430	20th-century French philosophers
.S33	The first Cutter number meaning the individual philosopher, Jean Paul Sartre (.S3), and the successive element (3) meaning a separate work
E813	The second Cutter number (E8) for the original title, *Etre et le néant* and the successive element (13 from the Translation Table) meaning an English translation
1994	The date of publication

It should be pointed out that the translations of a separate work are cuttered immediately following the original title. The method of distinguishing editions of a work has been discussed in chapter 4.

A collection containing interviews of Sartre is classed in B2430.S34A5 as follows:

Sartre, Jean-Paul. *Hope now : the 1980 interviews.* 1996

B	Subclass: Philosophy (general)
2430	20th-century French philosophers
.S34	The first Cutter number meaning the individual philosopher, Jean Paul Sartre (.S3), and the successive element (4) meaning a biographical work
A5	The second Cutter number for speeches according to Table B-BJ5
1996	The date of publication

General works of biography and criticism of Sartre as a philosopher are placed in the range of successive Cutter numbers ".S34A6-Z." The following examples show the use of this range of Cutter numbers:

Existentialist ethics. 1997

B	Subclass: Philosophy (general)
2430	20th-century French philosophers
.S34	The first Cutter number meaning the individual philosopher, Jean Paul Sartre (.S3), and the successive element (4) meaning general criticism

E94   The second Cutter number for the main entry under the
           title, *Existentialist ethics*
1997   The date of publication

Existentialist ontology and human consciousness.   1997
B   Subclass: Philosophy (general)
2430   20th-century French philosophers
.S34   The first Cutter number meaning the individual
           philosopher, Jean Paul Sartre (.S3), and the successive
           element (4) meaning general criticism
E95   The second Cutter number for the main entry under the
           title, *Existentialist ontology . . .*
1997   The date of publication

Note that since both titles begin with the same word, *Existentialist,* the second
Cutter numbers (E94 and E95) have to be adjusted to distinguish between
them and to ensure an alphabetical sequence.

Works by Sartre on specific philosophical topics or other subjects
are classed with the topics or subjects as appropriate, for example:

Sartre, Jean-Paul. *Troubled sleep.* 1992
PQ   Subclass: Romance literature
2637   20th-century French authors with names beginning with S
.A82   The first Cutter number for the individual author Jean
           Paul Sartre
M5613   The second Cutter number (M56) for the original title,
           Mort dans l'âme and the successive element (13 from the
           Translation Table) meaning an English translation
1992   The date of publication

Sartre, Jean-Paul. *Anti-Semite and Jew.* 1995
DS   Subclass: History of Asia
145   Antisemitism
.S2713   The Cutter number (.S27) for Jean Paul Sartre and the
           successive element (13) for an English translation
1995   The date of publication

Table B-BJ6, "Language Subdivisions," in Class B, Part I, B-BJ, is a
simple table requiring the matching of final digits and should present no
problem in use.

The index to B-BJ includes the names of many philosophers, broad categories with many subdivisions, and many compound entries. There are very few references to other schedules.

Subclasses BL, BM, BP, BQ

The schedule for subclasses BL, BM, BP, BQ: *Religion: Religions, Hinduism, Judaism, Islam, Buddhism* contains four subclasses: BL for general works on religion (captioned Religions, Mythology, Rationalism); BM for Judaism; BP for Islam, Bahaism, Theosophy, etc.; and BQ for Buddhism. Subclass BQ was first developed in 1972 and printed in *LC Classification, Additions and Changes*, List 168. In this version, the romanized names of sacred texts of Buddhism were also given in handwritten Chinese characters, but these characters were not included in the schedule published in 1984. Before the development of subclass BQ, Buddhism was classed in BL1400-1495, numbers which have since been canceled.

The subclasses for religion present certain problems in use. These were some of the last schedules to be developed and, as a result, much material related to religion had already been placed in other schedules, for example, Church and social problems in subclass HN; Education and the church in subclass LC; Church music in Class M; Art and architecture in Class N; Biblical languages in subclasses PA and PJ; and Bibliography in Class Z.

As usual, there are numerous tables for internal subarrangement, some of which are quite extensive, for example, Table I, in subclass BM (Judaism), for Special Orders and Tractates of the Mishnah and the Palestinian and Babylonian Talmuds (BM506) and Table III for special Midrashim (BM517). The most complicated tables are the eight tables used with subclass BQ, Buddhism. In addition, there are six Tables of Subdivisions used throughout the schedule.

The following examples illustrate the use of the schedule and, particularly, the tables:

Hembrom, T. *The Santals : anthropological-theological reflections on Santali & biblical creation traditions.* 1996

BL	Subclass: Religions, Mythology, Rationalism
2032	India, by ethnic group
.S24	The first Cutter number for Santals
H465	The second Cutter number for the main entry, Hembrom
1996	The date of publication

Neusner, Jacob. *The Talmud of the land of Israel : a complete outline of the second, third, and fourth divisions. III, The Division of Damages.* 1996

BM	Subclass: Judaism
506	Special orders and tractates of the Mishnah and the Palestinian and Babylonian Talmuds
.N63	The first Cutter number for the Nezikin Order
N45	The second Cutter number for the main entry, Neusner
1996	The date of publication

Midrash Tanhuma-Yelammedenu : an English translation of Genesis and Exodus from the printed version of Tanhuma-Yelammedenu with an introduction, notes, and indexes. 1995

BM	Subclass: Judaism
517	Special Midrashim
.T3613	Tanhuma-Yelammedenu version (.T36) according to Table III, followed by the element (13 from the Translation Table) for an English translation
1995	The date of publication

Eight tables were developed for use with subclass BQ, Buddhism. Examples are shown below:

Revatadhamma, Bhadanta. *The First Discourse of the Buddha : turning the wheel of Dhamma.* 1997

BQ	Subclass: Buddhism
1339	Saṃyuttanikaya
.5	Individual suttas
.D457	The first Cutter number .D45 for Dhammacakkapavattana sutta and the successive element (7 according to Table III) for a modern commentary
R48	The second Cutter number for the main entry, Revatadhamma
1997	The date of publication

Ernst, Judith. *The golden goose king : a tale told by the Buddha.* 1995

BQ	Subclass: Buddhism
1462	The number (in the range 1460-1469 for Jātakas for a translation or adaptation (-2 in Table I) in a Western language
.E5	The first Cutter number for the language, English
.E76	The second Cutter number for the main entry, Ernst
1995	The date of publication

Wray, Elizabeth. *Ten lives of the Buddha : Siamese temple painting and Jataka tales.* 1996

BQ	Subclass: Buddhism
1467	The number (in the range 1460-1469 for Jātakas for a modern commentary (-7 in Table I)
.W43	The Cutter number for the main entry, Wray
1996	The date of publication

Subclasses BR-BV

The separate schedule for subclasses BR-BV, *Religion: Christianity, Bible,* third edition, was published in 1987. It contains four subclasses: BR for Christianity, BS for the Bible, BT for Doctrinal theology, and BV for Practical theology. Following is an example of a work classed in subclass BR, Christianity:

The Christian's treasury of stories and songs, prayers and poems, and much more for young and old. 1995

BR	Subclass: Christianity
123	The integral number meaning Addresses, essays, etc. (Separates)
.E72	The Cutter number for the main entry under the title, *Christian's* . . .
1995	The date of publication

One advantage of Class B for libraries using the LC Classification is the detailed treatment of the Bible and exegesis in subclass BS. There are numerous internal tables in this schedule, and special tables are provided for the subarrangement of the texts of the Bible and works about the Bible. Examples illustrating the use of Table I for special parts of the Old Testament are shown below. In the schedule, the book of *Genesis* has been assigned the numbers BS1231-1235.5. In classing the following books, Table I for special parts of the Old Testament is used:

Bible. O.T. Genesis. English. Biddle. 1997. *Genesis.*   1997

BS	Subclass: The Bible
1233	The number (in the range 1231-1235.5) meaning the book of Genesis and English version (-3 from Table I)
.B53	The Cutter number for the name of the translator, Biddle
1997	The date of publication

Armstrong, Karen. *In the beginning : a new interpretation of Genesis.* 1996

BS	Subclass: The Bible
1235.2	The number meaning the book of Genesis (123-) and criticism (-5.2 from Table I)
.A76	The Cutter number for the main entry, Armstrong
1996	The date of publication

Visotzky, Burton L. *The Genesis of ethics.*   1996

BS	Subclass: The Bible
1235.6	The number meaning the book of Genesis (123-) and (-5.6 from Table I at the end of BS) for a commentary on a special topic
.E8	The first Cutter number for the topic Ethics (from Table I)
V57	The second Cutter number for the main entry, Visotzky
1996	The date of publication

Another example of using Table 1:

Thomason, Bill. *God on trial : the book of Job and human suffering.* 1997

BS	Subclass: The Bible
1415.2	The number meaning the book of Job (141-) and criticism (-5.2 from Table I)
.T47	The Cutter number for the main entry, Thomason
1997	The date of publication

Subclass BX

The schedule for subclass BX, *Religion: Christian Denominations*, is greatly enumerated and detailed. The third edition (1985) represents a cumulated edition, incorporating additions and changes since the second edition. There are five Tables of Subdivisions used for subarranging works about individual Christian denominations throughout subclass BX. In addition, there are a number of internal tables used with numbers for individual orders of the Roman Catholic Church. The use of the schedule and some of these tables is illustrated below.

Orthodox Church in America. *The Apostol : epistle readings, prokimena, alleluia verses, and antiphons for the entire liturgical year.* 1996

BX	Subclass: Christian denominations
375	Liturgical works of the Orthodox Eastern Church
.A65	Apostolos
A45	The second Cutter number (according to an internal table) for an English version
1996	The date of publication

The Benedictines are assigned the range of numbers BX3001-3056 in the schedule. An internal table with fifty-six numbers for Individual orders of men is used to subarrange works related to the Benedictines, as illustrated in the following example:

The rule of Benedict : a guide to Christian living : the full text of the rule in Latin and English. 1994

BX	Subclass: Christian denominations
3004	The number (chosen from the range BX3001-3056 according to the table preceding BX2890) for rules, instructions, constitution, etc., of the Benedictines
.A2	The Cutter number for a Latin version of the Rule of St. Benedict
1994c	The date of publication

Note that the letter "c" following the date in the call number indicates this is the third version or edition of the same work published in the same year.

Kardong, Terrence. *Benedict's Rule : a translation and commentary.* 1996

BX	Subclass: Christian denominations
3004	The number (chosen from the range BX3001-3056 according to the table preceding BX2890) for rules, instructions, constitution, etc., of the Benedictines
.Z5	The first Cutter number (according to the internal table · for a 56-number order) for a commentary
K34	The second Cutter number for the main entry, Kardong
1996	The date of publication

The following examples illustrate the use of one of the five tables for Christian denominations. These tables appear at the end of the schedule before the index.

Olbricht, Thomas H. *Hearing God's voice : my life with scripture in the Churches of Christ.*   1996

BX	Subclass: Christian denominations
7077	The number chosen from the range BX7075-7077, Churches of Christ, according to Table II for three numbers
.Z8	Individual biography, A-Z
O53	The Cutter number for the biographee and author, Olbricht
1996	The date of publication

The denomination of Uniting Church in Australia is assigned a Cutter number, BX9890.U34, with the instruction to use Table IV for subarrangement of works relating to it.

Owen, Michael. *Back to basics : studies on the basis of union of the Uniting Church.*   1996

BX	Subclass: Christian denominations
9890	United Missionary Church – Universal
.U345	The first Cutter number (.U34) meaning Uniting Church in Australia and the successive element (5) from Table IV meaning Doctrines, creeds, etc.
O94	The second Cutter number for the main entry, Owen
1996	The date of publication

The index to BX excludes names of popes but includes the names of the orders of the Roman Catholic Church, which were omitted from the index to the second edition of BL-BX. The detailed lists of religious orders and denominations make this schedule a useful reference tool.

CLASS C—AUXILIARY SCIENCES OF HISTORY

C
1-51   Auxiliary sciences of history (General)

CB
3-482   History of civilization
156   Terrestrial evidence of interplanetary
                                voyages
158-161   Forecasts of future progress
195-281   Civilization and race
305-430   By period
440-482   Relation to special topics
450   Geography and civilization
478   Technology
481   War and civilization
482   Water and civilization

CC
1-960   Archaeology
72-81   Philosophy.   Theory
73-81   Methodology
83-97   Study and teaching.   Research
135-137   Preservation, restoration, and
                                conservation of antiquities.
                                Antiquities and state
140   Forgeries of antiquities
200-260   Bells.   Campanology.   Cowbells
300-350   Crosses
600-605   Boundary stones
700-705   Stone heaps, cairns, etc., of
                                unknown purpose
710   Hill figures
960   Lanterns of the dead

CD
1-6471   Diplomatics.   Archives.   Seals
1-511   Diplomatics
70-79   Practice of special chancelleries
80-81   Formularies
87   Forgeries of documents
91-392   Collection of documents, facsimiles,
                                    etc., for study
501-511   Study and teaching
921-4280   Archives
995-4280   History and statistics
997   Biography of archivists
1000-4280   By region or country

5001-6471	Seals
5191	Iconography
5201-5391	Ancient
5501-5557	Medieval
5561	Renaissance
5575-6471	Modern

CE	
1-97	Technical chronology. Calendar
21-46	Ancient
51-85	Medieval and modern
91-92	Perpetual calendars. Century calendars, etc.

CJ	
1-6661	Numismatics
1-4625	Coins
153	Finds of coins
161	Symbols, devices, etc.
201-1397	Ancient
1509-4625	Medieval and modern
4801-5450	Tokens
4861-4889	By period
4901-5336	By region or country
5350-5450	Special uses of tokens
5501-6661	Medals and medallions
5581-5690	Ancient
5723-5793	Medieval and modern
5795-6661	By region or country

CN	
1-1355	Inscriptions. Epigraphy
120-740	Ancient inscriptions
750-753	Early Christian inscription
755	Medieval inscriptions (General)
760	Modern inscriptions (General)
805-865	By language
870-1355	By region or country

CR	
1-6305	Heraldry
51-79	Crests, monograms, devices, badges mottoes, etc.
91-93	Shields and supporters
101-115	Flags, banners, and standards
191-1020	Public and official heraldry
1101-1131	Ecclesiastical and sacred heraldry

Class C continues on page 176.

1179-3395	Family heraldry
3499-4420	Titles of honor, rank, precedence, etc.
4480-4485	Royalty. Insignia. Regalia, crown and coronets, etc.
4501-6305	Chivalry and knighthood (Orders, decorations, etc.)
4547-4553	Ceremonials, pageants, tournaments, etc.
4571-4595	Duels and dueling
4651-6305	Orders, etc.

CS
1-3090	Genealogy
23-35	Genealogical lists, etc., covering more than one country or continent
38-39	Family history covering more than one country
42-2209	By region or country
2300-3090	Personal and family names

CT
21-9999	Biography
21-22	Biography as an art or literary form
31-83	History of biographical literature. Lives of biographers
93-206	General collective biography
206	Portraits
210-3150	National biography
3200-3999	Biography. By subject
3200-3830	Biography of women (Collective)
3990	Academicians. Scholars. Savants
9960-9998	Other miscellaneous groups Including adventurers, eccentrics, misers, etc.
9999	Blank books for personal records, diaries, etc.

The schedule for **Class C: Auxiliary Sciences of History,** was first published in 1915. Subclass CN, Inscriptions, Epigraphy, was not included in the first edition, but was delayed until the completion of subclass PA (in 1942) to avoid any possible duplication. Subclass CN was completed in time for the second edition of Class C, published in 1947—the first appearance of Class C in its complete form. The third edition, published in 1974, introduced yet another subclass, labeled C, Auxiliary sciences of history (general). The fourth edition was published in 1993. Three years later, the 1996 edition was produced from the new automated system for the Library of Congress classification.

Class C, consisting of ten subclasses, may be considered the generalia and miscellanea class for history. The subclasses represent very precisely defined fields of study. There is little relationship among some of the subclasses, and each subclass is a complete development within itself.

There are thirty tables in Class C, numbered C1-C30. They appear between the schedule and the index. Each table is designated for use with a specific topic such as Archives, Seals, Coins, Genealogy, etc. Most of these tables require simply the matching of the final digits of the specific geographic area's range of numbers from the schedule with those in the table.

Tables C26-C30 are designed for biography. For example, Great Britain is a nineteen-number country, CT770-788; therefore, Table C26 is used for national biography of Great Britain. Its range of numbers may be matched to those in Table C26 in the following fashion:

CT 770-788	*Table C26*	
770	0	Periodicals. Societies. Serials
771	1	Collected works (nonserial)
772	2	Early works through 1800
773	3	Dictionaries. Encyclopedias
774	4	General works, 1801-
775	5	General special
777	7	Juvenile works
777.5	7.5	Portraits
		By period
		Ancient
		see class D
		Medieval
		see class D
		Modern
780	10	15th-16th centuries
781	11	17th-18th centuries
782	12	19th-20th centuries
783	13	20th century
(784)	(14)	Colonies
		see CT280-CT3090
(785)	(15.A-Z)	Local divisions, A-Z
		Class here collective biographies of persons not classed in classes D-F; for individual biography, *see* 18
		Cities
		see class D

		Rulers *see* Classes D-F
787	17.A-Z	Individual families, A-Z
788	18.A-Z	Individual persons, A-Z (Table C30) For individual biographies of political or historical persons, or of persons associated with particular cities, *see* classes D-F
788.Z9	18.Z9	Persons not known by name

A work about an individual family is classed in CT787.

Titford, Donald. *Moonrakers in my family.* 1995

CT	Subclass: Biography
787	A work about an individual family from Great Britain
.T58	The first Cutter number for the family Titford
T58	The second Cutter number for the main entry, Titford
1995	The date of publication

The following work is classed as an individual biography in the number, CT788, within Great Britain's range:

Pellow, James. *A lifetime on the Titanic : the biography of Edith Haisman.* 1995

CT	Subclass: Biography
788	A work about an individual person from Great Britain
.H22	The first Cutter number for the biographee, Haisman
P45	The second Cutter number for the biographer, Pellow
1995	The date of publication

Table C26 is also applied to national biography of France (CT1000-1018). For example:

Combes, Claudette. *Claire, ou, La vie de Claire Pradier.* 1994

CT	Subclass: Biography
1018	The number (-18.A-Z) based on Table C26 for a work about an individual person from France
.P69	The first Cutter number for the biographee, Pradier
C66	The second Cutter number for the main entry, Combes
1994	The date of publication

Journal d'un novice.   1996

CT	Subclass: Biography
1018	A work about an individual person from France
.Z9	The first Cutter number (based on number -18.Z9 from Table C26) for a person not known by name
J68	The second Cutter number for the main entry under the title, *Journal* ...
1996	The date of publication

Table C30, similar to the free-floating Biography Table, is used for subarrangement of individual biography. The following examples of individual American biography demonstrate the use of this table:

Ginzton, Edward L.   *Times to remember : the life of Edward L. Ginzton.* 1996 printing

CT	Subclass: Biography
275	Individual American biography
.G442	The first Cutter number for the subject of the biography, Ginzton
A3	The second Cutter number from Table C30 meaning an autobiographical work
1996	The date of publication

Frost, Alan.   *The precarious life of James Mario Matra : voyager with Cook, American loyalist, servant of empire.*   1995

CT	Subclass: Biography
275	Individual American biography
.M26	The first Cutter number for the subject of the biography, Matra
F76	The second Cutter number (based on Table C30) for the main entry of the biography, Frost
1995	The date of publication

A collection of letters between two individuals is classed in CT788 with the second Cutter number meaning letters from Table C30.

Morris, May.   *On poetry, painting, and politics : the letters of May Morris and John Quinn.*   1997

CT	Subclass: Biography
788	A work about an individual person from Great Britain

.M643	The first Cutter number for the first biographee, Morris
A4	The second Cutter number from Table C30, meaning Letters
1997	The date of publication

In the past, certain works of national biography were classed with History in Classes D and E-F. Current policy requires that works such as dictionaries of national biography and "Who's Who" types of works be classed in CT. For example:

Encyclopedia of American biography.   1996

CT	Subclass: Biography
213	An American biographical dictionary
.E53	The Cutter number for the main entry under the title, *Encyclopedia . . .*
1996	The date of publication

It is the policy of the Library of Congress to class biography by subject. Subclass CT, Biography, is used only for biography for which the subject is not readily discernible. This is true of both collective and individual biography, as the foregoing examples show. Examples in chapter 4 have shown biographies of literary writers and philosophers classed with their works in Classes P and B. For further discussion and examples of classifying biography by subject, see chapter 7, pages 444-57.

Classifiers are often faced with the question of whether certain types of historical works should be classed in the History Classes, C-F, or in other classes. Following is a summary of Library of Congress policies concerning some types of historical material:

1. *Archival inventories.* Archival inventories include records and papers of government bodies, families, and academic and religious institutions. Appropriate numbers in subclass CD are assigned to comprehensive inventories of archives of government bodies and academic or religious institutions; comprehensive inventories of materials deposited in national, state, provincial, or municipal archives; and inventories of the archives of several families or an individual family. However, archival inventories limited to a particular topic are classed in the appropriate numbers in Class K, M, or Z. Works containing the text of documents from an archive collection are assigned numbers from the regular classes.

2. *Manuscript catalogs.* Catalogs of manuscripts in one language, those held by an individual library or on a particular subject, and catalogs of the manuscripts or archives of an individual are classed in Z6605-6621, with alternate numbers assigned from the regular classes.[4] Texts of documents from a manuscript collection, on the other hand, are classed in Classes A-V.

3. *Historic preservation.*[5] Works on historic preservation are scattered in Classes C, D, E, F, and NA, depending on the emphasis of the work. A work treating collectively the preservation of sites, monuments, landmarks, historic buildings, etc. and not limited to a particular place is classed in CC135+. A general work on historic preservation limited to a particular place is classed with the place in D, E, or F, as are works on the history of a particular building or group of buildings. However, works on the architecture and preservation of historic buildings are classed in NA, Architecture. If the work covers both architecture and history, the number for the aspect emphasized in the work is assigned.

4. *Genealogy.* In general, genealogical materials are classed in CS, with the exception of works about the genealogy of individual American ethnic groups and local genealogy of the United States, which are classed in the appropriate numbers in Class E or F,[6] for example, F180, Genealogy of Maryland; and E184.G3, German Americans. Works about genealogy in general, including works on methodology, research, etc., are classed in CS1-CS21. Genealogical lists, etc., covering more than one country or continent are classed in CS23-35. Family history covering more than one country is classed in CS38-CS39. Genealogy of the United States in general is classed in CS42-CS71. Works about the genealogy of other countries and collections of records from these countries, including local genealogy and the genealogy of ethnic groups, are classed in CS80-CS2209. Personal and family names are classed in CS2300-CS3090.

5. *Biography.* For biographies classed with specific topics, see the discussion in chapter 7.

A work containing a mixture of family biography and genealogy is classed with genealogy unless the genealogical material is clearly a minor part of the work.

Collections of local court records intended for local historical or genealogical research are classified in appropriate numbers for local history or in CS. Those intended as primary legal source material are classified in Class K.[7]

The index to Class C is relatively brief. It does not include entries for geographic names, which appear extensively in the schedule.

CLASS D—HISTORY: GENERAL AND OLD WORLD

D

1-1075	History (General)
51-95	Ancient history
111-203	Medieval history
204-475	Modern history
501-680	World War I
731-838	World War II
839-850	Post-war history, 1945-
880-888	Developing countries
890-893	Eastern Hemisphere
901-1075	Europe (General)

DA

1-995	Great Britain
20-690	England
670	Local history and description
675-689	London
700-745	Wales
750-890	Scotland
900-995	Ireland

DAW

1001-1051	Central Europe

DB

1-879	Austria
881-898	Liechtenstein
901-999	Hungary
2000-3150	Czechoslovakia

DC

1-947	France
630-655.5	Alsace-Lorraine
701-790	Paris
921-930	Andorra
941-947	Monaco

DD

1-905	Germany
	Including West Germany
280-289	East Germany
301-454	Prussia
701-901	Local history and description

DE
1-100   The Mediterranean Region.   The Greco-Roman
                              World

DF
10-951   Greece
10-289   Ancient Greece
501-649   Medieval Greece.   Byzantine Empire, 323-1453
701-951   Modern Greece
915-936   Athens

DG
11-999   Italy
11-365   Ancient Italy.   Rome to 476
61-69   Rome (City)
401-583   Medieval and Modern Italy, 476-
670-684.72   Venice
791-800   Papal States.   Vatican City
803-817.3   Rome (Modern City)
861-869   Sicily
987-999   Malta

DH
1-925   Netherlands (Low Countries)
401-811   Belgium
901-925   Luxembourg

DJ
1-500   Netherlands (Holland)

DJK
1-77   Eastern Europe

DK
1-949   Russia.   Soviet Union.   Former Soviet Republics
541-579   Saint Petersburg.   Leningrad.   Petrograd
588-609   Moscow
751-781   Siberia
4010-4800   Poland

DL
1-1180   Northern Europe.   Scandinavia
101-291   Denmark
301-398   Iceland
401-596   Norway
601-991   Sweden
1002-1180   Finland

Class D continues on page 184.

DP
1-402	Spain
285-302	Local history and description
350-374	Madrid
501-900	Portugal
752-776	Lisbon

DQ
1-851	Switzerland
301-800	Cantons
820-841	Alps

DR
1-2285	Balkan Peninsula
51-98	Bulgaria
201-296	Romania
401-741	Turkey
716-739	Istanbul
901-998	Albania
1202-2285	Yugoslavia

DS
1-937	History of Asia
35.3-35.8	The Islamic World
36-39.2	Arab countries
	Including North Africa
41-66	Southwestern Asia. Ancient Orient. Near East
67-79.9	Iraq
80-90	Lebanon
92-99	Syria
101-151	Israel (Palestine). The Jews
133-151	Jews outside of Palestine
153-154.9	Jordan
155-156	Asia Minor
161-199	Armenia
201-248	Arabian Peninsula. Saudi Arabia
251-326	Iran
327-329	Ancient Western and Central Asia
331-339.9	Southern Asia. Indian Ocean Region
350-375	Afghanistan
376-392.2	Pakistan
393-396.9	Bangladesh
401-486.8	India
488-490	Sri Lanka
493-495.8	Nepal
498-498.8	Goa
501-519	East Asia. The Far East
527-530.9	Burma
554-554.98	Cambodia

555-555.98	Laos
556-560.72	Vietnam
557-559.8	Vietnamese Conflict
561-589	Thailand
591-599	Malaysia
600-605	Malay Archipelago
611-649	Indonesia
651-689	Philippines
701-799.9	China
777.545-779.29	People's Republic, 1949-
781-784.2	Manchuria
785-786	Tibet
798.92-799.9	Taiwan
801-897	Japan
901-937	Korea
930-937	Democratic People's Republic, 1948-

DT	
1-3415	History of Africa
43-154	Egypt
154.1-159.9	Sudan
160-177	North Africa
179.2-179.9	Northwest Africa
181-346	Maghrib. Barbary States
211-239	Libya
241-269	Tunisia
271-299	Algeria
301-330	Morocco
331-346	Sahara
348-363.3	Central, Sub-Saharan Africa
365-469	Eastern Africa
371-398	Ethiopia
401-409	Somalia
411-411.9	Djibouti
433.2-433.29	Uganda
433.5-434	Kenya
436-449	Tanzania
450-450.49	Rwanda
450.5-450.95	Burundi
468-469	Islands (East African coast)
	Including Madagascar, Mauritius, Reunion, Seychelles, etc.
470-671	West Africa
491-516.9	British West Africa
509-509.9	Gambia
509.97-512.9	Ghana
515-515.9	Nigeria
516-516.9	Sierra Leone

Class D continues on page 186.

521-555.9	French West Africa
541-541.9	Benin
543-543.9	Guinea
545-545.9	Ivory Coast
546.1-546.19	Gabon
546.2-546.29	Congo (Brazzaville)
546.3-546.39	Central African Republic
546.4-546.49	Chad
547-547.9	Niger
548	West Sahara
549-549.9	Senegal
551-551.9	Mali
554-554.9	Mauritania
555-555.9	Burkina Faso
561-581	Cameroon
582-582.9	Togo
591-615.9	Portuguese-speaking West Africa
613-613.9	Guinea-Bissau
615-615.9	Sao Tome and Principe
619-620.9	Spanish West Africa
620-620.9	Equatorial Guinea
621-637	Liberia
639	Congo (Kongo) River region
641-665	Zaire
669-671	Islands
1001-1190	Southern Africa
1251-1465	Angola
1501-1685	Namibia. South-West Africa
1701-2405	South Africa
1991-2054	Cape Province. Cape of Good Hope
2075-2145	Orange Free State. Oranje Vrystaat
2181-2278	Natal
2291-2378	Transvaal. South African Republic
2421-2525	Botswana. Bechuanaland
2541-2686	Lesotho. Basutoland
2701-2825	Swaziland
2831-2864	British Central Africa. Federation of Rhodesia and Nyasaland
2871-3025	Zimbabwe. Southern Rhodesia
3031-3145	Zambia. Northern Rhodesia
3161-3257	Malawi. Nyasaland
3291-3415	Mozambique

DU	
1-950	History of Oceania (South Seas)
80-398	Australia
400-430	New Zealand
490	Melanesia (General)
500	Micronesia (General)

510	Polynesia (General)
520-950	Smaller island groups
620-629	Hawaiian Islands. Hawaii
739-747	New Guinea
810-819	Samoan Islands

DX
101-301	History of Gypsies

Class D—History: General and Old World encompasses the history and topography of the world in general and of the continents and countries excluding those in the Western Hemisphere. The scheme was initially drafted by Charles Martel in 1901 and 1902. The first edition, with the title *Universal and Old World History*, was published in 1916, and the second edition in 1959. Prior to the publication of the second edition two separate supplements were issued for World War I and World War II. The first supplement, for World War I, was published in 1921, with a second edition in 1933. The supplement for World War II was published in 1947. The second edition of Class D incorporated these two supplements into the text.

Because of the extensive expansion of Class D since the second edition, it was decided that publication of the third edition of the schedule of Class D would be in separate parts. Currently Class D spreads over four volumes:

D-DJ, History (General), History of Europe, Part 1

DJK-DK, History of Eastern Europe (General), Soviet Union, Poland

DL-DR, History of Europe, Part 2

DS-DX, History of Asia, Africa, Australia, New Zealand, etc.

The first schedule to be produced from the MARC-based system was DS-DX, published in 1998.

To ensure consistency in the development of separate schedules for the subclasses in Class D, the Library of Congress has established model outlines for divisions within each schedule. The model for Class D is included in appendix B.

The separate schedules for Class D are discussed below.

Subclasses D-DJ

The main schedule for Class D, *D-DJ, History (General), History of Europe, Part 1*, covers world history, European history in general, and the history of Western European countries. In the third edition, a new subclass, DAW, was developed for Central Europe.

Historically, Class D was the first class to use a second letter in the notation for subclasses, a device designed to allow the development of whole subclasses without restriction to a specified range of numbers. The preface to the first edition of Class D is extremely helpful, not only as a guide to this class but as a sound general statement on the theory of classification for history. Unfortunately, this preface was not retained in later editions.

A major characteristic of Class D is that most division is by geographic rather than political areas. Similarly, geographic names are usually chosen in preference to political names. The reason, no doubt, is that the former are less prone to change.

One earlier criticism of Class D was that its general shape reflected the state of Europe at the time of the First World War. This situation is being gradually rectified to reflect current states of affairs. For example, the detailed development under the number DD491 for Provinces and regions of Prussia has been canceled and works previously classed in the subdivisions of DD491 are now classed at DD701+ (local history and description of Germany) and DK4600+ (local history and description of Poland), with local subdivisions of Germany and Poland.

The general pattern of arrangement of divisions under each country in the schedules for Class D is:

1. General works

2. Description and travel

3. Antiquities.   Social life and customs, etc.

4. History

5. Local history and description

The main exception to this pattern is subclass DA, Great Britain, in which the order is (1) General works; (2) History, including antiquities, etc.; (3) Description and travel; (4) Local history and description.

In the case of a few countries, cities are assigned numbers outside of the hierarchy of the larger entities of which they are a part. For example, cities in France other than Paris are classed in DC801 while regions, provinces, departments, and so forth, namely, the entities that encompass them, are classed in DC611. This placement results in two separate hierarchies where logically there should be one.[8]

The local history numbers for individual countries make use of extensive special tables within the schedules; the tables are accompanied by complete directions for their use. In most cases a careful analysis of LC practice with an individual number should show how to fit locally assigned call numbers into previously classed material.

French local history and description in subclass DC may be used as an example of special tables within the schedules. The history and description of the individual regions, provinces, departments, etc., of France is classed in the number DC611. Tables and instructions for subarrangement are given in the schedule under this one number. The following tables represent an updated version of the tables that appear in the published schedule:

DC		FRANCE		DC
		LOCAL HISTORY AND DESCRIPTION		

600	Islands of France (General)
	For individual islands, <u>see</u> DC611, DC801; DT469; etc.
	Larger geographical divisions
	For subarrangement, <u>see</u> table under DC611
601.1-9	North. Northeast
603.1-9	East
605.1-9	Central
607.1-9	South. Gulf of Lyons
608.1-9	Riviera
	Cf. DG975.R6, Italian Riviera
609.1-9	West. Southwest
611	Regions, provinces, departments, etc., A-Z
	For works limited to local history between 1589 and 1715, <u>see</u> DC121.9; for works limited to local history during the Revolution and Consulate, <u>see</u> DC195; for works limited to local history during the February Revolution of 1848, <u>see</u> DC271
	Under each (unless otherwise indicated):

9 nos.	7 nos.	6 nos.	5 nos.	3 nos.	2 nos.	
(1)	(1)	(1)	(1)	(1)	(1)	Periodicals. Societies. Serials
(13)	(13)	(13)	(13)	(13)	(13)	Museums, exhibitions, etc. Subarrange by author
(15)	(15)	(15)	(15)	(15)	(15)	Congresses
(2)	(2)					Sources and documents
(23)		(2)		(2)	(2)	Gazetteers, directories, dictionaries, etc.
(25)	(3)					Biography (Collective)

Table continues on page 190.

9 nos.	7 nos.	6 nos.	5 nos.	3 nos.	2 nos.	
(3)	(4)		(2)			General works. Description and travel. Guidebooks
						Antiquities
(4)	(5)		(3)			Social life and customs.
(45)	(55)		(35)			Civilization
						Ethnography
(46)						History (General)
(5)	(6)	(3)	(4)	(3)		By period
						Including history and description and travel
(6)		(4)				Early
(7)		(5)				Medieval and early modern
(8)		(6)				Modern
						Biography and memoirs
						Collective
(82)						Individual, A-Z
(83)						Special topics (not A-Z)
(9)	(7)	(65)	(5)			

Note: When only one Cutter number is indicated, subarrange by author

e.g.	.A16	Agenais
	.A26-27	Ain
	.A261	Sources and documents. Collections
	.A298-299	Aisne
		Including old district, Thiérache
	.A3	Alais
	.A33-35	Albigeois
	.A435-437	Allier
	.A553-557	Alpes (Basses-, Hautes-, Maritimes)
		Cf. DQ821+, Swiss Alps
	.A553	Periodicals. Societies. Serials
	.A554	Sources and documents. Collections
	.A555	Gazetteers. Dictionaries, etc.
	.A556	Description and history
	.A557	Other
		Alsace, <u>see</u> DC647+
	.A601-609	Anjou

The Pyrenees have been assigned the range of numbers DC611.P981-989. Therefore, the table for 9 nos. is used in classifying the following works:

Deloffre, R. *Châteaux et fortifications des Pyrénées-Atlantiques : dictionnaire.* 1996

DC	Subclass: History of France
611	Local history and description of individual regions, provinces, departments, etc.
.P983	The first Cutter number meaning (according to table of 9 nos.) description and travel in the Pyrenees
D45	The second Cutter number for the main entry, Deloffre
1996	The date of publication

Pays pyrénéens & pouvoirs centraux, XVIe-XXe s. : actes du colloque international organisé à Foix, les 1-2-3 octobre 1993. [1995?]

DC	Subclass: History of France
611	Local history and description of individual regions, provinces, departments, etc.
.P988	The first Cutter number meaning (according to table of 9 nos.) modern history
P3	The second Cutter number for the main entry under the title, *Pays* . . .
1995	The date of publication

Vaucluse has been assigned the range of numbers DC611.V356-357, and a history of Vaucluse is classed in the second Cutter number according to the table for 2 nos.

Vaucluse. [1995]

DC	Subclass: History of France
611	Local history and description of individual regions, provinces, departments, etc.
.V357	The first Cutter number meaning (according to table of 2 nos.) a history of Vaucluse
V38	The second Cutter number for the main entry under the title, *Vaucluse*
1995	The date of publication

Many of the better-known localities, for example, Alpes and Aquitaine, are fully developed in the schedules. Brittany (Bretagne) is given a range of successive Cutter numbers, "DC611.B841-9173." The successions are then clearly assigned in the schedule. The following is the first part of this assignment:

DC   FRANCE
                     Local history and description
611   Regions, provinces, departments, etc., A-Z
                         e.g.,   Brittany (Bretagne)
                         .B841   Periodicals.   Societies.   Serials
                         .B842   Sources and documents.   Collections
                         .B843   Collected works
                         .B844   Pamphlets, etc.
                         .B845   Biography (Collective)
                         .B846   Gazetteers.   Directories, etc.
                         .B847   General works
                         .B848   Description and travel
                                      Including the picturesque
                         .B85   Antiquities
                         .B851   Social life and customs.   Civilization
                         .B852   Ethnography
                         .B854   History
                         .B855   General special

For example, a work on the archaeology of Brittany is classed in DC611.B85, using the assigned successive Cutter number for a work on antiquities of Brittany:

> *Ateliers de potiers médiévaux en Bretagne.*   1996

DC	Subclass: History of France
611	Local history and description of an individual region, etc., of France
.B85	The first Cutter number meaning a work on antiquities of Brittany
A74	The second Cutter number for the main entry under the title, *Ateliers . . .*
1996	The date of publication

A work on social life and customs or civilization of Brittany is assigned the successive Cutter number, ".B851."

Bretagnes : art, négoce et société, de l'Antiquité à nos jours : mélanges offerts au professeur Jean Tanguy. 1996

DC	Subclass: History of France
611	Local history and description of an individual region, etc., of France
.B851	The first Cutter number meaning a work on social life and customs and civilization of Brittany
B77	The second Cutter number for the main entry under the title, *Bretagnes* . . .
1996	The date of publication

There are seven auxiliary tables in subclasses D-DJ. Tables I-III are used for subarrangement of material about countries or regions that have been assigned a single number (an integer or a number with decimal extension) or a Cutter number. Tables IV and V are used for cities with a single number or Cutter number. Tables VI and VII are used for subarranging individual biography, and the divisions in these tables correspond to those found in the table for biography in general, which is included in appendix A. The following examples illustrate the use of these tables:

Thatcher, Carol. *Below the parapet : the biography of Denis Thatcher.* 1996

DA	Subclass: History of Great Britain
591	Late 20th-century biography
.T467	The first Cutter number for the biographee, Thatcher (Denis)
T48	The second Cutter number for the main entry, Thatcher (Carol), assigned according to Table VII
1996	The date of publication

For an autobiography, the second Cutter number is A3, according to Table VII.

Maitland, Sir Donald. *Diverse times, sundry places.* 1996

DA	Subclass: History of Great Britain
591	Late 20th-century biography
.M325	The first Cutter number for the biographee, Maitland
A3	The second Cutter number for an autobiography, assigned according to Table VII
1996	The date of publication

Class D is one of several LC Classification schedules that have potential reference uses. The local history numbers for European countries contain comprehensive lists of countries, regions, and some cities. The index to subclasses D-DJ contains entries for many local place names, and so can serve as a useful reference tool.

Subclasses DJK-DK

The separate schedule for subclasses DJK-DK, *History of Eastern Europe (General), Soviet Union, Poland,* was last published in 1987, before the dissolution of the Soviet Union. Since then, the schedule has been revised to reflect the political changes, and the caption for DK was changed from *Soviet Union* to *Russia. Soviet Union. Former Soviet Republics.*

Subclass DJK contains general form divisions for works on Eastern Europe in general, and provisions for local history and description of the Black Sea Region and the Carpathian Mountain Region.

This schedule contains seven tables, similar to those found in subclasses D-DJ. In addition, it also includes the "List of Regions and Countries in One Alphabet," which is one of the free-floating tables used throughout the LC Classification scheme.

The following examples illustrate the use of this schedule:

Mason, David S. *Revolution and transition in East-Central Europe.* 1996

DJK	Subclass: Eastern Europe (General)
50	History since 1945
.M38	The Cutter number for the main entry, Mason
1996	The date of publication

Regionalismus und Nationalismus in Russland. 1996

DK	Subclass: Russia, Soviet Union, Former Soviet Republics
510.33	Ethnography of Russia
.R44	The Cutter number for the main entry under the title, *Regionalismus . . .*
1996	The date of publication

Regional identity, regional consciousness : the upper Silesian experience. 1995

DK	Subclass: Poland
4600	Provinces, counties, historical regions, etc., A-Z
.S4642	The first Cutter number (.S46) for Upper Silesia with the successive element (42 from Table III) for Ethnography
R44	The second Cutter number for the main entry under the title, *Regional* . . .
1995	The date of publication

Gutt-Mostowy, Jan. *Podhale : a companion guide to the Polish Highlands.* 1997

DK	Subclass: Poland
4600	Provinces, counties, historical regions, etc., A-Z
.P6	The first Cutter number (.P6) for Podhale Highlands
G88	The second Cutter number for the main entry, Gutt-Mostowy
1997	The date of publication

In addition to topical entries, the index contains names of monarchs and heads of state and names of countries, regions, and large cities.

Subclasses DL-DR

The schedule for DL-DR, *History of Europe, Part 2*, contains four subclasses:

> DL Northern Europe. Scandinavia. Denmark. Iceland. Norway. Sweden. Finland
> DP Spain. Portugal
> DQ Switzerland
> DR Balkan Peninsula. Bulgaria. Romania. Turkey. Albania. Yugoslavia

The caption for DR was originally "Eastern Europe. Balkan Peninsula," which was changed to "Balkan Peninsula." Eastern Europe is now classed in subclass DJK. There are seven auxiliary tables, which are similar to those found in subclasses D-DJ. The following examples illustrate the use of this schedule:

Thuesen, Nils Petter.   *Oslo : seks historiske vandringer.*   1996

DL	Subclass: Northern Europe and Scandinavia
581	Oslo, Norway
.A4	The first Cutter number (based on Table IV) for a guidebook
T48	The second Cutter number for the main entry, Thuesen
1996	The date of publication

Bohemene taler : tekster i utvalg.   1995

DL	Subclass: Northern Europe and Scandinavia
581	Oslo, Norway
.2	Social life and customs (based on Table IV)
B65	The Cutter number for the main entry under the title, *Bohemene . . .*
1995	The date of publication

Glick, Thomas F.   *From Muslim fortress to Christian castle : social and cultural change in medieval Spain.*   1995

DP	Subclass: Spain
99	A history published after 1801 on the Moorish domination and the Reconquest, 711-1516
.G46	The Cutter number for the main entry, Glick
1995	The date of publication

The new Switzerland : problems and policies.   1996

DQ	Subclass: Switzerland
208	A general history after 1945
.B5513	The Cutter number .B55 for the main entry under the original title, *Blickpunkt Schweiz* and the successive element (13 from the Translation Table) for an English translation
1996	The date of publication

Riedler, Michael.   *So veränderte sich Luzern.*   1993

DQ	Subclass: Switzerland
509.6	A modern guidebook (-9.6 in internal table for subarrangement of cantons in Switzerland) of Lucerne (DQ501-520.35)
.R54	The Cutter number for the main entry, Riedler
1993	The date of publication

Subclasses DS-DX

In the third edition of Class D, subclass DS, *History of Asia* (1987) and subclasses DT-DX, *History of Africa, Australia, New Zealand, etc.* (1989) were published as two separate schedules. In 1998, they were combined into one schedule, *DS-DX, History of Asia, Africa, Australia, New Zealand, etc.*

Initially, the classification of Western European history was more fully developed in Class D than the history of any other area. The subclasses for Africa and Asia, in particular, did not contain nearly as many numbers as the ten subclasses for Western Europe. This deficiency has been gradually rectified with extensive expansions for Asian and African history.

Changes in the history of African countries from colonial status to independence during the twentieth century have necessitated many adjustments in the classification schedule. Class numbers for southern Africa, for example, underwent substantial changes. The class numbers DT727-971, originally assigned to southern Africa, were replaced by the span DT1001 through DT3415 in the third edition in order to allow a more logical arrangement of southern African countries.

A notable characteristic of Class D is the detailed enumeration of historical periods under countries, under many local divisions, and in the provisions for large cities. This is true for newly developed areas as well as for countries and areas in Western Europe. The following examples show the detailed breakdown of Chinese history:

Ross, Robert S. *Managing a changing relationship : China's Japan policy in the 1990s.* 1996

DS	Subclass: Asia
779.27	Foreign relations of China since 1976
.R66	The Cutter number for the main entry, Ross
1996	The date of publication

Miles, James A. R. *The legacy of Tiananmen : China in disarray.* 1996

DS	Subclass: Asia
779.32	Tiananmen Square Incident, 1989, in China
.M54	The Cutter number for the main entry, Miles
1996	The date of publication

Stefoff, Rebecca. *Mao Zedong : founder of the People's Republic of China.* 1996

DS	Subclass: Asia
778	Individual Chinese biography, 1949-1976
.M3	The first Cutter number for the biographee, Mao
S762	The second Cutter number for the biographer, Stefoff
1996	The date of publication

Eberhardt, Isabelle. *Prisoner of dunes : selected writings.* 1995

DT	Subclass: Africa
294.7	Biography and memoirs of persons from Algeria during the period of 1901-1945
.E2	The first Cutter number for the biographee, Eberhardt
A25	The second Cutter number (according to the Biography Table) for selected works
1995	The date of publication

Kummer, Patricia K. *Côte d'Ivoire (Ivory Coast).* 1996

DT	Subclass: Africa
545.22	A general history of the Ivory Coast
.K86	The Cutter number for the main entry, Kummer
1996	The date of publication

Subclasses DS-DX contain seven tables, DS-DX1 to DS-DX7. The following examples illustrate the use of tables:

Watson, Virginia. *Anyan's story : a New Guinea woman in two worlds.* 1997

DU	Subclass: Oceania (South Seas)
740	Papua New Guinea
.42	The decimal extension (based on Table DS-DX1) meaning Ethnography
.W38	The Cutter number for the main entry, Watson
1997	The date of publication

Goncharoff, Nicko.   *Hong Kong : a Lonely Planet city guide.*   c1996

DS	Subclass: Asia
796	Cities, towns, etc. in China
.H73	The first Cutter number (H7) for Hong Kong with the successive element (3 based on Table DS-DX4) for guidebooks
G65	The second Cutter number for the main entry, Goncharoff
1996	The date of publication

History and description of Hawaii are classed in subclass DU rather than with United States in F, as shown in the following examples:

Hyun, Peter.   *In the new world : the making of a Korean American.* 1995

DU	Subclass: Oceania (South Seas)
624.7	Elements in the population of Hawaii
.K67	The first Cutter number for the element, Koreans
H983	The second Cutter number for the main entry, Hyun
1995	The date of publication

Clarke, Joan.   *Family traditions in Hawai'i : birthday, marriage, funeral, and cultural customs in Hawai'i.*   1994

DU	Subclass: Oceania (South Seas)
624.6	Ethnography of Hawaii
.C53	The Cutter number for the main entry, Clarke
1994	The date of publication

The detailed index contains topical entries; many geographic names; names of ethnic and national groups; and a small number of personal names, mainly names of monarchs.

Class E-F begins on page 200.

CLASS E-F—HISTORY: AMERICA

E	
11-143	America
11-29	General
29	Elements in the population
31-49.2	North America
51-73	Pre-Columbian America. The Indians
75-99	Indians of North America
81-83	Indian wars
99	Indian tribes and cultures
101-135	Discovery of America and early explorations
103-110	Pre-Columbian period
111-120	Columbus
121-135	Post-Columbian period. El Dorado
141-143	Descriptive accounts of America. Earliest to 1810
151-887	United States
151-169.12	General
171-183.9	History
171-180	General
173	Sources and documents
175-175.7	Historiography
176-176.8	Biography
179.5	Historical geography
181	Military history
182	Naval history
183-183.3	Political history
183.7-183.9	Diplomatic history. Foreign and general relations
183.8	Relations with individual countries
184-185.98	Elements in the population
184.5-185.98	Afro-Americans
185.2-185.89	Status and development since emancipation
185.96-185.98	Biography. Genealogy
186-199	Colonial history (1607-1775)
186-189	General
191-199	By period
191	1607-1689
195-199	1689-1775
196	King William's War, 1689-1697
197	Queen Anne's War, 1702-1713
198	King George's War, 1744-1748
199	French and Indian War, 1755-1763
201-298	The Revolution, 1775-1783
300-453	Revolution to the Civil War
300-302.6	General
302	Collected works of American statesmen
302.1	Political history

Class E-F continues on page 202.

456-655	Civil War period, 1861-1865
456-459	Lincoln's administrations, 1861-April 15, 1865
461-655	The Civil War, 1861-1865
482-489	Confederate States of America
491-586	Armies. Troops
591-600	Naval history
660-738	Late nineteenth century, 1865-1900
660-664	General
660	Collected works of American statesmen
661.7	Diplomatic history. Foreign and general relations
663-664	Biography
666-670	Johnson's administration, April 15, 1865-1869
668	Reconstruction, 1865-1877
669	Purchase of Alaska, 1867
671-680	Grant's administrations, 1869-1877
681-685	Hayes' administration, 1877-1881
686-687.9	Garfield's administration, March 4-September 19, 1881
691-695	Arthur's administration, September 19, 1881-1885
696-700	Cleveland's first administration, 1885-1889
701-705	Benjamin Harrison's administration, 1889-1893
706-710	Cleveland's second administration, 1893-1897
711-738	McKinley's first administration, 1897-1901
713	Annexation in 1898 of Hawaii, the Philippines, and Puerto Rico
714-735	War of 1898 (Spanish-American War)
740-837.7	Twentieth century
740-749	General
740.5	Sources and documents
742.5	Collected works of American statesmen
743-743.5	Political history
743.5	Un-American activities
744-744.5	Diplomatic history. Foreign and general relations
745	Military history
746	Naval history
747-748	Biography
751	McKinley's second administration, March 4-September 14, 1901
756-760	Theodore Roosevelt's administrations, September 14, 1901-1909
761-765	Taft's administration, 1909-1913
766-783	Wilson's administrations, 1913-1921
768	Purchase of Danish West Indies (Virgin Islands), 1917
780	Internal history during World War I
784-805	1919-1933. Harding-Coolidge-Hoover era. "The twenties"

Class E-F continues on page 204.

266-280	South Carolina
281-295	Georgia
296-301	Gulf States. West Florida
306-320	Florida
321-335	Alabama
336-350	Mississippi
350.5-355	Mississippi River and Valley. Middle West
366-380	Louisiana
381-395	Texas
396	Old Southwest. Lower Mississippi Valley
406-420	Arkansas
431-445	Tennessee
446-460	Kentucky
461-475	Missouri
476-485	Old Northwest. Northwest Territory
486-500	Ohio
516-520	Ohio River and Valley
521-535	Indiana
536-550	Illinois
550.5-553.2	The Lake Region. Great Lakes
561-575	Michigan
576-590	Wisconsin
590.3-596.3	The West. Trans-Mississippi Region. Great Plains
597	The Northwest
598	Missouri River and Valley
601-615	Minnesota
616-630	Iowa
631-645	North Dakota
646-660	South Dakota
661-675	Nebraska
676-690	Kansas
691-705	Oklahoma
721-722	Rocky Mountains. Yellowstone National Park
726-740	Montana
741-755	Idaho
756-770	Wyoming
771-785	Colorado
786-790	New Southwest. Colorado River, Canyon, and Valley
791-805	New Mexico
806-820	Arizona
821-835	Utah
836-850	Nevada
850.5-851.5	Pacific States
851.7	Cascade Range
852-854	Pacific Northwest. Columbia River and Valley. Northwest boundary since 1846
856-870	California
871-885	Oregon

886-900	Washington
901-951	Alaska
951	Bering Sea and Aleutian Islands
965	The territories of the United States (General)
970	Insular possessions of the United States (General)
975	Central American, West Indian, and other countries protected by, and having close political affiliations with the United States (General)
1001-1140	British America. Canada
1001-1140	Canada
1001-1035	General
1035.8	Maritime provinces. Atlantic coast of Canada
1036-1040	Nova Scotia. Acadia
1041-1045	New Brunswick
1046-1049.7	Prince Edward Island
1050	St. Lawrence Gulf, River and Valley (General)
1051-1055	Quebec
1056-1059.7	Ontario
1060-1060.97	Canadian Northwest. Northwest Territories
1061-1065	Manitoba
1067	Assiniboia
1070-1074.7	Saskatchewan
1075-1080	Alberta
1086-1089.7	British Columbia
1090	Rocky Mountains of Canada
1090.5	Arctic regions
1091-1095.5	Yukon
1096-1100.5	Mackenzie
1101-1105.7	Franklin
1106-1110.5	Keewatin
1121-1139	Newfoundland
1135-1139	Labrador
1140	The Labrador Peninsula
	Other than Canada
	Bahamas, *see* F1650 +
	Bermuda, *see* F1630 +
	British East and West Florida, 1763-1783 *see* F301, F314
	British Guiana, *see* F2361 +
	British Honduras (Belize), *see* F1441 +
	British West Indies, *see* F2131 +
	Falkland Islands, *see* F3031 +
	Thirteen North American Colonies before 1776, *see* E186 +

Class E-F continues on page 206.

Dutch America
 Colony in Brazil, 1625-1661, *see* F2532
 Dutch Guinea, *see* F2401
 Dutch West Indies, *see* F2141
 New Netherlands to 1664, *see* F122.1
 New Sweden (Dutch possession, 1655-1664), *see* F167

1170	French America
1170	Saint Pierre and Miquelon
	Other French America
	Colony in Brazil, 1555-1567, *see* F2529
	Colony in Florida, 1562-1565, *see* F314
	French Guiana, *see* F2441+
	French West Indies, *see* F2151
	Louisiana, 1698-1803, *see* F372
	New France and Acadia, 1600-1763, *see* F1030, F1038

1201-3799	Latin America. Spanish America
1201-1392	Mexico
1218.5-1221	Antiquities. Indians
1401-1419	Latin America (General)
1421-1440	Central America
1435-1435.3	Mayas
1441-1457	Belize
1461-1477	Guatemala
1481-1497	Salvador (El Salvador)
1501-1517	Honduras
1521-1537	Nicaragua
1541-1557	Costa Rica
1561-1577	Panama
1569.C2	Canal Zone. Panama Canal
1601-1629	West Indies
1630-1640	Bermudas
1650-1660	Bahamas
1741-1991	Greater Antilles
1751-1854.9	Cuba
1788-1788.22	Communist regime
1861-1896	Jamaica
1900-1941	Haiti (Island). Hispaniola
1912-1930	Haiti (Republic)
1931-1941	Dominican Republic
1951-1983	Puerto Rico
1991	Navassa
2001-2152	Lesser Antilles
	Groups of islands, by geographical distribution
2006	Leeward Islands
2011	Windward Islands
2016	Islands along Venezuela coast
2033-2129	Individual islands

	Groups of islands, by political allegiance
2131-2133	British West Indies
2136	Virgin Islands of the United States
2141	Netherlands West Indies. Dutch West Indies
2151	French West Indies
2155-2191	Caribbean area. Caribbean Sea
2201-3799	South America
2201-2239	General
2251-2299	Colombia
2301-2349	Venezuela
2351	Guiana
2361-2391	Guyana. British Guiana
2401-2431	Surinam
2441-2471	French Guiana
2501-2659	Brazil
2661-2699	Paraguay
2701-2799	Uruguay
2801-3021	Argentina
3031-3031.5	Falkland Islands
3051-3285	Chile
3301-3359	Bolivia
3401-3619	Peru
3701-3799	Ecuador

Class E-F—History: America, originally entitled *America: History and Geography*, was prepared by the Chief Classifier at the Library of Congress, Charles Martel, and was the first schedule to be published. It appeared in 1901. The second edition was published in 1913; and the third edition, with the title *History: America*, in 1958. Beginning with the 1995 edition, the schedule has been produced from the MARC-based version of the Classification.

The order of division in Class E is general American history, general North American history, and general United States history; Class F completes this sequence with United States local history followed by British America, Canada, Mexico, Latin American (General), Central America, West Indies, and South America.

Because double letters are not used for subclasses in classes E-F, room for expansion is a major problem in this schedule. Needed expansions have been created using decimal extensions, which tend to make the notation rather cumbersome. But basically this schedule should present no major problems to the classifier. A complete outline and a detailed index are provided in the schedule.

Class E

Class E includes history of America in general (E11-E143) and the history of the United States as a whole. With the exception of Cutter numbers for subarrangement of individual biographies and collected works of American statesmen, all topics relating to American and U.S. history are enumerated. Examples are shown below:

Bowen, Jeff. *Cherokee descendants : an index to the Guion Miller applications.* 1996-

E	Subclass: United States
99	Indians of North America
.C5	Cherokee Indians
B745	The second Cutter number for the main entry, Bowen
1996	The date of publication

Franklin, Jane. *Cuba and the United States : a chronological history.* 1997

E	Subclass: United States
183.8	Relations with individual countries
.C9	Cuba
F725	The second Cutter number for the main entry, Franklin
1997	The date of publication

Southern pamphlets on secession, November 1860-April 1861. 1996

E	Subclass: United States
458	Lincoln's administration
.1	Political history, March 4-December 31, 1861
.S68	The Cutter number for the main entry under the title, *Southern . . .*
1996	The date of publication

Three tables are included for use with Class E. Tables E1 and E2 are used for individual biographies, and Table E3 is used for collected works of American statesmen. They are used when instructed in the schedule as shown in the following examples.

In the schedule, general works of biography of Jimmy Carter are assigned the number E873 with the instruction to use Table E2. According to that table, autobiographical works by Jimmy Carter are therefore classed in E873.A3.

Carter, Jimmy. *Why not the best? : the first fifty years.* 1996

E	Subclass: United States
873	General biography of Jimmy Carter
.A3	The Cutter number (based on Table E2) for an autobiography
1997	The date of publication

A work about Carter by another person is assigned a Cutter number between .A6-.Z, based on the main entry.

Bourne, Peter G. *Jimmy Carter : a comprehensive biography from Plains to post-presidency.* 1997

E	Subclass: United States
873	General biography of Jimmy Carter
.B67	The Cutter number (based on Table E2) for the main entry, Bourne
1997	The date of publication

The following examples illustrate the use of Table E3:

Truman, Harry. *The wit & wisdom of Harry Truman.* 1995

E	Subclass: United States
742.5	Collected works of American statesmen of the 20th century
.T62	The Cutter number (.T6) for Harry S. Truman and the successive element (2 based on Table E3) for selected works including quotations
1995	The date of publication

Herbert Hoover Presidential Library. *Historical materials in the Herbert Hoover Presidential Library.* 1996

E	Subclass: United States
742.5	Collected works of American statesmen of the 20th century
.H669	The Cutter number (.H66) for Herbert Clark Hoover and the successive element (9 from Table E3) for special libraries
H47	The second Cutter number for the main entry, Herbert...
1996	The date of publication

Class F

Class F contains United States local history and the history of Canada, Central America, and South America. For example:

Barlow, Bernyce. *Sacred sites of the West.* 1996

F	Subclass: United States local history
590.3	Guidebooks to the West
.B37	The Cutter number for the main entry, Barlow
1996	The date of publication

Topics relating to U.S. local history are enumerated in great detail in the schedule. For example, New York City and County have been assigned the number F128.1-.9, with unique numbers for topics such as Chinatown, the Statue of Liberty, and Fifth Avenue.

Levinson, Lee Ann. *East Side, West Side : a guide to New York City parks in all five boroughs.* 1997

F	Subclass: United States local history
128.65	Parks, squares, circles, etc., in New York City
.A1	The first Cutter number for a general work
L48	The second Cutter number for the main entry, Levinson
1997	The date of publication

Holland, Gini. *The Empire State Building.* 1997

F	Subclass: United States local history
128.8	Individual buildings in New York City
.E46	The first Cutter number for the name of the building
H65	The second Cutter number for the main entry, Holland
1997	The date of publication

Details of the history of individual states are also provided in great depth. An example is the range of numbers assigned to the state of Wisconsin: F576-590. For example, the number F589 is used for the history of cities and towns of Wisconsin:

Dobberpuhl, Harold C. *Cedarburg, 1946-1964 : photographs.* 1995

F	Subclass: United States local history
589	Wisconsin: Cities, towns, etc., A-Z

.C4 The first Cutter number for the city, Cedarburg
D63 The second Cutter number for the main entry, Dobberpuhl
1995 The date of publication

In Class F, five auxiliary tables are used with class numbers for the Americas and for individual biography:

F1 Table for Cities with Single Number in the Americas

F2 Table for Cities with Cutter Number in the Americas

F3 Table for Countries, Islands, Regions with Single Number in the Americas

F4 Individual Biography (One No.)

F5 Individual Biography (Cutter No.)

The following examples illustrate the use of these tables:

Kasher, Robert J. *Passport's guide to ethnic Toronto : a complete guide to the many faces & cultures of Toronto.* 1997

F Subclass: British America
1059.5 Ontario, Canada: Cities and towns, etc., A-Z
.T683 The first Cutter number (.T68) meaning Toronto with the successive element (3 from Table F2) meaning guidebooks
K37 The second Cutter number for the main entry, Kasher
1997 The date of publication

Romero Estébanez, Leandro S. *La Habana arqueológica y otros ensayos.* 1995

F Subclass: Latin America, Spanish America
1799 Havana (province), Cuba: Cities and towns, etc., A-Z
.H357 The first Cutter number (.H3) for the city of Havana and the successive element (57 from Table F2) meaning a general history
R66 The second Cutter number for the main entry, Romero Estébanez
1995 The date of publication

Stout, Nancy. *Havana = La Habana.* [1994]

F	Subclass: Latin America, Spanish America
1799	Havana (province), Cuba: Cities and towns, etc., A-Z
.H34	The Cutter number (.H3) for the city of Havana and the successive element (4 from Table F2) meaning a general description
S86	The second Cutter number for the main entry, Stout
1994	The date of publication

Rice, Susan. *Milwaukee for free (or the next thing to it).* 1997

F	Subclass: United States local history
589	Wisconsin: Cities, towns, etc., A-Z
.M63	The first Cutter number (.M6) for the city, Milwaukee, and the successive element (3 from Table F2) for a guidebook
R53	The second Cutter number for the main entry, Rice
1997	The date of publication

Cantwell, Mary. *Manhattan, when I was young.* 1995

F	Subclass: United States local history
128.54	Individual biography of New Yorkers, 1951-1980
.C36	The first Cutter number for the biographee, Cantwell
A3	The second Cutter number for autobiography (Table F5)
1995	The date of publication

The classifier should remember that subject is paramount when classing in history. Although the complete works of a literary author may be carefully classed together, the works of a historian are usually not classed together. The works of a historian are classed by the subject content of each individual work. For example, Thomas Carlyle's *French Revolution* is classed in subclass DC for French history, and his *Early Kings of Norway* is classed in subclass DL for Scandinavian history. Only if a historian wrote solely on one subject would his or her works be classed together.

The extensive list of American Indian tribes and cultures under the number E99 is an important reference feature of Class E. It should be noted that the names of counties in the United States are not included in the index to this schedule; on the other hand, the names of cities, rivers, and regions are.

CLASS G—GEOGRAPHY. MAPS. ANTHROPOLOGY. RECREATION

G

1-9980	Geography (General). Atlases. Maps
	For geography and description of individual countries, *see* D-F
149-570	Voyages and travels (General)
	Including discoveries, explorations, shipwrecks, seafaring life. For travels in special continents and countries, *see* D-F
575-890	Polar regions
	Including exploration, history, description, travel
1000.3-3122	Atlases
3160-3182	Globes
3190-9980	Maps

GA

1-1776	Mathematical geography. Cartography

GB

3-5030	Physical geography
111-398.7	By region or country
400-649	Geomorphology
651-2998	Hydrology. Water
	Including ground water, rivers, lakes, glaciers
5000-5030	Natural disasters

GC

1-1581	Oceanography
109-149	Chemical oceanography
150-181	Physical oceanography
200-376	Dynamics of the ocean
377-399	Marine sediments
1000-1023	Marine resources. Applied oceanography
1080-1581	Marine pollution

GE

1-350	Environmental sciences

Class G continues on page 214.

GF
1-900	Human ecology. Anthropogeography
53-67	Man's relationship to specific environments
500-900	By region or country

GN
1-890	Anthropology
49-298	Physical anthropology. Somatology
301-673	Ethnology. Social and cultural anthropology
	For descriptions of individual ethnic groups, *see* D-F
700-890	Prehistoric archaeology
803-890	By region or country

GR
1-950	Folklore
72-79	Folk literature (General)
420-950	Folklore relating to special subjects

GT
1-7070	Manners and customs (General)
	For works limited to special countries, *see* D-F
170-476	Houses. Dwellings
500-2370	Customs relative to private and public life
	Including love, marriage, eating, smoking, treatment of the dead, town life, customs of chivalry, festivals and holidays
5320-6720	Customs relative to special classes. By birth, occupation, etc.

GV
1-1860	Recreation. Leisure
191.2-200.66	Outdoor life. Outdoor recreation
	Including camping for individuals or small groups, organized camps, trailer camping, hiking, mountaineering, wilderness survival, caving
201-555	Physical education and training
1199-1570	Games and amusements
1580-1799.3	Dancing
1800-1860	Circuses, spectacles, etc.

The first edition of **Class G—Geography. Maps. Anthropology. Recreation,** was published in 1910 under the title, *Geography, Anthropology, Sports and Games.* Subclasses GR, Folklore, and GT, Manners and customs, did not appear in the first edition but were first published separately in 1915. The second edition of Class G appeared in 1928 and included a provisional scheme for atlases (G1001-3035). In 1945 C. W. Buffum of the Map Division of the Library of Congress prepared a preliminary draft for a classification of maps using the numbers G3160-9999 from subclass G; this material was incorporated into the third edition of Class G issued in 1954. The fourth edition, with the title, *Geography. Maps. Anthropology. Recreation,* was published in 1976. In this edition, extensive revision was made in the atlas and map section of subclass G; many jurisdictions were realigned in order to reflect contemporary political situations. A new feature is the inclusion of many illustrative maps showing the new alignments.

In 1992, a new subclass GE, Environmental sciences, was developed for general works on the subject. Individual environmental sciences and specific topics relating to environmental sciences continue to be classed in appropriate classes, for example, pollution control in TD Environmental technology and Sanitary engineering; and environmental influences on man in GF Human ecology. The new subclass GE was published in *LC Classification, Additions and Changes,* list 247 (July-September 1992).[9]

Class G may be considered a connective schedule, lying between the history classes on one side and the remaining social sciences on the other. Five of its subclasses are related directly to geography; nevertheless, much geographical material, especially the topography and description of individual continents and countries, is placed in the history schedules, D-F.

The rationale for grouping Geography, Anthropology, Folklore, Manners and customs, Sports, and Games and amusements in Class G has been articulated by Charles Martel:

> This . . . group including on the one hand the material
> dealing with the earth as the abode of man and as the theater,
> the stage, of his history and his social activities, and on the
> other with primitive man himself, his being in social
> infancy and in transition to civilized states, has been found
> a most satisfactory association of subjects difficult to allo-
> cate. Physical Geography (GB) and Oceanography (GC)
> might have been excepted and placed with Geology (QE).
> Much and important material on these subjects is found,
> however, in the periodicals and collections in General
> Geography (class G) and certain aspects connect them with
> GF, Anthropogeography—their position in class G is not
> without its advantage.[10]

Geographic Cutters

In 1987, the Library of Congress published *Geographic Cutters*, a 24X microfiche publication containing thirty-two thousand Cutter numbers for geographic place names in the United States. A greatly expanded second edition, including more than sixty-five thousand Cutter numbers and accompanied by a printed introduction and a loose-leaf index, was issued in 1989.[11] The Cutter numbers are arranged in an order corresponding to that in Class G, and the alphabetic index provides access to each state and region larger than a state. Cutter numbers are also provided for physical and cultural features and regions, for the first order administrative divisions of each state, and for cities and towns. Geographic Cutters can be used as an extension of Class G to classify maps with greater specificity. They can also be used with tags 050 and 090 in MARC records to classify maps, with tag 052 to code the geographic areas identified in the subject analysis of any form of materials, and with tag 033 to indicate the location where a recording or interview took place.

Tables for Maps and Atlases

The main topic discussed in this section is the use of the detailed tables for atlases and maps, found at the end of subclass G. The other tables in this schedule are similar to previously discussed tables and should present no major problems.

Subclass G for atlases and maps is essentially a form class, in that all atlases and maps, regardless of subject matter, are classed here. Subdivisions are provided for individual areas and jurisdictions, which are further subdivided, when necessary, by subject. In other words, in this subclass, the citation order is form-place-subject. Subdivision of numbers assigned to specific places is carried out according to "Special Instructions and Tables of Subdivisions for Atlases and Maps," appearing on pages 206-223 of the fourth edition.

In call numbers for maps, furthermore, the date of map situation constitutes a part of the class number and precedes instead of follows the book number. An exception is made for historical maps when the date of map situation is implied in the subject letter-number "S+," in which case the date of publication is used in the call number.

Tables I and II contain instructions regarding map classification. Table III, "Area Subdivisions," provides subarrangement of atlases and maps of a particular area. The term *major area* refers to a general geographic area to which a specific range of integral numbers or decimal numbers is assigned in the schedule. For instance, a range of three numbers, G3700-3702, is assigned in the schedule to maps of the United States, and a range of five numbers, G3800-3804, is assigned to New York (State). Therefore, both the

United States and New York (State) are considered major areas. A *sub-area* is a specific geographic area within a major area; it may be a region or a natural feature of the major area, a major political division (e.g., province, county, etc.) of the major area, or a city or town in the major area.

There are five subdivisions in Table III:

AREA SUBDIVISIONS (abridged)

(1)	0 or 5	General
(2)	1 or 6	By subject
(3)	2 or 7	By region, natural feature, etc., when not assigned individual numbers, A-Z
(4)	3 or 8	By major political division (Counties, states, provinces, etc.) when not assigned individual numbers, A-Z
(5)	4 or 9	By city or town, A-Z

In the table, numbers enclosed in parentheses, (1), (2), etc., indicate the order of the numbers, whereas 0-4 or 5-9 are the actual final digits in the class numbers.

Major Areas

The first two numbers in Table III are used for major areas only. The first number, "0 or 5," matching the last digit of the number assigned to the area in the schedule, is used for general maps and atlases of the major area that have no special subject interest. The second number, "1 or 6," is used for maps and atlases of the major area that have special subject interest. This second number is further subarranged by Table IV, which will be discussed in the section on subject letter-numbers below.

For example, New York State has a specific range of numbers assigned for maps, G3800-3804, which makes New York State a major area. The first number of this range, G3800, is used for general maps of the state that have no special subject interest. The second number of this range, G3801, is used for maps of the major area that have special subject interest, such as a railroad map of New York State. The Special Instructions III: Area Subdivisions following G9980 in the schedule demonstrate the use of these numbers for both maps and atlases.

Sub-areas

The other three numbers (2-4 or 7-9) in Table III are used for sub-areas. The three types of sub-areas are: regions or natural features of the major area, major political divisions of the major area, and cities or towns in the major area. Through application of the table, each of these types is represented by an integral class number plus a Cutter number based on the name of the sub-area.

When the states or provinces of a country are given their own ranges of numbers, they are treated as major areas rather than as sub-areas of the country in question; this is the case for the states of the United States. In such cases, the country itself is given a span of only three numbers, without the last two numbers corresponding to the fourth and fifth numbers in Table III.

The third number of Table III, "2 or 7," is used for maps and atlases limited to only a region or natural feature of the major area. For example, a map of the Adirondack Mountains of New York State is classed in the third number of the range of numbers for New York State, G3802.A2. ".A2" is the Cutter number for the specific region, Adirondack Mountains, in the major area, New York State. The Adirondack Mountains are, in this case, a sub-area of New York State.

The fourth number in Table III, "3 or 8," is used for maps and atlases limited to only a major political division (such as a province or a county) of the major area. A map of Monroe County, New York, is classed in the fourth number of the range of numbers for New York State, G3803.M6. ".M6" is the Cutter number for the specific major political division, in this case, Monroe County. Monroe County is thus a sub-area of New York State.

The fourth edition of Class G introduces the use of the colon, a new feature in the LC Classification, to indicate further subdivisions of a sub-area. For example, under the fourth number in Table III, a colon (:) following the Cutter number for the political division and followed by the number 3 indicates an administrative subdivision. This is followed by a second Cutter number for the subordinate division. For example, the number G3823.A4:3A5 represents Pennsylvania, Allegheny County, Aleppo Township.[12]

The fifth number in Table III, "4 or 9," is used for maps and atlases limited to only a city or town of the major area. A map of Rochester, New York, is classed in the fifth number of the range of numbers for New York State, G3804.R6. ".R6" is the Cutter number for the specific city or town, in this case, Rochester, treated as a sub-area of New York State. All sub-areas are subarranged alphabetically by means of Cutter numbers.

Under the number assigned to a particular city, a colon (:) followed by the number 2 is used for further geographic subdivision, and a colon (:) followed by the number 3 is used for further political subdivision. For example, the number G3804.N4:2C4 means New York City, Central Park; and the number G3804.N4:3Q4 represents New York City, Queens.

Subject Letter-Numbers

The directions for the use of Table IV, "Subject Subdivisions," explain that this table is used for maps and atlases with specific subject interest. It is not used with general maps and atlases or maps covering several subjects or topics.

Table IV consists of seventeen form and subject divisions that are represented by capital letters, with subtopics designated by Arabic numerals. These symbols are called "subject letter-numbers." Although they resemble Cutter numbers in appearance, they are not Cutter numbers and are not based on names for topics, for example, .Q2 Business statistics. They are, however, treated as decimals. The summary of the seventeen categories of form and subject divisions and a typical development of the subject letter-number Q in Table IV are shown below.

Summary of Form and Subject Subdivisions

A	Special category maps and atlases
B	Mathematical geography
C	Physical sciences
D	Biogeography
E	Human and cultural geography. Anthropogeography. Human Ecology
F	Political geography
G	Economic geography
H	Mines and mineral resources
J	Agriculture
K	Forests and forestry
L	Aquatic biological resources
M	Manufacturing and processing. Service industries
N	Technology. Engineering. Public works
P	Transportation and communication
Q	Commerce and trade. Finance
R	Military and naval geography
S	Historical geography

Summary continues on page 220.

Q   Commerce and Trade.   Finance

.Q1	General
.Q2	Business statistics
.Q3	Movement of commodities

          Class here works on trade routes, caravan routes, etc.
          cf. Subdivision, .Q5, Tariffs and other trade barriers
          For maps and atlases that emphasize the carrier and
             show specific routes, *see* subdivision P

.Q4	Marketing
.Q42	Trade centers and trading areas
.Q44	Shopping centers. Shopping malls
.Q46	Retail sales outlets
.Q48	Fairs, exhibitions, etc.

          Class individual fairs and exhibitions as regions,
             e.g. New York Worlds Fair, and Transpo '72

.Q5	Tariffs and other trade barriers
.Q8	Finance

          Class here works on coins and currencies, foreign
             exchange credit, special types of financial
             institutions, individual finance firms, etc.

Examples of the Use of Tables III and IV

The following examples supplement those shown in Tables III and IV for maps and atlases.

General Maps and Atlases

Major-area Atlases. The complete call number for a major area atlas without specific subject interest consists of three parts:

Major-area number
Cutter number for person or authority responsible for, i.e., main
      entry of, the atlas
Date of publication

Nystrom (Firm) *The Nystrom atlas of our country.* 1996

G	Subclass: Geography (general), Atlases, Maps
1200	First (based on Table III) of the numbers (G1200-1202) assigned to major-area atlases of the United States
.N7	The Cutter number for the main entry, Nystrom (Firm)
1996	The date of publication

DeLorme Mapping Company. *Virginia atlas & gazetteer.* 1995

G	Subclass: Geography (general), Atlases, Maps
1290	First (based on Table III) of the numbers (G1290-1294) assigned to major-area atlases of Virginia
.D4	The Cutter number for the main entry, DeLorme . . . Mapping Company
1995	The date of publication

In the last example above, although Virginia is a state within the United States, it is treated as a major area in classification, indicated by the fact that a range of numbers has been assigned to it.

Sub-area Atlases. The complete call number for a sub-area atlas without specific subject interest consists of four parts:

Major-area number
Sub-area Cutter number
Cutter number for person or authority responsible for the atlas
Date of publication

Rand McNally and Company. *Memphis & vicinity StreetFinder.* 1995

G	Subclass: Geography (general), Atlases, Maps
1339	Fifth (based on Table III) of the numbers (G1335-1339) assigned to atlases of cities in Tennessee
.M3	Memphis
R3	The Cutter number for the main entry, Rand McNally and Company
1995	The date of publication

Atlas Nord-Pas-de-Calais. 1995

G	Subclass: Geography (general), Atlases, Maps
1844.23	Fourth (based on Table III) of the numbers (G1844.2-1844.24) assigned to atlases of major political divisions of France since 1976
.N65	Nord-Pas-de-Calais
A8	The Cutter number for the main entry under the title, *Atlas . . .*
1995	The date of publication

Major-area Maps. The complete call number for a major-area map consists of three parts:

Major-area number
Date of map situation
Cutter number for person or authority responsible for the map

Allan Cartography (Firm) *South Carolina.* 1994

G	Subclass: Geography (general), Atlases, Maps
3910	The first number (based on Table III) assigned to maps of South Carolina (G3910-G3914)
1994	The date of map situation
.A4	Cutter number for the main entry, Allan Cartography (Firm)

Sub-area Maps. The complete call number for a sub-area map consists of four parts:

Major-area number
Sub-area Cutter number
Date of map situation
Cutter number for person or authority responsible for the map

Quality Maps, Inc. *Horry County map, Myrtle Beach, Grand Strand area coverage : Conway, Socastee, Aynor, N. Myrtle Beach, and Surfside Beach.* 1995

G	Subclass: Geography (general), Atlases, Maps
3913	The fourth number (based on Table III) assigned to maps of counties in South Carolina (G3910-G3914)

.H6	Horry County
1995	The date of map situation
.Q3	Cutter number for the main entry, Quality Maps, Inc.

Subject Maps and Atlases

Major-area Subject Atlases. The complete call number of a major-area atlas with special subject interest consists of four parts:

Major-area number
Subject letter-number
Cutter number for the person or authority responsible for the atlas
Date of publication

Rand McNally and Company. *Rand McNally easy-to-read 1997 travel atlas : United States, Canada, Mexico.* 1997

G	Subclass: Geography (general), Atlases, Maps
1201	Second (based on Table III) of the numbers (G1200-1202) assigned to the subject atlases of the United States
.P2	The subject letter (based on Table IV) for roads
R3228	The Cutter number for the main entry, Rand McNally and Company
1997	The date of publication

Tarar, Tanya. *An administrative atlas for National Park Service eco-system management.* 1996

G	Subclass: Geography (general), Atlases, Maps
1201	Second (based on Table III) of the numbers (G1200-1202) assigned to the subject atlases of the United States
.G3	The subject letter (based on Table IV) for Conservation
T3	The Cutter number for the main entry, Tarar
1996	The date of publication

Collins (Firm) *Collins road atlas France, Belgium and Luxembourg : 1996.* 1996

G	Subclass: Geography (general), Atlases, Maps
1844.21	Second (based on Table III) of the numbers (G1844.2-1844.24) assigned to subject atlases of France published after 1976

.P2	The subject letter (based on Table IV) for Roads
C7	The Cutter number for the main entry, Collins (Firm)
1996	The date of publication

Sub-area Subject Atlases. The complete call number for a sub-area subject atlas consists of five parts:

Major area number
Sub-area Cutter number
Subject letter-number
Cutter number for the person or authority responsible for the atlas
Date of publication

ADC (Firm) *Northern Virginia street map : police data area, 1995.* 1995

G	Subclass: Geography (general), Atlases, Maps
1293	Fourth (based on Table III) of the numbers (G1290-1294) assigned to atlases of major political divisions in Virginia
.F2	The first Cutter number for Fairfax County (i.e., Northern Virginia)
F85	The subject letter from Table IV meaning Laws and law enforcement
A35	The second Cutter number for the main entry, ADC (Firm)
1995	The date of publication

Major-area Subject Maps. The complete call number for a major-area subject map consists of four parts:

Major-area number
Subject letter-number
Date of map situation (date of publication if subject letter-number is "S+")
Cutter number for the person or authority responsible for the map

South Carolina. Wildlife & Freshwater Fisheries Division. *South Carolina spring turkey season.* 1996

| G | Subclass: Geography (general), Atlases, Maps |
| 3911 | The second number (based on Table III) assigned to subject maps of South Carolina (G3910-G3914) |

.E63   The subject letter for Recreation, sports

1996   The date of map situation

.S6   Cutter number for the main entry, South . . .

Sub-area Subject Maps. The complete call number for a sub-area subject map consists of five parts:

Major-area number

Sub-area Cutter number

Subject letter-number

Date of map situation (date of publication if subject letter-number is
        "S+")

Cutter number for the person or authority responsible for the map

Color-Art, Inc. *San Francisco, CA and vicinity.*   1996

G   Subclass: Geography (general), Atlases, Maps

4362   The third number (based on Table III) assigned to maps
            of California (G4360-4364) for subdivision by region,
            natural feature, etc.

.S22   The sub-area Cutter number for San Francisco Bay Area

P2   The subject letter-number for Roads

1996   The date of map situation

.C6   The Cutter number for the main entry, Color-Art, Inc.

Series of Maps

In the call number for a series of maps, a lowercase letter "s" followed by the denominator of the scale minus the last three digits replaces the date. For example:

U.S. Lake Survey. *AAF cloth chart. [Indonesia].*   Advance ed. Scale
1:1,000,000.   1944-

G   Subclass: Geography (general), Atlases, Maps

8070   General maps (first number in the range G8070-8074) of
            Indonesia

s1000   The letter "s" followed by the denominator of the scale
            minus the last three digits

.U2   The Cutter number for the main entry, U.S. Lake Survey

United States. Agency for International Development. Afghanistan. *Health facilities & population (draft)*.   Scale [ca. 1:650,000].   1992

G	Subclass: Geography (general), Atlases, Maps
7631	Subject maps (second number in the range G7630-7634) of Afghanistan
s650	The letter "s" followed by the denominator of the scale minus the last three digits
.U5	The Cutter number for the main entry, United States

If the scale is larger than 1:1,000, the denominator of the fraction, treated as a decimal and preceded by 0 (zero), is used, for example, s05 for 1:500.[13]

Other Auxiliary Tables in Class G

The four tables of geographical subdivisions at the end of the schedule present no serious problems in use. The first of these tables provides a list of decimal extensions to be added to a topical number for further subdivision by place. The following is a part of this table:

.42	Europe
.425	Special regions . . .
.43	Great Britain
.44	England
.45	Scotland
.46	Northern Ireland
.465	Wales
.467	Ireland
.47	Austria

For example, a work about customs in England is assigned a number based on Table I:

Nikola-Lisa, W.   *Till year's good end : a calendar of medieval labors*. 1997

GT	Subclass: Manners and customs (General)
5856	Regions or countries other than the United States
.44	Number from Table I meaning England
.N56	The Cutter number for the main entry, Nikola-Lisa
1997	The date of publication

Similarly, the number for a work about ice skating in Canada contains the element .15 from Table I.

Wilkes, Debbi.   *Ice time : a portrait of figure skating.*   1994

GV	Subclass: Recreation, Leisure
849	Ice skating by regions or country
.15	Number from Table I meaning Canada
.W55	The Cutter number for the main entry, Wilkes
1994	The date of publication

A number of topics (such as folklore, social customs, and manners) that are classed in Class G also appear in other classes. Detailed instructions with regard to placement of specific topics or materials and cross references are provided at the beginning of the subclasses, under individual numbers, and in *Subject Cataloging Manual: Classification.*

The comprehensive index to the third edition of Class G, which included a large number of entries under geographic names (names of countries, provinces, states, counties, and many cities), has been pruned down considerably in the index to the fourth edition. In the fourth edition, geographic names are limited to those for the states, provinces, constituent countries, and larger regions in the United States, Canada, and Great Britain, and to the names of countries and larger or international regions for the rest of the world.

Class H begins on page 228.

CLASS H—SOCIAL SCIENCES

H
1-99   Social sciences (general)

HA
1-4737   Statistics
29-32   Theory and method of social science statistics
36-37   Organizations. Bureaus. Service
38-39   Registration of vital events. Registration
                      (General)
154-4737   Statistical data
154-155   Universal statistics
175-4737   By region or country

HB
1-3840   Economic theory. Demography
71-74   Economics as a science. Relation to other
                      subjects
75-130   History of economics. History of economic
                      theory
                        Including special economic schools
131-145   Methodology
135-145   Mathematical economics. Quantitative
                          methods
                            Including econometrics, input-output
                              analysis, game theory
201-206   Value. Utility
221-236   Price
238-251   Competition. Production. Wealth
501   Capital. Capitalism
522-715   Income. Factor shares
531-551   Interest
601   Profit
615-715   Entrepreneurship. Risk and uncertainty.
                          Property
801-843   Consumption. Demand
846-846.8   Welfare theory
848-3697   Demography. Vital events
3711-3840   Business cycles. Economic fluctuations

HC
10-1085   Economic history and conditions
79   Special topics, A-Z
                        Including air pollution, automation,
                          consumer demand, famines, flow of
                          funds, etc.

92	Economic geography of the oceans (General)
94-1085	By region or country

HD
28-9999	Economic history and conditions
28-88	Production
28-70	Organization of production. Management. Industrial management
39-40.7	Capital. Capital investments
41	Competition and cooperation. Regulation and restriction of output
45-45.2	Control of industry. Technological innovations. Automation
47-47.4	Costs
49-49.5	Crisis management and overproduction. Inflation
50-50.5	Delegation of authority. Decentralization
56-57.5	Industrial productivity
58	Location of industry
58.7-58.95	Organizational behavior, change and effectiveness. Corporate culture
59-59.6	Public relations. Industrial publicity
60-60.5	Social responsibilities. Corporate and social policies
61	Risk in industry. Risk management
62	Simplification. Standardization. Waste
62.2-62.8	Management of special enterprises
66	Work groups. Team work in industry. Quality circles
69	Other, A-Z
	Including business consultants, capacity, size of industries, etc.
72-88	Economic growth, development, planning
101-1395.5	Land use
	Land tenure
1241-1339	Policy. Theory of distribution of the land
1259-1265	Eminent domain. Expropriation. State domain
1286-1289	Communal ownership
1290-1291	Municipal ownership
1301-1313	Nationalization (Agrarian socialism)
1326-1329	Large holdings
1330-1331	Landlord and peasant
1332-1333.5	Land reform. Agrarian reform
1334-1335	Consolidation of land holdings
1336-1339	Small holdings. Peasant proprietors. Parcellation

Class H continues on page 230.

1361-1395.5	Real estate business
1401-2210	Agriculture
1428-1431	International cooperation
1470-1476	Size of farms
1478	Sharecropping
1483-1486	Agricultural associations, societies, etc.
1491-1491.5	Cooperative agriculture
1492-1492.5	Collective farms
1493	Government owned and operated farms. State farms. Sovkhozes
1501-1542	Agricultural classes
	Including farm tenancy, agricultural laborers
1549	Gleaning
1580	Melioration and reclamation of agricultural land
1635-1702	Utilization and culture of special classes of lands
	Including pasture lands, water resources development
1711-1741	Irrigation
2321-4730.9	Industry
2329	Industrialization
2330	Rural industry
2331-2336	House industry
2337-2339	Sweating system
2340.8-2346.5	Small and medium industry, artisans, handicrafts, trades
2350.8-2356	Large industry. Factory system. Big business
2365-2385	Contracting. Letting of contracts
2421-2429	Trade and industrial associations
2709-2930.7	Corporations. Cartels. Trusts
	Including international business enterprises, diversification, industrial concentration, public utilities
2951-3575	Industrial cooperation. Mutuality
3611-4730.9	The state and industrial organization
	Including licensing of occupations and professions, subsidies, inspection, government ownership, right of eminent domain, municipal industries
4801-8943	Labor
4861-4895	Labor systems
4906-5100.7	Wages
5106-5267	Hours
	Including overtime, shift work, sick leave, vacations
5306-5474	Labor disputes. Strikes. Lockouts

5481-5630.7	Arbitration and conciliation
5650-5660	Employees' representation in management. Shop councils. Employee ownership
5701-6000.7	Labor market. Labor supply and demand Including unemployment, manpower policy, occupational training, employment agencies
6050-6305	Classes of labor Including women, children, students, middle-aged and older persons, minorities
6350-6940.7	Trade unions. Labor unions. Workingmen's associations
6941-6948	Employers' associations
6951-6957	Industrial sociology. Social conditions of labor
6958.5-6976	Industrial relations
6977-7080	Wages and cost of living. Standard of living
7088-7250.7	Social insurance. Social security. Pension
7255-7256	Rehabilitation of the disabled
7260-7780.8	Industrial hygiene. Welfare work. Housing
7795-8027	Labor and the state. State labor
8031	Labor in politics
8038	Professions (General)
8039	By industry or trade, A-Z
8045-8942.5	By region or country
9000-9999	Special industries and trades
9000-9495	Agricultural and other plant and animal products. Food products
9502-9502.5	Energy industries (General). Energy policy
9506-9624	Mineral and metal industries
9650-9663	Chemical industries
9665-9675	Drugs
9680-9714	Mechanical industries Including electric utilities and industries and machinery
9715-9717.5	Construction industry and materials
9720-9975	Manufacturing industries
9999	Miscellaneous industries and trades, A-Z
HE	
1-9990	Transportation and communications
199-199.5	Freight (General)
199.9	Passenger traffic (General)
305-311	Urban transportation
323-328	Geography. Trade routes

Class H continues on page 232.

331-380	Traffic engineering. Roads and highways. Streets
369-373	Traffic surveys (General)
374-377	Bridges
379-380	Vehicular tunnels
380.8-971	Water transportation
380.8-560	Waterways
561-971	Shipping
730-943	Merchant marine. Ocean shipping. Coastal shipping
1001-5600	Railways. Rapid transit systems
5601-5720	Automotive transportation Including trucking, motor-bus lines, taxicab service
5746-5749	Stage lines
5751-5870	Ferries
5880-5990	Express service
6000-7496	Postal service. Stamps. Philately
7511-7549	Pneumatic service
7601-8700.9	Telecommunication industry. Telegraph
8660-8688	Radio. Wireless telegraph
8689-8700.9	Radio and television broadcasting
8701-9680.7	Telephone industry
9713-9715	Cellular radio. Wireless telephone industry
9719-9721	Artificial satellite telecommunications
9723-9737	Signaling
9751-9756	Messenger service
9761-9900	Air transportation

HF	
1-6182	Commerce
294-343	Boards of trade, chambers of commerce, merchants' associations, etc.
1014	Balance of trade
1021-1027	Commercial geography. Economic geography
1040-1054	Commodities. Commercial products
1701-2701	Tariff policy (Protection and free trade)
3000-4055	By region or country
5001-6182	Business
5381-5386	Vocational guidance. Career development
5387	Business ethics
5410-5417.5	Marketing. Distribution of products
5419-5422	Wholesale trade. Commission business, agencies. Brokers. Factors. Jobbers

5428-5429.6	Retail trade
5429.7-5430.6	Shopping centers
5437-5444	Buying. Selling. Sales personnel. Sales executives
5446-5459	Canvassing. Peddling
5460-5469.5	Department stores. Mail order business
5469.7-5481	Markets. Fairs
5482-5482.4	Secondhand trade
5482.6-5482.65	Black market
5484-5495	Warehousing and storage
5520-5541	Equipment
5546-5548.6	Office organization and management
5548.7-5548.85	Industrial psychology
5549-5549.5	Personnel management. Employment management
5601-5689	Accounting. Bookkeeping
5691-5716	Business mathematics. Commercial mathematics
	Including tables, etc.
5717-5746	Business communication
	Including business report writing, business correspondence, filing, indexing
5761-5780	Shipping of merchandise, etc. Delivery of goods
5801-6182	Advertising

HG		
1-9999	Finance	
178		Liquidity
179		Personal finance
201-1496		Money
261-312		Precious metals. Bullion
315		Small coins
321-329		Mints. Assaying
335-341		Counterfeiting
348-353.5		Paper money
361-363		The legal-tender power
381-395		International currency
401-421		International bimetallism, etc.
451-1496		By region or country
1501-3550		Banking
1621-1638		Rate of interest. Interest tables
1641-1643		Loans. Bank credit
1651-1654		Discount
1655		Acceptances
1656		Reserves. Liquidity

Class H continues on page 234.

1660	Accounts and deposits
1662	Insurance of deposits
1685-1703	Drafts. Checks
1706-1708	Accounting. Bookkeeping
1709	Electronic data processing
1710	Electronic funds transfers
1722	Mergers
1723	Bank stocks. Banking as an investment
1725-1778	Banks and the state. State supervision of banks
1811-2351	Special classes of banks and financial institutions
2401-3550	By region or country
3691-3769	Credit. Debt. Loans
	Including credit institutions, credit instruments, consumer credit, bankruptcy
3810-4000	Foreign exchange. International finance. International monetary system
4001-4280.7	Finance management. Business finance. Corporation finance
4301-4480.9	Trust services. Trust companies
4501-6051	Investment, capital formation, speculation
4530	Investment companies. Mutual funds
4538	Foreign investments
4551-4598	Stock exchanges
4621	Stock brokerage. Investment advisers
4701-4751	Securities
4950-5993	By region or country
6001-6051	Speculation
6105-6270.9	Lotteries
7920-7933	Thrift and saving
8011-9999	Insurance
8053.5-8054.45	Insurance for professions. Malpractice insurance
8059	Business insurance
8075-8107	Insurance business. Insurance management
8111-8123	Insurance and the state. State supervision
8205-8220	Government insurance
8501-8745	By region or country
8751-9271	Life insurance
8779-8793	Actuarial science. Statistical theory and methodology applied to insurance
8799-8830	By class insured, by risk, by plan
8835-8899	Life insurance business. Management
8901-8914	Life insurance and the state. State supervision
8941-9200.5	By region or country
9201-9245	Mutual life insurance. Assessment life

	insurance. Fraternal life insurance
9251-9262	Industrial life insurance
9271	Child insurance. Life insurance for children
9291-9295	Maternity insurance
9301-9343	Accident insurance
9371-9399	Health insurance
9651-9899	Fire insurance
9956-9969	Casualty insurance
9969.5-9999	Other insurance
	Including automobile, burglary, credit, disaster, title insurance

HJ	
9-(9995)	Public finance
9-99.8	Periodicals. Serials. By region or country
210-240	History
241-1620	By region or country
2005-2216	Income and expenditure. Budget
2240-(5957)	Revenue. Taxation. Internal revenue
2321-2323	Incidence, shifting, distribution, equality
2326-2327	Progressive, proportional taxation
2336-2337	Exemption
2338	Taxation of government property
(2341-2343)	Double taxation
(2347)	Taxation of aliens, nonresidents, etc.
(2348.5)	Tax evasion
2351	Inflation and taxation
2351.4	Tax revenue estimating
(2360)-3192.7	By region or country
(3231-3696)	Taxation. Administration and procedure
3801-3844	Revenue from sources other than taxation
3863-(4056.7)	Direct taxation
4113-4601	Property tax
4629-4830	Income tax
4919-4936	Poll tax
(5001-5009)	Internal revenue
5309-5510	Administrative fees, licenses, stamp tax
6603-7390	Customs administration
7461-7980	Expenditures. Government spending
8001-8899	Public debts
(8046-8049)	Government securities
8052	Sinking funds. Amortization
(8083-8086)	Foreign loans
8101-8899	By region or country
(8903-8963)	Claims
(9011)-9695	Local finance. Municipal finance

Class H continues on page 236.

	Including the revenue, budget, expenditure, etc., of counties, boroughs, communes, municipalities, etc.
9701-(9995)	Public accounting. Auditing

HM

1-299	Sociology (general)
101-121	Culture. Progress
126	Unity. Solidarity
131-134	Association. Mutuality. Social groups
	Including interpersonal relations, small groups
136-146	Individualism. Differentiation. Struggle
201-221	Social elements, forces, laws
251-291	Social psychology
	Including public opinion, communication, crowds

HN

1-991	Social history and conditions. Social problems. Social reform
30-40	The church and social problems
41-46	Community centers. Social centers
50-991	By region or country

HQ

1-2044	The family. Marriage. Women
12-449	Sexual life
19-30.7	Sexual behavior and attitudes. Sexuality
31-64	Sex instruction and sexual ethics
71-72	Sexual deviations
74	Bisexuality
75-76.8	Homosexuality. Lesbianism
77	Transvestism
77.7-77.9	Transsexualism
79	Sadism
101-440.7	Prostitution
447	Masturbation
449	Emasculation. Eunuchs, etc.
450-472	Erotica. Pornography
503-1064	The family. Marriage. Home
750-755.5	Eugenics
755.7-759.92	Parents. Parenthood
	Including parent and child, husbands, fathers, wives, mothers
760-767.7	Family size. Birth control. Abortion
767.8-792.2	Children. Child development
	Including child rearing, child life, play, socialization, children's rights

793-799.2	Youth. Adolescent. Teenagers
799.5-799.9	Young men and women
799.95-799.97	Adulthood
800-800.4	Single people
801-801.83	Man-woman relationships. Courtship. Dating
802	Matrimonial bureaus. Marriage brokerage
802.5	Matrimonial advertisements
803	Temporary marriage. Trial marriage. Companionate marriage
804	Breach of promise
805	Desertion
806	Adultery
809-809.3	Family violence
811-960.7	Divorce
961-967	Free love
981-996	Polygamy
997	Polyandry
998-999	Illegitimacy. Unmarried mothers
1001-1043	The state and marriage
1051-1057	The church and marriage
1058-1058.5	Widows and widowers. Widowhood
1060-1064	Aged. Gerontology (Social aspects). Retirement
1073-1073.5	Thanatology. Death. Dying
1075-1075.5	Sex role
1088-1090.7	Men
1101-2030.7	Women. Feminism
1871-2030.7	Women's clubs
2035-2039	Life skills. Coping skills. Everyday living skills
2042-2044	Life style

HS	
1-3371	Societies: secret, benevolent, etc.
101-330.7	Secret societies
351-929	Freemasons
951-1179	Odd Fellows
1201-1350	Knights of Pythias
1355	Other societies, A-Z
1501-2460.7	Other societies. By classes
1501-1510	Benevolent and "friendly" societies and mutual assessment fraternities
1525-1560	Religious societies
1601-2265	Race societies
2275	Occupation societies
2301-2460.7	Political and "patriotic" societies
2501-3371	Clubs and societies for special classes

Class H continues on page 238.

Including boys' societies, Boy scouts,
girls' societies

HT
51-1595	Communities. Classes. Races
51-65	Communities
101-395	Urban groups. The city. Urban sociology
161-165	Garden cities. "The city beautiful"
165.5-169.9	City planning. Zoning
170-178	Urban renewal. Urban redevelopment
201-221	City population
	Including children in cities, immigration
231	Effect of city life
251-265	Mental and moral life
281	Recreation. Amusements
321-325	The city as an economic factor. City promotion
330-334	Metropolitan areas
351-352	Suburban cities and towns
361-384	Urbanization. City and country
388	Regional economics
390-395	Regional planning
401-485	Rural groups. Rural sociology
601-1445	Classes
621-635	Origin of social classes
641-657	Classes arising from birth
	Including royalty, nobility, commons
675-690	Classes arising from occupation
713-725	Caste system
731	Freedmen
751-815	Serfdom
851-1445	Slavery
1501-1595	Races
	Including race as a social group and race relations in general

HV
1-9960	Social pathology. Social and public welfare. Criminology
40-69	Social service. Social work. Charity organization and practice
	Including social case work, private and public relief, institutional care, rural social work, work relief
70-72	State regulation of charities. Public welfare laws
85-525	By region or country
530	The church and charity

541	Women and charity
544	Charity fairs
544.5	International social work
547	Self-help groups
551.2-639	Emergency management
553-639	Relief in case of disasters
560-583	Red Cross
599-639	Special types of disasters
640-645	Refugee problems
650-670	Life saving
675-677	Prevention of accidents
680-696	Free professional services
	Including medical charities
697-4959	Protection, assistance and relief
697-1493	Special classes. By age
697-700.7	Families. Mothers. Widow's pensions
701-1420.5	Children
835-847	Foundlings
873-887	Destitute, neglected, and abandoned children
888-907	Handicapped children
931-941	Fresh-air funds
959-1420.5	Orphanages. Orphans
1421-1441	Young adults. Youth. Teenagers
1442-1448	Women
1449	Homosexuals
1450-1493	Aged
1551-3024	Handicapped
	Including blind, deaf, mentally handicapped, physically handicapped
3025-3174	Special classes. By occupation
3025-3163	Seamen
3165-3173	Shop women, clerks, etc.
3174	Other. By occupation, A-Z
3176-3199	Special classes. By race or ethnic group
4005-4013	Immigrants
4023-4470.7	Poor in cities. Slums
4480-4630	Mendicancy. Vagabondism. Tramps. Homelessness
4701-4959	Protection of animals. Animal rights. Animal welfare
4961-4995	Degeneration
5001-5720.5	Alcoholism. Intemperance. Temperance reform
5725-5770	Tobacco habit
5800-5840	Drug habits. Drug abuse
6001-7220.5	Criminology
6035-6197	Criminal anthropology

Class H continues on page 240.

	Including the criminal type, criminal psychology, prison psychology, causes of crime
6201-6249	Criminal classes
6250-6250.4	Victims of crimes. Victimology
6251-6773	Crimes and offenses
6774-7220.5	Crimes and criminal classes
7231-9920.5	Criminal justice administration
7428	Social work with delinquents and criminals
7431	Prevention of crime, methods, etc.
7435-7439	Gun control
7551-8280.7	Police. Detectives. Constabulary
7935-8025	Administration and organization
8031-8080	Police duty. Methods of protection
8035-8069	Special classes of crimes, offenses and criminals
8073-8079.3	Investigation of crimes. Examination and identification of prisoners
8079.2-8079.3	Police social work
8079.5-8079.55	Traffic control. Traffic accident investigation
8081-8099	Private detectives. Detective bureaus
8130-8280.7	Police: By region or country
8290	Private security services
8301-9025	Penology. Prisons. Corrections
9051-9230.7	The juvenile offender. Juvenile delinquency. Reform schools, etc.
9261-9430.7	Reformation and reclamation of adult prisoners
9441-9960	By region or country

HX

1-970.7	Socialism. Communism. Anarchism
519-550	Communism/socialism in relation to special topics
626-780.7	Communism: Utopian socialism, collective settlements
806-811	Utopias. The ideal state
821-970.7	Anarchism

Class H—Social Sciences covers the generalia class for the Social sciences and two individual social science disciplines: Economics and Sociology. The remaining social sciences disciplines are found in Schedules C, D, and E-F for History; G for Geography and Anthropology; J for Political science; K for Law; and L for Education.

The first edition of Class H was published in 1910 without subclass HT, which was published separately in 1915. A second edition including subclass HT was issued in 1920, and the third edition appeared in 1950.

With the fourth edition, the schedule was divided into two parts, H-HJ, *Social Sciences: Economics*, published in 1981; and HM-HX, *Social Sciences: Sociology*, published in 1980. After the schedule was converted to machine-readable form, the two parts were recombined in the 1994 edition. Another edition appeared in 1997.

Subclasses

Class H contains sixteen subclasses. The first subclass, H, for general works in the Social sciences is followed by subclass HA for general Statistics and seven subclasses for Economics: HB for Economic theory and demography; HC and HD for Economic history and conditions (including production and economic conditions of individual countries in HC, and land use, agriculture, industry, and labor in HD); HE for Transportation and communications; HF for Commerce; HG for Finance, including money, banking, and insurance; and HJ for Public finance, including revenue and taxation. These are followed by seven subclasses for the discipline of Sociology: HM for general works and theory of Sociology; HN for Social history and conditions, social problems, and social reform; HQ, HS, and HT for social groups (with HQ for the Family, marriage, and women; HS for Societies; and HT for Communities, classes, and races); HV for Social pathology, social and public welfare, and criminology; and HX for Socialism, communism, and anarchism. The position of this last subclass creates an interesting collocation with the following class, J, for Political science.

Internal Tables

Internal tables for subarrangement are used extensively throughout the schedule. The use of some of these is illustrated below:

Panduranga Rao, D.   *Rural bus transport operations* [in India].   1997

HE	Subclass: Transportation and communications
365	Roads and highways in regions or countries in Asia
.I42	The first Cutter number (.I4) for India and the successive element (2) meaning a general work according to the internal table for a Cutter-number country
P36	The second Cutter number for the main entry, Panduranga Rao
1997	The date of publication

Broderick, David. *An early toll-road : the Dublin-Dunleer Turnpike, 1731-1855.* c1996

HE	Subclass: Transportation and communications
363	Roads and highways in regions or countries in Europe
.I733	The first Cutter number (.I73) for Ireland and the successive element (3) meaning special topics according to the internal table for a Cutter-number country
T643	The second Cutter number (T64 listed under HE336) for the topic, Toll roads, and the successive element (3) for the main entry, Broderick
1996	The date of publication

Staff report, February modification, completion and implementation of the financial plan. [for New York, NY] 1994

HJ	Subclass: Public finance
9289	The third number in the range of numbers (9287-9289) assigned to New York State, meaning local subdivisions according to the internal table (found under HJ9191-9343) for a three-number state
.N46	The first Cutter number for the city of New York
S748	The second Cutter number for the main entry under the title, *Staff* ...
1994	The date of publication

Kellogg National Bank, 1874-1926 : Kellogg-Citizens National Bank, 1926-1993 : Associated Bank Green Bay, National Association, 1993-present. [1996?]

HG	Subclass: Finance
2613	Banking in the United States, by city
.G694	The first Cutter number (.G69) for the city of Green Bay, Wisconsin, with the successive element (4 from the internal table) for individual banks
A875	The second Cutter number for the individual bank, *Associated Bank* ...
1996	The date of publication

Auxiliary Tables

Many tables that appeared within the schedules in earlier editions of Class H have been converted to auxiliary tables placed at the end of schedules that are produced from MARC classification data. As a result, Class H now contains thirty-six auxiliary tables, H1-H36:

H1-H10	Tables of Geographical Divisions
H11-H14, H24	Tables of Statistics
H15-H17	Tables of Economic Subdivisions
H18-H23	Tables for Industries and Trades
H25-H27	Tables of Subdivisions under HJ3231
H28-H30	Tables of States
H31-H36	Tables for various topics in Public finance (HJ)

The application of some of these tables is discussed with examples below.

Tables of Geographical Divisions

The most common form of detailed enumeration in Class H is by geographic area. Some of the most typographically complex auxiliary tables in the LC Classification are the "Tables of Geographical Divisions" in this class. Thirteen auxiliary tables containing geographical subdivisions, H1-H10 and H28-H30, are used to subarrange ranges of numbers assigned to various topics. These tables appear after the class numbers and before the index in the schedule of Class H.

The tables in Class H present no great problems in use provided the following steps are followed:

1. Locate the appropriate class number or numbers in the schedule.

2. Identify the correct geographical table.

3. Determine the range of numbers within that table for a specific geographic area.

4. Apply that range of numbers to the appropriate internal table of subject subdivisions, if any.

5. Add the adjusted geographic number to the designated base number, usually given under the class number or range in question. Be careful to avoid simple errors in addition.

To become acquainted with the typographical features of these tables, it is important to follow carefully the examples given below. It should be noted that the use of these tables is further complicated by the fact that subject subdivisions under places are often represented by additional internal tables. For instance, works dealing with labor in geographical areas other than the United States are classed within the range of HD8101-8942.5 using Table H8. Following this range of numbers in the schedule are internal tables of subject subdivisions for twenty-number countries, ten-number countries, five-number countries, and one-number countries, as shown below.

HD	ECONOMIC HISTORY AND CONDITIONS	HD

	Labor. Work. Working class
	By region or country -- Continued
8101-8942.5	Other regions or countries (Table H8)
	Add country number in table to HD8100
	Under each country:
	20 nos.
1	*Periodicals. Societies. Serials*
	Including works about ministries, departments, bureaus of labor, etc.
3	*Associations, unions, etc., A-Z*
	Class here works about particular general trade unions.
	For official organs of general trade unions, see HD6521, subdivision (1)
	For unions belonging to individual industries and trades, including their official organs, see HD6521-HD6940.7 subdivision (8)
4	*Congresses*
5	*Yearbooks*
6	*Directories*
7	*Statistics*
8	*History (General)*
9-11	*General works and history. By period*
9	*Early through 1848*
10	*1849-1945*
11	*1945-*
13	*Biography*
13.A1	*Collective*
13.A2-Z	*Individual, A-Z*
15-17	*Labor in politics*
15	*General works*
16	*Chartists movement (Great Britain)*
17.A-Z	*Local, A-Z*
18	*Minority labor. By race or ethnic*

		origin, A-Z
18.A2		*General works*
18.B55		*Blacks*
19.A-Z		*By region or state, A-Z*
		Under each state:
.x		*Periodicals. Societies. Serials*
.x2		*General works. History*
.x3		*General special*
20.A-Z		*By city*
		Under each:
.x		*Early to 1848*
.x2		*1848-*

10 nos.

1	*Periodicals. Societies. Serials*
	Including works about ministries, departments, bureaus of labor, etc.
2	*Associations, unions, etc., A-Z*
	For official organs of general trade unions, see HD6521 subdivision (1)
	For unions belonging to individual industries and trades, including their official organs, see HD6521-HD6940.7 subdivision (4)
2.5	*Congresses*
3	*Yearbooks*
4	*History (General)*
5-6.5	*General works and history. By period*
5	*Early through 1848*
6	*1849-1945*
6.5	*1945-*
7	*Biography*
7.A1	*Collective*
7.A2-Z	*Individual, A-Z*
8	*Labor in politics*
8.5	*Minority labor. By race or ethnic origin, A-Z*
8.5.A2	*General works*
8.5.B55	*Blacks*
9	*By region or state, A-Z*
	Under each state:

Table continues on page 246.

.x		*Periodicals. Societies. Serials*
.x2		*General works. History*
.x3		*General special*
10		*By city, A-Z*
		Under each:
.x		*Early to 1848*
.x2		*1848-*
	5 nos.	

1   *Periodicals.   Societies.   Serials*
           Including works about ministries,
           departments, bureaus of labor,
           etc.

2   *Associations, unions, etc., A-Z*
           Class here works about particular
           general trade unions
           For official organs of general
           trade unions, see HD6521
           subdivision (1)
           For unions belonging to individual
           industries and trades, including
           their official organs, see
           HD6521-HD6940.7 subdivisions (8)
           and (4)

3   *History (General)*
3.5   *1945-*
4   *By region or state, A-Z*
             Under each state:
.x   *Periodicals.   Societies.   Serials*
.x2   *General works.   History*
.x3   *General special*
5   *By city, A-Z*
             Under each:
.x   *Early to 1848*
.x2   *1848-*

           1 no.

.A1-.A4   *Periodicals.   Societies.   Serials*
           Including works about ministries,
           departments, bureaus of labor,
           etc.

.A5   *Associations, unions, etc., A-Z*
           Class here works about particular
           general trade unions
           For official organs of general
           trade unions, see HD6521

*For unions belonging to individual
industries and trades, including
their official organs, see
HD6521-HD6940.7 subdivisions (8)
and (4)*

.A6-.Z7   *History (General)*
.Z8A-Z   *By region or state, A-Z*
            Under each state:
.x   *Periodicals. Societies. Serials*
.x2   *General works. History*
.x3   *General special*

Twenty-Number Countries. Before using these tables, however, the classifier must determine the range of numbers available to the geographic area in question. For example, a history of labor in Great Britain is classed in the following fashion. The numbers HD8101-8942.5 are used for works on labor by region or country. In Table H8 the numbers 281-300 are assigned to Great Britain. As Great Britain is a twenty-number country, the internal table for twenty numbers found under HD8101-8942.5 is used. The number "8" in the table is designated for a general history. The corresponding number in the range for Great Britain, therefore, is 288. This number is then added to the base number for labor in areas other than the United States. A note in the schedule instructs the classifier to add the country number directly to 8100. This yields the number HD8388, as shown below:

Fowler, Simon. *Sources for labour history.* 1995

HD   Subclass: Economic history and conditions
8100   The base number for foreign labor as given in the note under HD8101-8942.5
+ 288   The adjusted country number (i.e., the eighth number according to the twenty-number table) in the range 281-300 for Great Britain, meaning a history of labor in Great Britain
_____
8388

8388   The resulting number meaning a history of labor in Great Britain
.F67   The Cutter number for the main entry, Fowler
1995   The date of publication

Other works about labor in Great Britain are classed in a similar manner, as shown in the following examples:

Barrow, Logie. *Democratic ideas and the British Labour Movement, 1880-1914.* 1996

HD	Subclass: Economic history and conditions
8100	The base number for foreign labor as given in the note HD8101-8942.5
+ 290	The adjusted country number (i.e., the tenth number according to the twenty-number country table) in the range 281-300 for Great Britain, meaning a general work covering 1849-1945
8390	

8390	The resulting number meaning a work on late 19th- and early 20th-century British labor
.B274	The Cutter number for the main entry, Barrow
1996	The date of publication

The Era of the Reform League : English labour and radical politics 1857-1872. 1995

HD	Subclass: Economic history and conditions
8100	The base number for foreign labor as given in the note under HD8101-8942.5
+ 295	The adjusted country number (i.e., the fifteenth number according to the twenty-number country table) in the range 281-300 for Great Britain, meaning a general work on labor in politics
8395	

8395	The resulting number meaning a work on labor in British politics
.E73	The Cutter number for the main entry under the title, *Era . . .*
1995	The date of publication

Another example is the classification of a collective biography of working-class people in Great Britain, a work which is classed in HD8393.A1. The thirteenth number in this case is for biography, and the Cutter number ".A1" means a collective biography.

> *Useful toil : autobiographies of working people from the 1820s to the 1920s.* 1994

HD	Subclass: Economic history and conditions
8100	The base number for foreign labor as given in the note under HD8101-8942.5
+ 293	The adjusted country number (i.e., the thirteenth number according to the twenty-number country table) in the range 281-300 for Great Britain, meaning biography
———	
8393	

8393	A work of biography related to labor in Great Britain
.A1	The first Cutter number meaning a collective biography
.U8	The second Cutter number for the main entry under the title, *Useful . . .*
1994	The date of publication

Ten-Number Countries. An example of a ten-number geographic area is Canada, which is assigned the range of 1-10 in Table H8. Social history is assigned the range of numbers HN101-942.5 in the schedule, with the instruction to use Table H8, modified (the modification for Poland appears immediately after the internal tables). A work on the social history of Vancouver is classed in HN110.V36. Canada's ten numbers become HN101-HN110 when fitted into the range of numbers for social history. The range HN101-HN110 is then subdivided according to the internal table for a ten-number country appearing in the schedule following HN101-942.5. In this table, the tenth number, that is, HN110 for Canada, is to be further subdivided by local places and special topics, for example:

> *Violence : you can make a difference.* 1996?

HN	Subclass: Social history and conditions
100	The base number for regions or countries other than the United States, as given in the schedule
+ 10	The last number in the range 1-10 (according to Table H8) assigned to Canada
———	
110	

110	The number meaning a work on the social history of Canada
.Z9	The first Cutter number meaning special topics, A-Z, according to the internal table for a ten-number country
V577	The second Cutter number (V5 listed in the internal table for twenty numbers) for the topic Violence and the successive element (77) added to distinguish works on the same topic
1996	The date of publication

Under some numbers, the tables are modified to accommodate special needs of certain regions or countries. For example, Table H5 is used with the numbers HD5721-5851 for Labor market, with the numbers for the United States and Canada modified as enumerated in the schedule. While only three of the four numbers indicated in Table H5 are actually assigned meanings in the internal table for a four-number country, all four numbers assigned to the United States are used as specified in the schedule in order to separate works on individual states from those on individual cities. This portion of the schedule is reproduced below:

HD   ECONOMIC HISTORY AND CONDITIONS
  Labor
  Labor market. Labor supply and demand
5721-5851 By region or country (Table H5 modified)
   Add country number in table to HD5720
   For United States use:
   HD5723 Periodicals. Societies. Serials
   HD5724 General works
   HD5725 By region or state, A-Z
   HD5726 By city, A-Z

   For Canada use:
   HD5727 Periodicals. Societies. Serials
   HD5728 General works
   HD5729 By province, A-Z
    Under each (local numbers used under countries only):
    4 nos.

1	*Periodicals. Societies. Serials*
3	*General works*
4.A-Z	*Local, A-Z*

> *1 no.*
>
> *.A1-.A5*   *Periodicals. Societies. Serials*
> *.A6*   *General works*
> *.A7-.Z*   *Local, A-Z*

In many cases, an auxiliary table is used, when instructed, in conjunction with an internal table such as the one shown above. For instance, when classifying in HD5721-5851, Table H5 is used along with the internal tables within the schedule. As a result, the following work on labor projection in Oregon is classed in HD5725.O7:

Oregon occupational projections, 1995-2005.   1995-1996

HD	Subclass: Economic history
5725	The number meaning a work on Labor supply and demand in a state of the United States (according to Table H5 and the internal table for four numbers)
.O7	The first Cutter number for the state, Oregon, based on the free-floating table for states of the United States
O765	The second Cutter number for the main entry under the title, *Oregon* . . .
1995	The date of publication

Tables of Subdivisions Under Regions or Countries

Tables H11-H17 are used with main numbers that represent geographic areas. The tables provide form and topical subdivisions under places. An example is a work about economic conditions in China, which is assigned the range of numbers HC426-430 in the schedule, with the instruction to use Table H16. The five numbers assigned to China are therefore used as laid out in Table H16. For example:

Becker, Jasper.   *Hungry ghosts : Mao's secret famine.*   1996

HC	Subclass: Economic history and conditions
430	The fifth number in the range HC426-430 assigned to China meaning special topics, A-Z (according to Table H16)
.F3	The first Cutter number for the topic, Famine (from list under HC79)
B33	The second Cutter number for the main entry, Becker
1996	The date of publication

Tables of Subdivisions of Industries and Trades

Tables H18-H23 are used when the main numbers represent industries or trades. The tables provide form and geographic subdivisions. The following examples illustrate the use of some of these tables:

Rodengen, Jeffrey L. *The legend of Honeywell.* 1995

HD	Subclass: Economic history and conditions
9729	The tenth number in the range 9720-9739 assigned to Manufacturing industries, to be subdivided by firm (in the United States, according to Table H18 for a twenty-number industry)
.H66	The first Cutter number for the firm, Honeywell
R63	The second Cutter number for the main entry, Rodengen
1995	The date of publication

Chanderbali, David. *Kayman Sankar : the ultimate rice magnate* [from Guyana]. c1995

HD	Subclass: Economic history and conditions
9066	The rice industry
.G952	The first Cutter number (G95) for Guyana, with the successive element (2) meaning a biography (according to Table H20)
S263	The second Cutter number for the biographee, Sankar
1995	The date of publication

The herbal supplements market. [1995]

HD	Subclass: Economic history and conditions
9019	Special industry products, A-Z
.H472	The first Cutter number (H47) for the product, herbs, with the successive element (2) meaning a general work (based on Table H21)
H47	The second Cutter number for the main entry under the title, *herbal* . . .
1995	The date of publication

Redverse-Mutton, Anthony. *Protein ingredients in foods : a western European perspective.* 1996

HD	Subclass: Economic history and conditions
9019	Special industry products
.P753	The first Cutter number (P75) for the product, proteins, with the successive element (3) meaning local subdivisions (according to Table H22)
E857	The second Cutter number for Europe
1996	The date of publication

Perhaps the greatest single problem in the use of Class H and the other social science classes is where to class material dealing with more than one of the disciplines in the social sciences. The safest solution to this problem is to ascertain a precedent in LC practice for a particular type of material. This can be done by examining LC cataloging records for similar material.

Because much of the geographic subdivision in the class is accomplished by auxiliary tables, the index has very few geographic entries.

Class J begins on page 254.

CLASS J—POLITICAL SCIENCE

J

(1)-981	General legislative and executive papers
(1)-(9)	Gazettes
(10)-(98)	United States
80-82	Presidents' messages and other executive papers
100-981	Other regions and countries

JA

1-92	Political science (General)
1-26	Periodicals
27-34	Societies
35.5	Congresses
60-64	Dictionaries and encyclopedias
71-(80.2)	Theory. Relations to other subjects
81-84	History
86-88	Study and teaching. Research
92	Collective biography of political scientists

JC

11-(607)	Political theory
11-(607)	State. Theories of the state
47	Oriental state
49	Islamic state
51-93	Ancient state
109-121	Medieval state
131-273	Modern state
177-(178)	Thomas Paine
311-314	Nationalism. Nation state
319-323	Political geography
327	Sovereignty
328.2	Consent of the governed
328.6	Violence. Political violence
329	Patriotism
345-347	Symbolism
348-497	Forms of the state
(501)-(607)	Purpose, functions, and relations of the state

JF

20-2112	Political institutions and public administration
20-1177	General. Comparative government
51-56	General works. History
(201)-619	Organs and functions of government
251-289	Executive. Heads of state

331-341	Parliamentary government
(441)-619	Legislation. Legislative process. Law-making
800-1177	Political rights. Political participation
1338-2112	Public administration
(1411)-1521	Civil service
2011-2112	Political parties

JK

1-9993	Political institutions and public administration
1-9593	United States
(401)-1685	Government. Public administration
501-(901)	Executive branch
631-(873)	Civil Service. Departments and agencies
(1001)-(1443)	Congress. Legislative branch
1154-1276	Senate
1308-(1443)	House of Representatives
1606-1685	Government property, etc.
1717-(2248)	Political rights. Practical politics
(1756)-1761	Citizenship
1846-(1936)	Suffrage
(1961)-(2248)	Electoral system
2255-2391	Political parties
2403-9593	State government
9663-9993	Confederate States of America

JL

1-3899	Political institutions and public administration
1-500	Canada
599.5-839	West Indies. Caribbean Area
1200-1299	Mexico
1400-1679	Central America
1850-3899	South America

JN

1-9689	Political institutions and public administration
1-97	Europe (General)
101-1179	Great Britain
1187-1371	Scotland
(1400)-1571.5	Ireland
1601-2191	Austria-Hungary. Austria. Hungary
2210-2229	Czech Republic. Czechoslovakia
2240	Slovakia
2301-3007	France
3201-(4980)	Germany
5001-5191	Greece
5201-5690	Italy

Class J continues on page 256.

5701-5999	Netherlands
6101-6371	Belgium
6500-6598	Soviet Union. Russia. Former Soviet Republics
6615	Estonia
6630-6639	Ukraine
6640-6649	Belarus
6680-6689	Moldova
6690-6699	Russia (Federation)
6730-6739	Latvia
6745	Lithuania
6750-6769	Poland
7011-7066	Scandinavia. Northern Europe
7101-7367	Denmark
7370-7379	Greenland
7380-7389	Iceland
7390-7399	Finland
7401-7695	Norway
7721-(7997)	Sweden
8101-8399	Spain
8423-8661	Portugal
8701-9599	Switzerland
9600-9689	Balkan States

JQ

(1)-6651	Political institutions and public administration
(1)-1849	Asia
200-620	India
1070-1199	Central Asia
	Including former republics of the Soviet Union
1499-1749	East Asia
	Including China, Japan, Korea
1758-1852	Middle East
	Including Turkey, Iran, Israel, Arabian Peninsula
1850	Arab countries
1852	Islamic countries
1870-3981	Africa
3981.5-3986.7	Atlantic Ocean islands
3995-6651	Australia. New Zealand. Pacific Ocean islands

JS

(3)-8500	Local government. Municipal government
55-67	History
141-271	Municipal government and local government other than municipal
300-1583	United States

1701-1800	Canada
1840-2058	West Indies. Caribbean Area
2101-2148	Mexico
2145-2219	Central America
2300-2778	South America
3000-6949.8	Europe
6950-7509	Asia
7510	Arab countries
7520	Islamic countries
7525-7819	Africa
7820-7827	Atlantic Ocean islands
7900-7906	Indian Ocean islands
8001-8490	Australia. New Zealand. Pacific Ocean islands

JV

1-9480	Colonies and colonization. Emigration and immigration. International migration
1-5399	Colonies and colonization
1-9	Periodicals. Serials
10-19	Societies
61-151	History
412-461	Administration and organization
500-5399	Colonizing nations
6001-9480	Emigration and immigration. International migration
6001-6006	Periodicals. Serials
6021-6032	History
(6061)-(6149)	Emigration
6201-(6348)	Immigration
6403-7127	United States
7200-7539	Canada, Latin America, etc.
7590-(8349)	Europe
8490-8758	Asia
8760	Arab countries
8762	Islamic countries
8790-(9025)	Africa
9029-9036	Atlantic Ocean islands
9040-9047	Indian Ocean islands
9100-9269	Australia. New Zealand
9290-9470	Pacific Ocean islands

JX

(1)-(6650)	International law
(63)-(191)	Collections. Documents. Cases
(221)-(1195)	Collections, cases, etc. By country
(1261)-(1283)	Codification of international law

Class J continues on page 258.

(1305)-(1598)	Foreign relations
(1621)-(1896)	Diplomacy
(1901)-(1995)	International arbitration, organization, etc.
(2001)-(6650)	International law

JZ
(2)-6530	International relations
5.5-18	Periodicals
24-38	Societies. Associations, etc.
63-1153	Sources
221-1153	By region or country
1249-1254	Relation to other disciplines and topics
1305-2060	Scope of international relations
(1328)-1395	By period
1400-1454	Diplomatic and consular service
1464-2060	By country, territory, or region
3675-3875	State territory and its different parts
(3684)-3685	Boundaries
3686-3875	International waters
4835-5490	International organizations and associations
4841-4848	Political non-governmental organizations. NGOs
4850-5490	Intergovernmental organizations. IGOs
4853-4934	The League of Nations
4935-5160	The United Nations
5511.2-(6299)	Promotion of peace. Peaceful change
5514-5526	Societies. Associations, etc.
5527-5532	Congresses and conferences
(5586)-6009	International security. Disarmament
6010-(6299)	Pacific settlement of international disputes
6360-6377	Non-military coercion
(6378)-6405	The armed conflict. War and order
6422-6422.5	Neutrality
6530	Humanitarian aspects of war

Class J—Political Science was first published in 1910. The second edition was issued in 1924 and reprinted in 1966 with supplementary pages of additions and changes as of October 1965. The schedule was not fully revised until the 1995 edition, which was produced from the machine-readable database. This edition provides updated captions that reflect current terminology and realigns geographic breakdowns that reflect the geopolitical situation of the late twentieth century.

The original schedule for Class J was completed before Class K, Law, was fully developed. As work proceeded on the K schedules, many legal topics formerly classed in J were relocated to the law schedules. Originally, International law and International relations were classed in JX. With the completion of two new subclasses, JZ, International relations, and KZ, Law of nations, subclass JX was discontinued as of May 1, 1997. Because work on the new subclasses was still in process as the 1995 edition of Class J went to print, numbers in subclass JX were retained in the 1995 edition but enclosed in parentheses in anticipation of the impending schedule changes. In 1997, another new edition of Class J was issued; this edition cumulates all changes made since the 1995 edition, and includes for the first time the new subclass JZ, International relations, developed by Jolande Goldberg. Subclass JZ and another new subclass KZ, Law of nations, thus replace the former subclass JX, but to assist libraries in the migration to the new subclasses, the 1997 edition includes, for the last time, the defunct subclass JX, with all numbers in this subclass enclosed in parentheses.

Subclasses

Class J contains twelve subclasses. Unlike other main classes, subclass JA Political science (General) for general works on the discipline as a whole is preceded by subclass J General legislative and executive papers. Subclass JC contains Political theory.

W. C. Berwick Sayers described Class J as the most revolutionary notion used in the entire system: "It is no less than the application of the 'national' method of grouping (familiar in the treatment of literature), conjoined with a chronological development, in complete contrast to the 'topical' method so familiar to users of the Decimal scheme."[14] This method of inserting geographical divisions between topical or subject divisions of a subject may be seen in the scheme for Political institutions and public administration (formerly Constitutional history and administration). Subclass JF is for General works, but subclasses JK, JL, JN, and JQ are all for geographic areas: the United States; Canada and Latin America; Europe; and Asia, Africa, Australia, and Pacific Area. This device allows the further subdivisions under geographic areas to be designed specifically and directly in relation to what is pertinent to an individual area. Not only do political institutions and topics vary from one country to another, but so does the amount of material the Library of Congress has or is likely to have on a given political topic. For example, the range of numbers JK1880-1911 has been assigned to suffrage for women in the United States, while the similar topic under France has only one number, JN2954; similarly, Germany also has only one number for this topic, JN3825. Another example is political parties: more than one hundred numbers are assigned for political parties in the United States, JK2255-2391; France has only two numbers, JN2997 and JN3007; and Germany has three numbers, JN3931, JN3933, and JN3946. In each case the size of the span of numbers assigned is related to the amount of material in the LC collections.

Subclass JS contains Local government, including municipal government. Subclass JV is used for works on colonies and colonization, emigration and immigration, and international migration. Subclass JZ, the newly developed schedule, is used for international relations.

Tables

There are thirty-six auxiliary tables, numbered J1-J21, JX1-JX11, and JZ1-JZ4, in Class J, which are similar to the tables already discussed in chapter 4. These include the five internal tables previously located within subclass JS for subarranging material about local government.

Chicago is a city that is assigned twenty numbers in the schedule, JS701-720, with the instruction to use Table J14 for subdivisions. The number "13" in Table J14 is designated for local government other than municipal (county, township, and village governments), as illustrated in the following example:

Ferman, Barbara. *Challenging the growth machine : neighborhood politics in Chicago and Pittsburgh.*   1996

JS	Subclass: Local government
713	The number (13 in Table J14) meaning local government other than municipal in the range of numbers JS701-720 assigned to Chicago
.F47	The Cutter number for the main entry, Ferman
1996	The date of publication

Other cities are treated similarly:

Pecorella, Robert F. *Community power in a postreform city : politics in New York City.*   1994

JS	Subclass: Local government
1228	The number (8 in Table J14) meaning a 20th-century history in the range of numbers JS1221-1240 assigned to New York City
.P43	The Cutter number for the main entry, Pecorella
1994	The date of publication

Ethington, Philip J. *The public city : the political construction of urban life in San Francisco, 1850-1900.* 1994

JS	Subclass: Local government
1437	The number (7 in Table J14) meaning a 19th-century history in the range of numbers JS1431-1449 assigned to San Francisco
.E84	The Cutter number for the main entry, Ethington
1994	The date of publication

Works about state governments are classed with the use of Table J7. For example:

Tannahill, Neal R. *Texas government : policy and politics.* c1997

JK	Subclass: Political institutions and public administration (United States)
4816	The number (16 in Table J7), meaning General works in the range JK4801-4893 assigned to Texas
.T36	The Cutter number for the main entry, Tannahill
1997	The date of publication

State of Minnesota telecommuting program. [1996]

JK	Subclass: Political institutions and public administration (United States)
6160	The number (60 in Table J7), meaning Civil service in the range JK6101-6193 assigned to Minnesota
.P44	The first Cutter number for the topic, Personnel management
S75	The second Cutter number for the main entry under the title, *State . . .*
1996	The date of publication

An example illustrating the use of an "A" Cutter number under number 88, Supplies, government property, government purchasing, in Table J7 is given below:

Let us guide you : marketing guide for doing business with the Commonwealth of Virginia. 1996

JK	Subclass: Political institutions and public administration (United States)

3988	The number (88 in Table J7), meaning Government purchasing, in the range 3901-3993 assigned to Virginia
.A1	The "A" Cutter number for a general work
L48	The second Cutter number for the main entry under the title, *Let . . .*
1996	The date of publication

The city of Washington, D.C., is classed with the numbers JK2701-2793 assigned to the District of Columbia with governments of individual states and territories. Table J7 is used for subarrangement.

A vision for America's first city : a transformed government for the people of Washington, D.C. [1996]

JK	Subclass: Political institutions and public administration (United States)
2716	The number (16 in Table J7), meaning General works in the range 2701-2793 assigned to District of Columbia
.V57	The Cutter number for the main entry under the title, *vision . . .*
1996	The date of publication

Other examples of Class J include:

Mims, Julian. *Records management : a practical guide for cities and counties.* 1996

JS	Subclass: Local government
344	U.S. local and municipal government
.P77	The first Cutter number for the topic Public records management
M56	The second Cutter number for the main entry, Mims
1996	The date of publication

Victoria. Office of the Auditor-General. *Equality in the workplace : women in management.* 1995

JQ	Subclass: Political institutions and public administration (Asia, Africa, Australia, Pacific Area)
5349	The number (49 in Table J8) meaning Civil service, in the range of numbers JQ5300-5399 assigned to Victoria, Australia

.W6	The first Cutter number for the topic Women in the civil service
V53	The second Cutter number for the main entry, Victoria
1995	The date of publication

The New Asian immigration in Los Angeles and global restructuring. 1994

JV	Subclass: Emigration and immigration
6926	Local subdivisions of California
.L67	The first Cutter number for Los Angeles
N49	The second Cutter number for the main entry under the title, *New . . .*
1994	The date of publication

Spencer, Ian R. G. *British immigration policy since 1939 : the making of multi-racial Britain.* 1997

JV	Subclass: Emigration and immigration
7633	The number (33 in Table J20) meaning Immigration policy in the range of numbers JV7600-7699 assigned to Great Britain
.S64	The Cutter number for the main entry, Spencer
1997	The date of publication

McCarthy, Kevin F. *Immigration in a changing economy : California's experience.* 1997

JV	Subclass: Emigration and immigration
6920	First of two numbers (JV6920-6921) assigned to General works (according to Table J19) on California
.M33	The Cutter number for the main entry, McCarthy
1997	The date of publication

Parker, Richard A. *Illegal immigration in San Diego County : an analysis of costs and revenues.* 1993

JV	Subclass: Emigration and immigration
6926	Local places in California, A-Z
.S26	The first Cutter number for the place, San Diego County
P37	The second Cutter number for the main entry, Parker
1993	The date of publication

The following examples illustrate the use of the newly developed subclass JZ:

> Schmidt, Brian C.   *The political discourse of anarchy : a disciplinary history of international relations.*   c1998

JZ	Subclass: International relations
1237	Study and teaching
.S35	The Cutter number for the main entry, Schmidt
1998	The date of publication

> Jack, Homer Alexander.   *Homer's odyssey : my quest for peace and justice.* [1996]

JZ	Subclass: International relations
5540.2	Promotion of peace, individual biography, A-Z
.J33	The Cutter number for the biographee, Jack
A3	The second Cutter number for an autobiography according to the Biography Table
1996	The date of publication

In general, Class J does not pose any unusual problems. However, it should be noted that materials in political and diplomatic history are often classed in the appropriate history class in D or E-F, and not in J.

The index for Class J contains many entries for geographic names and detailed enumeration of United Nations documents.

CLASS K—LAW

K	
1-7720	Law (General)
201-487	Jurisprudence. Philosophy and theory of law
520-5582	Comparative law. International uniform law
7000-7720	Conflict of laws

Law of the United Kingdom and Ireland

KD	
51-9500	England and Wales
8850-9312	Local laws of England
9320-9355	Local laws of Wales
9400-9500	Wales

KDC	
51-990	Scotland

KDE	
21-580	Northern Ireland

KDG	
26-540	Isle of Man. Channel Islands

KDK	
21-1950	Ireland (Eire)

KDZ	
0-4999	America. North America
1100-1199	Organization of American States

Law of Canada

KE	
1-9450	Federal law. Common and collective provincial law

Individual provinces and territories

KEA	
1-599	Alberta

KEB	
1-599	British Columbia

Class K continues on page 266.

KEM
1-599   Manitoba

KEN
1-599   New Brunswick
1201-1799   Newfoundland
5401-5999   Northwest Territories
7401-7999   Nova Scotia

KEO
1-1199   Ontario

KEP
1-599   Prince Edward Island

KEQ
1-1199   Quebec

KES
1-599   Saskatchewan

KEY
1-599   Yukon Territory

KEZ
1-9999   Individual cities, A-Z

Law of the United States

KF
1-9827   Federal law.   Common and collective state law

Individual states

KFA
1-599   Alabama
1201-1799   Alaska
2401-2999   Arizona
3601-4199   Arkansas

KFC
1-1199   California
1801-2399   Colorado
3601-4199   Connecticut

KFD
1-599   Delaware
1201-1799   District of Columbia

KFF
1-599   Florida

KFG
1-599   Georgia

KFH
1-599   Hawaii

KFI
1-599   Idaho
1201-1799   Illinois
3001-3599   Indiana
4201-4799   Iowa

KFK
1-599   Kansas
1201-1799   Kentucky

KFL
1-599   Louisiana

KFM
1-599   Maine
1201-1799   Maryland
2401-2999   Massachusetts
4201-4799   Michigan
5401-5999   Minnesota
6601-7199   Mississippi
7801-8399   Missouri
9001-9599   Montana

KFN
1-599   Nebraska
601-1199   Nevada
1201-1799   New Hampshire
1801-2399   New Jersey
3601-4199   New Mexico
5001-6199   New York
7401-7999   North Carolina
8601-9199   North Dakota

KFO
1-599   Ohio
1201-1799   Oklahoma
2401-2999   Oregon

Class K continues on page 268.

KFP
1-599   Pennsylvania

KFR
1-599   Rhode Island

KFS
1801-2399   South Carolina
3001-3599   South Dakota

KFT
1-599   Tennessee
1201-799   Texas

KFU
1-599   Utah

KFV
1-599   Vermont
2401-2999   Virginia

KFW
1-599   Washington
1201-1799   West Virginia
2401-2999   Wisconsin
4201-4799   Wyoming

KFX
1-9999   Individual cities, A-Z

KFZ
1801-2399   Northwest Territory
8601-9199   Confederate States of America

KG
1-999   Latin America (General)
3001-3999   Mexico and Central America (General)

KGA
1-9000   Belize

KGB
1-9000   Costa Rica

KGC
1-9800   El Salvador

KGD
1-9990   Guatemala

KGE
1-9990   Honduras

KGF
1-9900   Mexico

KGG
1-9800   Nicaragua

KGH
1-8000   Panama
9001-9499   Panama Canal Zone

                          West Indies.   Caribbean area
KGJ
1-999   General
7001-7499   Anguilla

KGK
1-499   Antigua and Barbuda
1001-1499   Aruba

KGL
1-499   Bahamas
1001-1499   Barbados
2001-2499   Bonaire
3001-3499   British Leeward Islands
4001-4499   British Virgin Islands
5001-5999   British West Indies
6001-6499   British Windward Islands

KGM
1-499   Cayman Islands

KGN
1-9800   Cuba

KGP
1-499   Curacao
2001-2499   Dominica

KGQ
1-9800   Dominican Republic

Class K continues on page 270.

KGR
1-499	Dutch Leeward Islands (General)
1001-1499	Dutch West Indies (Netherlands Antilles)
2001-2499	Dutch Windward Islands (General)
3001-3499	French West Indies (General)
4001-4499	Grenada
5001-5499	Guadeloupe

KGS
1-9000	Haiti

KGT
1-499	Jamaica
1001-1499	Martinique
2001-2499	Montserrat

KGU
1-499	Navassa Islands

KGV
1-8200	Puerto Rico

KGW
1-499	Saba
2001-2499	Saint Christopher (Saint Kitts), Nevis, and Anguilla
3001-3499	Saint Lucia
5001-5499	Saint Vincent and the Grenadines
7001-7499	Saint Eustatius
8001-8499	Saint Maarten

KGX
1-499	Trinidad and Tobago

KGY
1-499	Turks and Caicos Islands

KGZ
1-499	Virgin Islands of the United States

KH
1-999	South America (General)

KHA
1-9800	Argentina

KHC 1-8200	Bolivia
KHD 1-9900	Brazil
KHF 1-9800	Chile
KHH 1-9900	Colombia
KHK 1-9990	Ecuador
KHL 1-9000	Falkland Islands
KHM 1-9000	French Guiana
KHN 1-9000	Guyana
KHP 1-9700	Paraguay
KHQ 1-9800	Peru
KHS 1-9000	Surinam
KHU 1-9800	Uruguay
KHW 1-9900	Venezuela

Europe

KJ 2-1040	History of Law
160-1040	Germanic law

Class K continues on page 272.

KJA
2-3660   Roman law

KJC
2-9799   Regional comparative and uniform law

KJE
5-7975   Regional organization and integration.
                             Comparative law

KJG
1-4999   Albania

KJH
1-499   Andorra

KJJ
1-4999   Austria

KJK
1-4999   Belgium

KJM
1-4999   Bulgaria

KJN
1-499   Cyprus

KJP
1-4999   Czechoslovakia

KJR
1-4999   Denmark

KJS
1-4985   Estonia

KJT
1-4999   Finland

                          France

KJV
2-9158   National laws

KJW
51-4360   Individual regions, provinces, departments,
                                 etc.
5201-9600   Individual cities

                               Germany
KK
2-9799.3   Germany and West Germany

KKA
7-9796   East Germany

KKB-KKC
                               Individual states, provinces, and cities

KKE
1-4999   Greece

KKF
1-4999   Hungary

KKG
1-499   Iceland

KKH
1-4999   Italy

KKI
1-4890   Latvia

KKJ
1-499   Liechtenstein
501-9890   Lithuania

KKK
1-499   Luxembourg
1001-1499   Malta

KKL
1-499   Monaco

KKM
1-4999   Netherlands

KKN
1-4999   Norway

Class K continues on page 274.

KKP
1-4999   Poland

KKQ
1-4999   Portugal

KKR
1-4999   Romania

KKS
1-499   San Marino

KKT
1-4999   Spain

KKW
1-4999   Switzerland

KKX
1-4999   Turkey

KKY
1-4999   Ukraine (1991-   )

KKZ
1-4999   Yugoslavia

                      Asia and Eurasia, Africa, Pacific Area, and
                         Antarctica
KL
2-5915   History of law.   The ancient orient
2-135   General
147-177   Ancient legal systems compared
190-420   Sources
700-2215   Mesopotamia.   Assyro-Babylonian law
1000-1299   Sumer
1600-1899   Assyria
2200-2499   Babylonia
2800-3099   Egypt
3500-3799   Elam
4110-4399   Greek law
4700-4999   Hittite law
5300-5599   Persia
5900-6199   Phoenicia

KLA-KLW	Eurasia
	Turkey, *see* KKX
KLA 1-9999	Russia. Soviet Union
KLB 1-6499	Russia (Federation, 1992-)
KLD 1-490	Armenia (Republic)
KLE 1-490	Azerbaijan
KLF 1-490	Belarus (Republic)
	Estonia, *see* KJS
KLH 1-490	Georgia (Republic)
	Latvia, *see* KKI Lithuania, *see* KKJ
KLM 1-490	Moldova
KLN 1-489	Russian S.F.S.R. (to 1991)
KLP 1-4989 9001-9499	Ukraine (1919-1991) Zakavkazskaia Sotsialisticheskaia Federativnaia Sovetskaia Respublika (to 1936)
KLQ 1-499	Bukharskaia Narodnaia Sovetskaia Respublika (to 1924)
KLR 1-490	Kazakhstan

Class K continues on page 276.

1001-1499	Khorezmskaia Sovetskaia Sotsialisticheskaia Respublika (to 1924)

KLS
1-490   Kyrgyzstan

KLT
1-490   Tadjikistan

KLV
1-490   Turkmenistan

KLW
1-490   Uzbekistan

KM-KPZ   Asia

KM
1-999   General

KMC-KMY   Middle East.   Southwest Asia

KMC
1-799   Regional comparative and uniform law

KMF
1-293.5   Armenia (to 1921)
1001-1490   Bahrain

KMG
1-489   Gaza

KMH
1-4990   Iran

KMJ
1-4990   Iraq

KMK
1-4990   Israel

KML
1-490   Jerusalem

KMM
1-490   Jordan

501-994	West Bank (Territory under Israeli occupation, 1967-)
KMN 1-499	Kuwait
KMP 1-490	Lebanon
KMQ 1-490 1001-1499	Oman Palestine (to 1948)
KMS 1-490	Qatar
KMT 1-4990	Saudi Arabia
	Southern Yemen, *see* KMY
KMU 1-490	Syria
KMV 1-9870	United Arab Emirates
KMX 1001-1526	Yemen
KMY0-489	Yemen (People's Democratic Republic) (to 1990)
KNC-KPW	South Asia. Southeast Asia. East Asia
KNC 1-999	Regional comparative and uniform law
KNE 150-499	Regional organization and integration
KNF 1-4990	Afghanistan
KNG 1-4990	Bangladesh

Class K continues on page 278.

KNH
1-490   Bhutan

KNK
1-490   Brunei

KNL
1-4990   Burma

KNM
1-4990   Cambodia

KNN
1-9000   China

KNP
1-599   China (Republic, 1949-   ).   Taiwan

KNQ
1-9665   China (People's Republic, 1949-   )

KNR
1-489   Hong Kong

KNS
1-4999   India

KNT-KNU   States, cities, etc.

KNV
1-489   French Indochina

KNW
1-4990   Indonesia

KNX
1-4999   Japan

KNY
10-220   Cities, etc.

KPA
1-4990   Korea.   South Korea

KPC
1-4990   Democratic People's Republic of Korea.
                           North Korea

KPE
1-4990   Laos

KPF
1-489   Macao

KPG
1-6999   Malaysia
7001-9999   States of East and West Malaysia
                                 (1957-   )

KPH
1-4990   States of East and West Malaysia
                                 (1957-   )
5001-5490   Maldives

KPJ
1-490   Mongolia

KPK
1-490   Nepal

KPL
1-4990   Pakistan

KPM
1-4990   Philippines

KPP
1-499   Singapore

KPS
1-4990   Sri Lanka

KPT
1-4990   Thailand

KPV
1-8094   Vietnam

KPW
1-489   Vietnam.   South Vietnam

Class K continues on page 280.

KQ-KTZ	Africa
KQ	
2-197	History of law
2010-9000	Law of indigenous peoples
KQC	
1-999	Regional comparative and uniform law
KQE	
10-1249	Regional organization and integration
KQG	
1-4990	Algeria
KQH	
1-4990	Angola
KQJ	
1-490	Benin
KQK	
1-490	Botswana
KQM	
1-499	British Central Africa Protectorate
KQP	
1-499	British Indian Ocean Territory
1001-1499	British Somaliland
KQT	
1-490	Burkina Faso
KQV	
1-490	Burundi
KQW	
1-8020	Cameroon
KQX	
1-490	Cape Verde
KRB	
1-490	Central African Republic
KRC	
1-490	Chad

KRE
1-490   Comoros

KRG
1-490   Congo

KRK
1-490   Djibouti

KRL
1-499   East Africa Protectorate

KRM
1-4990   Egypt

KRP
1-4990   Ethiopia

KRR
1-499   French Equatorial Africa

KRS
1-499   French West Africa

KRU
1-490   Gabon

KRV
1-489   Gambia

KRW
1-499   German East Africa

KRX
1-4990   Ghana

KRY
1-499   Gibraltar

KSA
1-490   Guinea

KSC
1-490   Guinea-Bissau

Class K continues on page 282.

KSE
1-490   Equatorial Guinea
601-699   Ifni

KSG
1-499   Italian East Africa
1001-1499   Italian Somaliland

KSH
1-4990   Ivory Coast

KSK
1-4990   Kenya

KSL
1-490   Lesotho

KSN
1-490   Liberia

KSP
1-4990   Libya

KSR
1-490   Madagascar

KSS
1-490   Malawi

KST
1-490   Mali

KSU
1-490   Mauritania

KSV
1-490   Mauritius
5001-5490   Mayotte

KSW
1-4990   Morocco

KSX
1-4990   Mozambique

KSY
1-4990   Namibia

KSZ 1-490	Niger
KTA 1-9150	Nigeria
KTC 1-499	Reunion
KTD 1-490	Rwanda
KTE 1-490	Saint Helena
KTF 1-490	Sao Tome and Principe
KTG 1-4990	Senegal
KTH 1-490	Seychelles
KTJ 1-490	Sierra Leone
KTK 1-490	Somalia
KTL 1-9560	South Africa, Republic of
KTN 1-499 601-699	Spanish West Africa (to 1958) Spanish Sahara (to 1975)
KTQ 1-4990	Sudan
KTR 1-490	Swaziland
KTT 1-9910	Tanzania

Class K continues on page 284.

KTU 1-490	Togo
KTV 1-4990	Tunisia
KTW 1-490	Uganda
KTX 1-4990	Zaire
KTY 1-490 1501-1599	Zambia Zanzibar (to 1964)
KTZ 1-490	Zimbabwe
KU-KWW	Pacific Area
KU 1-4999	Australia
KUA-KUH	States and territories
	External territories
KUN 501-599 3001-3050	Norfolk Island Cities, communities, etc.
KUQ 1-4990	New Zealand
KV-KWW	Pacific area jurisdictions
KVC 1-999	Regional comparative and uniform law
KVE 200-349	Regional organization and integration
KVH 1-490 1001-1499	American Samoa British New Guinea (Territory of Papua)

KVL
1-489   Cook Islands

KVM
1-489   Easter Island

KVN
1-490   Fiji

KVP
1-100   French Polynesia
1001-1099   German New Guinea (to 1914)

KVQ
1-490   Guam

KVR
1-490   Kiribati

KVS
1-490   Marshall Islands
501-990   Micronesia (Federated States)
2501-2999   Midway Islands

KVU
1-499   Nauru
1001-1099   Netherlands New Guinea (to 1963)

KVW
1-490   New Caledonia

KWA
1-489   Niue

KWC
1-490   Northern Mariana Islands

KWE
1-499   Pacific Islands (Trust Territory)

KWG
1-490   Palau

KWH
1-490   Papua New Guinea

Class K continues on page 286.

KWL
1-499	Pitcairn Island
2001-2490	Solomon Islands

KWP
1-490	Tonga

KWQ
1-490	Tuvalu

KWR
1-490	Vanuatu

KWT
1-489	Wake Island
2001-2490	Wallis and Futuna Islands

KWW
1-490	Western Samoa

KWX   Antarctica

KZ
1-6785	Law of nations
2-5.5	Bibliography
24-38	Societies, etc.
27-37	By region or country
(60)-62.5	Intergovernmental congresses and conferences
(63)-1152	Sources. Fontes juris gentium
118-194	Treaties and other international agreements
119-165	To 1920
170-173	1920-
176-182.5	Boundary treaties
183-183.5	Treaties of arbitration, investigation, etc.
184-194	Peace treaties
199-218	Judicial decisions and arbitral awards
221-1152	By region or country
1165-1208	Trials
1168-1208	War crime trials
1234-1236	Legal research. Legal bibliography
1249-1252	International law and other disciplines
1255-1273	Theory and principles
1267-1273	Domain of the law of nations
1284-1285.5	Methodology
1287-1296	Codification of the law of nations

Class K continues on page 288.

6350-6785	Enforced settlement of international disputes
6360-6373	Non-military coercion
6374-(6377)	Threat of force
6378-6785	Law of war and neutrality. Jus belli
6427-6437	Warfare on land
6440-6530	Humanitarian law
6540-6660	Warfare on sea
6665-6714	Air warfare
6730-6785	The end of war. Armistice. Surrender. Postliminy

KZA

1002-(4205)	Law of the sea
1040-1065	Intergovernmental congresses and conferences
1118-1122	Treaties and other international agreements
1340-1417	Concepts and principles
1340	Mare clausum doctrine
1348-1405	Mare liberum doctrine
1430-1690	Maritime boundaries
1630-1664	Continental shelf
(3481)-(3900)	Marine resources conservation and development
(3891)-(3900)	High-seas fisheries and fisheries regimes
4130-(4205)	Public order of the oceans

KZD

1002-6715	Space law. Law of outer space
1040-1065	Intergovernmental congresses and conferences
1118-1122	Treaties and other international agreements
1340-1400	Concepts and principles. Theory
1390-1400	Regulated use theory
1410	The source of the law of space
1420-1455	Boundaries
3489-4406	Peaceful uses of outer space
3489.5-3608	Space resources
4030-4326	Public order in space and outer space
4080-4210	Space flight
(4301)-4310	Space communication
4320.2-4326	Rescue operations in outer space
4400-4406	Liability for accidents
5614-6715	Un-peaceful uses of outer space
5620-5622.2	Treaties and other international agreements
5648-5680.2	Disarmament and demilitarization regimes in outer space

The schedules for **Class K—Law** represent the most recent development in the Library of Congress Classification. *Subclass KF: Law of the United States*, the first K schedule to be published, did not appear until 1969. Although Class K was included in the original outline for the Classification, at the beginning little work was done on its development. There were several reasons for this. First, much of the material to be classed in K was already assigned by subject in Martel's seven points, for example, school law in Class L for Education, library law in Class Z for Library science, etc. Second, because the Library of Congress maintains a separate Law Library, which utilized the traditional form arrangement of law libraries, a subject classification for law was not deemed vital.

In 1948 a scheme constructed by Elizabeth Benyon for the Law Library of the University of Chicago was published by the Library of Congress but was not adopted by the Library. In 1949, a joint meeting of the Library of Congress Committee on a Classification for Law and the Committee on Cooperation with the Library of Congress of the American Association of Law Libraries began work on developing Class K. Its content was projected and a tentative outline and notation were developed. Between 1953 and 1960 nine working papers were prepared at the Library and distributed to librarians and scholars. The papers covered the following topics: (1) German law; (2) Roman law; (3) History of German law; (4) Canon law; (5) Chinese law; (6) English law; (7) Law of Japan; (8) Classification of American law (A Survey); and (9) Law of the United States. Subclass KF is the result of Working Paper No. 9.

In 1979,[15] the Library of Congress found it necessary to revise the draft outline of Class K (which had been published in 1970) in order to take into account the political developments of the late 1960s and the Library's increased acquisitions of Asian and African legal materials. It was decided at that time to rearrange the order of countries into an alphabetical sequence instead of into geographic sequence clusters that had been planned earlier. Countries covered by KJ-KZ in the original outline were revised to an arrangement by continent or other major geographic area. Within each major area, regions and regional organizations are classed first, followed by individual countries in an alphabetical order. The basic groups were determined as follows:

Europe
Soviet Union
Asia
    Southwest Asia.   Near East
    South and Southeast Asia.   The Far East
    Islands of the Indian and Pacific Ocean

Africa
North Africa
Sub-Saharan Africa
Offshore Africa.   Islands of the Atlantic and Indian Ocean
Australia
New Guinea
New Zealand
Oceania
Antarctica

Development work on the schedules for Class K took place over a long period of time, during which considerable effort was made to ensure that they were consistent with each other. Many adjustments of positions and notation were and continue to be made. The more recent schedules include lengthy introductions; these not only outline the principles and policies governing Class K in general, but address the specific schedules as well, with discussions on the background for the development of each particular schedule. Users will find these introductions very helpful in understanding and applying the K schedules.

In the Introduction to subclasses KL-KWX, Jolande E. Goldberg summarizes the Class K policies:[16]

A.   Jurisdiction Policy

B.   Synchronized Tables

C.   Legal History

D.   Regionalism

With regard to the jurisdiction policy, Goldberg remarks, "Arrangement by jurisdiction takes precedence over arrangement by topic or form because of differences in the legal systems, nomenclature, public policies and intellectual tradition from one jurisdiction to the next" (p. viii). This policy in a way entails the detailed enumeration of topics under many of the jurisdictions. Nevertheless, forms of publications are fairly uniform among legal publications. Tables are used extensively for subarranging materials on the same topic but in different forms. The general *form division tables* first used in subclass KF were implemented in subsequent subclasses with modifications where necessary. In the course of developing the schedules, it was decided to use legal history with its corpus of sources as the opening *topical* chapter for all schedules and tables, and constitutional history, originally placed in Class J, was relocated to the pertinent K schedules. The policy of regionalism, first adopted with the schedules KJ-KKZ, refers to the practice of classing works on the law of two or more countries with the region to which such jurisdictions belong and in subclass K when the jurisdictions in question belong to different regions.[17] It was later applied to regional intergovernmental organizations (IGOs) and the European treaty law as well. Thus, in Class K, particularly in the more recently developed schedules, there is a conscientious effort to achieve consistent and parallel treatment of legal materials among the subclasses.

Tables for subject divisions and form divisions are used throughout the law schedules. They appeared in individual schedules. Because form division tables have much in common across the subclasses, the Library of Congress decided to develop a set of uniform form tables, numbered K1-K24, to be used throughout Class K. For ease of maintenance and update, they were published in a separate volume entitled *K Tables: Form Division Tables for Law* (1999). These tables replace the form division tables found in individual schedules except KD, KE, and KF.

Subclass K

The schedule for subclass K, *Law [General]*, was first published in 1977. A new, MARC-based edition was issued in 1998. This subclass contains the philosophy and theory of law, comparative law, international uniform law, and conflict of laws. As pointed out in the preface to the schedule, public international law as a discipline remained in subclass JX. With the development and publication of subclasses, JZ, International relations, and KZ, Law of nations, in 1997, much of the material pertaining to international relations and international law, particularly treaties, previously classed in subclasses JX and K, has been relocated to subclasses JZ and KZ.

Subclass KD

The schedule for subclass KD, *Law of the United Kingdom and Ireland*, was first published in 1973. A new, MARC-based edition was issued in 1998. Werner B. Ellinger's Working Paper No. 6 (English law), used originally as the basis for arrangement of the subject matter, was substantially modified in order to conform as far as possible to the systematic order established in Schedule KF, Law of the United States. The arrangement of the law of the United Kingdom and Ireland is shown in the following synopsis:

SYNOPSIS

KD	Law of England and Wales
KDC	Law of Scotland
KDE	Law of Northern Ireland
KDG	Law of Isle of Man. Channel Islands
KDK	Law of Ireland (Éire)

Subclass KD includes the law of the United Kingdom as a whole and the common law system (Anglo-American law) in general. There are five form tables. Also included are the "Table of Regnal Years of English Sovereigns" and a list of "Greater London Boroughs." The index provides detailed topical entries and a few geographic name entries.

Subclasses *KDZ, KG-KH*

The schedule for subclasses KDZ, KG-KH, *Law of the Americas, Latin America and the West Indies*, was published in 1984. The subarrangement is shown in the following synopsis:

SYNOPSIS

KDZ	1-1000	America. North America (General)
	2001-4500	America. North America—Individual Countries
KG	1-1000	Latin America
	3001-4000	Mexico and Central America (General)
KGA-KGH		Mexico and Central America—Individual Countries
KGJ		West Indies. Caribbean Area
KGK-KGZ		West Indies. Caribbean Area—Individual Islands and Island Groups
KH		South America (General)
KHA-KHW		South America—Individual Countries

With this schedule, the Library of Congress began the use of generalized tables for the subarrangement of the law of individual countries. In this and subsequent law schedules, individual countries and their political divisions are assigned ranges of numbers to be divided according to a set of tables, instead of enumerating the subdivisions under each country (as is the case for the law of the United States, Canada, Great Britain, and Germany). As a result, the bulk of this schedule consists of tables, with a small section at the beginning of the schedule listing the ranges of numbers assigned to individual countries, provinces, cities, etc. There are seven tables (Tables

A-G) for subject divisions: Tables A-D for entities larger than cities, Tables E-F for cities, and Table G for the Organization of American States (OAS). Form tables I-VI have been replaced by Tables K8, K12, K9b, K11, K12, and K15 in *K Tables* respectively. Use of Table VII has been discontinued.

The index to this schedule contains references to topics listed in the tables. There are no entries for geographic or jurisdictional names.

Subclass KE

The schedule for subclass KE, *Law of Canada*, published in 1976, represents a joint effort between the Library of Congress and the National Library of Canada. In general, the schedule for KE follows the pattern of subclass KF, Law of the United States, except where subclass KD, Law of the United Kingdom and Ireland, provides a better model because of the structure of Canadian law. A new edition was published in 1999.

The arrangement of the subclasses is shown in the following synopsis:

	SYNOPSIS
KE	Law of Canada
KEO	Law of Canada - Ontario
KEQ	Law of Canada - Quebec
KEA-KEY	Canada - Provinces and territories
KEZ	Canada - Cities, towns, etc.

The notation follows closely that of subclass KF. Law of provinces is represented by triple capital letters, the third letter being a mnemonic based on the name of the province, for example, KEQ Quebec. Law of cities, towns, etc., is classed in KEZ with integral numbers apportioned to individual cities and towns in an alphabetical sequence. Similar types of auxiliary form tables and internal tables as found in KF are used. A detailed index includes topical entries and a few geographic name entries.

Subclass KF

The schedule for subclass KF, *Law of the United States*, was issued in a preliminary edition in 1969. This was the first of the schedules of Class K to appear, and it introduced a new feature to the Library of Congress notation: triple capital letters.

The arrangement of the subclasses is shown in the following synopsis:

SYNOPSIS

KF	Federal law
KFA-KFW	Law of states
KFX	Cities, towns, etc.
KFZ	Territories and Confederate States of America

The general arrangement of the subclass begins with KF, Federal law, followed by the law of individual states in KFA-KFW. The third letter is mnemonic, based on the initial letter of the name of the state, for example, KFA for law of Alabama, Alaska, Arizona, and Arkansas; KFL for law of Louisiana; etc. Each state is assigned six hundred numbers, for example, KFA0-599, Alabama; KFO2400-2999, Oregon; etc., with the exception of California and New York, each of which is assigned twelve hundred numbers: KFC0-1199, California; and KFN5000-6199, New York. The subdivisions of the law of California and New York are individually developed. For the other states, a uniform "Table of Subject Divisions for the Law of the States and Territories of the United States" containing six hundred integral numbers (some with decimal extensions) is provided. The law of individual states is followed by the law of cities, KFX0-9999. The numbers are apportioned to all cities in the United States in an alphabetical sequence, for example:

KFX	1097	Austin, Texas
	1098	Austin to Baltimore
	1101-1119	Baltimore, Maryland
	1121	Baltimore to Bangor

Each city is assigned twenty numbers, one number, or a Cutter number, based on literary warrant. The only exception is the city of New York, which is assigned the numbers KFX2001-2099, with specially developed subject divisions enumerated in the schedule. Three tables (twenty-number, one-number, and Cutter-number) are provided for subject divisions of the law of individual cities. Following KFX, the law of cities, is KFZ, the law of territories of the United States and the law of the Confederate States of America.

In subclass KF there are nine auxiliary form division tables: Table I, twenty-number subjects; Table II, ten-number subjects; Tables III and IV, five-number subjects; Table V, two-number subjects; Table VI, one-number subjects; Table VII, Cutter-number subjects; Table VIII, single-number captions for general works; and Table IX, modified form divisions for state law.

Because of the unique nature of the publications of the Supreme Court and other courts of individual states, a set of supplementary KF entries was developed after the publication of subclass KF and published in *LC Classification, Additions and Changes*. In this supplementary development, such publications are enumerated under the number assigned to the Supreme Court and other courts of each state. Examples are shown below:

SUBCLASS KF

KFM			*MARYLAND*	KFM
1245			Court of Appeals.	
			Official series and predecessors.	
	.A19	1658	Harris and McHenry (General Court) (1658-1799) 4 v.	
	.A19	1800	Harris and Johnson (1800-1826) 7 v.	
	.A19	1826	Harris and Gill (1826-1829) 2 v.	
	.A19	1829	Gill and Johnson (1829-1842) 12 v.	
	.A19	1843	Gill and Miller (1843-1851) 9 v.	
	.A195	1811	Bland (Chancery) (1811-1832) 3 v.	
		1847	Maryland Chancery decisions (1847-1854) 4 v.	
	.A2		Maryland Reports (1851-).	
	.A3-39		Unofficial series.	
	.A3		Maryland reporter (1942-).	
	.A4		Abridged, selected, defunct.	
			.P7 Proceedings (1695-1729) 1 v.	
1248			Court of Special Appeals.	
			Official series.	
	.A2		Maryland appellate reports (1967-).	

KFM			*MASSACHUSETTS*	KFM
	2445		Supreme Judicial Court.	
			Official series and predecessors.	

N.S. (1873-)	O.S.	Separate editions of nominative reports making up vols. 1-100 of Massachusetts Reports.
.A2 v. 1	.A19 1804	Williams (1804-1805) 1 v.
.A2 v. 2-17	.A19 1806	Tyng (1806-1822) 16 v.
.A2 v. 18-41	.A19 1822	Pickering (1822-1839) 24 v.
.A2 v. 42-54	.A19 1840	Metcalf (1840-1844) 13 v.
.A2 v. 55-66	.A19 1848	Cushing (1848-1853) 12 v.
.A2 v. 67-82	.A19 1854	Gray (1854-1860) 16 v.
.A2 v. 83-96	.A19 1861	Allen (1861-1867) 14 v.
.A2 v. 97-100	.A19 1867	Browne (1867-1872) 13 v.
	v. 1-4	

Table continues on page 296.

.A2 v. 101-   --   --
.A3-39	Massachusetts Reports (1873-).
.A32	Unofficial series.
.A33	Massachusetts decisions (1885-).
2448	Massachusetts decisions (2d) (West, 1936-).
	Appeals Court.
.A22	Official series.
	Massachusetts Appeals Court reports
2451	(1972/1974-).
.A4A-Z	Lower courts.

Abridged, selected, defunct.
.M36   Massachusetts appellate decisions
(1941-1978) 59 v.
.M37   Massachusetts appellate divisions
(1942-   ).

Subclasses KJ-KKZ

The schedule for subclasses KJ-KKZ, *Law of Europe*, was published in 1989. It was prepared by Jolande E. Goldberg with the assistance of Gabriel Horchler. The following synopsis indicates the scope of this schedule:

SYNOPSIS

KJ	History of law (General). Celtic law. Germanic law. Slavic law
KJA	Roman law (Occident and Orient)
KJC	Regional comparative and uniform law
KJE	Regional organization and integration. Community law
KJG-KKZ	List of jurisdictions and number assignments

The jurisdictions covered by this schedule include European countries with the exception of Great Britain, France, Germany, and the former Soviet Republics, which are provided for in separate schedules.

The schedule for KJ-KKZ contains an "Introduction to the Application of the Schedule," outlining the principles and structure of each of the segments as well as the entire schedule. Also discussed is the provision of tables for the subdivision of ranges of numbers assigned to individual jurisdictions.

It was indicated earlier that when the law schedules were developed, some topics originally provided for in Class J were shifted to Class K. Such shifts include treaties and conventions by subject, for example, treaties on the right of asylum or extradition, the law of regional organizations with their treaties, and regional treaty law, which were moved to the appropriate subclasses of law. Comprehensive treaty sets and treaties truly concerning international public law issues are now classed in KZ.

Internal tables for form division are found throughout the schedule at appropriate points of application in the schedule; for example, Tables A and B (page 4 of schedule) used with KJ200-580, sources of German law; Tables C and D (page 23 of schedule) used with KJA211-1622, sources of Roman law; and Tables E and F (page 26 of schedule). These have been replaced by tables in *K Tables*. For the division of ranges of numbers assigned to individual jurisdictions (including cities) in Europe, a series of six subject tables is used. They are designated A-F (pages 210-451 of the schedule) and range from 5000 numbers to a Cutter number. Tables for Form Divisions, numbered I-XVIII have been replaced by various tables in *K Tables*.

A detailed subject index to schedule numbers and table numbers is provided with this schedule, including many vernacular terms. Jurisdictional names are not indexed.

Subclasses *KJV-KJW*

The schedule for subclasses KJV-KJW, *Law of France*, was published in 1985. This schedule is the last one developed that is unique to a single country. All subsequent law schedules were planned to conform to generalized tables for subarrangement.

Following is the synopsis for subclasses KJV-KJW:

		France
KJV	2-9158	National laws
KJW	51-4360	Individual regions, provinces, departments, etc.
	5201-9600	Individual cities

Each region, province, or department is assigned a range of ten numbers to be divided uniformly according to an established pattern of division. Major cities, each also assigned a range of ten numbers, are treated in a similar manner with an established pattern of division for cities. Other cities are classed in KJW9600 with a Cutter number assigned to each, subarranged by means of successive elements. The ranges of numbers originally assigned to regions, etc., and cities and communities have been revised since the publication of the main schedule, with the revision published in *LC Classification, Additions and Changes*. The last two digits in each ten-number sequence were changed from 1-10 to 0-9 to facilitate the matching of table numbers with schedule numbers. For example, the range of numbers KJW6821-6830 originally assigned to Dijon were changed to KJW6820-6829.

The four tables of form divisions (for ten numbers, five numbers, one number, and Cutter number) have been replaced by Tables K9b-K12 in *K Tables*. The index contains entries in both English and French. It does not include geographic names.

Subclasses KK-KKC

The schedule for subclasses KK-KKC, *Law of Germany*, was published in 1982. As the first LC Classification schedule to cover a major civil law system, it serves as the model for developing subsequent foreign law schedules and tables for civil law jurisdictions.

This schedule covers the law of both East and West Germany as well as Germany as a whole. The subarrangement of the subclass is shown in the following synopsis:

SYNOPSIS

KK	Law of Germany and West Germany
KKA	Law of East Germany
KKB-KKC4999	German states, provinces, and territories
KKC5000 +	German cities, towns, etc.

In developing the subclass KKA for the law of East Germany, a "derivation technique" was used. This means that, as far as possible, the development of the law of East Germany was kept in parallel with that for the law of West Germany, with modifications made as needed to accommodate unique features of East German law. As a result, most of the integral numbers in subclasses KK and KKA carry the same meanings; for example, both KK6130 and KKA6130 mean Land reform and land policy legislation.

Both English and German terms are used in the captions in the schedule in order to facilitate the classification of legal materials written in German. Ample scope notes are provided, particularly under numbers related to the distribution of material among history of law, constitutional history, and modern law; the distribution of material among federal law, state law, and city law; and the division of material between West Germany and East Germany. The schedule includes a helpful "Introduction to the Application of the Schedule," outlining features that are peculiar to subclass KK-KKC.

As in other law schedules, numerous tables are used in subclasses KK-KKC. There are many tables for internal subarrangement scattered throughout the schedule. The five form division tables (I-V) have been replaced by Tables K9a, K9c, K10, K11, and K12 in *K Tables*. In addition, Table

VI for form divisions in History of law and Constitutional history, has been replaced by Table K22. It uses "A" Cutter numbers, for example, ".A2--.A55" for legal texts, such as law collections, statutes, and court decisions, and ".A7--Z79" for General works.

A detailed bilingual index contains English and German terms interfiled in one alphabetical arrangement. Terms in German are used as *see* references to those in English, under which class numbers are found. In cases where there are no English equivalents, class numbers are given under the German terms only.

Subclasses *KL-KWX*

The schedule for subclasses KL-KWX, *Law of Asia and Eurasia, Africa, Pacific Area, and Antarctica*, was published in two volumes in 1993. The subarrangement of the subclasses is shown in the following synopsis:

SYNOPSIS

KL	History of Law. The Ancient Orient
KLA-KLW	Eurasia
KM-KPZ	Asia
KQ-KTZ	Africa
KU-KWW	Pacific Area
KWX	Antarctica

As in other schedules for Class K, tables are used extensively in this schedule. In fact, volume two consists entirely of tables. The tables are listed below:

Table A	Ancient Law
Table B	Regional, Comparative and Uniform Law
Table C	Regional and Subregional Organizations
Tables D&E	Civil Law
Tables F&G	Common Law
Table H	States, Territories, Provinces, etc.
Tables J&K	Cities, Communities, etc.
Tables I-XIX	Form Divisions

Table A, containing 299 numbers used for subarranging topics for different systems of ancient law, such as Greek law and Hittite law, follows subclass KL in volume one. The remaining tables appear in volume two. Form Tables I-XIX have been replaced by various tables in *K Tables*.

Subclass KZ

Subclass KZ, *Law of Nations*, a new subclass developed in conjunction with subclass JZ, International relations, was published in 1997. These two new subclasses replace the former subclass JX, International law. The background and development of these subclasses is given in a separate publication prepared by Jolande E. Goldberg.[18]

Currently, subclass KZ consists of the following divisions:

KZ	Law of nations
KZA	Law of the sea
KZD	Space Law. Law of outer space

There are nine tables, KZ1-KZ9 in the schedule; they have been replaced by the following tables in *K Tables*:

K Tables	Schedule KZ	
K23	(KZ1)	Table for Sources (10 nos.)
K24	(KZ2)	Table for Sources (1 no.)
K1	(KZ3)	Table for War Crime Trials (1 no.)
K2	(KZ4)	Table for War Crime Trials (Cutter no.)
K3	(KZ5)	Table for Works of Jurists (1 no.)
K4	(KZ6)	Table for Works of Jurists (Cutter no.)
K5	(KZ7)	Table for Treaties, Conventions, etc. (1 no.)
K6	(KZ8)	Table for Treaties, Conventions, etc. (Cutter no.)
K8	(KZ9)	Table for Regional Comparative and Uniform law (1 no.)

Tables K23-K24 and K1-K4 (formerly KZ1-KZ6) are revisions of tables previously appearing in subclass JX. Tables K5 and K6 (formerly KZ7 and KZ8) are used for subarrangement of materials relating to treaties, conventions, etc.; and Table K8 (formerly KZ9) is a form table used throughout Class K. According to Goldberg, form divisions in subclasses JZ and KZ were kept to a minimum because, based on a recent study, "it was found that application of comprehensive form division tables in the major subdivisions obscures important information."[19] As a result, organizations, conferences, and treaties under individual topics are enumerated in the schedule.

Revised Form Division Tables in Class K

In the process of converting Class K to the *USMARC Format for Classification Data*, efforts were made to introduce current language and subject headings, to restructure schedules to reflect recent developments, and to restore pattern conformity throughout the class. In addition, a full review of Class K form division tables was undertaken: many tables were condensed, and redundant entries were eliminated. As a result, a set of generic form division tables has been designed, which are to be applied uniformly to all Class K schedules except the common law schedules of KF, KD, and KE. This smaller set of uniform and simplified tables have been published in a separate volume, *K Tables: Form Division Tables for Law* (1999). Some of these revised and newly created tables also appeared in *Cataloging Service Bulletin*.[20]

Examples of Classification of Law

Rhyne, Charles S. *Working for justice in America and justice in the world : an autobiography.* 1995

KF	Subclass: Law of the United States
373	An individual biography (see internal table in the schedule) in the range of numbers, KF371-374, assigned to the recent history of U.S. Law
.R48	The first Cutter number for the biographee, Rhyne
A3	The second Cutter number (based on the Biography Table) for an autobiography
1995	The date of publication

Geltman, Elizabeth Glass. *Modern environmental law : policy and practice.* 1997

KF	Subclass: Law of the United States
3775	The Public health and sanitation in general
.A7	The first Cutter number from Table VI meaning a casebook or readings
G45	The second Cutter number for the main entry, Geltman
1997	The date of publication

Diamond, Michael. *If you can keep it : a constitutional roadmap to environmental security.* 1996

KF	Subclass: Law of the United States
3775	The Public health and sanitation in general
.Z9	The Cutter number from Table VI meaning a popular work
D53	The second Cutter number for the main entry, Diamond
1996	The date of publication

	Alabama. *Alabama insurance laws.* 1996- 1 v. (loose-leaf)
KFA	Subclass: Law of states of the United States with names beginning with "A"
185	The number (based on the Table of Subject Divisions for the Law of the States and fitted into the range of numbers KFA000-599 assigned to Alabama) meaning general insurance law
.A34	The first Cutter number based on Table IXA, meaning a particular act of state legislation
A2	The second Cutter number meaning monographs
1996	The date of publication

In the example above, the Cutter number ".A34" is based on Table IXA. Although the instruction in the schedule calls for Table VI, an instruction in Table VI refers to Table IXA for Modified Form Divisions for State Law. Because the topic is represented by a whole number (185), Table IXA is used. The Cutter number .A34 falls within the range of .A33-349 particular acts arranged chronologically according to date of original enactment or revision of law. The second Cutter number A2, meaning monographs, comes from an internal table within Table IXA. The date of publication is added to complete the call number as instructed.

	Connecticut. *Connecticut related laws to the insurance laws.* c1997-
KFC	Subclass: Law of states of the United States with names beginning with "C"
3785	General insurance laws of Connecticut, derived from the following procedure:

KFC 3600-4199   Numbers assigned to Connecticut

+ 185   Number from the Table of Subject Divisions for the Law of the States general insurance laws

_____

KFC 3785

.A3	The Cutter number (from Table IXA) meaning a collection or compilation of state statutes
1997	The date of publication

Oklahoma. *Political Subdivisions Ethics Act : Title 51 O.S. Supp. 1996, [sections] 301 through 325 including other related statutory provisions governing the ethical conduct of county officers and employees and campaigns for county, municipal, and school board office and county and municipal propositions.* [1996?]

KFO	Subclass: Law of states of the United States with names beginning with "O"
1620.6	The integral number meaning Local election law derived from the following procedure:

KFO 1200-1799		Numbers assigned to Oklahoma
	420	Number from the Table of Subject Divisions for the Law of the States with the caption: Election law
+	.6	Local elections (subarranged by Table VI)

KFO 1620.6

.A336	The first Cutter number (from Table IXA via Table VI) meaning a particular act
A2	The second Cutter number (from a table within Table IXA) meaning a monograph
1996	The date of publication

In the example above, although 420.6 local elections is to be subdivided according to Table VI, the Cutter numbers are based on those found in Table IXA, which contains modifications of the range of numbers .A24-.A49, specifically designed for state law when the topics are represented by whole or decimal numbers.

Michigan. *Constitution of the state of Michigan of 1963.* [1995]

KFM	Subclass: Law of states of the United States with names beginning with "M"
4601	The number (401 in the Table of Subject Divisions for the Law of the States fitted into the range of numbers KFM4200-4799 assigned to Michigan) meaning a particular constitution, subarranged by date of constitution
1963	The date of the constitution
.A35	The Cutter number chosen from the range .A3-399, based on an internal table meaning Official editions
1995	The date of publication

A commentary on this constitution is classified in the following manner:

> Fino, Susan P.   *The Michigan state constitution : a reference guide.*
> 1996

KFM	Subclass: Law of states of the United States with names beginning with "M"
4601	The number (401 in the Table of Subject Divisions for the Law of the States fitted into the range of numbers KFM4200-4799 assigned to Michigan) meaning a particular constitution, subarranged by date of constitution
1963	The date of the constitution
.A6	The Cutter number based on an internal table meaning an annotated text or a commentary
F56	The second Cutter number for the main entry, Fino
1996	The date of publication

Additional examples:

> Hill, Melvin B.   *The Georgia state constitution : a reference guide.* 1994

KFG	Subclass: Law of states of the United States with names beginning with "G"
401	The number (based on the Table of Subject Divisions for the Law of the States and fitted into the range of numbers KFG000-599 assigned to Georgia) meaning a particular constitution, subarranged by date of constitution
1983	The date of the constitution
.A6	The first Cutter number based on an internal table meaning a commentary
H55	The second Cutter number for the author, Hill
1994	The date of publication

> Los Angeles (Calif.)   *Los Angeles municipal code* / compiled under the direction of James K. Hahn.   1990-

KFX	Subclass: Law of cities of the United States
1621	The number (1 in Table A for Divisions under 20-number cities fitted into the range of numbers KFX1621-1639 assigned to Los Angeles) meaning Collections of charters, ordinances, and local laws
.A6	The Cutter number for Codes of ordinances
1990	The date of publication

Rolph, Elizabeth S. *Escaping the courthouse : private alternative dispute resolution in Los Angeles.* 1994

KFX	Subclass: Law of cities of the United States
1624.1	The number (based on the number 4.1 in Table A for Divisions under 20-number cities and fitted into the range of numbers KFX1621-1639 assigned to Los Angeles) meaning Special topics, A-Z, relating to city government
.J83	The first Cutter number for the special topic, Judicial functions; Court organization and procedure
R65	The second Cutter number for the main entry, Rolph
1994	The date of publication

Mexico. *Sociedades mercantiles y cooperativas.* 1996

KGF	Subclass: Law of Mexico
1295	The number (based on Table B) meaning Business associations and Commercial companies law
.A28	The Cutter number (based on Table K11 for Form subdivisions) for Statutes in monographic form
1996	The date of publication

Civil practice in the Virgin Islands : recent legal changes and the new rules : ALI-ABA course of study materials, March 10, 1994, St. Thomas, Virgin Islands. 1994

KGZ	Subclass: Law of the Virgin Islands of the United States
222	The number (based on Table C) meaning Civil procedure
.Z9	The first Cutter number based on Table K11 meaning General works
C58	The second Cutter number for the main entry under the title, *Civil . . .*
1994	The date of publication

Otamendi, Jorge. *Derecho de marcas.* [1995]

KHA	Subclass: Law of Argentina
1670	The number (based on Table B) meaning Trademarks
.O87	The Cutter number (based on Table K11 for Form Divisions) for a work about the law arranged by the main entry, Otamendi
1995	The date of publication

Social rights as human rights : a European challenge.   1994

KJC	Subclass: Law of Europe
2837	Social reform and policies
.S63	The Cutter number for the main entry under the title, *Social . . .*
1994	The date of publication

European employment law : a country by country guide.   1995

KJC	Subclass: Law of Europe
2855	A general work on Labor law (derived by fitting the number 5, General works, from Table K7 into the range of numbers 2851-2855, Labor law)
.E95	The Cutter number for the main entry under the title, *European . . .*
1995	The date of publication

Monhemius, Jurgen.   *Beamtenrecht : eine Darstellung der beim Bund und in den Bundesländern geltenden Regelungen.*   1995

KK	Subclass: Law of Germany and West Germany
5932	A general work on Civil service
.Z85	The first Cutter number (based on Table K11 for Form divisions) meaning a general work
M66	The second Cutter number for the main entry, Monhemius
1995	The date of publication

Fox, James R.   *Dictionary of international and comparative law.*   c1997

KZ	Subclass: Law of nations
1161	Dictionaries
.F69	The Cutter number for the main entry, Fox
1997	The date of publication

A New Zealand guide to international law and its sources.   [1996]

KZ	Subclass: Law of nations
1242	General works
.N49	The Cutter number for the main entry under the title, *New Zealand guide . . .*
1996	The date of publication

Rohn, Peter H.   *World treaty index.*   1997

KZ	Subclass: Law of nations
173	Indexes to treaties
.R64	The Cutter number for the main entry, Rohn
1997	The date of publication

Valencia, Mark J.   *Sharing the resources of the South China Sea.*   c1997

KZA	Subclass: Law of the sea
1146	Position of legislative or executive branch on the law of the sea
.C6	The first Cutter number for China
V35	The second Cutter number for the main entry, Valencia
1997	The date of publication

Bender, R.   *Launching and operating satellites : legal issues.*   c1998

KZD	Subclass: Space law
4080	General work on space flight
.B46	The Cutter number for the main entry, Bender
1998	The date of publication

Class L begins on page 308.

CLASS L—EDUCATION

L

7-991	Education (General)
7-97	Periodicals. Societies
101	Yearbooks
107	Congresses
111-791	Official documents, reports, etc.
797-898	Educational exhibitions and museums
899	School fairs
900-991	Directories of educational institutions

LA

5-2396	History of education
5-25	General
31-135	By period
173-186	Higher education
201-398	United States
410-2284	Other regions or countries
2301-2396	Biography

LB

5-3640	Theory and practice of education
5-45	General
51-885	Systems of individual educators and writers
1025-1050.75	Teaching (Principles and practice)
1049.9-1050.75	Reading (General)
1050.9-1091	Educational psychology
1101-1139	Child study
1139.2-1139.5	Early childhood education
1140-1140.5	Preschool education. Nursery schools
1141-1489	Kindergarten
1501-1547	Primary education
1555-1602	Elementary or public school education
1603-1696.6	Secondary education. High schools
1705-2286	Education and training of teachers and administrators
1771-1773	Certification of teachers
1775-1785	Professional aspects of teaching and school administrators. Vocational guidance
1805-2151	State teachers colleges
1811-1987	United States
1991-2151	Other regions or countries
2165-2278	Teacher training in universities and colleges
2300-2430	Higher education
2326.4-2330	Institutions of higher education
2331.7-2335.8	Teaching personnel

2335.86-2335.885	Trade unions
2335.95-2337	Endowments, trusts, etc.
2337.2-2340.8	Student financial aid
2341-2341.95	Supervision and administration. Business management
2351-2359	Admissions and entrance requirements
2361-2365	Curriculum
2366-2367.75	College examinations
2371-2372	Graduate education
2381-2391	Academic degrees
2799-2799.3	Educational consultants and consulting
2801-3095	School administration and organization
2831.6-2831.99	Administrative personnel
2832-2844.1	Teaching personnel
2844.52-2844.63	Trade unions
3011-3095	School management and discipline
3045-3048	Textbooks
3050-3060.87	Educational tests, measurements, evaluations and examinations
3201-3325	School architecture and equipment. School physical facilities. Campus planning
3401-3495	School hygiene. School health services
3497-3499	Hygiene in universities and colleges
3525-3575	Special days
3602-3640	School life. Student manners and customs

LC	
8-6691	Special aspects of education
8-59	Forms of education
8	General works
15	Conversation and culture
25-33	Self-education. Self-culture
37-44.3	Home education
45-45.8	Nonformal education
47-58.7	Private school education
58-58.7	Preparatory schools. Preparatory school education
59	Public school education
65-245	Social aspects of education
65-67.68	Economic aspects of education
68-70	Demographic aspects of education
71-120.4	Education and the state
72-72.5	Academic freedom
107-120.4	Public school question. Secularization. Religious instruction in the public schools

Class L continues on page 310.

2630-2638	Asian Americans. Asians in the United States
2667-2698	Latin Americans. Hispanic Americans
2680-2688	Mexican Americans. Mexicans in the United States
2690-2698	Puerto Ricans. Puerto Ricans in the United States
2699-2913	Blacks. Afro-Americans
3001-3501	Asians
3503-3520	Gipsies
3530-3540	Lapps
3551-3593	Jews
3701-3740	Immigrants or ethnic and linguistic minorities. Bilingual schools and bilingual education
3745-3747	Children of immigrants (First generation)
3950-4806.5	Exceptional children and youth. Special education
3991-4000	Gifted children and youth
4001-4806.5	Handicapped children and youth. Learning disabled children and youth
4812-5160.3	Other special classes
5161-5163	Fundamental education
5201-6660.4	Education extension. Adult education. Continuing education
5451-5493	Aged education
5501-5560	Evening schools
5701-5771	Vacation schools. Summer schools
5800-5808	Distance education
5900-6101	Correspondence schools
6201-6401	University extension
6501-6560.4	Lyceums and lecture courses. Forums
6571-6581	Radio and television extension courses. Instruction by radio and television
6601-6660.4	Reading circles and correspondence clubs
6681	Education and travel
6691	Traveling educational exhibits

LD

13-7501	Individual institutions
13-7501	United States
13-7251	Universities. Colleges
6501	Community colleges. Junior colleges
7020-7251	Women's colleges
7501	Secondary and elementary schools

Class L continues on page 312.

LE

3-78	Individual institutions
3-78	America (except United States)
3-5	Canada
7-9	Mexico
11-13	Central America
15-17	West Indies
21-78	South America
21-23	Argentina
27-29	Bolivia
31-33	Brazil
36-38	Chile
41-43	Colombia
46-48	Ecuador
51-59	Guianas
61-63	Paraguay
66-68	Peru
71-73	Uruguay
76-78	Venezuela

LF

14-5627	Individual institutions
14-1257	Great Britain
14-797	England
800-957	Ireland
960-1137	Scotland
1140-1257	Wales
(1311)-1537	Austria
1541-1549	Czech Republic
1550-1550.8	Slovakia
1561-1697	Hungary
1705-1709	Finland
1711-2397	France
2402-3197	Germany
3211-3247	Greece
3248-3897	Italy
3899	Malta
3911-4067	Belgium
4069	Luxembourg
4071-4197	Netherlands
4203-4209	Poland
(4211)-4437	Russia (Federation)
4440-4441	Estonia
4443-4444	Latvia
4445-4446	Lithuania
4447.2-4447.5	Belarus
4448-4448.5	Moldova
4449.2-4449.5	Ukraine
4451-4487	Denmark

4489-4491	Iceland
4493-4537	Norway
4539-4607	Sweden
4610-4827	Spain
4831-4887	Portugal
4901-5047	Switzerland
5051-5627	Turkey and the Baltic states

LG

21-961	Individual institutions
21-395	Asia
21	Afghanistan
51-53	China
55-57	Taiwan
60-170.2	India. Pakistan. Bangladesh. Burma. Sri Lanka. Nepal
171-172	Indochina
173	Malaysia
181-184	Indonesia
185-187	Papua-New Guinea (Ter.)
200-227	Philippines
240-277	Japan
281-285	Korea
291	Iran
302.2-320	Former Soviet republics in Asia
321	Asia Minor
331-331.5	Armenia (Republic)
332.2-332.5	Azerbaijan
332.7-332.9	Georgia (Republic)
333	Bahrain
338	Iraq
341-345	Israel. Palestine
346	Jordan
347	Kuwait
351-357	Lebanon
358	Qatar
359	Saudi Arabia
361-367	Syria
370	Yemen (Yemen Arab Republic)
395	Other
401-681	Africa
401	Ethiopia
405-411	South Africa
416	Botswana
418	Kenya
419	Lesotho
421-423	Uganda

Class L continues on page 314.

431-438	Natal
441-443	Malawi
451	Orange Free State
454	Swaziland
457	Transkei
459	Venda
461-462	Zimbabwe
468	Tanzania
469	Zambia
471-475	Transvaal
478	Zululand
481-505	West Africa
481-483	Nigeria
497-499	Ghana
511	Egypt
513-514	Sudan
521	Algeria and Tunisia
525	Burundi
531-536	French Equatorial Africa. French Congo
541-543	Madagascar
545-547	Rwanda
551-552	Senegal
553-554	Benin
559-560	Ivory Coast
561	Mali
581-593	German Africa (Former)
601-611	Italian Africa (Former)
615	Zaire
621	Liberia
631-632	Morocco
641-651	Portuguese Africa (Former)
671	Spanish Africa
681	Libya
690	Indian Ocean islands
715-720	Australia
741-745	New Zealand
961	Pacific islands

LH

1-9	College and school magazines and papers

LJ

3-165	Student fraternities and societies, United States

LT

6-(1001)	Textbooks

Class L—Education, originally developed by J. C. Bay and W. D. Johnston, was first published in 1911, with a second edition in 1928, a third in 1951, and a fourth edition in 1984. Beginning with the 1995 edition, the schedule has been produced from the electronic version.

This schedule presents no serious problems to the classifier. There are thirteen tables, numbered L1-L13. Tables L1-L2 are used for subdivisions under the history of education in different countries, and Tables L3-L13 contain subdivisions for subarranging numbers assigned to individual institutions of education around the world. For the most part, Class L tables are relatively easy to use, the most complex being Tables L3-L6 for subdivisions of individual institutions in America including the United States, which are classed in subclasses LD and LE. Even these tables are similar to those already covered and so need little further discussion. The only exception is Table L3, which is used for institutions to which a series of successive Cutter numbers have been assigned. The use of this table, which may appear confusing to the beginner, is illustrated in the following examples.

Wesleyan University, Middletown, Connecticut, is assigned a range of Cutter numbers, ".W27-W36," under the class number LD5901.

LD	INDIVIDUAL INSTITUTIONS
	United States
5901.W27-W36	Wesleyan University, Middletown, Connecticut (Table L3)
5901.W4	West Chester State College, West Chester, Pennsylvania (Table L7)
5901.W46	West Hartford, Connecticut. University of Hartford (Table L7)

Following are examples of numbers listed in table L3:

.x17	Charter (and founding)
.x173	Heraldry. Seal
.x175	College statutes, by-laws, etc.
	Administration
.x177	General works. Office reports
.x18	Board of regents, trustees, etc.
.x19	President (or head of the institution)

★★★★★

	History and description
.x22	History (including early descriptions)
.x23	Description (including guidebooks)

.x233	Views.　Pictorial works
.x234	Dormitories, residence halls, etc.

The instruction for use is given at the head of the table:

> Use Table 3 as follows: substitute for x1 or x2 of the initial and first digit(s) of the cutter assigned to them in the schedule, and add a second cutter for author . . .

In the case of Wesleyan University, W2 is substituted for x1, and W3 is substituted for x2.

A general history is represented in Table L3 by x22, therefore the following work on the history of Wesleyan University is classed in LD5901.W32 P68.

> Potts, David B.　*Wesleyan University, 1831-1910 : collegiate enterprise in New England.*　1992

LD	Subclass: Colleges and universities in the United States
5901	Individual institutions whose names begin with "Wes"
.W32	The first Cutter number meaning a history (.x22 in Table L3) of Wesleyan University
P68	The second Cutter number for the main entry, Potts
1992	The date of publication

Similarly, Table L3 is used for Brigham Young University, which is assigned the numbers LD571.B667-B676. A history of housing at Brigham Young is classed in LD571.B6734. B6734 has been substituted for x234 in Table L3.

> Barrett, Bruce A.　*Brigham Young University housing through the years.*　1994

LD	Subclass: Colleges and universities in the United States
571	Individual institutions whose names begin with "Br"
.B6734	The first Cutter number meaning Dormitories (.x234 in Table L3) of Brigham Young University
B37	The second Cutter number for the main entry, Barrett
1994	The date of publication

The University of North Carolina at Chapel Hill has been assigned the range of numbers LD3930-3949 with the instruction to use Table L4. In Table L4, the number 16.4 carries the caption "Freshman." As a result, a work about a freshman class at the university is classed in LD3946.4, matching the number 16.4 in Table L4.

> Devane, Mary M. *Tracking the 1979 freshmen class* [University of North Carolina at Chapel Hill]. [1995]
>
> LD   Subclass: Colleges and universities in the United States
>
> 3946.4   Freshman at the University of North Carolina at Chapel Hill
>
> .D48   The Cutter number for the main entry, Devane
>
> 1995   The date of publication

Textbooks

Subclass LT for textbooks is designed only for those textbooks covering several subjects; textbooks on a particular subject are classed with the subject in Classes B-K and M-Z. For examples see the discussion on school textbooks at the end of chapter 7.

If a library wishes to bring all textbooks together, as might be the case for a curriculum library, it could affix a locational label such as "LT" to the spine of the book in addition to its subject call number. Without using such a device, however, it would be impossible under the LC Classification to collocate all textbooks in one place.

Works on Teaching Methods in Special Subjects

The numbers LB1572 through LB1599 provide for works on teaching methods in special subjects; other material of similar nature is classed with individual subjects. Where a given item is placed depends in part on the teaching level addressed and in part on whether its subject is listed in LB1572-1599.[21] In respect to teaching level, works that deal with teaching a subject at the elementary level are classed in LB1572 through LB1599 if their subjects are listed; this policy holds even if they also include material on teaching the subject at the secondary level. Almost all other works, aimed at the secondary level or higher or treating subjects not listed in this schedule, are classed in the subject schedules; the two exceptions are noted below. The following examples illustrate how works on teaching methods are handled:

> *Cooperative learning in science : a handbook for teachers.*   1996
>
> LB   Subclass: Theory and practice of education
>
> 1585   A general work on teaching of science

.C665	The Cutter number for the main entry under the title, *Cooperative* . . .
1996	The date of publication

Harlen, Wynne. *The teaching of science in primary schools* [in Great Britain]. 1996

LB	Subclass: Theory and practice of education
1585.5	Teaching of science on the elementary level in regions and countries other than the United States
.G7	The first Cutter number for Great Britain
.H38	The second Cutter number for the main entry, Harlen
1996	The date of publication

Works on the study and teaching of science other than at the elementary level are classed in Q181.

Astronomy is a subject that does not appear in the LB1572-1599 list. A work on teaching astronomy at any level, therefore, is classed with other material on the study and teaching of astronomy in QB61-62.7, for example:

Fraknoi, Andrew. *The cosmos in the classroom : a resource guide for teaching astronomy.* 1995

QB	Subclass: Astronomy
61	Study and teaching
.F7	The Cutter number for the main entry, Fraknoi
1995	The date of publication

There are, however, two exceptions to the rule that works on teaching special subjects at secondary or higher levels are classed with the subject: English and composition (in the mother tongue only) is classed at LB1631, and Reading is classed at LB1632.

Writers INC : school to work : a student handbook. 1996

LB	Subclass: Theory and practice of education
1631	Teaching English and composition in high schools
.W68	The Cutter number for the main entry under the title, *Writers* . . .
1996	The date of publication

Irvin, L. Lennie.   *Writing skills : preparing for the TASP test.*   1997

LB	Subclass: Theory and practice of education
1631	Teaching English and composition in high schools
.5	Examinations
.I78	The Cutter number for the main entry, Irvin
1997	The date of publication

Into focus : understanding and creating middle school readers.   c1998

LB	Subclass: Theory and practice of education
1632	Reading in high schools
.I58	The Cutter number for the main entry under the title, *Into focus* . . .
1998	The date of publication

Class M begins on page 320.

CLASS M—MUSIC

M

1-5000	Music
1.A1-1.A15	Music printed or copies in manuscript in the United States or the colonies before 1860
1.A5-2.3	Collections
3-3.3	Collected works of individual composers
5-1490	Instrumental music
6-175.5	Solo instruments
176	Instrumental music for motion pictures
176.5	Instrumental music for radio and television
177-990	Music for two or more solo instruments
1000-1075	Orchestra
1100-1160	String orchestra
1200-1269	Band
1270	Fife (bugle) and drum music, field music, etc.
1350-1353	Reduced orchestra
1356-1356.2	Dance orchestra and instrumental ensembles
1360	Mandolin and similar orchestras of plucked instruments
1362	Accordion band
1363	Steel band
1365	Minstrel music
1366	Jazz ensembles
1375-1420	Instrumental music for children
1450	Dance music
1470	Chance compositions
1473	Electronic music
1480	Music with color or light apparatus
1490	Music printed before 1700 or copied in manuscript before 1700
1495-5000	Vocal music
1497-1998	Secular vocal music
1999-2199	Sacred vocal music
5000	Unidentified compositions

ML

1-3930	Literature on music
25-28	Societies and organizations
32-33	Institutions
35-38	Festivals. Congresses
40-44	Programs
47-54.8	Librettos. Scenarios
62-90	Special aspects
93-96.5	Manuscripts, autographs, etc.
100-109	Dictionaries. Encyclopedias

110-111.5	Music librarianship
112-112.5	Music printing and publishing
112.8-158.8	Bibliography
159-3799	History and criticism
3800-3923	Philosophy and physics of music
3928-3920	Literature for children

MT	
1-960	Musical instruction and study
1-5	History and criticism
5.5-7	Music theory
20-32	Special methods
40-67	Composition. Elements and techniques of music
68	Improvisation. Accompaniment. Transposition
70-74	Instrumentation and orchestration
90-146	Analysis and appreciation of musical works
170-810	Instrumental techniques
820-915	Singing and vocal technique
918-948	School music
955-956	Musical theater

Class M—Music was developed in 1902 by Oscar G. Sonneck, the first Chief of the Music Division of the Library of Congress.[22] The first edition was published in 1904, with a revised edition in 1917; and the third edition appeared in 1978. The 1998 edition, produced from the machine-readable database, was published in 1999.

In the prefatory note to the first edition, Sonneck described the development of the class:

> As a matter of course the scheme, at least so far as it concerns music proper, took a form leaning toward the classified catalogues of publishers, and somewhat different from the schemes adopted by the notable American and European libraries. But care was taken to profit by the experience of these. In its present form the scheme embodies many valuable suggestions of the Chief Classifier of the Library, Mr. Charles Martel, besides such modifications as he considered necessary in conformity with the arrangement of other classes of books in the library.

This schedule differs in several ways from other schedules. There are only three subclasses: M, Music; ML, Literature on music; and MT, Musical instruction and study. Subclass M also contains a section devoted to definitions of musical terms and special rules.

In fact, subclass M is a scheme based on physical form rather than on subject classification. Separate numbers are given to different musical forms, that is, M450-454 for string quartets, M1001 for symphonies, M1500 for operas, and so on. As a result of classification by form, not all of the works by and about a composer, for instance, are found in one place. In other words, a composer's works are scattered according to form, as illustrated in the following examples of works by Joseph Haydn. (The variations in the Cutter numbers will be explained later.)

Haydn, Joseph. *Il maestro e lo scolare : sonata a quattro mani, Hob.XVIIa:1 : Klavier vierhändig - piano duet.*   1996

M	Subclass: Music
202	Piano sonatas for four hands
.H38	The first Cutter number for the composer, Haydn
M3	The second Cutter number for the title, *maestro . . .*
1996	The date of publication

Haydn, Joseph. *Cäcilienmesse.*   1997

M	Subclass: Music
2013	Vocal scores of masses with organ, piano or other instrument
.H4	The Cutter number for the composer, Haydn
H. XXII, 5	The Hoboken Thematic Catalog number
1997	The date of publication

Haydn, Joseph.   *Sinfonie in D : Londoner Sinfonie : Nr. 12 = Symphony in D major : London Symphony : no. 12 : Hob. I:104.*   1995

M	Subclass: Music
1001	Symphonies
.H4	The Cutter number for the composer, Haydn
H. I, 104	The Hoboken Thematic Catalog number
1995	The date of publication

Haydn, Joseph. *Stabat Mater.* 1996

M	Subclass: Music
2023	Vocal scores for sacred choruses with piano or organ accompaniment
.H42	The first Cutter number for the composer, Haydn
S6	The second Cutter number for the title, *Stabat . . .*
1996	The date of publication

Arrangement of Class M by physical form rather than by subject raises some criticism. Such an arrangement of material is probably more helpful to the musician than to the musicologist. However, because all the works by a composer can be retrieved from the catalog by the composer's name, the Classification provides another access route to the material.

There are ten auxiliary tables, numbered M1-M10, in Class M. An example is shown below:

M2   TABLE OF ORIGINAL WORKS AND ARRANGEMENTS

Assign the five numbers in the span as follows:

1	Miscellaneous collections
	Original compositions
2	Collections
3	Separate works
	Arrangements
4	Collections
5	Separate works

Haydn, Joseph. *Divertimento, zwei Flöten, zwei Hörner, zwei Violinen und Basso, D-Dur.* 1995

M	Subclass: Music
762	The third number in the span M760-764 for a separate work (according to Table M2) of String and wind septet
.H38	The Cutter number for the composer, Haydn
H. II, 8	The Hoboken Thematic Catalog number
1995	The date of publication

Cutter Numbers

Over the years, LC practice in shelflisting musical materials has varied, as explained in the *Shelflisting* manual:

The Music Shelflist was begun in the Music Division in 1904. At that time, a system of Cuttering, different from that used in other classes, was devised for subclasses M, ML, and MT.... the music shelflist was transferred in 1943 to the Subject Cataloging Division, where the main part of the shelflist was housed. There was an effort made to coordinate music shelflisting methods with those used in the main shelflist. The result was that new methods of shelflisting were created, adding to those inherited from the Music Division. Several methods of Cuttering may be found in the same class, and it is difficult to determine which pattern to follow when a new entry is introduced.... Where the introduction of new procedures would have meant extensive changes to older entries, new entries were made to fit into the old system. For example, if some of a composer's works are provided with opus numbers, some with serial numbers, and still others with keys, three methods of cuttering may be found, not only in the same class but for the same composer.[23]

Currently, Cutter numbers for music materials are assigned according to the following procedures:[24]

Instrumental Music

After the class number, the first element is almost always a Cutter number for the main entry. For a work entered under the composer, the following additions are made:

1.   Opus or thematic index number when given in the uniform title. For example:

Bach, Johann Sebastian. *Two-part inventions.* c1995 [uniform title: *Inventions, harpsichord, BWV 772-786*]

M	Subclass: Music
22	Piano music
.B11	The first Cutter number for the composer, Bach
BWV 772-786	The *Bachs Werke Verzeichnis* number
1995	The date of publication

Bach, Johann Sebastian. *Kantate Nr. 190, am Neujahrstag : Singet dem Herrn ein neues Lied, BWV 190.*   1996

M	Subclass: Music

2020	Full scores for sacred choruses with orchestral accompaniment
.B16	The Cutter number for the composer, Bach
BWV 190	The *Bachs Werke Verzeichnis* number
1996	The date of publication

Boccherini, Luigi. *Sei trii op. 14 (G. 95-100) per violino, viola e violoncello.* 1996

M	Subclass: Music
351	String trios, separate works (according to Table M2)
.B663	The Cutter number for the composer, Boccherini
G. 95-100	The Gerard *Thematic Catalog* numbers
1996	The date of publication

Mozart, Wolfgang Amadeus. *Concerto, B♭ major, for piano and orchestra, K450.* c1995

M	Subclass: Music
1011	Piano concerto
.M93	The first Cutter number for the composer, Mozart
K. 450	The *Köchel Verzeichnis* number
1995	The date of publication

When thematic catalog numbers are not identified, the key of the composition or the opus number may be included as part of the call number.

Beethoven, Ludwig van. *Klaviersonate op. 2/1 = Piano sonata op. 2/1.* 1995

M	Subclass: Music
23	Piano sonatas
.B414	The Cutter number for the composer, Beethoven
op. 2, no. 1	The designation of the particular sonata, op. 2, no. 1, by opus number
1995	The date of publication

Beethoven, Ludwig van. *Piano concertos nos. 4 and 5 : Emperor.* 1995

M	Subclass: Music
1006	Organ solo(s) with piano
.B4	The Cutter number for the composer, Beethoven

op. 58	The opus number
1995	The date of publication

Note that in the example above, an opus number rather than the concerto numbers is included in the call number.

2.   Other additions. If the opus number or thematic index number is not given, and the class number is based on the individual title or uniform title of the work, the following additions are made in the following order of preference:

serial number

key (maj. for major and min. for minor, e.g., A min. or D maj.)

date of composition in parentheses (to distinguish it from dates used for editions)

second Cutter based on title, editor, etc.

For example:

Beach, H. H. A.   *Mass in E-flat, SATB chorus with soloists and piano.* c1995

M	Subclass: Music
2013	Vocal scores with organ or piano or other instrument for masses
.B354	The first Cutter number for the composer, Beach
M3	The second Cutter number for the title, *Mass . . .*
1995	The date of publication

Mozart, Wolfgang Amadeus.   *Ouvertüre zum Dramma giocoso Don Giovanni : KV527 = Overture to the dramma giocoso.*   c1995

M	Subclass: Music
1004	Overtures
.M93	The first Cutter number for the composer, Mozart
D55	The second Cutter number for the uniform title, *Don Giovanni*
1995	The date of publication

Beethoven, Ludwig van.   *Sonatas for violin and piano : with separate violin part* / edited by Joseph Joachim.   1996

M	Subclass: Music

219	Piano and violin sonatas
.B416	The first Cutter number for the composer, Beethoven
J7	The second Cutter number for the editor, Joachim
1996	The date of publication

If none of these elements is available, a single Cutter number is assigned.

Collections

Complete editions of collected works by one composer classed in M3 are assigned a single Cutter number.

Brahms, Johannes. *Neue Ausgabe sämtlicher Werke.* 1996-

M	Subclass: Music
3	Complete editions of collected works of individual composers
.B835	The Cutter number for the composer, Brahms
1996	The date of publication

A collection of miscellaneous works by one composer with a uniform title (e.g., works, songs, quartets, piano works, etc.) represented in the class number is assigned double Cutter numbers. The first Cutter number is based on the composer and the second on the compiler, editor, arranger, or publisher, if given. If not, the second Cutter number is based on the title.

Selections

The second Cutter number for selections from a composer's work is based on the type of music named in the uniform title, for example, *Pièces en trio*, with another digit for the editor, arranger, publisher, or title. If the uniform title is *Selections*, the second Cutter number is based on the editor, arranger, publisher, or title.

Mozart, Wolfgang Amadeus. *Complete sonatas and fantasies for solo piano.*
Mineola, N.Y. : Dover, 1996   [uniform title: *Piano music. Selections*]

M	Subclass: Music
22	Collections of piano music by one composer
.M93	The first Cutter number for the composer, Mozart
D68	The second Cutter number for the publisher, Dover
1996	The date of publication

Arrangements

The first Cutter number for an arrangement is based on the composer, with the second Cutter number for the title with additional digits representing the arranger.

Bach, Johann Sebastian. *Brandenburg concerto : no. 3, first movement* / arranged by Robert J. Bardeen. c1995

M	Subclass: Music
216	Two or more pianos
.B13	The first Cutter number for the composer, Bach
B76312	The second Cutter number for the title, *Brandenburg,* adjusted for the arranger, Bardeen
1995	The date of publication

If the name of the arranger is not given, the second Cutter is based on the editor or publisher. If the composer and the arranger happen to be the same, the second Cutter number is not assigned.

Vocal Music

Anthologies of vocal music are classified in the regular manner.

Cantares tradicionales del Tucumán : antología. 1994

M	Subclass: Music
1687	Secular vocal music from South America
.A7	The first Cutter number for the country, Argentina
C17	The second Cutter number for the main entry under the title, *Cantares . . .*
1994	The date of publication

For vocal music by individual composers, double Cutter numbers based on the name of the composer and the title are used, for example:

Berlioz, Hector. *Roméo et Juliette.* 1995

M	Subclass: Music
1533	Vocal scores for choruses with orchestra or other ensemble for mixed voices with piano accompaniment
.B515	The first Cutter number for the composer, Berlioz

R4   The second Cutter number for the title, *Roméo* . . .

1995   The date of publication

Bach, Johann Sebastian. *Mein Gott, wie lang, ach lange : BWV 155 : Kantate zum 2. Sonntag nach Epiphanias für Soli (SATB), Chor (SATB) under Orchester (2 Violinen, Viola und Basso continuo).* c1996.

M   Subclass: Music

2023   Vocal scores for sacred choruses for mixed voices with piano or organ accompaniment

.B12   The first Cutter number for the composer, Bach

M732   The second Cutter number for the title, *Mein Gott,* . . .

1996   The date of publication

Schubert, Franz. *Stabat Mater in g, D 175, per coro (SATB) ed orchestra.* 1995

M   Subclass: Music

2020   Vocal scores for sacred choruses for mixed voices with orchestral accompaniment

.S34   The first Cutter number for the composer, Schubert

S73   The second Cutter number for the title, *Stabat* . . .

1995   The date of publication

However, existing patterns including thematic index numbers as part of the call number are followed.

Schubert, Franz. *Salve Regina in F, D 27 : soprano solo ed orchestra.* 1994

M   Subclass: Music

2103   Vocal scores for sacred songs with orchestral accompaniment

.S38   The Cutter number for the composer, Schubert

D. 27   The Deutsch index number

1994   The date of publication

The Cutter number for the original with an additional digit is assigned to an excerpt. If the excerpt has been expressed by a number, this number is used as the additional digit.

Works About Music

Works about music in general and about individual composers are classed in subclass ML. For example, bio-bibliographical dictionaries are classed in ML105-107:

Candé, Roland de. *Dictionnaire des compositeurs.* 1996

ML	Subclass: Literature on music
105	International bio-bibliographical dictionaries
.C35	The Cutter number for the main entry, Candé
1996	The date of publication

The Harvard biographical dictionary of music. 1996

ML	Subclass: Literature on music
105	International bio-bibliographical dictionaries
.H38	The Cutter number for the main entry under the title, *Harvard* . . .
1996	The date of publication

Subclass ML also includes history and criticism of music.

Dawidoff, Nicholas. *In the country of country : people and places in American music.* 1997

ML	Subclass: Literature on music
3524	General works on country music
.D39	The Cutter number for the main entry, Dawidoff
1997	The date of publication

Smith, Michael B. *Carolina dreams : the musical legacy of upstate South Carolina.* c1997

ML	Subclass: Literature on music
3477.7	Popular music in the United States, by state, A-Z (according to Table M9)
.S6	The first Cutter number for the state, South Carolina
S65	The second Cutter number for the main entry, Smith
1997	The date of publication

The number ML410 is assigned to all biographies of individual composers. Under ML410 is a complete expansion for the German composer Richard Wagner.

Examples of biographies of musicians are shown below:

Dieckmann, Friedrich. *Franz Schubert : eine Annäherung.* 1996

ML	Subclass: Literature on music
410	Biographies of composers
.S3	The first Cutter number for the subject of the biography, Schubert
D73	The second Cutter number for the main entry, Dieckmann
1996	The date of publication

Breton, Tomas. *Diario (1881-1888).* 1995

ML	Subclass: Literature on music
410	Biographies of composers
.B844	The first Cutter number for the subject of the biography, Breton
A3	The second Cutter number, according to the Biography Table, for an autobiographical work
1995	The date of publication

Bernardin, Claude. *Rocket man : Elton John from A-Z.* 1996

ML	Subclass: Literature on music
410	Biographies of composers
.J64	The first Cutter number for the subject of the biography, John
B4	The second Cutter number for the main entry, Bernardin
1996	The date of publication

Coleman, Ray. *McCartney : yesterday--and today.* 1996

ML	Subclass: Literature on music
410	Biographies of composers
.M115	The first Cutter number for the subject of the biography, McCartney
C65	The second Cutter number for the main entry, Coleman
1996	The date of publication

Works about individual performers of instrumental music are classed in ML416-419, and those about individual performers of vocal music are classed in ML420. For example:

O'Meilia, Matt.   *Garth Brooks : the road out of Santa Fe.*   c1997

ML	Subclass: Literature on music
420	Biographies of individual performers of vocal music
.B7796	The first Cutter number for the subject of the biography, Brooks
O45	The second Cutter number for the main entry, O'Meilia
1997	The date of publication

Discography

The range of numbers ML112.8-158 is provided for bibliography, including discography, of music. This is one of the few instances in the LC Classification where bibliography is classed with the subject rather than separately in Class Z.

General discographies of music sound recordings, as well as topical discographies of music, are classed in ML156-156.9.

Cook, Richard.   *The Penguin guide to jazz on compact disc.*   1996

ML	Subclass: Literature on music
156.4	A list of sound recordings arranged by topic
.J3	The first Cutter number for the topic, Jazz music
C67	The second Cutter number for the main entry, Cook
1996	The date of publication

Garrod, Charles.   *Columbia Dallas master numbers.*   1995

ML	Subclass: Literature on music
156.4	A list of sound recordings arranged by topic
.P6	The first Cutter number for the topic, Popular music
G376	The second Cutter number for the main entry, Garrod
1995	The date of publication

Garrod, Charles.   *AFRS one night stands, 1001 thru 2000 : working draft.*   1996

ML	Subclass: Literature on music
156.4	A list of sound recordings arranged by topic
.B5	The first Cutter number for the topic, Big band music
G36	The second Cutter number for the main entry, Garrod
1996	The date of publication

Garrod, Charles. *Bob Crosby and his orchestra.* [1996]

ML	Subclass: Literature on music
156.7	A list of sound recordings of individual performers, A-Z
.C75	The first Cutter number for the performer, Crosby
G3	The second Cutter number for the main entry, Garrod
1996	The date of publication

The classification of non-music discographies is discussed on pages 502-503 in chapter 7.

The "Glossary and General Guidelines" at the beginning of Class M contains definitions of a number of key terms such as *Continuo, Instructive edition, Piece,* and *Teaching piece* and their placements in Class M. The index is detailed, although it does not include names of composers or performers. The detailed special scheme within the schedule for Richard Wagner under ML410.W1 is a useful reference feature.

Class N begins on page 334.

CLASS N—FINE ARTS

N

1-9165	Visual arts (General)
	For photography, *see* TR
400-4042	Art museums, galleries, etc.
	Arranged by country, subarrangement by city
4390-5098	Exhibitions
5198-5299	Private collections and collectors
5300-7418	History of art
7429.7-7433	Technique, composition, style, etc.
7475-7483	Art criticism
7575-7624.5	Portraits
7790-8199	Religious art
8554-8585	Examination and conservation of works of art
8600-8675	Economics of art
8700-9165	Art and the state. Public art

NA

1-9428	Architecture
190-1614	History. Historical monuments
2695-2793	Architectural design and drawing
2835-4050	Architectural details, motives, decoration, etc.
4100-8480	Special classes of buildings
9000-9428	Aesthetics of cities. City planning and beautification

NB

1-1952	Sculpture

NC

1-1940	Drawing. Design. Illustration
997-1003	Commercial art. Advertising art
1300-1766	Caricature. Pictorial humor and satire
1800-1850	Posters

ND

25-3416	Painting
1290-1460	Special subjects
	Including human figure, landscapes, animals, still life, flowers
1700-2495	Watercolor painting
2550-2888	Mural painting
2890-3416	Illuminating of manuscripts and books

NE
1-3002	Print media
1-978	Printmaking and engraving
1000-1352	Wood engraving. Woodcuts. Xylography. Block printing
1400-1879	Metal engraving. Copper, steel, etc. Including color prints
1940-2232.5	Etching and aquatint
2236-2239.7	Serigraphy
2250-2570	Lithography
2800-2890	Printing of engravings

NK
1-9955	Decorative arts. Applied arts. Decoration and ornament Including antiques in general
1135-1149.5	Arts and crafts movement
1700-3505	Interior decoration. House decoration
3600-9955	Other arts and art industries
3700-4695	Ceramics. Pottery. Porcelain
4700-4890	Costume and its accessories
4997-6060	Enamel. Glass. Glyptic arts Including gems, jade, ivory, bone
6400-8459	Metalwork Including armor, jewelry, plate, brasses, pewter
8800-9505.5	Textile arts and art needlework
9600-9955	Woodwork Including carvings, fretwork, inlaying

NX
1-820	Arts in general Including works dealing with two or more of the fine arts media, i. e. literature, performing arts, and the visual arts. For works on any one of these subjects, *see* the subject, e.g., GV, M, N, P, TR
654-694	Religious arts
700-750	Patronage of the arts
798-820	Special arts centers

Class N—Fine Arts was prepared under the direction and supervision of Charles Martel. The first edition was published in 1910, a second edition in 1917, a third edition in 1922, and a thoroughly revised fourth edition in 1970. In 1996, a long-awaited new edition was published using the automated system.

This schedule was influenced by the fine arts sections of both the *Dewey Decimal Classification* and Cutter's *Expansive Classification*. In addition, the catalog of the Library of the Kunstgewerke-Museum of Berlin was used for special features; also, the Library of the Art Institute of Chicago recommended ideas derived from its modification of the *Dewey Decimal Classification*. The close relationship of this schedule to the other two classification schemes may be observed in its use of subclasses for different artistic forms or media: NA, Architecture; NB, Sculpture, NC, Graphic arts in general; ND, Painting; and NE, Engraving. Because of this division, the patterns in fine arts differ from those in literature and philosophy: not all works by and about an individual artist are classed in the same place.

Eight subclasses make up Class N: subclass N for the visual arts in general; NA for architecture; NB for sculpture; NC for drawing, design, and illustration; ND for painting, including illuminated manuscripts and books; NE for print media, including printmaking and engraving; NK for the decorative arts, the applied arts, decoration and ornament; and NX, a subclass added in the fourth edition, for arts in general, including works dealing with two or more fine arts media, that is, literature, performing arts (dance, motion pictures, music, opera, theater), and the visual arts.

In the 1996 edition, the use of the schedule was simplified by enumerating many areas that were previously covered by "Divided like" notes.

Order of Precedence

Art materials, particularly reproductions of works of art that can be classed in several numbers manifesting different aspects treated in the works, are classified according to the following order of preference:

1. Individual artists under the country number

2. Genre by nationality or period (e.g., Italian sculpture; Medieval caricature)

3. Genre (General) (e.g., Sculpture)

4. Special topics (e.g., Roses in art)

Examples:

1. A collection of the paintings of one artist all on the theme of roses is classed with the individual artist.

2. A collection of paintings by Italian artists using roses as a theme is classed with Italian painting.

A work on horses in Degas's works is classed with the number for the artist instead of the number for horses in art.

> Boggs, Jean Sutherland. *Degas at the races.* c1998

N	Subclass: Visual arts
6853	The number for French artists
.D33	The first Cutter number for the artist, Degas
A4	The Cutter number (from Table N6) for reproductions and exhibition catalogs
1998b	The date of publication

A work on the portrayal of Buddha in Indic sculpture is classed with the number for sculpture from India instead of with the topic.

> Klimburg-Salter, Deborah E. *Buddha in Indien : die frühindische Skulptur von König Ásoka bis zur Guptazeit.* 1995

NB	Subclass: Sculpture
1002	The number (802 in Table N5 added to the base number NB200) meaning Indic art before 1800
.K57	The first Cutter number for the author, Klimburg-Salter
1995	The date of publication

However, there are exceptions to the order of preference given above. If written directions in various locations of the N schedule contradict the established order, the written directions should be observed. For example, under NC101-377, Drawing, design, illustration in special countries, a note states: "Prefer classification by subject except for special artists." In other words, in classifying drawing, design, and illustration in special countries, individual artists take precedence over subject, which, in turn, is preferred to genre.

Tables

Fourteen auxiliary tables, numbered N1-N14, are found at the end of the schedule. Tables N1-N5 are relatively simple tables of geographic subdivisions. Tables N6-N7, discussed under the section "Artists" below, are used to subarrange works by and about individual artists. Table N8 lists English counties with their Cutter numbers. Tables N9-N14 were previously internal tables; they have now been converted to auxiliary tables placed at the end of the schedule.

The following example illustrates the use of Table N2:

20th century American ceramics price guide.   c1996

NK	Subclass: Decorative arts
4008	The number (08 in Table N2 added to base number NK4000) meaning 20th-century ceramics in the United States
.A13	The Cutter number for the main entry under the title, *20th*. . . [For Cutter numbers for numerals, see chapter 3]
1996	The date of publication

Table N5, a table of geographic subdivisions, contains 1000 numbers with special added elements such as collective and individual biography of artists. For example, this table is called for at the range of numbers for Modern art, N6501-7414:

N	VISUAL ARTS
	History
6501-7414	Special countries (Table N5 modified)

(The numbers in the table that have been modified for a particular range of numbers are enumerated under the pertinent range of numbers in the schedule.)

The example below shows a book on art in the United States, classed in N6505. The number 05 from Table N5, meaning the geographic area of the United States, when fitted into the range of numbers N6501-7414, results in the number N6505. A simple way of arriving at the number is to add the table number, 05 in this case, to the base number, N6500.

Hughes, Robert.   *American visions : the epic history of art in America.* 1997

N	Subclass: Visual arts
6505	The number (05 in Table N5 added to the base number 6500) for a general work on art in the United States
.H84	The Cutter number for the main entry, Hughes
1997	The date of publication

A work on art in an individual state in the United States makes use of the number 30 in Table N5. A work about art in Hawaii is therefore classed in N6530.H3.

Artists/Hawaii. 1996

N	Subclass: Visual arts
6530	The number (30 in Table N5 added to the base number 6500) for a work on art in one of the states in the United States
.H3	The first Cutter number for Hawaii
A76	The second Cutter number for the main entry under the title, *Artists . . .*
1996	The date of publication

Similarly, the number 35 in Table N5 is designated for art in individual cities in the United States. A work about art in Savannah, Georgia, is therefore classed in N6535.S34.

King, Pamela D. *Looking back : art in Savannah, 1900-1960.* 1996

N	Subclass: Visual arts
6535	The number (35 in Table N5 added to the base number 6500) for a work on art in the cities of the United States
.S34	The first Cutter number for Savannah
K56	The second Cutter number for the main entry, King
1996	The date of publication

The following example illustrates the use of the number 261 from Table N5, meaning a general work on British art:

Graham-Dixon, Andrew. *A history of British art.* 1996

N	Subclass: Visual arts
6761	The number (261 in Table N5 added to base number 6500) meaning a general work on British art
.G73	The Cutter number for the main entry, Graham-Dixon
1996	The date of publication

Works on British art in specific periods are classed in the following manner:

Ayres, James. *Two hundred years of English naive art, 1700-1900.* 1996

N	Subclass: Visual arts
6766	The number (266 in Table N5 added to base number 6500) meaning a work on 17th-18th century British art

| .A97 | The Cutter number for the main entry, Ayres |
| 1996 | The date of publication |

Begde, Prabhakar V. *Living sculpture : classical Indian culture as depicted in sculpture and literature.* 1996

NB	Subclass: Sculpture
1002	The number (802 in Table N5 added to base number 200) meaning Indic art before 1800
.B426	The Cutter number for the main entry, Begde
1996	The date of publication

The city of Rome is listed in Table N5 as 420. Therefore, a work on art in Rome is classed in N6920, a result of adding 420 to the base number N6500.

Partridge, Loren W. *The art of Renaissance Rome, 1400-1600.* 1996

N	Subclass: Visual arts
6920	The number (420 in Table N5 added to the base number 6500) meaning art in the city of Rome
.P28	The Cutter number for the main entry, Partridge
1996	The date of publication

Internal Tables

Many internal tables appear within the schedule, including some which use a prescribed range of successive numbers. The schedule provision for the architecture of government buildings, NA4410-4510, includes such a table.

NA	ARCHITECTURE
	Special classes of buildings
	Classed by use
	Public buildings
	National, state, municipal, etc. Government buildings
	Capitols. Parliament buildings
4410	General works
4411	United States
4412.A-W	States, A-W
4413.A-Z	Cities, A-Z

4415.A-Z	Other countries, A-Z

Under each country:

.x	General
.x2A-.x2Z	Local, A-Z

★ ★ ★ ★ ★ ★ ★

4420-4427	Government office and bureaus. Prefectures, etc.

★ ★ ★ ★ ★ ★ ★

	City halls. Townhalls
4430	General works
	Official residences. Embassies
4440	General works
4441	United States
4442.A-W	States, A-W
4443.A-Z	Cities, A-Z
4445.A-Z	Other countries, A-Z
	Apply table at NA4415.A-Z

For example, a work on the architecture of the German embassy in Washington, D.C., is classed in NA4443.W3:

Ungers, O. M.   *Deutsche Botschaft Washington : Neubau der Residenz = German Embassy Washington : the new residence.*   1995

NA	Subclass: Architecture
4443	Architecture of official residences and embassies in U.S. cities
.W3	The first Cutter number for the city, Washington, D.C.
U54	The second Cutter number for the main entry, Ungers
1995	The date of publication

Hnatyshyn, Gerda.   *Rideau Hall : Canada's living heritage.*   1994

NA	Subclass: Architecture
4445	Architecture of official residences and embassies in countries other than the U.S.
.C22	The first Cutter number, C2, for Canada and the successive element 2 (indicated by .x2 in the internal table under NA4415) for local subdivision, A-Z
O865	The second Cutter number for Ottawa, Ontario
1994	The date of publication

Artists

Works by and about an individual artist[25] are classed in the class of persons representing the medium in which the artist is best known. Tables N6 and N7 are used for subarranging works by and about individual artists. These tables are often used in conjunction with Tables N1-N5. The free-floating Translation Table may also be used with both artists tables. It may be applied to the numbers ".xA8-.xZ" in Table N6 and to the numbers x3-39 in Table N7. It is not used, however, with those Cutter numbers that carry instructions to subarrange by date, that is, ".xA2" to ".xA6-79" in Table N6, and x to x2 in Table N7.

Table N6 is used for numbers with the caption "Special artists, A-Z," with the first Cutter number designating the artist, and the second Cutter number selected according to Table N6, which is reproduced below.

N6	TABLE OF CUTTERS FOR ARTISTS (FIRST CUTTER)
.xA2	Autobiography. By date
.xA3	Letters. By date
.xA35	Speeches, essays, interviews, etc. of the artist. By date
.xA4	Reproductions (Collections). By date Including exhibition catalogs *[even if main entry is not the artist]*
.xA6-.xA79	Individual works of art. Alphabetically by title of work of art and date
.xA8-.xZ	Biography and criticism

The following examples illustrate the use of Table N6:

McGough, Stephen C.   *Thiebaud selects Thiebaud : a forty-year survey from private collections.*   1996

N	Subclass: Visual arts
6537	The number (37 in Table N5 added to the base number N6500) for individual artists in the United States
.T472	The first Cutter number for the artist, Thiebaud
A4	The second Cutter number (from Table N6) for reproductions and exhibition catalogs
1996	The date of publication

Picasso, Pablo. *Picasso and drawing : April 28-June 2, 1995.* c1995

NC	Subclass: Drawing, Design, Illustration
248	The number (148 in Table N3 added to the base number NC100) meaning special artists in France
.P5	The first Cutter number for the artist, Picasso
.A4	The second Cutter number (from Table N6) for reproductions and exhibition catalogs
1995	The date of publication

Picasso, Pablo. *Picasso : suite Vollard.* 1996

NE	Subclass: Print media
2049	The number (49 in Table N1 added to the base number NE2000) meaning History and collections in France
.5	Special artists, A-Z
.P5	The first Cutter number for the artist, Picasso
.A76	The second Cutter number (from Table N6) for an individual work of art: *Suite Vollard*
1996	The date of publication

Krauss, Rosalind E. *The Picasso papers.* 1998

N	Subclass: Visual arts
6853	Special artists in France
.P5	The first Cutter number for the artist, Picasso
.K73	The second Cutter number (from Table N6) for a work of criticism, based on the main entry, Krauss
1998	The date of publication

None of the tables in Class N should present any major difficulties, as there are many extensive directions and notes in the schedule. More frequently, problems with Class N center on basic classification: a work may appear to fit into more than one category within Class N, or a work may be classed in either Class N or another class, such as T, Technology. For instance, material on aesthetics may be classed in subclass N or NX, or it may be classed in subclass BH if the work deals with the theory and philosophy of aesthetics and the arts in general. Works on photoengraving may be classed in subclass NE, Engraving, or in subclass TR, Photography. A work on alphabets may be classed in NK3600 or P211, depending on its approach; both numbers are valid locations for material on alphabets—one from an artistic viewpoint and the other from a philological one. When the question arises of whether or not a work should be classed in N, it is helpful to compare the work with similar books already cataloged, whether in N or elsewhere. Such a comparison will provide guidance to the best placement choice and will maintain consistency within established practice. The improved index in the new edition provides guidance in solving many placement problems.

The index to the 1996 edition was greatly expanded; it now includes entries for individual artists and for many corporate bodies and buildings.

CLASS P—LANGUAGE AND LITERATURE

P	
1-1091	Philology. Linguistics
1-85	General
87-96	Communication. Mass media
94.7	Interpersonal communication
95-95.6	Oral communication. Speech
98-98.5	Computational linguistics. Natural language processing
99-99.4	Semiotics
99.5-99.6	Nonverbal communication
101-410	Language. Linguistic theory. Comparative grammar
118-118.7	Language acquisition
121-149	Science of language (Linguistics)
201-299	Comparative grammar
301-301.5	Style. Composition. Rhetoric
302-302.87	Discourse analysis
306-310	Translating and interpreting
321-324.5	Etymology
325-325.5	Semantics
326-326.5	Lexicology
327-327.5	Lexicography
375-381	Linguistic geography
501-769	Indo-European (Indo-Germanic) philology
901-1091	Extinct ancient or medieval languages
PA	
1-199	Classical philology
(201)-(899)	Greek philology and language
1000-(1179)	Medieval and modern Greek language
2001-2915	Latin philology and language
(3000)-(3049)	Classical literature
(3050)-4505	Greek literature
(3051)-3285	Literary history
3300-3516	Collections
3520-3564	Criticism, interpretation, etc.
3601-3681	Translations
3818-4505	Individual authors
3825-3849	Aeschylus
3851-3858	Aesophus
3890-3926	Aristoleles
3949-3964	Demosthenes
3973-3992	Euripedes
4018-4209	Homerus

Class P continues on page 346.

4279-4333	Plato
4367-4389	Plutarchus
4413-4434	Sophocles
4452-4486	Thucydides
4494-4499	Xenophon
5000-5660	Byzantine and modern Greek literature
5301-5637	Individual authors
(6000)-6971	Roman literature
6001-(6097)	Literary history
(6100)-6140	Collections
6141-6144	Criticism, interpretation, etc.
6155-6191	Translations
6202-6971	Individual authors
6235-6269	Caesar, C. Julius
6278-6370	Cicero
6393-6444	Horatius
6482-6496	Lucretius
6501-6510	Martialis
6519-6553	Ovidius Naso
6568-6609	Plautus
6611-6637	Plinius
6661-6693	Seneca, Lucius Annaeus
6705-6753	Tacitus
6755-6785	Terentius
6801-6961	Virgilius
8001-8595	Medieval and modern Latin literature
8200-8595	Individual authors

	Modern European languages
PB	
1-431	General works
	Celtic languages and literatures
1201-1449	Irish
1501-1709	Gaelic. Scottish Gaelic
1801-1867	Manx
1950	Pict
2001-3029	Brythonic group
	Including Welsh, Cornish, Breton, Gallic

PC	
1-5498	Romance languages
601-872	Romanian language and literature
1001-1977	Italian
2001-3761	French. Provencal
3801-3976	Catalan language and literature
4001-4977	Spanish
5001-5498	Portuguese

PD
	Germanic languages
1001-1350	Old Germanic dialects
	Including Gothic, Vandal, Burgundian, Langobardian
1501-5929	Scandinavian. North Germanic
2201-2392	Old Norse. Old Icelandic and Norwegian
2401-2489	Icelandic
2571-2999	Norwegian
3001-3929	Danish
5001-5929	Swedish

PE
1-3729	English

PF
1-5999	West Germanic
1-979	Dutch
1001-1184	Flemish
1401-1541	Friesian language and literature
3001-5999	German

PG
	Slavic. Baltic, Albanian languages and literature
1-7925	Slavic
615-716	Church Slavic
801-1199	Bulgarian. Macedonian
1201-1696	Serbo-Croatian
1801-1962	Slovenian
2001-3987	Russian. White Russian. Ukrainian
4001-5546	Czech. Slovak
5631-7446	Polish. Sorbian
8001-9146	Baltic
8501-8772	Lithuanian
8801-9146	Latvian
9501-9665	Albanian

PH
1-5490	Finno-Ugrian, Basque languages and literatures
101-1109	Finnish
101-405	Finnish (Proper)
601-671	Estonian
701-735	Lapp
801-836	Mari

Class P continues on page 348.

1201-3445	Ugrian. Hungarian
5001-5490	Basque

Oriental languages and literatures

PJ

1-995	General works
1001-2199	Egyptian. Coptic
2353-2367	Libyan group
2369-2399	Berber
2401-2594	Cushitic

PJ

3001-9293	Semitic
3101-4083	Assyrian. Sumerian
4501-5192	Hebrew
5201-5329	Aramaic
5403-5909	Syriac
6001-8517	Arabic
8991-9293	Ethiopian

PK

1-6996	Indo-Iranian
	Including Vedic, Sanskrit, Pali,
	Assamese, Bengali, Hindi, Urdu,
	Hindustani, Sinhalese, Persian
8001-8835	Armenian
9001-9201	Caucasian. Georgian

PL

1-8844	Languages and literatures of Eastern Asia,
	Africa, Oceania
1-481	Ural-Altaic languages
501-889	Japanese language and literature
901-998	Korean language and literature
1001-3207	Chinese language and literature
5001-7511	Oceanic languages and literatures
8000-8844	African languages and literatures

PM

	Hyperborean, Indian, and Artificial languages
1-95	Hyperborean languages of America
101-7356	American Indian languages
8001-9021	Artificial languages

PN

1-6790	Literature (General)
1-9	Periodicals
20-30	Societies

45-57	Theory. Philosophy. Esthetics
59-72	Study and teaching
80-99	Criticism
101-245	Authorship
172-239	Technique. Literary composition, etc.
241-241.5	Translating as a literary pursuit
441-1009.5	Literary history
451-497	Biography
500-519	Collections
597-605	Special relations, movements, and currents of literature
610-779	By period
611-649	Ancient
661-694	Medieval (to 1500)
683-687	Legends
688-691	Poetry
692-693	Prose. Prose fiction
695-779	Modern
715-749	Renaissance (1500-1700)
801-820	Romance literature
821-840	Germanic literature
841	Black literature (General)
842	Jewish literature in various languages
851-(884)	Comparative literature
(905)-1008	Folk literature
980-995	Fables
1008.2-1009.5	Juvenile literature
1010-1525	Poetry
1031-1049	Theory, philosophy, relations, etc.
1065-1085	Relations to, and treatment of, special subjects
1110-1279	History and criticism
1301-1333	Epic poetry
1341-1347	Folk poetry
1351-1389	Lyric poetry
1530	The monologue
1551	The dialogue
1560-1590	The performing arts. Show business
1585-1589	Centers for the performing arts
1600-3307	Drama
1635-1650	Relation to, and treatment of, special subjects
1660-1693	Technique of dramatic composition
1720-1861	History
1865-1988	Special types
1990-1992.92	Broadcasting
1991-1991.9	Radio broadcasts
1992-1992.92	Television broadcasts

Class P continues on page 350.

1992.93-19 92.95	Nonbroadcast video recordings
1993-1999	Motion pictures
1997-1997.85	Plays, scenarios, etc.
2000-3307	Dramatic representation. The theater
2061-2071	Art of acting
2085-2091	The stage and accessories
2131-2193	By period
2131-2145	Ancient
2152-2160	Medieval
2171-2179	Renaissance
2181-2193	Modern
2219.3-3030	Special regions or countries
3035	The Jewish theater
3151-3171	Amateur theater
3175-3191	College and school theatricals
3203-3299	Tableaux, pageants, "Happenings," etc.
3311-3503	Prose. Prose fiction
3329-3352	Philosophy, theory, etc.
3355-3383	Technique. Authorship
3427-3448	Special kinds of fiction. Fiction genres
3451-3503	History
4001-4355	Oratory. Elocution, etc.
4071-4095	Study and teaching
4177-4191	Debating
4199-4321	Recitations (in English)
4331-4355	Recitations in foreign languages
4390	Diaries
4400	Letters (Literary history)
4500	Essays (Literary history)
4699-5650	Journalism. The periodical press, etc.
4735-4748	Relation to the state. Government and the press. Liberty of the press
4775-4784	Technique. Practical journalism
4825-4830	Amateur journalism
4832-4836	Magazines and other periodicals
4840-5648	By region or country
5650	The Jewish press
6010-6790	Collections of general literature
6066-6069	Special classes of authors
6080-6095	Quotations
6081-6084	English
6086-6089	French
6090-6093	German
6099-6110	Poetry
6110.5-6120	Drama
6120.15-6120.95	Fiction
6121-6129	Orations
6130-6140	Letters

6141-6145	Essays
6146.5-6231	Wit and humor
6157-6222	By region or country
6233-6238	Anacreontic literature
6244-6246	Literary extracts. Commonplace books
6249-6258	Ana
6259-6268	Anecdotes. Table talk
6269-6278	Aphorisms. Apothegms
6279-6288	Epigrams
6288.5-6298	Epitaphs
6299-6308	Maxims
6309-6318	Mottoes
6319-6328	Sayings, bon mots, etc.
6329-6338	Thoughts
6340-6348	Toasts
6348.5-6358	Emblems, devices
6361	Paradoxes
6366-6377	Riddles, acrostics, charades, conundrums, etc.
6400-6525	Proverbs
6700-6790	Comic books, strips, etc.

PQ

	Romance literatures
1-3999	French literature
4001-5999	Italian literature
6001-8929	Spanish literature
9000-9999	Portuguese literature

PR

1-9680	English literature

PS

1-3576	American literature

PT

	Germanic literatures
1-4897	German literature
5001-5980	Dutch literature
6000-6471	Flemish literature
6500-6592.36	Afrikaans literature
	Scandinavian literature
7001-7099	General works
7101-7338	Old Norse. Old Icelandic
7351-7550	Modern Icelandic literature
7601-8260	Danish literature

Class P continues on page 352.

8301-9155	Norwegian literature
9201-9999	Swedish literature

PZ
5-90   Juvenile belles lettres
                       Works classed here are in English and in
                       foreign languages

Class P—Language and Literature took nearly forty years to construct. Much of the work was done by Walter F. Koenig, who began it in 1909. It was completed in 1948 with the publication of subclass PG (in part), *Russian literature*. Class P is made up of thirteen different schedules and tables as shown below, with dates of first publication and most recent edition enclosed in parentheses:

P-PA, *Philology and Linguistics (General), Greek Language and Literature, Latin Language and Literature*   (1928; 1997)

PA Supplement: *Byzantine and Modern Greek Literature.   Medieval and Modern Latin Literature (1942; 1968)*

PB-PH, *Modern European Languages (1933; 1966)*

PG, *Russian Literature (1948; 1965)*

PJ-PK, *Oriental Philology and Literature, Indo-Iranian Philology and Literature (1933; 1988)*

PL-PM, *Languages of Eastern Asia, Africa, Oceania; Hyperborean, Indian, and Artificial Languages (1933; 1988)*

P-PM, *Supplement: Index to Languages and Dialects (1936; 1991)*

PN, *Literature (General) (1997)*

PR, PS, PZ, *English and American Literature, Juvenile Belles Lettres* (1915; 1988; 1998)

PQ, *French, Italian, Spanish, and Portuguese Literatures* (part 1, 1936, part 2, 1937; combined 1998)

PT, part 1, *German Literature (1938; 1989)*

PT, part 2, *Dutch and Scandinavian Literatures (1941; 1992)*

P-PZ Tables, *Language and Literature Tables (1998)*

Classification of Literature

Before examining the individual schedules of Class P, it is important to consider two related but different factors: how the LC Classification handles languages and literatures, and how the Library of Congress classifies literature under the schedules' provisions. One thing to note is that classification of literature differs from classification in other subjects in that languages and forms take precedence over topic. Furthermore, literatures written in major languages are represented by subclasses.

Pattern of Subarrangement

For each individual literature, such as American literature and French literature, a recurring plan or pattern for subarrangement of materials is used:

1. History and criticism

2. Collections or anthologies of more than one author

3. Individual authors

4. Non-national (local) literature, including collections and criticism (may precede individual authors in some cases)

Literary Collections

In general, a work is classed as a collection if it consists of two or more independent literary works by different authors not written specifically for the publication in hand, regardless of whether the publication has a collective title.[26] The determining factor in the classification of such collections is the treatment given the publication in accordance with *AACR2R*. A Cutter number based on the main entry is assigned.

Publications with Collective Titles. These are classed as a collection, in spite of the fact that author-title added entries may have been made for individual works. Such works are cuttered under the title.

Publications Without Collective Titles. The Cutter number is taken from the main entry heading. However, if the work named first on the title page is the essential or most important aspect of the publication, with the remaining works being only supplementary in nature, the collection is classed as an individual work in the literary author number for the first-named work.

Individual Authors

The third element in the pattern of subarrangement given above, individual authors, is an important characteristic of the LC Classification. Works written in a particular language by a literary author and works about the author are arranged in a single group regardless of literary form; in other words, although subdivision by literary form is common in other classification systems, the LC Classification does not use form divisions under individual authors. The one exception is Elizabethan drama in subclass PR, English literature, which is treated as a separate form.

Individual authors are grouped by period under each national literature. Under each period, they have been assigned individual numbers in an alphabetical sequence. Authors prior to the twentieth century are assigned ranges of numbers according to the amount of material by and about them. Major authors, such as William Shakespeare (PR2750-3112) and Johann Wolfgang von Goethe (PT1891-2239), have been assigned more than three hundred numbers each. Other important authors, such as Robert Browning and Friedrich von Schiller, receive up to forty-nine numbers each. Most of the authors receive one number or a Cutter number each.

All twentieth-century authors are assigned a Cutter number each, regardless of the amount of material, for example, PS3511.A86 for William Faulkner, a twentieth-century American author. The Cutter number for the author is based on the second letter of the author's last name. This is necessary because the class number is based on the first letter of the author's last name. In other words, PS3511 is used for twentieth-century American authors whose names begin with the letter "F."

Because many authors have written in more than one language or have been citizens of more than one country, the same author may be assigned numbers in different national literatures. The following statement issued by the Library of Congress explains the placement of literary authors:

> The principal factors to be considered in determining the location of individual literary author numbers in Class P are the language in which the author wrote, the author's nationality, and, if required, the time period during which the author was productive. The simplest situation encountered in establishing an author's number is the author who wrote in one language only and was a citizen of only one country. Authors living in the country most commonly associated with a particular language are classed with the general literature area for that language.

Authors of a country other than the one most commonly associated with the language in which they write may be classed by country in the area developed for that literature in other countries. Many literatures, however, have no geographic development, may be only partially expanded (such as literature of former colonies), or may have special locations for collections but not for individual authors. The literature of the United States is the exception to the standard arrangement of keeping the literature of a particular language together in the same subclass. No special section for United States literature exists in subclass PR, **English Literature**. Instead, subclass PS has been reserved for literature in English of the United States.[27]

Authors Writing in More Than One Language. If an author writes in more than one language, a number for the author is provided under the literature of each language; no effort is made to keep all the works of the author together. (For example, Vladimir Nabokov wrote works in both Russian and English; his Russian-language works are classed with Russian literature in PG3476.N3 and his English-language works are classed with American literature in PS3527.A15.)

Translations and critical studies of individual works in each case are classed with the original works. A collective criticism of several works is classed according to the general emphasis of the group of works studied, for example, a criticism of Nabokov's English works should be classed in his subclass PS number. General criticism, and all bibliographical works, however, are classed in one predetermined number that best represents the total literary output of the author, for example, for Nabokov, the Russian literature number is used.[28]

Authors Associated with More Than One Country. After determining with which particular language an author should be classed, the particular country of that literature under which the author's number should be established also may need to be determined. Under any particular literature representing a particular language, for example, German literature or French literature, an author is classed under one country only, and only one literature number is assigned for each language used by the author. The author is classed with the country of his or her citizenship, if the literature of his or her language provides for arrangement of individual authors by country, such as Britain and the United States. If the author was a citizen of several countries, the preferred classification is under the country in which the author's most productive years were spent or under the country usually associated with the author by scholars in the field. For example, Henry James and T. S. Eliot, both citizens of the United States and later

Britain, are classed in PS, American literature. If no preference can be determined, an arbitrary selection is made. Once a decision has been made to class a living author with a particular country, however, this number will usually continue to be used regardless of subsequent changes of residence by the author; an author is moved from one place to another in the schedule only when absolutely necessary, for example, in case of errors.

For living authors whose works are being cataloged for the first time and about whom there is little information (citizenship is not known), the selection of the country is based on available information, such as birthplace, parentage, residences, place of publication of the work(s) being cataloged. If this information does not justify the choice of one country over another, an arbitrary decision is made.[29]

Name Changes. Changes in personal names may occur as a result of individuals' own decisions or as a result of changes in cataloging rules. With each name change, the form of the heading is affected. In this circumstance, a decision must be made with regard to the Cutter number assigned to the author in question. With the implementation of *AACR2R*, many personal name headings have been changed. It is the policy of the Library of Congress to keep all works by a single author together regardless of heading changes under *AACR2R* by continuing to use the author numbers and Cutter numbers previously established.[30] For example, works by and about Mark Twain continue to be classed in PS1300-1348, based on his real name, Samuel Langhorne Clemens; and O. Henry continues to be classed in PS2649.P5, the number based on his real name, William Sydney Porter. These author numbers are printed in the P schedules, with *see* references from *AACR2R* forms of the names. For authors whose numbers are being established for the first time, author numbers are based on the *AACR2R* forms of headings.

Subarrangement of Works by and About Individual Authors. Regardless of the range of numbers assigned to an author, works written by and about the author are generally subarranged according to a recurring pattern:

1. Collected works, collected fiction, collected essays, etc.

2. Translations (collective)

3. Selected works.   Selections.   By date

4. Separate works, alphabetically by title

5. Biography and criticism

When both *Selected works* and *Selections* are provided under an author, *Selected works* refer to collections of two or more complete works of an author, but not the author's entire literary output. *Selections* refer to collections of isolated excerpts, quotations, etc., from different works of the author. *Separate works* include individual titles as well as collections consisting of works such as poems, stories, etc., that are published for the first time while the author is still living.[31] In some cases, the second and third items in the list above appear in reverse order.

Exhibitions on Individual Literary Authors. Previously, exhibitions focusing on individual literary authors and their writings were classed in Z under "Personal bibliography." Now they are classed under the individual author numbers in the P schedules.

Language and Literature Tables

Previously, numerous author tables based on ranges of numbers assigned to the authors were included in individual schedules for subarrangement of works written by and about an author according to the pattern above. Special tables were also included for individual works that have appeared in numerous texts and translations, and for works about those works. In 1982, the tables in individual schedules in Class P were consolidated and published in a single volume entitled *Language and Literature Tables*, which supersedes the tables in all P schedules. A new edition was published in 1998, in which the numbering system was again changed, from Table I–Table XLIV to Table P-PZ1–Table P-PZ44, with the addition of a new Table P-PZ50.

As a result of consolidating and renumbering language and literature tables, the references to tables in many of the older P schedules do not agree with the revised numbering. Before using them, therefore, the classifier must be careful to convert the schedule references to tables to the correct table numbers. Examples of using the author tables and tables for individual works appear in chapter 4, and further examples appear later in this chapter.

In most cases, there are special provisions in the author tables for biographies of an author and for translations of his or her works. These specific provisions or instructions take precedence over the floating tables for translations and biography. The general pattern is to class a translation of a work with the original work.

Subclasses P-PA

The schedule for subclasses P-PA, *Philology, Linguistics, Classical Philology, Classical Literature*, was prepared by Walter F. Koenig. The first edition was published in 1928. It was reissued in 1968 with supplementary pages. A new edition, under the title, *Philology and Linguistics (General), Greek Language and Literature, Latin Language and Literature*, was published in 1997.

The first edition of this schedule contained a detailed introduction to the schedule, giving directions for its use with many bibliographical references, an appendix that included a list of subjects in other classes that were related to classical philology, auxiliary tables with complete explanations and examples, a list of authorities used in the preparation of the schedule, and an extensive list of classical authors. These features are omitted in the 1997 edition.

The index does not include the names of individual authors.

Topical Greek and Roman Classics

Original texts of topical Greek and Roman classics[32] are, in general, classed in subclass PA, as are translations into all languages except English. English translations are classed with the appropriate discipline in Classes B through Z.

An exception is made for works in the field of philosophy. Translations, including those accompanied by the original text, are classed in Class B, unless they contain textual criticism or are translations into Latin, both of which are classed in subclass PA.

The following examples of Aristotle's works demonstrate the classification of topical Greek and Roman classics:

> Aristotle
> *Aristoteles Athenaion politeia.* 1986
> PA3893 .P6 1986
>
> *Aristotelis Ethica Eudemia.* 1991
> PA3893 .E7 1991
>
> *Politics.* c1998
> JC71.A41 R4413 1998
>
> *Poetics.* 1997
> PN1040 .A513 1997
>
> *Physics.* 1996
> Q151 .A72 1996

Subclasses PB-PH

The schedule for subclasses PB-PH, *Modern European Languages*, was first published in 1933. Walter F. Koenig, under the supervision of Charles Martel, was chiefly responsible for its preparation. Subclasses PB-PH cover the following European language groups:

PB: Modern European languages (General). Celtic languages and literatures

PC: Romance languages

PD: German languages (General). Scandinavian languages

PE: English language

PF: West Germanic languages, including Dutch, Flemish, Friesian, and German

PG: Slavic languages, and Baltic and Albanian languages and literatures

PH: Finno-Ugrian and Basque languages and literatures

Although the predominant pattern throughout the P schedules is for literature to be classed apart from treatment of the language as such, some of the provisions in the PB-PH schedule include literature in the language as well as material on the language. Among these are Celtic; Romanian; Catalan; Friesian; the Slavic, Baltic, and Albanian languages; and the Finno-Ugric (including Hungarian) and Basque languages.

The thirty-one auxiliary tables in the original PB-PH schedule have been replaced by the consolidated tables in the separate volume, *P-PZ, Language and Literature Tables*.

There is no index in the current edition of this schedule. However, an index to the languages and dialects covered in subclasses P-PM has been published separately under the title, *P-PM Supplement: Index to Languages and Dialects* (4th edition, 1991), which provides some index access to the various PB-PH subclasses.

Subclass PG

The schedule for subclass PG, *Russian Literature*, developed by L. Belle Voegelein, was first published in 1948. In 1965, it was reissued with supplementary pages. This subclass was first begun by Clarence Perley in the 1930s to serve as a system for classing translations of Russian literature. Perley's prefatory note to the schedule states:

This discontinuance of the Slavic Division and incorporation of the Library's Russian collections, of which the Yudin Collection was the nucleus, into the general collections made it necessary to develop a scheme to cover Russian literature in the original as well as in translation.

The Yudin Collection had in part been classified according to a scheme devised by Alexis V. Babine, which could not be applied to the combined collection, since it took no account of translations and did not follow the notation used in other sections of the Library of Congress classification.

There is neither an individual index nor a detailed outline to this schedule. Its lists of Russian names are transcribed in accordance with the LC system of transliteration and contain full names and dates and many syndetic devices. The auxiliary tables in the original issue of the schedule have been replaced by the consolidated tables in *P-PZ, Language and Literature Tables*. The separately published *P-PM Supplement: Index to Languages and Dialects* gives some index access.

Subclasses *PJ-PK, PL-PM*

The schedule for subclasses PJ-PM, *Languages and Literatures of Asia, Africa, Oceania, America, Mixed Languages, Artificial Languages*, was first published in 1933, the work of Walter F. Koenig. Because of the considerable expansion of the schedule since the first edition, particularly in Chinese and Japanese literatures, the second edition, published in 1988, was divided into two schedules: PJ-PK, *Oriental Philology and Literature, Indo-Iranian Philology and Literature*; and PL-PM, *Languages of Eastern Asia, Africa, Oceania; Hyperborean, Indian, and Artificial Languages*. As in the case of other schedules in Class P, the auxiliary tables appearing in the first edition of PJ-PM have been replaced by the consolidated tables in *P-PZ, Language and Literature Tables*.

These schedules do not contain indexes.

Subclass *PN*

Subclass PN, *Literature (General)*, was originally published with subclasses PR, PS, and PZ in one schedule (see discussion below). In 1997, a new edition, produced from the automated system, was published separately.

Subclass PN contains the following topics:

PN	1-1551	Literature (General)
	1560-3307	Performing arts. Drama. Motion pictures. The theater
	3311-4500	Prose. Oratory
	4699-5650	Journalism
	6010-6790	Collections of general literature

The interspersion of performing arts, motion pictures, the theater, and journalism amidst literary topics may appear somewhat unusual. The reason is probably historical rather than logical. Performing arts, motion pictures, and the theater were placed here apparently because of their affinity to drama; and journalism was placed near prose and oratory because of its relationship to writing.

Subclasses PR, PS, PZ

The schedule for subclasses PN, PR, PS, PZ, formerly entitled *Literature (General), English and American Literature, Fiction in English, Juvenile Belles Lettres*, was the first of the Class P schedules issued; it appeared in 1915. Originally, subclass PZ also included fiction in English and topical juvenile works. Current LC policy is to classify fiction in English in the appropriate subclasses of literature and topical juvenile works in the appropriate subject classes.

The first edition was reissued with supplementary pages in 1964; the second edition was published in 1978, and the third in 1988. The 1998 edition, produced from the automated system, was published in 1999. With the separate publication of subclass PN, the 1998 edition appeared under the title *PR, PS, PZ English and American Literature and Juvenile Belles Lettres*.

Two features of the first edition—personal names in the index, and author Cutter numbers—were removed from subsequent editions. Exceptions were made for Geoffrey Chaucer and William Shakespeare. The personal name entries were deleted from the index because it was felt that listing such names would amount to a replication of the schedule. The author Cutter numbers that were listed in the 1964 reissue of the first edition did not appear in later editions because those Cutter numbers had never been incorporated into the official schedules in LC's Subject Cataloging Division, and it was from those schedules that the second edition was prepared.[33]

Subclass PZ

Subclass PZ was first developed in 1906. At that time PZ consisted of two numbers only—PZ1 and PZ3. PZ1 was used for collections of fiction in English; for example, anthologies or short stories. PZ3 was used for individual or separate works of individual authors. Later, PZ3 was qualified to include individual authors to 1950 and restricted to the period 1750-1950, and PZ4 was developed for individual authors after 1950.

Until July 1, 1980, the Library of Congress classed all works of fiction in English, including translations into English, in subclass PZ. The only exceptions were made for works assigned to the Rare Book Division, in which case they were classed with the regular literature subclasses. Even though many special class numbers exist under literary authors for individual novels in English, these numbers were used only for books assigned to the Rare Book Division and for discussions about their English translations. In 1980, the Library of Congress changed its policy with regard to the treatment of fiction in English.[34] Since then, American fiction has been classed in PS, English fiction in PR, and translations into English with the original national literatures.

Previously, juvenile non-fiction was also classed in PZ. This has also been changed. Now all juvenile non-fiction is classed with the topic in the appropriate subject classes, except in rare cases of amorphous children's works that do not lend themselves to subject classification.

Chapter 7 gives examples of classifying juvenile belles lettres.

Auxiliary Tables in PR, PS, PZ

The schedule for subclasses PR, PS, PZ contains many references to the tables found in the separately published *P-PZ, Language and Literature Tables*. Tables are used extensively with individual authors and their works. Only in a few cases are the subdivisions worked out within the schedules, for William Shakespeare and Geoffrey Chaucer, for instance.

For authors enumerated in the schedule, specific table references are given after their names, for example:

PR
3550-3598	Milton, John (Table P-PZ31)
5810-5828	Wilde, Oscar (Table P-PZ32)
6019.09	Joyce, James, 1882-1941 (Table P-PZ40)

Subclass PQ

Subclass PQ was originally published in two parts in separate schedules: subclass PQ, part 1, *French Literature* (1936), and subclass PQ, part 2, *Italian, Spanish, and Portuguese Literature* (1937). Koenig prepared the original scheme, and C. K. Jones developed many of the details in these schedules, particularly the Spanish and Portuguese names. The two schedules were combined in the new 1998 edition, with an index for the first time.

Subclass PT

Subclass PT appears in two separate schedules: subclass PT, part 1, *German literature* (1938) and subclass PT, part 2, *Dutch and Scandinavian literatures* (1941). Neither part 1 nor part 2 of PT has an index, although they each contain long outlines.

The auxiliary tables appearing in these schedules have been replaced by the consolidated tables in *P-PZ, Language and Literature Tables*.

Examples of Call Numbers in Languages and Literature

There are twenty tables designed for use with class numbers for various languages. The tables in the schedules have been replaced by those in the separately published *P-PZ, Language and Literature Tables*.

For literature, there are tables for the subdivision of various ranges of numbers assigned to collections and/or history and criticism. For works by and about individual authors, each author is assigned a range of numbers appropriate to the amount of material written by and about him or her. There are tables for authors assigned forty-nine numbers, nineteen numbers, nine numbers, five numbers, four numbers, two numbers, one number, or only a Cutter number. Separate works with one number or with successive Cutter numbers have separate tables, as do anonymous literary works.

When using schedules published before the consolidation of the tables, care must be taken to convert the table references appearing in the schedules to those corresponding to the renumbered tables in *P-PZ, Language and Literature Tables*. The correct table numbers are given in *LC Classification, Additions and Changes* and incorporated into later editions of each schedule.

Chapter 4 (pages 99-111) includes a discussion of author tables in general and gives specific examples illustrating the use of a number of literature tables (pages 104-111).

Further examples of classifying works in Class P are given below:

Homer. *L'odissea.* 1993

PA	Subclass: Greek literature
4024	Translations of Homer in modern languages
.C2	Catalan
A4	*Odyssea* (according to Table PA3)
1993	The date of publication

Sansweet, Stephen J.   *Tomart's price guide to worldwide Star wars collectibles.*   1997

PN	Subclass: Literature (General)
1995.9	Special topics in motion pictures
.S695	The first Cutter number for the special topic, *Star Wars* films
S25	The second Cutter number for the main entry, Sansweet
1997	The date of publication

Mercier, Arnaud.   *Le journal télévisé : politique de l'information et information politique.*   1996

PN	Subclass: Literature (General)
5184	The number (14 in internal table for 20 nos.) from the range PN5171-5190 assigned to Journalism in France, meaning special topics
.T4	The first Cutter number for the special topic, Television journalism
M47	The second Cutter number for the main entry, Mercier
1996	The date of publication

Samuel Taylor Coleridge is a nineteenth-century English author with a range of nineteen numbers, PR4470-4488. Coleridge's entry in the schedule includes the following elements:

PR	ENGLISH LITERATURE
4470-4488	Coleridge, Samuel Taylor (Table P-PZ32)
	For Coleridge as philosopher, *see* B1583
	Separate works
4476	Biographia literaria
4477	Biographia epistolaria
4478	Poems
4479	Rime of the ancient mariner
4480.A-Z	Other, A-Z

To use Coleridge's entire range of nineteen numbers, the appropriate auxiliary table must be identified. Following Coleridge's name in the schedule is "(Table P-PZ32)", a table for nineteen-number authors. The following examples illustrate the use of this table to classify works by and about Coleridge:

Coleridge, Samuel Taylor. *The Collected Works of Samuel Taylor Coleridge.* 1984-

PR	Subclass: English literature
4470	The number, being the first assigned to Coleridge, meaning collected works (according to Table P-PZ32) to be arranged by date, since no editor is given
.F84	The date letter representing the date of publication, 1984

According to Table P-PZ32, date letters are used for subarrangement of Collected works. Date letters consist of a letter that represents a particular century, followed by the last two digits of the year of publication, for example, D80 for 1780 and E84 for 1884. Perhaps the greatest advantage of this device is that it provides a figure that resembles a Cutter number in the book's call number. In the case of Coleridge's collected works shown above, the date of publication, 1984, is represented by the Cutter-like number .F84, and no further notation for the date of publication is needed.

According to Table P-PZ32, a work containing selections from Coleridge's works is classed in the third number, PR4472.

Coleridge, Samuel Taylor. *Selected poems.* 1994

PR	Subclass: English literature
4472	The number (2 in Table P-PZ32) in the range PR4470-4488, meaning selected works by Coleridge
1994	The date of publication

The number above is derived from the number 2 (Selected works.   Selections) in Table P-PZ32. The instruction given in Table P-PZ32 reads: "Subarranged by editor, if given, or date." Since no editor is given, only the date is added to the class number, resulting in a call number without a Cutter number.

Coleridge, Samuel Taylor. *Coleridge : selected poems* / [edited by] Richard Holmes.   1996

PR	Subclass: English literature
4472	The number (2 in Table P-PZ32) in the range PR4470-4488, meaning selected works by Coleridge
.H65	The Cutter number for the editor, Holmes
1996	The date of publication

Coleridge, Samuel Taylor. *Coleridge : poems and prose* / [selection by Peter Washington].   1997

PR	Subclass: English literature

4472	The number (2 in Table P-PZ32) in the range PR4470-4488, meaning selected works by Coleridge
.W37	The Cutter number for the editor, Washington
1997	The date of publication

Separate works by Coleridge are assigned the numbers PR4475-4480 (i.e., numbers 5-10 in Table P-PZ32). Under Coleridge's separate works both his major literary and his non-literary works are listed alphabetically. Four of his more important or famous works are given their own special numbers, which are listed in the schedules. An example is PR4479, *Rime of the ancient mariner*:

Coleridge, Samuel Taylor. *The rime of the ancient mariner : in seven parts.* 1994

PR	Subclass: English literature
4479	*Rime of the ancient mariner* by Coleridge
.A1	The Cutter number from Table P-PZ41 meaning Texts
1994	The date of publication

The lesser literary works together are assigned one number, PR4480, A-Z, with a unique Cutter number for each title. For further subdivisions of these numbers Table P-PZ41, Separate Works with One Number, and Table P-PZ43, Separate Works with Successive Cutter Numbers, are used.

A minor work by Coleridge entitled, *Kubla Khan* is classed in PR4480, the number for "Other" works by Coleridge, that is, works other than those assigned single numbers, with the Cutter number based on the individual title.

Coleridge, Samuel Taylor. *Kubla Khan : a pop-up version of Coleridge's classic.* 1994

PR	Subclass: English literature
4480	Other works by Coleridge
.K8	The Cutter number assigned to the individual work, *Kubla Khan*, being the first of three successive numbers (K8, K82, and K83) for the text
1994	The date of publication as required by the schedule

PR4483.A4 (corresponding to the number 13.A4 in Table P-PZ32) is the number for collections of letters of Coleridge. The following example illustrates the use of this number:

Coleridge, Samuel Taylor. *Four letters to Anna and Basil Montagu.*
1995

PR	Subclass: English literature
4483	Biography, criticism, etc., of Coleridge
.A4	The Cutter number (according to Table P-PZ32) meaning collections of letters
1995	The date of publication

PR4484 (corresponding to the number 14 in Table P-PZ32) is the number for general criticism about Coleridge.

Paley, Morton D. *Coleridge's later poetry.* 1996

PR	Subclass: English literature
4484	General criticism of Coleridge
.P33	The Cutter number for the main entry, Paley
1996	The date of publication

Criticism of specific aspects of Coleridge's works is classed in PR4487, according to Table P-PZ32, as illustrated in the following example:

Zuccato, Edoardo. *Coleridge in Italy.* 1996

PR	Subclass: English literature
4487	A critical work about Coleridge on an aspect other than sources
.I8	The first Cutter number for the special topic, Italy
Z83	The second Cutter number for the main entry, Zuccato
1996	The date of publication

Chapter 3 contains a discussion and demonstration of shelflisting different manifestations (editions, translations, etc.) of a particular work. For literary works, special tables are used. Chapter 4 (page 106) provides examples of using Table P-PZ43 in subclasses PR, PS, PZ for subarranging separate literary works with a Cutter number.

Twentieth-century authors are uniformly assigned a Cutter number each. Because the first Cutter number represents the author, the second Cutter number is used for various manifestations of the author's works, including separate works and their commentaries. The following examples show how these manifestations are accommodated according to Table P-PZ40 for authors with a Cutter number:

Ayala, Francisco. *En qué mundo vivimos.* 1996

PQ	Subclass: Spanish literature
6601	Individual authors, 1868-1960, whose names begin with the letter "A"
.Y3	The first Cutter number for the author, Ayala
E6	The second Cutter number (according to Table P-PZ40) for the separate work *En qué . . .*
1996	The date of publication

Antolín, Enriqueta. *Ayala sin olvidos.* 1993

PQ	Subclass: Spanish literature
6601	Individual authors, 1868-1960, whose names begin with the letter "A"
.Y3	The first Cutter number for the Spanish author, Ayala
Z54	The second Cutter number (chosen from the range Z5-999 in Table P-PZ40) for general works of criticism arranged alphabetically by main entry (in this case Antolín) by means of successive Cutter numbers
1993	The date of publication

The selection of the Cutter number Z54 for the title above is determined by the position of the critic's name, Antolín, in the alphabetical sequence, relative to works already existing in the shelflist. Similarly, a critical work on Ayala by Elisabeth Kollatz is classed in PQ6601.Y3 Z683 1995.

Further examples:

Arniches y Barrera, Carlos. *Obras completas.* 1995-

PQ	Subclass: Spanish literature
6601	20th-century authors whose names begin with the letter "A"
.R5	The Cutter number for the text of complete works by the author, Arniches y Barrera
1995	The date of publication

Arniches y Barrera, Carlos. *La señorita de Trevélez ; Que viene mi marido.* 1995

PQ	Subclass: Spanish literature
6601	20th-century authors whose names begin with the letter "A"
.R5	The first Cutter number for the author, Arniches y Barrera

S4   The second Cutter number (according to Table P-PZ40) for the separate work *Señorita . . .*

1995   The date of publication

Vonnegut, Kurt. *Timequake.* 1997

PS   Subclass: American literature

3572   Late 20th-century authors whose names begin with the letter "V"

.O5   The first Cutter number for Kurt Vonnegut based on the second and third letters of his last name

T56   The second Cutter number (for separate works according to Table P-PZ40) based on the title, *Timequake*

1997   The date of publication

Vonnegut, Kurt. *Fates worse than death : an autobiographical collage of the 1980s.* 1991

PS   Subclass: American literature

3572   Late 20th-century authors whose names begin with the letter "V"

.O5   The first Cutter number for Kurt Vonnegut based on the second and third letters of his last name

Z465   The second Cutter number (within the range of .xZ46-479 given in Table P-PZ40) for autobiography, based on the title, *Fates . . .*

1991   The date of publication

Klinkowitz, Jerome. *Vonnegut in fact : the public spokesmanship of personal fiction.* c1998

PS   Subclass: American literature

3572   Late 20th-century authors whose names begin with the letter "V"

.O5   The first Cutter number for Kurt Vonnegut based on the second and third letters of his last name

Z748   The second Cutter number (within the range of .xZ5-999 given in Table P-PZ40) for criticism, based on the main entry, Klinkowitz

1998   The date of publication

The Vonnegut chronicles : interviews and essays.   1996

PS	Subclass: American literature
3572	Late 20th-century authors whose names begin with the letter "V"
.O5	The first Cutter number for Kurt Vonnegut based on the second and third letters of his last name
Z895	The second Cutter number (within the range of .xZ5-999 given in Table P-PZ40) for criticism, based on the main entry under the title, *Vonnegut chronicles*
1996	The date of publication

Works about an individual work are classed with the work by means of successive Cutter numbers designated in the tables, for example:

Vonnegut, Kurt.   *Slaughterhouse-five, or, The children's crusade : a duty-dance with death.*   1994

PS	Subclass: American literature
3572	Late 20th-century authors whose names begin with the letter "V"
.O5	The first Cutter number for Kurt Vonnegut based on the second and third letters of his last name
S6	The second Cutter number for separate works (according to Table P-PZ40) based on the title, *Slaughterhouse-five*
1994	The date of publication

A work about *Slaughterhouse-five* is assigned the call number for the original work plus a successive element (3) for a criticism:

Wiswell, Tonnvane.   *Kurt Vonnegut, Jr.'s Slaughterhouse-five.*   1996

PS	Subclass: American literature
3572	Late 20th-century authors whose names begin with the letter "V"
.O5	The first Cutter number for Kurt Vonnegut based on the second and third letters of his last name
S639	The second Cutter number S6 for *Slaughterhouse-five* plus the successive elements (3 based on Table P-PZ42) for a criticism and (9) for the main entry, Wiswell
1996	The date of publication

In the example above, the successive element (9) is used because the author's name, Wiswell, begins with a letter coming late in the alphabet. In other words, works about *Slaughterhouse-five* are assigned a second Cutter number S63-S639.

As mentioned earlier, the index to this schedule does not include the names of individual authors.

Class Q begins on page 372.

CLASS Q—SCIENCE

Q	
1-390	Science (General)
1-295	General
300-390	Cybernetics
350-390	Information theory
QA	
1-939	Mathematics
1-43	General
47-59	Tables
71-90	Instruments and machines
75-76.95	Calculating machines
75.5-76.95	Electronic computers. Computer science
76.75-76.765	Computer software
101-(145)	Elementary mathematics. Arithmetic
150-272.5	Algebra
273-280	Probabilities. Mathematical statistics
299.6-433	Analysis
440-699	Geometry. Trigonometry. Topology
801-939	Analytic mechanics
QB	
1-991	Astronomy
1-139	General
140-237	Practical and spherical astronomy
275-343	Geodesy
349-421	Theoretical astronomy and celestial mechanics
455-456	Astrogeology
460-466	Astrophysics
468-480	Non-optical methods of astronomy
495-903	Descriptive astronomy
500.5-785	Solar system
799-903	Stars
980-991	Cosmogony. Cosmology
QC	
1-999	Physics
1-75	General
81-114	Weights and measures
120-168.85	Descriptive and experimental mechanics
170-197	Atomic physics. Constitution and properties of matter
	Including molecular physics, relativity, quantum theory, and solid state physics
221-246	Acoustics. Sound
251-338.5	Heat

310.15-319	Thermodynamics
350-467	Optics. Light
450-467	Spectroscopy
474-496.9	Radiation physics (General)
501-766	Electricity and magnetism
501-(721)	Electricity
669-675.8	Electromagnetic theory
676-678.6	Radio waves (Theory)
701-715.4	Electric discharge
717.6-718.8	Plasma physics. Ionized gases
750-766	Magnetism
770-798	Nuclear and particle physics. Atomic energy. Radioactivity
793-793.5	Elementary particle physics
794.95-798	Radioactivity and radioactive substances
801-809	Geophysics. Cosmic physics
811-849	Geomagnetism
851-999	Meteorology. Climatology Including the earth's atmosphere
974.5-976	Meteorological optics
980-999	Climatology and weather
994.95-999	Weather forecasting

QD

1-999	Chemistry
1-65	General Including alchemy
71-142	Analytical chemistry
146-197	Inorganic chemistry
241-441	Organic chemistry
415-436	Biochemistry
450-801	Physical and theoretical chemistry
625-655	Radiation chemistry
701-731	Photochemistry
901-999	Crystallography

QE

1-996.5	Geology
1-350.62	General Including geographical divisions
351-399.2	Mineralogy
420-499	Petrology
500-639.5	Dynamic and structural geology
521-545	Volcanoes and earthquakes
601-613.5	Structural geology
640-699	Stratigraphy
701-760	Paleontology

Class Q continues on page 374.

760.8-899.2	Paleozoology
901-996.5	Paleobotany

QH
1-278.5	Natural history (General)
1-(199.5)	General
	Including nature conservation, geographical distribution
201-278.5	Microscopy

QH
301-705.5	Biology (General)
359-425	Evolution
426-470	Genetics
471-489	Reproduction
501-531	Life
540-549.5	Ecology
573-671	Cytology
705-705.5	Economic biology

QK
1-989	Botany
1-474.5	General
	Including geographical distribution
474.8-495	Spermatophyta. Phanerogams
494-494.5	Gymnosperms
495	Angiosperms
504-(638)	Cryptogams
640-(707)	Plant anatomy
710-899	Plant physiology
900-989	Plant ecology

QL
1-991	Zoology
1-355	General
	Including geographical distribution
360-599.82	Invertebrates
461-599.82	Insects
605-739.8	Chordates. Vertebrates
614-639.8	Fishes
640-669.3	Reptiles and amphibians
671-699	Birds
700-739.8	Mammals
750-795	Animal behavior
791-795	Stories and anecdotes
799-799.5	Morphology
801-950.9	Anatomy
951-991	Embryology

QM
1-695	Human anatomy
1-511	General
531-549	Regional anatomy
550-577.8	Human and comparative histology
601-695	Human embryology

QP
1-(981)	Physiology
1-345	General
	Including influence of the environment
351-495	Neurophysiology and neuropsychology
501-801	Animal biochemistry
(901)-(981)	Experimental pharmacology

QR
1-502	Microbiology
1-74.5	General
75-99.5	Bacteria
99.6-99.8	Cyanobacteria
100-130	Microbial ecology
171	Microorganisms in the animal body
180-189.5	Immunology
355-502	Virology

The first edition of **Class Q—Science** was published in 1905, under the editorship of James David Thompson. Six more editions appeared before 1996: 1913, 1921, 1948, 1950, 1973, and 1989. Class Q is thus the most frequently updated schedule in the system. Beginning with the 1996 edition, the printed schedule has been produced from the automated system.

Geographic subdivisions are common in subclasses QE, Geology, QH, Natural history (General), Biology (General), QK, Botany, and QL, Zoology. For example, the geology of each state in the United States is assigned two numbers, the first of which is used for the state in general:

Geologic field trips in Nebraska and adjacent parts of Kansas and South Dakota. [1995]

QE	Subclass: Geology
135	Nebraska
.G35	The Cutter number for the main entry under the title, *Geologic . . .*
1995	The date of publication

The second number assigned to a state is used for specific regions of the state, as shown in the following examples:

Diffendal, R. F. (Robert Francis)   *Geologic history of Ash Hollow State Historical Park, Nebraska.*   [1996]

QE	Subclass: Geology
136	A local place in Nebraska
.A88	The first Cutter number for the special locality, Ash Hollow State Historical Park
D54	The second Cutter number for the main entry, Diffendal
1996	The date of publication

Gentile, Richard J.   *A geologic cross section of the Missouri River Valley at Kansas City, Missouri.*   1995

QE	Subclass: Geology
132	A local place in Missouri
.K36	The first Cutter number for Kansas City
G46	The second Cutter number for the main entry, Gentile
1995	The date of publication

Cutter numbers are often used for subject subdivisions in Class Q. For instance, Cutter numbers representing individual proteins are enumerated under QP552, special proteins in physiology:

Calmodulin and signal transduction.   c1998

QP	Subclass: Physiology
552	Special proteins
.C28	The first Cutter number for the protein, Calmodulin
C344	The second Cutter number for the main entry under the title, *Calmodulin* . . . .
1998	The date of publication

This device is also used under QE516, Geochemistry, and extensively in subclass QL, Zoology, for systematic divisions by order and family, for example:

Geochemistry of noble gases in natural gases.   c1996

QE	Subclass: Geology
516	Special elements in geochemistry
.R23	The first Cutter number for the element, Rare gases

G46   The second Cutter number for the main entry under the title, *Geochemistry . . .*

1996   The date of publication

Moutran, Julia Spencer.   *Only one : becoming a giant panda.*   1997

QL   Subclass: Zoology

737   Systematic divisions of mammals

.C214   The first Cutter number for Ailuropidae (Pandas), a subdivision under .C2 Carnivora

M685   The second Cutter number for the main entry, Moutran

1997   The date of publication

Carwardine, Mark.   *Whales, dolphins, and porpoises.*   c1998

QL   Subclass: Zoology

737   Systematic divisions of mammals

.C4   The first Cutter number for Cetacea

C275   The second Cutter number for the main entry, Carwardine

1998   The date of publication

Tables

There are three auxiliary tables, numbered Q1-Q3. They were converted from internal tables that appeared in editions published before 1996. Q1 is a table of chemical elements, used with numbers in subclass QD, Chemistry. Q2 is a table for particles and rays, used with numbers in subclass QC, Physics. Q3 is a brief table of geographic subarrangement used throughout the schedule. For example:

The borane, carborane, carbocation continuum.   c1998

QD   Subclass: Chemistry

181   Special elements

.B1   The first Cutter number for Boron (according to Table Q1)

B64   The second Cutter number for the main entry under the title, *borane . . .*

1998   The date of publication

Department of Energy review of the National Spallation Neutron Source Project. [1997]

QC	Subclass: Physics
793.5	Special nuclear and subnuclear particles
.N4622	The first Cutter number (in the range .N462-N4629) for Particle source (.x22 in Table Q2)
D47	The second Cutter number for the main entry under the title, *Department* . . .
1997	The date of publication

Allen, Bruce Hampton. *Moss flora of Central America.* 1994-

QK	Subclass: Botany
542	Mosses in Central America
.A1	The first Cutter number for general works (according to Table Q3)
A55	The second Cutter number for the main entry, Allen
1994	The date of publication

There are still a few internal tables scattered throughout the schedule. Their application is relatively simple and straightforward, for example:

Hamilton, Bruce Taylor. *Human nature : the Japanese Garden of Portland, Oregon.* c1996

QK	Subclass: Botany
73	Botanical gardens, by region or country, A-Z
.U62	The first Cutter number (.U6) for the United States with the successive element (2 from an internal table) for individual gardens
J365	The second Cutter number for the garden, Japanese Garden . . .
1996	The date of publication

Book Numbers

One unusual classification device used in Class Q is referred to as *book numbers*. One use of these numbers is shown under QB543-545, for Solar eclipses.

QB	ASTRONOMY
	Solar eclipses
541	General works, treatises, and textbooks
541.5	Juvenile works
542	Through 1799
543	1800-1899
	Book number = last two figures of the year, followed by author number
544	1900-1999
	Book number = last two figures of the year, followed by author number, e.g. QB544.47U6, U.S. National Almanac Office, Total eclipse of the sun, May 20, 1947
545	2000-2099
	Book number = last two figures of the year, followed by author number

In the case of QB543-545, "Book numbers" are decimal extensions of integral numbers indicating a particular decade and year of a predetermined century. An example of the use of "book numbers" to subdivide an integral number chronologically by year is shown below:

Chou, B. Ralph.   *Your complete guide to the solar eclipse of May 10, 1994.*   1993

QB	Subclass: Astronomy
544	Solar eclipses, 1900-1999
.94	The "book number" meaning 1994, the date of the eclipse
.C48	The Cutter number for the main entry, Chou
1993	The date of publication

The index to Class Q is detailed and specific. The exhaustive lists of the various taxa in subclasses QK, Botany, and QL, Zoology, are useful as reference sources.

Class R begins on page 380.

CLASS R—MEDICINE

R
5-920	Medicine (General)
5-130.5	General works
131-687	History of medicine. Medical expeditions
690-697	Medicine as a profession. Physicians
702-703	Medicine and the humanities. Medicine and disease in relation to history, literature, etc.
711-713.97	Directories
722-722.32	Missionary medicine. Medical missionaries
723-726	Medical philosophy. Medical ethics
726.5-726.8	Medicine and disease in relation to psychology. Terminal care. Dying
727-727.5	Medical personnel and the public. Physician and the public
728-733	Practice of medicine. Medical practice economics
735-854	Medical education. Medical schools. Research
855-855.5	Medical technology
856-857	Biomedical engineering. Electronics. Instrumentation
858-859.7	Computer applications to medicine. Medical informatics
864	Medical records
895-920	Medical physics. Medical radiology. Nuclear medicine

RA
1-1270	Public aspects of medicine
1-418.5	Medicine and the state
396	Regulation of medical education. Licensure
398	Registration of physicians, pharmacists, etc.
399	Regulation of medical practice. Evaluation and quality control of medical care. Medical audit
405	Death certification
407-409.5	Health status indicators. Medical statistics and surveys
410-410.9	Medical economics. Economics of medical care. Employment
411-415	Provisions for personal medical care. Medical care plans
418-418.5	Medicine and society. Social medicine. Medical sociology
421-790.95	Public health. Hygiene. Preventive medicine

428-428.5	Public health laboratories, institutes, etc.
440-440.87	Study and teaching. Research
565-600	Environmental health
	Including sewage disposal, air
	pollution, nuisances, water supply
601-602	Food and food supply in relation to public
	health
604-618	Parks, public baths, public carriers,
	buildings, etc.
619-637	Disposal of the dead. Undertaking. Burial.
	Cremation. Cemeteries
638	Immunity and immunization in relation to
	public health
639-642	Transmission of disease
643-645	Disease (Communicable and noninfectious) and
	public health
645.3-645.37	Home health care services
645.5-645.9	Emergency medical services
646-648.3	War and public health
648.5-767	Epidemics. Epidemiology. Quarantine.
	Disinfection
771-771.7	Rural health and hygiene. Rural health
	services
773-788	Personal health and hygiene
	Including clothing, bathing, exercise,
	travel, nutrition, sleep, sex hygiene
790-790.95	Mental health. Mental illness prevention
791-954	Medical geography. Climatology. Meteorology
960-1000.5	Medical centers. Hospitals. Dispensaries.
	Clinics
	Including ambulance service, nursing
	homes, hospices
1001-1171	Forensic medicine. Medical jurisprudence.
	Legal medicine
1190-1270	Toxicology. Poisons

RB	
1-214	Pathology
1-17	General works
24-33	Pathological anatomy and histology
37-56.5	Clinical pathology. Laboratory technique
57	Post-mortem examination. Autopsies
127-150	Manifestations of disease
151-214	Theories of disease. Etiology. Pathogenesis

Class R continues on page 382.

RC

31-1245	Internal medicine
49-52	Psychosomatic medicine
71-78.7	Examination. Diagnosis
	Including radiography
81-82	Popular medicine
86-88.9	Medical emergencies. Critical care.
	Intensive care. First aid
91-103	Disease due to physical and chemical agents
109-216	Infectious and parasitic diseases
251	Constitutional diseases (General)
254-282	Neoplasms. Tumors. Oncology
	Including cancer and carcinogens
306-320.5	Tuberculosis
321-571	Neurosciences. Biological psychiatry.
	Neuropsychiatry
346-429	Neurology. Diseases of the nervous system
	Including speech disorders
435-571	Psychiatry
475-489	Therapeutics. Psychotherapy
490-499	Hypnotism and hypnosis. Suggestion
	therapy
500-510	Psychoanalysis
512-569.5	Psychopathology
512-528	Psychoses
530-552	Neuroses
554-569.5	Personality disorders. Behavior
	problems
	Including sexual problems, drug
	abuse, suicide, child abuse
569.7-571	Mental retardation. Developmental
	disabilities
581-951	Specialties of internal medicine
581-607	Immunologic diseases. Allergy
620-627	Nutritional diseases. Deficiency diseases
627.5-632	Metabolic diseases
633-647.5	Diseases of the blood and blood-forming
	organs
648-665	Diseases of the endocrine glands. Clinical
	endocrinology
666-701	Diseases of the circulatory (Cardiovascular)
	system
705-779	Diseases of the respiratory system
799-869	Diseases of the digestive system.
	Gastroenterology
870-923	Diseases of the genitourinary system.
	Urology
924-924.5	Diseases of the connective tissues
925-935	Diseases of the musculoskeletal system

952-1245	Special situations and conditions
952-954.6	Geriatrics
955-962	Arctic medicine. Tropical medicine
963-969	Industrial medicine. Industrial hygiene
970-986	Military medicine. Naval medicine
1000-1020	Submarine medicine
1030-1160	Transportation medicine
	Including automotive, aviation, and space medicine
1200-1245	Sports medicine

RD	
1-811	Surgery
1-31.7	General works
32-33.9	Operative surgery. Technique of surgical operations
49-52	Surgical therapeutics. Preoperative and postoperative care
57	Surgical pathology
58	Reparative processes after operations (Physiological)
59	Surgical shock. Traumatic shock
63-76	Operating rooms and theaters. Instruments, apparatus, and appliances
78.3-87.3	Anesthesiology
91-91.5	Asepsis and antisepsis. Sterilization (Operative)
92-97.8	Emergency surgery. Wounds and injuries
98-98.4	Surgical complications
99-99.35	Surgical nursing
101-104	Fractures (General)
118-120.5	Plastic surgery. Reparative surgery
120.6-129.8	Transplantation of organs, tissues, etc.
130	Prosthesis. Artificial organs
137-145	Surgery in childhood, adolescence, pregnancy, old age
151-498	Military and naval surgery
520-599.5	Surgery by region, system, or organ
651-678	Neoplasms. Tumors. Oncology
680-688	Diseases of the locomotor system (Surgical treatment)
701-811	Orthopedic surgery
792-811	Physical rehabilitation

RE	
1-994	Ophthalmology
75-79	Examination. Diagnosis

Class R continues on page 384.

80-87	Eye surgery
88	Ophthalmic nursing
89	Eye banks
91-912	Particular diseases of the eye
918-921	Color vision tests, charts, etc.
925-939	Refraction and errors of refraction and accommodation
939.2-981	Optometry. Opticians. Eyeglasses
986-988	Artificial eyes and other prostheses
991-992	Ocular therapeutics

RF

1-547	Otorhinolaryngology
110-320	Otology. Diseases of the ear
341-437	Rhinology. Diseases of the nose, accessory sinuses, and nasopharynx
460-547	Laryngology. Diseases of the throat

RG

1-991	Gynecology and obstetrics
104-104.7	Operative gynecology
133-137.6	Conception. Artificial insemination. Contraception
138	Sterilization of women
159-208	Functional and systemic disorders. Endocrine gynecology
211-483	Abnormalities and diseases of the female genital organs
484-485	Urogynecology and obstetric urology. Urogynecologic surgery
491-499	Diseases of the breast
500-991	Obstetrics
551-591	Pregnancy
600-650	The embryo and fetus
648	Spontaneous abortion. Miscarriage
651-721	Labor. Parturition
725-791	Obstetric operations. Operative obstetrics
801-871	Puerperal state
940-991	Maternal care. Prenatal care services

RJ

1-570	Pediatrics
47.3-47.4	Genetic aspects
50-51	Examination. Diagnosis
52-53	Therapeutics
59-60	Infant and neonatal morbidity and mortality
91	Supposed prenatal influence. Prenatal culture. Stirpiculture
101-103	Child health. Child health services

125-145	Physiology of children and adolescents
206-235	Nutrition and feeding of children and adolescents
240	Immunization of children (General)
242-243	Hospital care
245-247	Nursing of children. Pediatric nursing
250-250.3	Premature infants
251-325	Newborn infants
	Including physiology, care, treatment, diseases
370-550	Diseases of children and adolescents
499-507	Mental disorders. Child psychiatry

RK

1-715	Dentistry
58-59.3	Practice of dentistry. Dental economics
60.7-60.8	Preventive dentistry
280	Oral and dental anatomy and physiology
301-493	Oral and dental medicine. Pathology. Diseases
501-519	Operative dentistry. Restorative dentistry
520-528	Orthodontics
529-535	Oral surgery
641-667	Prosthetic dentistry. Prosthodontics

RL

1-803	Dermatology
87-94	Care and hygiene
95	Pathological anatomy
110-120	Therapeutics
130-169	Diseases of the glands, hair, nails
201-331	Hyperemias, inflammations, and infections of the skin
391-489	Atrophies. Hypertrophies
675	Chronic ulcer of the skin. Bedsores
701-751	Diseases due to psychosomatic and nerve disorders. Dermatoneuroses
760-785	Diseases due to parasites
790	Pigmentations. Albinism
793	Congenital disorders of the skin. Nevi. Moles

RM

1-950	Therapeutics. Pharmacology
138	Drug prescribing
139	Prescription writing
146-146.7	Misuse of therapeutic drugs. Medication errors

Class R continues on page 386.

147-180	Administration of drugs and other therapeutic agents
182-190	Other therapeutic procedures
	Including acupuncture, pneumatic aspiration, spinal puncture, pericardial puncture
214-258	Diet therapy. Dietary cookbooks
259	Vitamin therapy
260-263	Chemotherapy
265-267	Antibiotic therapy. Antibiotics
270-282	Immunotherapy. Serotherapy
283-298	Endocrinotherapy. Organotherapy
300-666	Drugs and their actions
671-671.5	Nonprescription drugs. Patent medicines
695-893	Physical medicine. Physical therapy
	Including massage, exercise, occupational therapy, hydrotherapy, phototherapy, radiotherapy, thermotherapy, electrotherapy
930-931	Rehabilitation therapy
950	Rehabilitation technology

RS
1-441	Pharmacy and materia medica
125-131.9	Formularies. Collected prescriptions
139-141.9	Pharmacopoeias
151.2-151.9	Dispensatories
153-441	Materia medica
160-167	Pharmacognosy. Pharmaceutical substances (Plant, animal, and inorganic)
189-190	Assay methods. Standardization. Analysis
192-199	Pharmaceutical technology
200-201	Pharmaceutical dosage forms
250-252	Commercial preparations. Patent medicines
355-356	Pharmaceutical supplies
400-431	Pharmaceutical chemistry
441	Microscopical examination of drugs

RT
1-120	Nursing
89-120	Specialties in nursing

RV
1-431	Botanic, Thomsonian, and eclectic medicine

RX
1-681	Homeopathy
211-581	Diseases, treatment, etc.
601-675	Materia medica and therapeutics

RZ
201-999   Other systems of medicine
201-275   Chiropractic
301-397.5   Osteopathy
399   Osteo-magnetics, neuropathy, etc., A-Z
400-408   Mental healing
409.7-999   Miscellaneous systems and treatments
                              Including magnetotherapy, mesmerism,
                              naturopathy, organomic medicine,
                              phrenology, radiesthesia

Class R—Medicine was developed by J. Christian Bay in 1904. The first edition was not published until 1910, and the second edition was issued in 1921. The third edition, representing a complete revision reflecting the many advances in the medical sciences during the long interval between the second and third editions, appeared in 1952. A fourth edition was published in 1980, and the fifth edition in 1986. Since 1995, the schedule has been produced from the automated system.

Class R has seventeen subclasses. There is only one auxiliary table, a simple one used for subarranging works about medical education and schools. On the other hand, there are many internal tables that employ both double and successive Cutter numbers. An example of an internal table is shown below:

RA   PUBLIC ASPECTS OF MEDICINE
         Medical centers.   Hospitals.   Dispensaries.   Clinics
           By region or country
              America
                United States
982.A-Z   By city, A-Z
                     Each city subarranged like New York City:
                     .N49-.N5   *New York City*
                     .N49A-.N49Z   *General works*
                     .N5A-.N5Z   *Special institutions.*
                                       By name, A-Z

The following examples illustrate the Cutter numbers used for New York City:

Opdycke, Sandra. *No one was turned away : the role of public hospitals in New York City since 1900.* 1999

RA   Subclass: Public aspects of medicine

982   Medical centers in a city in the United States

.N49   The first Cutter number for General works on New York City

O63	The second Cutter number for the main entry, Opdycke
1999	The date of publication

Edson, John N. *Brooklyn first : a chronicle of the Long Island College Hospital, 1858-1990.* c1993

RA	Subclass: Public aspects of medicine
982	Medical centers in a city in the United States
.N5	The first Cutter number for special institutions in New York City
L664	The second Cutter number based on the name of the institution, Long Island College Hospital
1993	The date of publication

The pattern in the schedule shown above indicates that class numbers for medical centers and hospitals in U.S. cities are to be subarranged like those for New York City institutions.

Lehr, Teresa K. *To serve the community : a celebration of Rochester General Hospital, 1847-1997.* c1997

RA	Subclass: Public aspects of medicine
982	Medical centers in a city in the United States
.R56	The first Cutter number (following the pattern established for New York City in the internal table) for special institutions in the city of Rochester
R634	The second Cutter number based on the name of the institution, Rochester General Hospital
1997	The date of publication

The following examples illustrate the use of the internal table given under RA984.A-.Z:

Gómez Mampaso, Valentina. *La unificación hospitalaria en Castilla : su estudio a través de la Casa de San Lázaro de Sevilla.* 1996

RA	Subclass: Public aspects of medicine
989	Medical centers or hospitals in Europe
.S73	The first Cutter number (.S7) for Spain with the successive element (3) based on the internal table under RA984, meaning subdivision by province
C364	The second Cutter number for Castilla
1996	The date of publication

Gómez Rodríguez, Ma. Soledad (María Soledad)   *El Hospital de la Misericordia de Toledo en el siglo XIX.*   1995

RA	Subclass: Public aspects of medicine
989	Medical centers or hospitals in Europe
.S74	The first Cutter number (.S7) for Spain with the successive element (4) based on the internal table under RA984, meaning subdivision by city
T7354	The second Cutter number for the city, Toledo
1995	The date of publication

National Library of Medicine Classification

Class R was developed to classify medical literature within a general library, not a medical library. There are specialized classifications that are more suitable for medical libraries than Class R in the LC Classification. A scheme directly related to the Library of Congress Classification is that of the National Library of Medicine (NLM), another federal library. This library was formerly the U.S. Army Medical Library. In the early 1940s a survey showed the need for a special classification for the Army Library, and in 1948 a preliminary edition of such a classification was prepared by Mary Louise Marshall. This edition was modified and revised by Dr. Frank B. Rogers in 1950 and issued as the first edition of the *Army Medical Library Classification*[35] in 1951. This edition established the basic structure of the classification for subsequent editions and set the pattern of classification practices at the National Library of Medicine. The second edition was published in 1956 as the *National Library of Medicine Classification*, followed by the third edition in 1964. The fourth edition was published in 1978, and a revised fourth edition was issued in 1981. The fifth edition, under the editorship of Wen-min Kao, appeared in 1994.[36]

The National Library of Medicine (NLM) Classification makes use of the vacant Class W and subclasses QS-QZ, which have been permanently excluded from the LC Classification. Class W is used for Medicine and related subjects, and Classes QS-QZ for Preclinical sciences. By adopting the LC notation with slight modifications, the National Library of Medicine and other medical libraries can use the remainder of the LC Classification for their nonmedical books, excluding Class R (Medicine) and subclasses QM (Anatomy) and QR (Microbiology).

Because the NLM Classification is mainly a system for shelf-location of library materials, the structure remains fairly broad. The index, on the other hand, is detailed and comprehensive. Where feasible, index terms reflect the current forms of MeSH (Medical Subject Headings) descriptors.

The following is a synopsis of the NLM Classification:

PRECLINICAL SCIENCES

QS	Human Anatomy
QT	Physiology
QU	Biochemistry
QV	Pharmacology
QW	Microbiology and Immunology
QX	Parasitology
QY	Clinical Pathology
QZ	Pathology

MEDICINE AND RELATED SUBJECTS

W	Health Professions
WA	Public Health
WB	Practice of Medicine
WC	Communicable Diseases
WD100	Nutrition Disorders
WD200	Metabolic Diseases
WD300	Immunologic and Collagen Diseases. Hypersensitivity
WD400	Animal Poisons
WD500	Plant Poisons
WD600	Diseases and Injuries Caused by Physical Agents
WD700	Aviation and Space Medicine
WE	Musculoskeletal System
WF	Respiratory System
WG	Cardiovascular System
WH	Hemic and Lymphatic Systems
WI	Digestive System
WJ	Urogenital System
WK	Endocrine System
WL	Nervous System
WM	Psychiatry
WN	Radiology. Diagnostic Imaging
WO	Surgery
WP	Gynecology
WQ	Obstetrics
WR	Dermatology
WS	Pediatrics
WT	Geriatrics. Chronic Disease
WU	Dentistry. Oral Surgery
WV	Otolaryngology
WW	Ophthalmology
WX	Hospitals and other Health Facilities
WY	Nursing
WZ	History of Medicine 19th Century Schedule

As a classification scheme, Class W employs many original features. For example, serials are not classified but rather are separated by form and placed in one of six broad categories. General divisions, beginning with a group of numbers ranging generally from 1-49, are provided in each main schedule and in some sections within a schedule. They are used for types of publication such as dictionaries, atlases, laboratory manuals, etc., and other general topics such as research, equipment and supplies, and medical informatics. For specific topics, division by organ usually has priority.

In the NLM Classification, early printed books are separated from the main schedule. Books published before 1801 and Americana, that is, early imprints from North, South, and Central America and the Caribbean Islands, are classed in WZ 220-270. Books within this range are arranged alphabetically by author within each century or in the Americana number. Monographs published in the nineteenth (and the very early part of the twentieth) century (1801-1913) are provided for in a separate schedule called *19th Century Schedule*. Only twentieth-century material from 1914 on is classed in schedules QS-QZ, W-WY, and WZ (excluding WZ 220-270).

Unlike the LC Classification, Cutter numbers are not used widely for subject subdivisions but are usually reserved for authors; the *Cutter-Sanborn Three-Figure Author Table*[37] is used to formulate them. There are brief outlines at the beginning of each class. The call number for a bibliography in medicine begins with the letter Z, followed by the class number for the particular subject of the bibliography. For example, an annotated bibliography of recent literature on interviewing and physical examination entitled *Bedside Diagnosis* is classed in ZWB 200 S359b. "Z" means the work is bibliographic in nature; WB 200 is the class number for "Physical diagnosis (General)"; S359 is the Cutter number for the author, Henry Schneiderman; and "b" is the work mark for the title.

There is only one auxiliary table, Table G for geographic subdivisions. It is used mainly with serial publications of governments and with hospital publications.

Most of the major medical libraries in this country use the NLM Classification. There are several advantages to using this scheme: (1) currency in arrangement of material and in terminology; (2) compatibility with the *Medical Subject Headings List*; and (3) easy access to NLM call numbers through the National Library of Medicine's catalog and its online databases. The MARC records, furthermore, of all shared cataloging of medical literature prepared by the National Library of Medicine for the Library of Congress carry both Class R and Class W numbers. The following examples illustrate the provision of alternate NLM numbers on LC MARC records:

Pfeiffer, Ronald P.   *Concepts of athletic training.*   1998

RC	Subclass: Internal medicine
1210	General works on Sports medicine
.P45	The Cutter number for the main entry, Pfeiffer
1998	The date of publication

[NLM call no.:   QT 261 P528c 1998]

Comprehensive adolescent health care.   c1998

RJ	Subclass: Pediatrics
550	Diseases of adolescents
.C67	The Cutter number for the main entry under the title, *Comprehensive . . .*
1998	The date of publication

[NLM call no.: WS 460 C7375 1998]

Dunne, Patrick J.   *Respiratory home care : the essentials.*   c1998

RC	Subclass: Internal medicine
735	Special therapies
.H65	The first Cutter number for Home care
D86	The second Cutter number for the main entry, Dunne
1998	The date of publication

[NLM call no.:   WF 145 D923r 1998]

Clinical chemistry : theory, analysis, and correlation.   c1996

RB	Subclass: Pathology
40	Chemical examination used in clinical pathology
.C58	The Cutter number for the main entry under the title, *Clinical . . .*
1996	The date of publication

[NLM call no.:   QY 90 C6415 1996]

CLASS S—AGRICULTURE

Class S continues on page 394.

419.5	Roof gardening. Balcony gardening
421-439.8	Classes of plants
	Including annuals, climbers, ferns, lawns, perennials, shrubs
441-441.75	Flower shows. Exhibitions
442.5	Care and preparation of cut flowers and ornamental plants for market
442.8-443.4	Marketing. Cut flower industry. Florists
446-446.6	Horticultural service industry
447	Preservation and reproduction of flowers, fruits, etc.
447.5	Bonkei. Tray landscapes
449-450.87	Flower arrangement and decoration
450.9-467.8	Gardens and gardening
469-(476.4)	Landscape gardening. Landscape architecture
481-486	Parks and public reservations
	Including theory, management, history
599-990.5	Pests and diseases
608	Individual or types of plants or trees
610-615	Weeds, parasitic plants, etc.
617-618	Poisonous plants
621-795	Plant pathology
818-945	Economic entomology
950-990.5	Pest control and treatment of diseases. Plant protection
950.9-970.4	Pesticides
973-973.5	Soil disinfection
974-978	Organic plant protection. Biological control
979.5-985	Inspection. Quarantine
992-998	Economic zoology applied to crops. Agricultural zoology
	Including animals injurious and beneficial to plants

SD	
1-669.5	Forestry
11-115	Documents
119	Voyages, etc.
131-247.5	History of forestry. Forest conditions

Class S continues on page 396.

250-363.3	Forestry education
388	Forestry machinery and engineering
388.5	Tools and implements
389	Forest roads
390-390.43	Forest soils
390.5-390.7	Forest meteorology. Forest microclimatology
391-410.9	Sylviculture
411-428	Conservation and protection Including forest influences, damage by elements, fires, forest reserves
430-(559)	Exploitation and utilization Including timber trees, fuelwood, logging, transportation, valuation
561-669.5	Administration. Policy

SF	
1-1100	Animal culture
41-55	History
84-84.64	Economic zoology
84.82-85.6	Rangelands. Range management. Grazing
87	Acclimatization
89	Transportation
91	Housing and environmental control
92	Equipment and supplies
94.5-99	Feeds and feeding. Animal nutrition
101-103.5	Brands and branding, and other means of identifying
105-109	Breeding and breeds
111-113	Cost, yield, and profit. Accounting
114-121	Exhibitions
170-180	Working animals
191-275	Cattle
221-250	Dairying
250.5-275	Dairy processing. Dairy products
277-360.4	Horses
294.2-297	Horse sports. Horse shows
304.5-307	Driving
308.5-310.5	Horsemanship. Riding
311-312	Draft horses
315-315.5	Ponies
321-359.7	Racing
360-360.4	Feral horses. Wild horses
361-361.73	Donkeys
362	Mules

371-379	Sheep. Wool
380-388	Goats
391-397.83	Swine
402-405	Fur-bearing animals
405.5-407	Laboratory animals
408-408.6	Zoo animals
409	Small animal culture
411-459	Pets
421-440.2	Dogs. Dog racing
441-450	Cats
451-455	Rabbits and hares
456-458.83	Fishes. Aquariums
459	Other animals
461-473	Birds. Cage birds
481-507	Poultry. Eggs
508-(510.6)	Game birds
511-511.5	Ostrich
512-513	Ornamental birds
515-515.5	Reptiles
518	Insect rearing
521-539.8	Bee culture
541-560	Sericulture. Silk culture
561	Lac-insects
600-1100	Veterinary medicine
756.5-769.5	Special preclinical sciences
	Including veterinary genetics, ethology, anatomy, physiology, embryology, pathology
780.2-780.7	Veterinary microbiology, bacteriology, virology, mycology
780.9	Veterinary epidemiology. Epizootiology
781-809	Communicable diseases of animals (General)
810	Veterinary parasitology
810.5-810.7	Predatory animals and their control
811-909	Veterinary medicine of special organs, regions, and systems
910	Other diseases and conditions
910.5	Veterinary orthopedics
911-914.4	Veterinary surgery
914.3-914.4	Veterinary traumatology. Veterinary emergencies
914.5	Veterinary acupuncture
915-919.5	Veterinary pharmacology
925	Veterinary physical medicine
951-997.5	Diseases of special classes of animals

Class S continues on page 398.

SH
1-691	Aquaculture. Fisheries. Angling
20.3-191	Aquaculture
33-134.6	By region or country
138	Mariculture
151-179	Fish culture
171-179	Diseases and adverse factors
185-191	Frogs, leeches, etc.
201-399	Fisheries
213-216.55	By oceans and seas
219-321	By region or country
327.5-327.7	Fishery resources. Fishery conservation
328-329	Fishery management. Fishery policy
334	Economic aspects. Finance
334.5-334.7	Fishery technology
334.9-336.5	Fishery processing
337	Packing, transportation, and storage
337.5	Fishing port facilities
343.2-343.3	Fishery oceanography. Fishery meteorology
343.4	Fishery research vessels
343.5	Exploratory fishing
343.8	Navigation
343.9	Safety measures
344-344.8	Methods and gear. Catching of fish
346-351	Fishery for individual species
360-363	Seal fisheries. Fur sealing
364	Sea otter
365-380.92	Shellfish fisheries. Shellfish culture
381-385	Whaling
387	Porpoises. Dolphins
388.7-391.5	Algae culture
393	Seagrasses
396	Sponge fisheries
400-400.8	Seafood gathering
401-691	Angling
	Including tackle, casting, methods of angling, angling for special kinds of fish

SK
1-664	Hunting sports
37-39.5	Shooting
40-268	By country
281-293	Special methods and types of hunting Including bolos, game calling, tracking, trapping, dressing

284-287	Fox hunting
291-292	Coursing
293	Ferreting
295-305	Big game
311-335	Bird hunting. Fowling
336	Varmint hunting (General)
337	Predator hunting
341	Other game
351-579	Wildlife management. Game protection
	Including annual reports of game
	commissioners
590-593	Wild animal trade
650-664	Wildlife-related recreation

S. C. Stuntz of the United States Department of Agriculture developed **Class S—Agriculture—Plant and Animal Industry** on a plan outlined by the Chief Classifier at the Library of Congress, Charles Martel. Stuntz used existing bibliographies and classification schemes to formulate the details of the subclasses. According to the preface to the third edition, one subclass, SD, Forestry, was based on "corresponding sections of the systematic catalog of the K. Sächsische Forstakademie (more recently known as the Forstliche Hochschule) at Tarandt."

The first edition of Class S was published in 1911, the second in 1927, the third in 1948, and the fourth in 1982. Beginning with the 1996 edition, the schedule has been produced from the electronic version.

Class S, a relatively simple schedule, consists of six subclasses. There are only two auxiliary tables, both for geographical distribution. These tables were used as examples of auxiliary tables in chapter 4; they are discussed and illustrated on pages 113-16 of that chapter. Further examples include:

Ireland. Dept. of Agriculture, Food, and Forestry.   *Growing for the future : a strategic plan for the development of the forestry sector in Ireland.* [1996]

SD	Subclass: Forestry
607	Forest administration and policy in Ireland
.I734	The Cutter number for the main entry, Ireland
1996	The date of publication

The number 607 is the result of adding the number 41 from Table S2, meaning a general work on Ireland to the base number SD566 in the schedule for forest administration and policy. The second number, 42, assigned to Ireland is used for local subdivision.

Northern Ireland. Forest Service. *Forest Service tactical plan, 1993-1997.* [1993?]

SD	Subclass: Forestry
606.5	Forest administration and policy in Northern Ireland
.N67	The Cutter number for the main entry, Northern Ireland
1993	The date of publication

The number 606.5 is the result of adding the first of two numbers, 40.5-6 assigned to Northern Ireland in Table S2 to the base number SD566.

Not all geographic division in the schedule requires the use of these tables. The following examples show geographic division by means of Cutter numbers:

Robertson, S.A. *Kenya coastal forests : the report of the NMK/WWF Coast Forest Survey : WWF Project 3256 : Kenya, Coast Forest Status, Conservation, and Management.* [1993]

SD	Subclass: Forestry
414	Conservation and protection by region or country
.K4	The first Cutter number for the country, Kenya
R635	The second Cutter number for the main entry, Robertson
1993	The date of publication

Attaway, John A. *A history of Florida citrus freezes.* 1997

SB	Subclass: Plant culture
369.2	Citrus fruits in the United States
.F6	The first Cutter number for Florida
A88	The second Cutter number for the main entry, Attaway
1997	The date of publication

Hunting and Fishing

The sports of hunting and fishing are included in the schedules for subclasses SH, Aquaculture, Fisheries, Angling; and SK, Hunting sports. This is probably a more useful location for this material than classing hunting and fishing with other sports in subclass GV.

Mathews, Craig. *The Yellowstone fly-fishing guide.* 1997

SH	Subclass: Aquaculture, Fisheries, Angling
464	Angling in regions in the United States

.Y45   The first Cutter number for Yellowstone

M38   The second Cutter number for the main entry, Mathews

1997   The date of publication

Davies, Gordon E.   *The living rivers : British Columbia and the Yukon : river stories & fishing guide.*   1996

SH   Subclass: Aquaculture, Fisheries, Angling

572   Angling in Canada

.B8   The first Cutter number for British Columbia

D38   The second Cutter number for the main entry, Davies

1996   The date of publication

In the following example, geographic subdivision is built into the class number rather than represented by a Cutter number:

Richmond, Scott.   *Fishing in Oregon's endless season.*   1996

SH   Subclass: Aquaculture, Fisheries, Angling

539   Angling in Oregon

.R53   The Cutter number for the main entry, Richmond

1996   The date of publication

The index of Class S is detailed and specific. It was completely revised in the fourth edition and further developed for the 1996 edition.

Class T begins on page 402.

CLASS T—TECHNOLOGY

T
1-995	Technology (General)
10.5-11.9	Communication of technical information
11.95-12.5	Industrial directories
55-55.3	Industrial safety. Industrial accident prevention
55.4-60.8	Industrial engineering. Management engineering
57-57.97	Applied mathematics. Quantitative methods
57.6-57.97	Operations research. Systems analysis
58.4	Managerial control systems
58.5-58.64	Information technology
58.6-58.62	Management information systems
58.7-58.8	Production capacity. Manufacturing capacity
59-59.2	Standardization
59.5	Automation
59.7-59.77	Human engineering in industry. Man-machine systems
60-60.8	Work measurement. Methods engineering
61-173	Technical education. Technical schools
173.2-174.5	Technological change
175-178	Industrial research. Research and development
201-342	Patents. Trademarks
351-385	Mechanical drawing. Engineering graphics
391-995	Exhibitions. Trade shows. World's fairs

TA
1-2040	Engineering (General). Civil engineering (General)
164	Bioengineering
165	Engineering instruments, meters, etc. Industrial instrumentation
166-167	Human engineering
168	Systems engineering
170-171	Environmental engineering
174	Engineering design
177.4-185	Engineering economy
190-194	Management of engineering works
197-198	Engineering meteorology
213-215	Engineering machinery, tools, and implements
329-348	Engineering mathematics. Engineering analysis
349-359	Mechanics of engineering. Applied mechanics
365-367	Acoustics in engineering. Acoustical engineering
401-492	Materials of engineering and construction. Mechanics of materials

495	Disasters and engineering
501-625	Surveying
630-695	Structural engineering (General)
703-712	Engineering geology. Rock mechanics. Soil mechanics. Underground construction
715-787	Earthwork. Foundations
800-820	Tunneling. Tunnels
1001-1280	Transportation engineering
1501-1820	Applied optics. Photonics
2001-2040	Plasma engineering

TC

1-978	Hydraulic engineering
160-181	Technical hydraulics
183-201	General preliminary operations. Dredging. Submarine building
203-380	Harbors and coast protective works. Coastal engineering. Lighthouses
401-506	River, lake, and water-supply engineering (General)
530-537	River protective works. Regulation. Flood control
540-558	Dams. Barrages
601-791	Canals and inland navigation. Waterways
801-978	Irrigation engineering. Reclamation of wasteland. Drainage

TC

1501-1800	Ocean engineering

TD

1-1066	Environmental technology. Sanitary engineering
159-168	Municipal engineering
169-171.8	Environmental protection
172-193.5	Environmental pollution
194-195	Environmental effects of industries and plants
201-500	Water supply for domestic and industrial purposes
419-428	Water pollution
429.5-480.7	Water purification. Water treatment and conditioning. Saline water conversion
481-493	Water distribution systems
511-780	Sewage collection and disposal systems. Sewerage
783-812.5	Municipal refuse. Solid wastes
813-870	Street cleaning. Litter and its removal

Class T continues on page 404.

878-894	Special types of environment
	Including soil pollution, air pollution, noise pollution
895-899	Industrial and factory sanitation
896-899	Industrial and factory wastes
920-934	Rural and farm sanitary engineering
940-949	Low temperature sanitary engineering
1020-1066	Hazardous substances and their disposal

TE

1-450	Highway engineering. Roads and pavements
175-176.5	Highway design. Interchanges and intersections
177-178.8	Roadside development. Landscaping
200-205	Materials for roadmaking
206-209.5	Location engineering
210-228.3	Construction details
	Including foundations, maintenance, equipment
250-278.8	Pavements and paved roads
279	Streets
279.5-298	Pedestrian facilities
280-295	Sidewalks. Footpaths. Flagging
298	Curbs. Curbstones

TF

1-1620	Railroad engineering and operation
200-320	Railway construction
340-499	Railway equipment and supplies
501-668	Railway operation and management
670-851	Local and light railways
840-851	Elevated railways and subways
855-1127	Electric railways
1300-1620	High speed ground transportation

TG

1-470	Bridge engineering

TH

1-9745	Building construction
845-895	Architectural engineering. Structural engineering of buildings
900-915	Construction equipment in building
1000-1725	Systems of building construction
	Including fireproof construction, concrete construction
2025-3000	Details in building design and construction
	Including walls, roofs
3301-3411	Maintenance and repair

4021-4977	Buildings: Construction with reference to use Including public buildings, dwellings
5011-5701	Construction by phase of the work (Building trades)
6014-6081	Environmental engineering of buildings. Sanitary engineering of buildings
6101-6887	Plumbing and pipefitting
7005-7699	Heating and ventilation. Air conditioning
7700-7975	Illumination. Lighting
8001-8581	Decoration and decorative furnishings
9025-9745	Protection of buildings Including protection from dampness, fire, burglary

TJ

1-1570	Mechanical engineering and machinery
163.13-163.25	Power resources
163.26-163.5	Energy conservation
170-179	Mechanics applied to machinery. Dynamics
181-210	Mechanical movements
210.2-211.47	Mechanical devices and figures. Automata. Ingenious mechanisms. Robots (General)
212-225	Control engineering systems. Automatic machinery (General)
227-240	Machine design and drawing
241-254.7	Machine construction (General)
255-265	Heat engines
266-267.5	Turbines. Turbomachines (General)
268-740	Steam engineering
603-695	Locomotives
751-805	Miscellaneous motors and engines Including gas, gasoline, diesel engines
807-830	Renewable energy sources
836-927	Hydraulic machinery
940-940.5	Vacuum technology
950-1030	Pneumatic machinery
1040-1119	Machinery exclusive of prime movers
1125-1345	Machine shops and machine shop practice
1350-1418	Hoisting and conveying machinery
1425-1475	Lifting and pressing machinery
1480-1496	Agricultural machinery. Farm machinery
1501-1519	Sewing machines

TK

1-9971	Electrical engineering. Electronics. Nuclear engineering
301-399	Electric meters

Table continues on page 406.

452-454.4	Electric apparatus and materials. Electric circuits. Electric networks
1001-1841	Production of electric energy or power. Powerplants. Central stations
2000-2891	Dynamoelectric machinery and auxiliaries Including generators, motors, transformers
2896-2985	Production of electricity by direct energy conversion
3001-3521	Distribution or transmission of electric power
4001-4102	Applications of electric power
4125-4399	Electric lighting
4601-4661	Electric heating
5101-6720	Telecommunication Including telegraphy, telephone, radio, radar, television
7800-8360	Electronics
7885-7895	Computer engineering. Computer hardware
8300-8360	Photoelectronic devices (General)
9001-9401	Nuclear engineering. Atomic power
9900-9971	Electricity for amateurs. Amateur constructors' manuals

TL

1-4050	Motor vehicles. Aeronautics. Astronautics
1-484	Motor vehicles. Cycles
500-777	Aeronautics. Aeronautical engineering
780-785.8	Rocket propulsion. Rockets
787-4050	Astronautics. Space travel

TN

1-997	Mining engineering. Metallurgy
263-271	Mineral deposits. Metallic ore deposits. Prospecting
275-325	Practical mining operations. Safety measures
331-347	Mine transportation, haulage and hoisting. Mining machinery
400-580	Ore deposits and mining of particular metals
600-799	Metallurgy
799.5-948	Nonmetallic minerals
950-997	Building and ornamental stones

TP

1-1185	Chemical technology
155-156	Chemical engineering
200-248	Chemicals: Manufacture, use, etc.
248.13-248.65	Biotechnology
250-261	Industrial electrochemistry
267.5-301	Explosives and pyrotechnics
315-360	Fuel

368-456	Food processing and manufacture
480-498	Low temperature engineering. Cryogenic engineering. Refrigeration
500-660	Fermentation industries. Beverages. Alcohol
670-699	Oils, fats, and waxes
690-692.5	Petroleum refining. Petroleum products
700-746	Illuminating industries (Nonelectric)
751-762	Gas industry
785-869	Clay industries. Ceramics. Glass
875-888	Cement industries
890-933	Textile bleaching, dyeing, printing, etc.
934-945	Paints, pigments, varnishes, etc.
1080-1185	Polymers and polymer manufacture

TR

1-1050	Photography
250-265	Cameras
287-500	Photographic processing. Darkroom technique
504-508	Transparencies. Diapositives
510-545	Color photography
550-581	Studio and laboratory
590-620	Lighting
624-835	Applied photography Including artistic, commercial, medical photography, photocopying processes
845-899	Cinematography. Motion pictures
925-1050	Photomechanical processes

TS

1-2301	Manufactures
155-194	Production management. Operations management
195-198.8	Packaging
200-770	Metal manufactures. Metalworking
780-788	Stonework
800-937	Wood technology. Lumber
840-915	Wood products. Furniture
920-937	Chemical processing of wood
940-1047	Leather industries. Tanning
1060-1070	Furs
1080-1268	Paper manufacture and trade
1300-1865	Textile industries
1870-1935	Rubber industry
1950-1982	Animal products
2120-2159	Cereals and grain. Milling industry
2220-2283	Tobacco industry
2284-2288	Animal feeds and feed mills. Pet food industry

Class T continues on page 408.

TT
1-999	Handicrafts. Arts and crafts
161-170.7	Manual training. School shops
174-176	Articles for children
180-200	Woodworking. Furniture making. Upholstering
201-203	Lathework. Turning
205-267	Metalworking
300-382.8	Painting. Wood finishing
387-410	Soft home furnishings
490-695	Clothing manufacture. Dressmaking. Tailoring
697-927	Home arts. Homecrafts
	Including sewing, embroidery, decorative crafts
950-979	Hairdressing. Beauty culture. Barbers' work
980-999	Laundry work

TX
1-1110	Home economics
301-339	The house
	Including arrangement, care, servants
341-641	Nutrition. Foods and food supply
642-840	Cookery
851-885	Dining-room service
901-946.5	Hospitality industry. Hotels, clubs, restaurants, etc. Food service
950-953	Taverns, barrooms, saloons
955-985	Building operation and housekeeping
1100-1105	Mobile home living
1110	Recreational vehicle living

The first edition of **Class T—Technology** appeared in 1910, the second in 1922, the third in 1937, the fourth in 1948, and the fifth in 1971. Beginning with the 1995 edition, the schedule has been produced from the automated system.

There are seventeen subclasses in Class T. The scope of the class covers all the engineering disciplines plus other technology fields such as photography and manufactures. In addition, home economics, handicrafts, and arts and crafts are also found in this class.

Auxiliary Tables

Class T contains four auxiliary tables numbered T1-T4. They should create few serious problems in application and are often used as an introduction to the study and use of auxiliary tables in the LC Classification. A portion of Table T1, "History and Country Divisions," is reproduced below.

| T1 | HISTORY AND COUNTRY DIVISIONS | T1 |

	History
15	General works
16	Ancient
17	Medieval
18	Modern
19	19th century
20	20th century
	Special countries
	The special provision for local or special subdivision does not apply to single number or Cutter number countries, which remain undivided
	The numbers for "Cities or other special," "Local or special," "Province or special" may be used in some cases for local subdivision, and in other cases for special canals, rivers, harbors, railroads, or bridges, as appropriate for the subject matter to which the table is applied
	America
21	General works
	North America
22	General works
	United States
23	General works
23.1	Eastern states. Atlantic coast
23.15	New England
23.2	Appalachian region
23.3	Great Lakes region
23.4	Midwest. Mississippi Valley
23.5	South. Gulf states
23.6	West
23.7	Northwest
23.8	Pacific coast
23.9	Southwest
24.A-W	States, A-W
	e.g.
24.A4	Alaska
24.H3	Hawaii

Table continues on page 410.

25.A-Z	Cities (or other special), A-Z
	Canada
26	General works
27.A-Z	Provinces (or other special), A-Z
27.5	Latin America
	Mexico
28	General works
29.A-Z	Local or special, A-Z
	Central America
30	General works
31.A-Z	Special countries, A-Z
	West Indies
32	General works
33.A-Z	Special islands, A-Z
	South America
34	General works

This table is used, for instance, to classify works about generating electric power in plants using heat energy. In the schedule, the following numbers are designated for this subject:

TK	ELECTRICAL ENGINEERING. ELECTRONICS. NUCLEAR ENGINEERING
	Production of electric energy or power
	Electric power plants (General)
	Special
1221-1327	Power plants utilizing heat energy (Table T1)
	Add country number in table to TK1200

For example, a book on power generation using heat energy in East Central Europe is classed in TK1255. "55" is the number in Table T1 for Europe. "55" added to TK1200 gives the number TK1255.

Least-Cost Economic Power Generation in East Central Europe Workshop (1994 : Prague, Czech Republic) *Proceedings of the Least-Cost Economic Power Generation in East Central Europe Workshop : October 31 — November 1, 1994, Hotel Atrium, Prague, Czech Republic.* [c1995]

TK	Subclass: Electrical engineering, Electronics, Nuclear engineering
1200	The designated base number in the schedule
+ 55	The number for Europe from Table T1

1255

1255	Power plants in Europe utilizing heat energy
.L33	The Cutter number for the main entry, Least-Cost . . .
1994	The date of conference

As shown in the example above, when the main entry is under the name of a conference, the date of conference rather than that of publication is used in the call number.

Similarly, a work on power plants using waterpower in India is classed in TK1503, the result of adding the number 103 (meaning general works on India) from Table T1 to the base number 1400 given in the schedule for water-powered power plants.

Naidu, B. S. K.   *Planning and management of hydropower resources in India.*   1992

TK	Subclass: Electrical engineering, Electronics, Nuclear engineering
1503	Power plants in India utilizing waterpower
.N29	The Cutter number for the main entry, Naidu
1992	The date of publication

Table T1 is also used with TX171-277, Study and teaching of Home economics in special countries. "24" is the number in Table T1 for states in the United States. "24" added to 150 gives the number TX174 for the study and teaching of home economics in a particular state.

Mounter, Clyde T.   *The quiet revolution : a seventy-five year history of women's extension clubs in South Carolina.*   1995

TX	Subclass: Home economics
174	Study and teaching in a state in the United States
.S6	The Cutter number for South Carolina
.M68	The second Cutter number for the main entry, Mounter
1995	The date of publication

Beginning with the 1995 edition, many of the class numbers previously derived by means of the "divided like" procedure are enumerated. An example is shown below:

Earlier editions:

TK ELECTRICAL ENGINEERING. ELECTRONICS.
   NUCLEAR ENGINEERING
   Production of electric energy or power
    Powerplants. Central stations
     Special
1341-1375   Powerplants utilizing atomic power
      Divided like TK171-205

1995 edition:

TK ELECTRICAL ENGINEERING. ELECTRONICS.
   NUCLEAR ENGINEERING
   Electric power plants (General)
    Special
     Power plants utilizing nuclear power
      America
1341   General works
      United States
1343   General works
1344.A-W   States, A-W

       ★★★★★★

      Europe
1361   General works
1362.A-Z   Special countries, A-Z

A book about the Chernobyl nuclear accident in Ukraine is classed in TK1362.

  Yaroshinska, Alla. *Chernobyl, the forbidden truth.* c1995

  TK   Subclass: Electrical engineering, Electronics, Nuclear
      engineering

  1362   Power plants utilizing nuclear power

  .U38   The first Cutter number for Ukraine

  Y3713 The second Cutter number for the main entry,
      Yaroshinska, with the successive element (13 from
      the Translation Table) for an English translation

  1995   The date of publication

In using this schedule it is important to make the distinction between pure and applied sciences. Class Q, Science, is normally used for pure sciences, while applied sciences are classed in Class T, Technology. For example, works on computers may be classed in Q or T, depending on their orientation:

Capron, H. L. *Computers : tools for an information age.* c1998

QA	Subclass: Mathematics
76.5	General works on digital computers
.C363	The Cutter number for the main entry, Capron
1998	The date of publication

Software without frontiers : a multi-platform, multi-cultural, multi-nation approach. c1997

QA	Subclass: Mathematics
76.754	General works on computer software
.S64724	The Cutter number for the main entry under the title, *Software . . .*
1997	The date of publication

Hardware-software co-design of embedded systems : the POLIS approach. 1997

TK	Subclass: Electrical engineering, Electronics, Nuclear engineering
7895	Special components and auxiliary equipment of computers
.E42	The first Cutter number for Embedded computer systems
H37	The second Cutter number for the main entry under the title, *Hardware-software . . .*
1997	The date of publication

Optics in computing : March 18-21, 1997, Hyatt Regency Lake Tahoe, Incline Village, Nevada. 1997

TK	Subclass: Electrical engineering, Electronics, Nuclear engineering
7895	Special components and auxiliary equipment of computers
.O6	The first Cutter number for Optical equipment
O68	The second Cutter number for the main entry under the title, *Optics in . . .*
1997	The date of publication

Moreover, other science schedules create further distinctions. For example, works about wool may be classed in Class T or Class S as shown in the following examples:

Parker, Julie. *All about wool : a fabric dictionary & swatchbook.* c1996

TS	Subclass: Manufactures
1625	General works on woolen manufactures
.P37	The Cutter number for the main entry, Parker
1996	The date of publication

Wool in the Australian imagination. 1994

SF	Subclass: Animal culture
377	Wool
.W66	The Cutter number for the main entry under the title, *Wool*...
1994	The date of publication

Other examples of works classed in T include:

McNicoll, Dan M. *Bioremediation of petroleum-contaminated soils : an innovative, environmentally friendly technology.* 1995

TD	Subclass: Environmental technology, Sanitary engineering
879	Soil pollutants
.P4	The first Cutter number for petroleum
M36	The second Cutter number for the main entry, McNicoll
1995	The date of publication

Lindley, James A. *Agricultural buildings and structures.* 1996

TH	Subclass: Building construction
4911	General works on farm buildings
.L56	The first Cutter number for the main entry, Lindley
1996	The date of publication

Burgess, Colin. *Oceans to orbit : the story of Australia's first man in space : Dr. Paul Scully-Power.* 1995

TL	Subclass: Motor vehicles, Aeronautics, Astronautics
789.85	Individual biography in the field of astronautics
.S38	The first Cutter number for the biographee, Scully-Power
B87	The second Cutter number for the main entry, Burgess
1995	The date of publication

CLASS U-V—MILITARY SCIENCE.   NAVAL SCIENCE

U

1-900	Military science (General)
21-22.3	War. Philosophy. Military sociology
27-43	History of military science
45	Historiography
56-59	Army clubs
150-155	Military planning
161-163	Strategy
164-167.5	Tactics
168	Logistics
250-255	Maneuvers (combined arms)
260	Joint operations. Combined operations
261	Amphibious warfare
262	Commando tactics
263-264.5	Atomic warfare. Atomic weapons
300-305	Artillery and rifle ranges
310-310.2	War games
320-325	Physical training of soldiers
400-714	Military education and training
750-773	Military life, manners and customs, antiquities, etc.
799-897	History of arms and armor

UA

10-997	Armies: Organization, distribution, military situation
21-885	By region or country
910-915	Mobilization
920-925	Plans for attack and defense
926-929	Civil defense
929.5-929.95	War damage in industry. Industrial defense
940-945	Military communication
950-979	Routes of travel. Distances
985-997	Military geography

UB

1-900	Military administration
160-165	Records, returns, muster rolls, etc.
170-175	Adjutant generals' offices
180-197	Civilian personnel departments
250-271	Intelligence
273-274	Sabotage
275-277	Psychological warfare. Propaganda

Class U-V continues on page 416.

320-338	Enlistment, recruiting, etc.
340-345	Compulsory service. Conscription and exemption
356-369.5	Provision for veterans
370-375	Military pensions, etc.
380-385	Soldiers' and sailors' homes
407-409	Warrant officers. Noncommissioned officers
410-415	Officers
416-419	Minorities, women, etc. in armed forces
420-425	Furloughs
440-449.5	Retired military personnel

UC

10-780	Maintenance and transportation
20-258	Organization of the service. By region or country
260-267	Supplies and stores
270-360	Transportation
400-440	Barracks. Quarters. Camps
460-535	Clothing and equipment
540-585	Equipage. Field kits
600-695	Horses. Mules. Remount service
700-780	Subsistence

UD

1-495	Infantry
157-302	Tactics. Maneuvers. Drill regulations
320-325	Manual of arms
330-335	Firing. Military sharpshooting
340-345	Bayonet drill
380-425	Small arms. Swords, etc.
450-455	Mounted infantry
460-464	Mountain troops
470-475	Ski troops
480-485	Airborne troops. Parachute troops
490-495	Airmobile operations

UE

1-500	Cavalry. Armor
	Including horse cavalry, armored cavalry, mechanized cavalry
144-145	Horse cavalry
147	Armored cavalry
157-302	Tactics. Maneuvers. Drill regulations
420-425	Cavalry sword exercises
460-475	Horses

UF
1-910	Artillery
157-302	Tactics. Maneuvers. Drill regulations
400-405	Field artillery
450-455	Seacoast artillery
460-465	Siege artillery
470-475	Howitzer artillery. Mortar batteries
480-485	Garrison artillery
500-515	Weapons systems
520-537	Ordnance and small arms
540-545	Arsenals, magazines, armories, etc.
560-780	Ordnance material (Ordnance proper)
820-830	Ballistics. Velocities and motions of projectiles
848-856	Artillery instruments. Fire control, etc.

UG
1-620	Military engineering
160-302	Tactics and regulations
335	Bridges
340	Tunnels
360-390	Field engineering
400-442	Fortification
443-449	Attack and defense. Siege warfare
470-474	Military surveying, topography, and mapping
490	Land mines, etc.
500-565	Technical troops and other special corps
570-582	Military signaling
590-613.5	Military telegraphy and telephony
614-614.5	Military electric lighting
615-620	Military motor vehicles
622-1435	Air forces. Air warfare
633-635	By region or country
637-639	Education and training
640-645	Military aeronautical research
700-705	Tactics
730-735	Air defenses
760-765	Aerial reconnaissance
770-1045	Organization. Personnel management
1097	Air bases
1100-1435	Equipment and supplies
1500-1530	Military astronautics. Space warfare. Space surveillance
1523-1525	By region or country

Class U-V continues on page 418.

UH

20-910	Other services
20-25	Chaplains
201-515	Medical and sanitary services
520-(560)	Care of sick and wounded. Relief societies
600-629.5	Military hygiene and sanitation
700-705	Public relations. Press. War correspondents
750-769	Military social work. Social welfare services
800-910	Recreation and information services

V	
1-995	Naval science (General)
25-55	History and antiquities of naval science
66-69	Navy clubs
160-165	Strategy
167-178	Tactics
200	Coast defense
210-214.5	Submarine warfare
390-395	Naval research
396-396.5	Military oceanography
399	Automation in the naval sciences
400-695	Naval education
720-743	Naval life, manners and customs, antiquities, etc.
750-995	War vessels: Construction, armament, etc.

VA	
10-750	Navies: Organization, distribution, naval situation
49-395	United States
400-750	Other regions or countries

VB	
15-(955)	Naval administration
21-124	By region or country
170-187	Civil department
260-275	Enlisted personnel
307-309	Warrant officers
310-315	Officers
320-325	Minorities, women, etc. in navies

VC	
10-580	Naval maintenance
20-258	Organization of service
260-268	Supplies and stores
270-279	Equipment of vessels, supplies, allowances, etc.
280-345	Clothing and equipment
350-410	Subsistence. Provisioning
412-425	Navy yards and stations. Shore facilities

VD	
7-430	Naval seamen
21-124	By region or country

Class U-V continues on page 420.

160-302	Drill regulations
330-335	Shooting
360-390	Small arms
400-405	Small boat service

VE
7-500	Marines
23-124	By region or country
160-302	Drill regulations
330-335	Shooting
360-390	Small arms
420-425	Barracks, quarters, etc.
430-435	Training camps

VF
1-580	Naval ordnance
21-124	By region or country
160-302	Ordnance instructions and drill books
310-315	Target practice
346-348	Naval weapons systems
350-375	Ordnance and arms (General)
390-510	Ordnance material (Ordnance proper)

VG
20-2029	Minor services of navies
20-25	Chaplains
50-55	Coast guard and coast signal service
70-85	Naval communication by telegraphy, telephone, etc.
90-95	Naval aviation
100-475	Medical service
500-505	Public relations. Press. War correspondents
2000-2005	Social work. Social welfare services
2020-2029	Recreation and information service

VK
1-1661	Navigation. Merchant marine
15-124	History, conditions, etc.
321-369.8	Harbors. Ports
381-397	Signaling
401-529	Study and teaching
549-572	Science of navigation
573-587	Nautical instruments
588-597	Marine hydrography. Hydrographic surveying
600-794	Tide and current tables
798-997	Sailing directions. Pilot guides
1000-1249	Lighthouse service
1250-1299	Shipwrecks and fires

1299.5-1299.6	Icebreaking operations
1300-1491	Saving of life and property
1500-1661	Pilots and pilotage

VM
1-989	Naval architecture. Shipbuilding. Marine engineering
15-124	History
165-276	Study and teaching
295-296	Contracts and specifications
298.5-301	Shipbuilding industry. Shipyards
311-466	Special types of vessels
595-989	Marine engineering
975-989	Diving

Like the schedule for Classes E-F, this schedule contains two main classes, U and V. These are discussed below.

Class U—Military Science was originally developed by Charles Martel in 1903 and was first issued in 1910. The preface to the second edition stated: "The extensive additions incident to the military developments of the First World War made it necessary to issue a second edition in 1928." The third edition was published in 1952. The fourth edition, published in 1974, included the revision and expansion of subclass UG to provide for material on aerial warfare and the air forces of the world.

Class V—Naval Science was first planned in 1904 by S. C. Stuntz under the direction of Charles Martel. In 1905, Clarence Perley took charge of this schedule and served as the editor of the first edition in 1910. The second edition was issued in 1953 and the third, with no major rearrangement, in 1974. A fourth edition was published in 1993.

With the 1996 edition, the schedules for Classes U and V were combined into a single volume.

The *Classification and Index* of the Military Information Division of the Adjutant-General's Office of the former U.S. War Department served as the basis for Class U, as well as for most of Class V. Subclass VK, Navigation, was based on the order of the publications of the British Hydrographic Office.

Class U contains nine subclasses: subclass U for Military science (general); UA for Armies; UB for Military administration; UC for Maintenance and transportation; UD for Infantry; UE for Cavalry and armor; UF for Artillery; UG for Military engineering; and UH for Other services.

Class V contains ten subclasses: subclass V for Naval science (general); VA for Navies; VB for Naval administration; VC for Naval maintenance; VD for Naval seamen; VE for Marines; VF for Naval ordnance; VG for Minor services of navies; VK for Navigation and the merchant marine; and VM for Naval architecture, shipbuilding, and marine engineering.

Neither of these two brief classes poses significant problems in use. Class U contains three auxiliary tables, numbered U1-U3. Table U1 replaces many of the "Divided like" notes used in earlier editions. Table U2, Table of Region and Country Subdivisions, is a table for geographic subdivisions by means of numbers. Table U3 is called Table for Organization of the Service, Other Regions or Countries. The following examples illustrate the use of auxiliary tables:

Belfiglio, Valentine J. *Honor, pride, duty : a history of the Texas State Guard.* 1995

UA	Subclass: Armies: organization, distribution, military situation
470	The first number in the range UA470-479 assigned to United States Militia in Texas, meaning a general work (according to Table U1)
.B45	The Cutter number for the main entry, Belfiglio
1995	The date of publication

Hawaii. Legislature. Office of the Legislative Auditor. *Financial audit of the Department of Defense : a report to the Governor and the Legislature of the State of Hawaii.* 1996

UA	Subclass: Armies: organization, distribution, military situation
159.8	The number in the range UA159.1-.9 assigned to United States Militia in Hawaii, meaning organizations (according to Table U1)
.D47	The first Cutter number for the name of the organization, Department of Defense
H39	The second Cutter number for the main entry, Hawaii
1996	The date of publication

Internal tables are used throughout the schedule. An example is shown below:

Livingston, Gary. *Cradled in glory : Georgia Military Institute, 1851-1865.* 1997

U	Subclass: Military science (general)
430	Private military schools in the United States, by name, A-Z
.G4	The first Cutter number for the name of the school, Georgia Military Institute

L57	The second Cutter number for a non-official work (according to the internal table) based on the main entry, Livingston
1997	The date of publication

Many of the internal tables in earlier editions have been replaced by enumeration of subdivisions. For example, the very detailed internal table using Cutter numbers for material concerning West Point has been eliminated, and the subdivisions under U410 are now listed in the schedule. A class history of West Point is classed in the number U410.N1 (by date).

McWhorter, John C.   *West Point revisited : reminiscences of the Class of 1946, 50 years later.*   1996

U	Subclass: Military science (general)
410	U.S. Military Academy, West Point
.N1	The Cutter number meaning a class history
1946a	The date of the class

In the example above, the date of publication is not added. The letter "a" in 1946a indicates a second work on the subject.

Maihafer, Harry J.   *Oblivion : the mystery of West Point cadet Richard Cox.*   1996

U	Subclass: Military science (general)
410	U.S. Military Academy, West Point
.M1	The first Cutter number meaning a biography
C69	The second Cutter number for the biographee, Cox
1996	The date of publication

Similarly, various kinds of works about the Naval Academy are classed in the number V415 subarranged by form using Cutter numbers.

McNitt, Robert W.   *Sailing at the U.S. Naval Academy : an illustrated history.*   1996

V	Subclass: Naval science (general)
415	United States Naval Academy
.L1	The first Cutter number for a history or general work
M36	The second Cutter number for the main entry, McNitt
1996	The date of publication

The Cutter number .P1 is designated for descriptive works and works about "Life at Annapolis," for example:

Mackenzie, Ross. *Brief points : an almanac for parents and friends of U.S. Naval Academy midshipmen.* 1996

V	Subclass: Naval science (general)
415	United States Naval Academy
.P1	The first Cutter number for a descriptive work
M33	The second Cutter number for the main entry, Mackenzie
1996	The date of publication

Gantar, Jeffrey. *A question of honor : the cheating scandal that rocked Annapolis and a midshipman who decided to tell the truth.* 1996

V	Subclass: Naval science (general)
415	United States Naval Academy
.P1	The first Cutter number for a work on "Life at Annapolis"
G36	The second Cutter number for the main entry, Gantar
1996	The date of publication

Alphabetically arranged topical subdivisions are very common in Classes U and V, as shown in the following examples:

Gibson, James N. *The Navaho Missile Project : the story of the "know-how" missile of American rocketry.* 1996

UG	Subclass: Air forces
1312	Missiles and rockets, by type
.C7	The first Cutter number for the type, Cruise
G53	The second Cutter number for the main entry, Gibson
1996	The date of publication

Hill, Tracie L. *Thompson, the American legend : the first submachine gun.* 1996

UF	Subclass: Artillery
620	Machine guns
.T5	The first Cutter number for the type, Thompson
H55	The second Cutter number for the main entry, Hill
1996	The date of publication

A work on machine guns in general is assigned the Cutter number .A2.

Ford, Roger. The grim reaper : the machine-gun and machine-gunners. 1996

UF	Subclass: Artillery
620	Machine guns
.A2	The first Cutter number for a general work
F64	The second Cutter number for the main entry, Ford
1996	The date of publication

Sometimes, for a type of object, the special instruction "(not A-Z)" is given, which means that a single number is used for various types of the object. For example, in the schedule, the number V895 is designated for types of war vessels other than the types enumerated in the schedule. A work about the Jeffersonian gunboat is classed in the number V895 without a special Cutter number for the type of vessel because the caption of the number reads "Other types (not A-Z)."

Smith, Gene A. For the purposes of defense : the politics of the Jeffersonian gunboat program. 1995

V	Subclass: Naval science (general)
895	War vessels other than the types enumerated in the schedule
.S63	The Cutter number for the main entry, Smith
1995	The date of publication

The index combines the entries for Classes U and V. In addition to topics, it includes entries for many corporate bodies, particularly military colleges and academies in the United States and Great Britain and a number of U.S. military agencies.

Class Z begins on page 426.

CLASS Z—BIBLIOGRAPHY.   LIBRARY SCIENCE

Z
4-115.5	Books (General). Writing. Paleography
4-8	History of books and bookmaking
40-104.5	Writing
41-42.5	Autographs. Signatures
43-45	Calligraphy. Penmanship
48	Processes of duplicating (manifolding)
	Including mimeographing, multilithing
49-51	Typewriters. Typewriting. Keyboards.
	Keyboarding
52-52.5	Word processing
53-102	Shorthand. Stenography. Phonography
102.5-104.5	Cryptography. Ciphers. Invisible writing
105-115.5	Manuscripts. Paleography
116-659	Book industries and trade
116.A2	Treatises on the modern printed book
116.A3	Book design
116.A5-265.5	Printing
124-228	History
231-232	Printers and printing establishments
234	Medallic history of printing. Tokens
235-236	Printer's marks, mottoes, etc.
237	Paper. Watermarks, etc.
240-241.5	Incunabula. Block books
	Including broadsides, playing cards
242.9-264.5	Practical printing
	Including printing as a business, layout, paper and ink, machinery, type and type founding, electrotyping, desktop publishing, typesetting, presswork
265	Reproduction of books, documents, etc., by photography, microphotography, etc.
266-276	Bookbinding. Book decoration
278-549	Bookselling and publishing
551-656	Copyright
657-659	Freedom of the press. Censorship
662-1000.5	Libraries
662-664	Collections
665-718.8	Library science. Information science
668-669.7	Library education. Research
672	Library cooperation and coordination
674.7-674.83	Library information networks
675	Classes of libraries
678-678.88	Library administration and organization. Constitution

678.89-678.892	Library service agencies
678.9	Automation
679-680	Library buildings. Library architecture
	Including planning, space utilization,
	security, safety, lighting, etc.
680.3-680.6	Library communication systems
681-681.3	Reproduction of library materials. Storage
	media of library materials
681.5-681.7	Trustees. Library boards, committees, etc.
682-682.4	Personnel
683-683.5	Finance. Insurance
684-685	Supplies. Shelving. Bookstacks
686	Branches. Delivery stations. Bookmobiles
687-718.8	The collections. The books
688	Special collections
688.5	Processing
689-689.8	Acquisition (selection, purchase, gifts,
	duplicates)
690	Exchanges
691-692	Special classes of materials
	Including manuscripts, maps,
	microforms,serials
693-695.83	Cataloging
695.85	Library handwriting
695.87	Printing of catalogs
695.9-695.94	Indexing. Abstracting
695.95	Alphabetizing. Filing
695.98	Recataloging. Reclassification
696-697	Classification and notation
698	Shelflisting. Author notation
699-699.5	Machine methods of information and
	retrieval. Mechanized bibliographic
	control
699.7	Physical processing. Shelf preparation
700	Bookbinding
700.9-701.5	Preservation, conservation and restoration
	of books, etc.
702	Thefts and losses of books
703.5-703.6	Moving. Disposition of books on shelves,
	etc.
	Including discarding, weeding
711-711.92	Reference work. Library service to
	special groups
712-714	Circulation. Loans. Charging systems
716-716.1	Library extension. Library commissions.
	Traveling libraries

Class Z continues on page 428.

716.2-718.8	Libraries in relation to special topics Including libraries and community, libraries and television, children's libraries, libraries and students
719-725	Libraries (General)
729-871	Library reports. History. Statistics
881-980	Library catalogs and bulletins
987-997	Private libraries. Book collecting Including bibliophilism, bookplates
998-1000.5	Booksellers' catalogs. Book prices
1001-8999	Bibliography
1001-1121	General bibliography
1001	Introduction to bibliography. Documentation
1003-1003.5	Choice of books. Books and reading. Book reviews
1004	Biography of bibliographers
1011-1017	General bibliographies
1019-1033	Special classes of books Including prohibited books, rare books, paperbacks, reprints
1035-1035.9	Best books
1036	Booksellers' general catalogs of modern books
1037-1039	Books for special classes of persons, institutions, etc.
1040	Databases. Computer files
1041-1121	Anonyms and pseudonyms
1201-4980	National bibliography
1201-1946	America
1215-1363	United States
1365-1401	Canada. British North America
1411-1939	Latin America
1975	Eastern Hemisphere
2000-2959	Europe
3001-3496	Asia
3501-3975	Africa
4001-4980	Australia. Oceania
5051-7999	Subject bibliography Subjects arranged in alphabetical sequence
8001-8999	Personal bibliography Names of individuals arranged in alphabetical sequence
ZA	
3040-5185	Information resources (General)
3150-3159	Information services. Information centers
3201-3250	Information superhighway

4050-4750	Information in specific formats or media
4050-4460	Electronic information resources
4150-4390	Computer network resources
4450-4460	Databases
4550	Motion pictures. Video recordings
4650-4675	Pictures. Photographs
4750	Sound recordings
	Information from specific providers
5050-5185	Government information

Class Z—Bibliography and Library Science was the first schedule of LC Classification to be prepared. Even before the debate in 1897 on whether to develop an original scheme for the Library of Congress or to adopt an existing system, it was decided that " 'Bibliography' would constitute a basic reference collection separate from the general collections" and that the development of Class Z would proceed "regardless of the uncertainty about the new classification system."[38]

Class Z was completed in 1898 and published in 1902. Charles Martel developed the original schedule for this class. The second edition was issued in 1910 and the third in 1926. The fourth edition was published in 1959, and a fifth edition in 1980. Beginning with the 1995 edition, the schedule has been produced using the automated system.

In addition to subjects relating to the book and the discipline of library and information science, Class Z is designed to contain all bibliographies (except bibliographies in Classes K and M and lists of films or sound recordings). There are separate ranges of numbers for National Bibliography (Z1201-4980), Subject Bibliography (Z5051-7999), and Personal Bibliography (Z8001-8999). Class M, Music, and Class K, Law, contain numbers for bibliographies on these subjects. The Library of Congress uses these numbers instead of those in Class Z.

A new subclass, ZA, Information resources, was added to Class Z in 1995. This is the first time that double letters are used for subclasses in Class Z.

Tables

There are nine auxiliary tables, some of which were converted from internal tables in earlier editions. The following example illustrates the use of tables:

Oberlé, Gérard.   *Auguste Poulet-Malassis, un imprimeur sur le Parnasse : ses ancêtres, ses auteurs, ses amis, ses écrits.*   1996

Z	Subclass: Bibliography and library science
305	A history or biography relating to bookselling and publishing in France

.P67   The first Cutter number for the biographee, Poulet-
            Malassis

O25   The second Cutter number for the main entry, Oberlé

1996   The date of publication

In the example above, the number Z305 is chosen from the range of numbers
Z303-310 assigned to France according to Table Z7 for an "eight-number"
country. The third number (i.e., 2) in the table represents history and biography
subarranged by name of individual or firm in the case of individual biographies
or histories of individual firms.

Book Industries and Trade and Libraries and Library Science

The numbers used for Book industries and trade (Z116-659) and
Libraries and Library and information science (Z662-1000.5) are enumerated
in the schedules and should not present problems in application. For example:

From database networking to the digital library.   c1997

Z   Subclass: Bibliography and library science
674.7   General works on library information networks
.F76   The Cutter number for the main entry under the title,
            From . . .
1997   The date of publication

*Up and running : implementing Z39.50 : proceedings of a symposium
sponsored by the State Library of Iowa, November 26, 1996, Ames, Iowa.*
c1997

Z   Subclass: Bibliography and library science
674.8   Library information networks in the United States
.U62   The Cutter number for the main entry under the title,
            Up and running
1997   The date of publication

Dewey, Melvil.   *Abridged Dewey decimal classification and relative index.*
Ed. 13 / edited by Joan S. Mitchell . . . [et al.].   1997

Z   Subclass: Bibliography and library science
696   Classification and notation
.D54   The Cutter number for abridged Decimal Classification
1997   The date of publication

Chan, Lois Mai. *Dewey decimal classification : a practical guide.* 1996

Z	Subclass: Bibliography and library science
696	Classification and notation
.D7	The first Cutter number meaning a general work on the Dewey Decimal Classification
C48	The second Cutter number for the main entry, Chan
1996	The date of publication

Library of Congress, Cataloging Policy and Support Office. *Library of Congress Classification. Z. Bibliography. Library science.* 1995 ed. 1995

Z	Subclass: Bibliography and library science
696	Classification and notation
.U5	The Cutter number (based on United States), meaning (according to an internal table) the official edition of an individual schedule of the LC Classification
Z	The letter representing Class Z
1995	The date of publication

The unusual notation resulted from the instruction in the schedule:

Z696.U5A-Z   Official editions.   By class, A-Z, and date

The Cutter number .U5 was based on the main entry for earlier editions under "United States."

National Bibliography

Six of the nine auxiliary tables are used with the classification of bibliographies in Class Z: Tables Z1-Z3 for National bibliography and imprints, and Tables Z4-Z6 for Subject bibliography. The basic use of all six of these tables essentially involves direct numerical transfer or matching of final digits. Table Z1 serves as an illustration.

The following is an excerpt from Table Z1:

Z1	NATIONAL BIBLIOGRAPHY. IMPRINTS
0.A1	Bibliography
0.A2	Theory, method, etc.
0.A3-Z	General bibliography
1	Bibliography of early works
1.5	History of bibliography
2	Publishers' catalogs
4	Periodicals
5	Societies
6	Collections
8	Government publications
9	Biobibliography
	Literature (General)
10.A1	Bibliography of bibliography
10.A3-Z	General bibliography
	By period
11	Early to 1800
12	1801-1950
12.3	1951-
12.5.A-Z	Special classes or groups of writers, A-Z
12.5.E42	Emigre authors. Authors in foreign countries

★★★★★

12.5.W6	Women authors
13.A-Z	Special topics, A-Z
13.A5	Almanacs
13.A7	Argot

★★★★★

	History and description (General)
	Including geography
	By period
16	To 1500
16.5	16th century
17	17th-18th centuries
18	19th century
19	Early 20th century
19.3	1945-
20.A-Z	Special topics not in 16-19, A-Z

★★★★★

	Local
22	General
23.A-Z	Special, A-Z

In the schedule, national bibliography of Great Britain and Ireland is assigned a range of numbers Z2001-2029. The classifier is instructed in the schedule to use Table Z1 with this range of numbers. In Table Z1, government publications are classed in the number 8. Adding the number 8 to the first number Z2001 in the range assigned to Great Britain results in Z2009. If the matching method is used, Z2009, the ninth number in the range, corresponds to the number 8, the ninth number in Table Z1. This is one of the rare cases where the last digits of schedule numbers do not match exactly the numbers in the tables.

National Library of Canada. *Great Britain official publications : collection guide.* 1996

Z	Subclass: Bibliography and library science
2009	Government publications of Great Britain
.N35	The Cutter number for the main entry, National Library of Canada
1996	The date of publication

Literature, philology, and history are all treated as subdivisions of national bibliography in Table Z1. This material, if of a national scope, is then classed by the Library of Congress as national bibliography and not subject bibliography. The eleventh number (10.A3-Z) in Table Z1 is for a general national bibliography of literature. Therefore, Z2011, the eleventh number in Great Britain's range, is assigned to a bibliography of British literature.

Roy Davids Ltd. *Manuscripts, annotated books, literary and historical portraits, and artefacts.* [1996?]

Z	Subclass: Bibliography and library science
2011	A general bibliography of British literature
.R69	The Cutter number for the main entry, Roy Davids Ltd.
1996	The date of publication

Likewise, the twelfth number (11) in Table Z1 is used for a bibliography of early (through 1800) literature. When fitted into the span of numbers assigned to the literature of Great Britain and Ireland, it becomes Z2012.

Simonds, Peggy Munoz. *Iconographic research in English Renaissance literature : a critical guide.* 1995

Z	Subclass: Bibliography and library science
2012	A general bibliography of British literature through 1800

.S56	The Cutter number for the main entry, Simonds
1995	The date of publication

In Table Z1, the number for women authors is 12.5.W6. Therefore, a bibliography of British women authors is classed in Z2013.5.W6

Horwitz, Barbara Joan. *British women writers, 1700-1850 : an annotated bibliography of their works and works about them.* 1997

Z	Subclass: Bibliography and library science
2013.5	A general bibliography of special classes or groups of writers from Great Britain, A-Z
.W6	The first Cutter number meaning women authors
H67	The second Cutter number for the main entry, Horwitz
1997	The date of publication

A general national bibliography of history covering the twentieth century is classed in the twentieth number (19) in Table Z1, as illustrated in the following example:

Robbins, Keith. *A bibliography of British history. 1914-1989.* 1996

Z	Subclass: Bibliography and library science
2020	A general bibliography of early 20th-century British history
.R63	The Cutter number for the main entry, Robbins
1996	The date of publication

In this case, the first of the two numbers (19 and 19.3) in Table Z1 covering the twentieth century is chosen according to the first-of-two rule, that is, choosing the first of two equally applicable numbers. Further example:

Creaton, Heather. *London.* 1996

Z	Subclass: Bibliography and library science
2024	A general bibliography of a local place in Great Britain, A-Z
.L8	The first Cutter number for the place, London
C74	The second Cutter number for the main entry, Creaton
1996	The date of publication

Alternate Class Numbers

Class Z has received considerable criticism, mainly because it groups all subject bibliographies together in Z and thus separates them from the subject materials to which they pertain. On the other side of the coin is the consideration that where all bibliographies are shelved in a reference collection, a separate class for them is most useful.

In recognition of the problem, the Library of Congress provides alternate class numbers for certain bibliographical materials. Alternate subject class numbers appear in LC MARC records immediately following the call numbers and are coded as subfield "a." Alternate numbers are provided for all bibliographies with LC call numbers falling within the following ranges of numbers in Class Z:[39]

> Z1201-4980, National bibliography (except in the case of bibliographies having no topical focus)
>
> Z5051-7999, Subject bibliography
>
> Z8001-8999, Personal bibliography

Following are examples of alternate numbers for bibliographies:

> Kost, I. L.   *The international aspects of natural and industrial catastrophes : selective bibliography / prepared by I.L. Kost = Les aspects internationaux des catastrophes naturelles et industrielles : bibliographie selective.*   1995

Z6004.N3 K68 1995	LC call number
[GB5014]	Alternate number in subclass GB, Physical geography

> *A bibliography on writing and written language.*   1996

Z7004.W69 B53 1996	LC call number
[P211]	Alternate number in subclass P, Philology and linguistics (General)

> *What fantastic fiction do I read next? : a reader's guide to recent fantasy, horror, and science fiction.*   c1998

Z5917.F3 W53 1998	LC call number
[PN3435]	Alternate number in subclass PN, Literature (General)

Shaw, Gareth.   *British directories : a bibliography and guide to directories published in England and Wales (1850-1950) and Scotland (1773-1950).* 1997

| Z5771.4.G7 S47 1997 | LC call number |
| [DA27.5] | Alternate number in subclass DA, History of Great Britain |

Architecture sourcebook : a guide to resources on the practice of architecture. c1997

| Z5943.A72 A75 1997 | LC call number |
| [NA2750] | Alternate number in subclass NA, Architecture |

Romi, Rivka.   *China shipping & ports : bibliography.*   [1996]

| Z7164.S55 R558 1996 | LC call number |
| [HE565.C6] | Alternate number in subclass HE, Transportation and communications |

As a rule, the alternate number does not include the book number since it is not a valid LC call number. The Cutter number ".C6" in the last example above is a geographic Cutter number for China, not an item number.

Normally, the class number in Classes A-J, L, N-V, or Z1-Z1200 that most closely corresponds to the topic of the bibliography is assigned as the alternate number. Even when various form numbers have been established under the appropriate subject, there is usually none for bibliographies. Therefore, the most general number for the subject (often with the caption "General works," "Treatises," or a variation thereof) is selected. The numbers for special forms, for example, periodicals, directories, picture works, etc., are not used for bibliographies.

The alternate number is given even if the Z number itself is an alternate number, as in the case of an analytic of a collected monographic series.

Alternate numbers for special types of bibliographies are selected according to the following table:[40]

Alternate numbers for specific types of materials.

TYPE OF MATERIAL	ALTERNATE NUMBER
Belles lettres	**General works** number under **History and criticism** in class P, as appropriate for the language, form, and period of the bibliography
Children's literature	PN1009, and numbers in specific P subclasses
Dissertations from a single institution	AS11+
Dissertations from many institutions, not limited to a specific topic	None
Government publications, not limited to a specific topic or agency	Appropriate number in subclass J
Government publications on a specific topic or limited to a specific agency	Appropriate topical number
National bibliography with no topical focus, e.g. list of imprints of a specific country	None
Newspapers	PN4700+
Personal bibliography	Number for biographies of the person
Subject bibliography, including topical bibliographies classed in national bibliography numbers	**General works** number for the topic in classes A-J, L, N-V, Z1-1200
University bibliography, i.e. publications issued by a university, not limited to a specific topic	AS11+

Source: Library of Congress, *Subject Cataloging Manual: Classification.*

Subclass ZA

In 1995, recognizing the deficiency of Class Z in accommodating general works on information resources, the Library of Congress proposed a new subclass, ZA, Information Resources. A tentative draft[41] was published with an invitation for comments from the library community. The schedule, finalized in spring 1996, was published in *LC Classification, Additions and Changes*, List 261 (January-March 1996); it will be incorporated into future editions of Class Z. It is also available on LC Marvel on the World Wide Web.[42]

Following are examples of works classed in ZA:

Ellis, David. *Progress and problems in information retrieval.* 1996

ZA	Subclass: Information resources
3075	General works on how to find information
.E43	The Cutter number for the main entry, Ellis
1996	The date of publication

Mackall, Joe. *Information management.* 1998

ZA	Subclass: Information resources
3080	Juvenile works on how to find information
.M33	The Cutter number for the main entry, Mackall
1998	The date of publication

Nieuwenhuizen, John. *Asleep at the wheel : Australia on the super-highway.* 1997

ZA	Subclass: Information resources
3250	Information superhighway, by region or country, A-Z
.A8	The first Cutter number for Australia
N53	The second Cutter number for the main entry, Nieuwenhuizen
1997	The date of publication

Basch, Reva. *Secrets of the super Net searchers : the reflections, revelations, and hard-won wisdom of 35 of the world's top Internet researchers.* 1996

ZA	Subclass: Information resources
4201	General works on the Internet
.B37	The Cutter number for the main entry, Basch
1996	The date of publication

The Internet international directory. 1995- [1995]-

ZA	Subclass: Information resources
4201	General works on the Internet
.I57	The Cutter number for the main entry under the title, *Internet . . .*

Library of Congress Publications

A detailed expansion of the class number Z663, Library of Congress, was developed by the Library to enable it to class and maintain copies of its own publications together in a separate archival collection in the Rare Book Division.[43] Libraries that do not possess an extensive collection of LC publications may wish to class them by subject in Classes B-Z. For LC publications, in addition to the regular LC call numbers, numbers based on the expansion under Z663 are also assigned, as shown in the following examples:

Library of Congress. *Financial statements for fiscal 1995.* [1996]
Call number: Z733.U58 L38 1996
[Special LC number: Z663 .F55 1996]

Library of Congress. *Women come to the front : journalists, photographers, and broadcasters during World War II.* [1995?]
Call number: PN471 .L53 1995
[Special LC number: Z663 .W66 1995]

ALA-LC romanization tables : transliteration schemes for non-Roman scripts. 1997 ed. 1997
Call number: P226 .A4 1997
[Special LC number: Z663.72 .A4 1997]

In the numbers based on the special scheme, the decimal extension represents a department or division of the Library of Congress, and the Cutter number is taken from the first word or a key word in the title.

NOTES

1. Library of Congress, Office for Subject Cataloging Policy, *LC Classification Outline*, 6th ed. (Washington, DC: Library of Congress, 1990).

2. "Societies," in Library of Congress, Cataloging Policy and Support Office, *Subject Cataloging Manual: Shelflisting*, 2nd ed. (Washington, DC: Library of Congress, 1995), G240.

3. Jean M. Perreault, "The Classification of Philosophy," *Libri* 14 (1964):32-39.

4. "Archival Inventories and Manuscript Catalogs," in Library of Congress, Office for Subject Cataloging Policy, *Subject Cataloging Manual: Classification*, 1st ed. (Washington, DC: Cataloging Distribution Service, Library of Congress, 1992), F495.

5. "Historic Preservation," Library of Congress, *Subject Cataloging Manual: Classification*, F595.

6. "Genealogy," Library of Congress, *Subject Cataloging Manual: Classification*, F600.

7. "Local Court Records," Library of Congress, *Subject Cataloging Manual: Classification*, F635.

8. Jean M. Perreault, "Lois Mai Chan's New Edition of Immroth's Manual on the Library of Congress Classification," *International Classification* 7, no. 3 (1980):126-30.

9. "Subclass GE, Environmental Science," *Cataloging Service Bulletin* 58 (Fall 1992):53.

10. Charles Martel, "The Library of Congress Classification: Some Considerations Regarding the Relation of Book or Library Classification to the 'Order of the Sciences'," in *Essays Offered to Herbert Putnam by His Colleagues and Friends on His Thirtieth Anniversary As Librarian of Congress: 5 April 1929*, ed. William Warner Bishop and Andrew Keogh (New Haven, CT: Yale University Press, 1929), 329.

11. Library of Congress, Geography and Map Division, *Geographic Cutters*, 2nd microfiche ed. (Washington, DC: Cataloging Distribution Service, Library of Congress, 1989).

12. "Change in Notation in the Classification for Maps and Atlases of Minor Political and Geographic Units," *Cataloging Service* 106 (May 1973):5.

13. Mary Lynette Larsgaard, *Map Librarianship: An Introduction*, 3rd ed. (Englewood, CO: Libraries Unlimited, 1998), 126.

14. W. C. Berwick Sayers, *A Manual of Classification for Librarians and Bibliographers*, rev. 3rd ed. (London: Grafton, 1955), 160.

15. "Law Classification Schedules," *Cataloging Service Bulletin* 23 (Winter 1983):47-48.

16. Jolande E. Goldberg, "Introduction to the Application of the Schedule," in Library of Congress, Cataloging Policy and Support Office, *Classification. Class KL-KWX. Law of Asia and Eurasia. Africa, Pacific Area, and Antarctica* (Washington, DC: Library of Congress, 1993), I, viii-ix.

17. Jolande E. Goldberg, "Introduction to the Application of the Schedule," in Library of Congress, Subject Cataloging Division, *Classification. Class KJ-KKZ. Law of Europe* (Washington, DC: Library of Congress, 1988), xii.

18. Jolande E. Goldberg, *Library of Congress Classes JZ and KZ: Historical Notes and Introduction to Application* (Washington, DC: Cataloging Distribution Service, Library of Congress, 1997).

19. Ibid., 28.

20. "Class K Form Division Tables," *Cataloging Service Bulletin* 72 (Spring 1996):10-18.

21. "Teaching of Particular Subjects," Library of Congress, *Subject Cataloging Manual: Classification*, F730.

22. Fred Bindman, "Classification of Musical Materials," in *Proceedings of the Institute on Library of Congress Music Cataloging Policies and Procedures, January 26-27, 1971, Coolidge Auditorium, Library of Congress, Washington, D.C.*, transcribed and compiled with editorial comments by David Sommerfield, Music Library Association Technical Reports, No. 3 (Ann Arbor, MI: Music Library Association, 1975), 63.

23. "Music Materials," Library of Congress, *Subject Cataloging Manual: Shelflisting*, G800, p. 1.

24. "Music Materials," Library of Congress, *Subject Cataloging Manual: Shelflisting*, G800.

25. "Artists," Library of Congress, *Subject Cataloging Manual: Shelflisting*, G330.

26. "Literary Collections," Library of Congress, *Subject Cataloging Manual: Classification*, F634.

27. "Literary Authors," Library of Congress, *Subject Cataloging Manual: Classification*, F632, p. 1.

28. Ibid., 2.

29. Ibid., 3.

30. Ibid., 2.

31. "Literary Authors: Subarrangement of Works," Library of Congress, *Subject Cataloging Manual: Classification*, F633, p. 2.

32. "Topical Greek and Roman Classics," *Cataloging Service* 121 (Spring 1977):19.

33. "Class P: Subclasses PN, PR, PS, PZ," *Cataloging Service Bulletin* 2 (Fall 1978):45.

34. "Cataloging Change Announced," *Library of Congress Information Bulletin* 38 (August 24, 1979):335.

35. United States Army Medical Library, *Army Medical Library Classification: Medicine. Preclinical Sciences: QS-QZ, Medicine and Related Subjects: W*, 1st ed. (Washington, DC: Government Printing Office, 1951).

36. National Library of Medicine (U.S.), *National Library of Medicine Classification: A Scheme for the Shelf Arrangement of Library Materials in the Field of Medicine and Its Related Sciences*, 5th ed. (Bethesda, MD: U.S. Dept. of Health and Human Services, Public Health Service, National Institutes of Health, National Library of Medicine, 1994).

37. Charles Ammi Cutter, *Cutter-Sanborn Three-Figure Author Table (Swanson-Swift revision, 1969)* (Chicopee, MA: H. R. Huntting Company, 1969?).

38. "Preface," in Library of Congress, Subject Cataloging Division, *Classification. Class Z. Bibliography and Library Science*, 5th ed. (Washington, DC: Library of Congress, 1980), [iii].

39. "Alternate Class Numbers: Bibliography," Library of Congress, *Subject Cataloging Manual: Classification*, F150.

40. Ibid., 2.

41. "Subclass ZA, Information Resources," *Cataloging Service Bulletin* 70 (Fall 1995):7-10.

42. "Subclass ZA, Information Resources," *Cataloging Service Bulletin* 72 (Spring 1996):18.

43. "Library of Congress Publications," Library of Congress, *Subject Cataloging Manual: Classification*, F620.

Classification of Special Types of Library Materials

Chapter 6 discusses the individual classes in the Library of Congress (LC) Classification. There are certain types of library materials, however, that occur in more than one subject area and that require special treatment because of their unique characteristics. This chapter presents current LC practice on classifying and shelflisting such materials. It should be noted that LC policies have varied over the years and older cataloging records may reflect practices that are no longer in force. At the same time, some current records may reflect apparently obsolete policy in part because Cutter numbers established in the shelflist under patterns that prevailed earlier may still be used in new records in order to keep materials together.

The types of materials covered in this chapter are biography; serial publications, including monographic series, collections, collected works, etc.; materials cataloged under corporate headings; works from special sources, including society publications, government documents, congresses, and conferences; works related to other works, including editions, translations, abridgments, commentaries, supplements, and indexes; works requiring special treatment, including incunabula, "bound-with" books, comic books, abstracts and annotated bibliographies, nonprint materials, software, and microforms; and juvenile materials. As these categories are not mutually exclusive, much information would have to be repeated if each were discussed in full. References to other accounts, both within chapter 7 and to earlier chapters, are made to the fullest extent possible.

BIOGRAPHY

Biographies[1] are writings that present accounts of the lives of individuals or groups of individuals. There are several ways that the LC Classification provides for biographical works:

1. under "Collective biography" numbers throughout the schedules;

2. under "Individual biography" numbers throughout the schedules;

3. under "General works" numbers throughout the schedules; and,

4. in Class C (Auxiliary sciences of history), particularly in subclass CT (Biography).

How a particular biographical work is treated depends in part on its nature and in part on the provisions in the schedule at the point where it is most appropriately placed.

Most works that are considered biographies cover the whole lives of their subjects and include personal details as well as accounts of the activities for which the biographees, that is, the subjects of the biographies, are known. Many works, however, are not full personal accounts but rather confine themselves to one or another aspect of a person's life; particularly, they treat how an individual or individuals relate to a topic. In classification, special-aspects biographies are not distinguished from biographies as such except insofar as their subject matter indicates different classification placement. But two other differences do matter in classification: those between individual biography and collective biography, and those between general and topic-related biography.

Collective Biography. The term *collective biography* is defined as a work dealing with the lives and/or contributions of two or more individuals, provided that a discrete section in the work is devoted to each individual.[2] For example, a work with a title like *Men and Women Who Have Led [particular] College*, with a chapter on each college president since the institution was founded, is considered collective biography; so is a publication reproducing obituaries from a given newspaper.

Individual Biography. The term *individual biography* is defined as a work containing a continuous narrative that discusses the life of a single individual or the contributions of a single individual to a particular discipline or field. Works of the type *My Life with [a famous person]*, as well as combined biographies of two closely related individuals (husband and wife or brother and sister), are also considered individual biography for classification purposes, as is a single continuous text that covers several disparate lives if the author's intent is to tell a single story with emphasis on one person. In these cases, the class number is assigned on the basis of the individual emphasized or the more famous one.

An account of travel is not considered a biography unless more than half the work is devoted to personal details of the life of the traveler.

General and Topic-Related Biography. Most biographical works are written about persons or groups of persons who are known for their connection with a field or topic or event. The term *topic-related biography* is used for these. But some biographical works are not associated with a particular subject field. The latter are called general biography. General biography may be either individual biography or collective biography; there are examples of both types of general biography in the previous chapter, in the discussion of Class C, Auxiliary sciences of history. See chapter 6, pages 177-80.

It is a characteristic of the LC Classification system that biographies of persons associated with particular fields are classed with the subjects represented in the various schedules. As noted briefly above, in some of the LC schedules there are special numbers for biography (in most cases, different numbers for collective biography and for individual biography) under both major disciplines and under broad topics within those disciplines. Also, there are usually biography provisions wherever personal names appear in the schedules, such as philosophers in B, musicians in M, artists in N, and literary authors in P. Often, however, there is no biography provision under the topic with which a given biographee is associated; in that case, biographical works about him or her are treated as general works on that topic. And again as noted above, there is provision for biography in subclass CT, Biography, in Schedule C, Auxiliary sciences of history. Placement there, however, is restricted to material that cannot reasonably be placed within a subject class, in other words, to general biography.

In classing a biographical work, classifiers must first find its appropriate place in the schedules. Then, the main concern is subarrangement. There is a separate table for the subarrangement of biographical works about a person; this table was introduced in chapter 4, page 98. The following discussion and examples cover further situations that arise in assigning class numbers and item numbers to biographical material.

Collective Biography

As indicated in the discussion of terminology above, collective biography may center on a topic, or its coverage may be general. General collective biography is classed in subclass CT in Schedule C. Its treatment there, with examples, is covered in chapter 6 in the unit on Class C and is also shown in the examples below. Collective biographies of persons who are associated with particular subject fields are classed under the numbers for those fields. If there is no special provision for collective biography at the appropriate place in the schedules, it is classed under the "General works" numbers. In many fields, however, there are special provisions for collective biography as well as for individual biography. The Biography Table is not used for collective biography; subarrangement of collective biographies under an explicit provision for collective biography is through Cutter numbers based on their main entries. For example:

Five thousand personalities of the world. 1996

CT	Subclass: Biography
120	General collective biography in the English language of persons from the 20th century
.F58	The Cutter number for the main entry under the title, *Five thousand . . .*
1996	The date of publication

The Cambridge dictionary of American biography. 1995

CT	Subclass: Biography
213	A biographical dictionary of persons from the United States
.C36	The Cutter number for the main entry under the title, *Cambridge . . .*
1995	The date of publication

Scher, Jon. *Baseball's best sluggers.* 1997

GV	Subclass: Recreation and leisure
865	Biography in the field of baseball
.A1	The first Cutter number for a collective biography as indicated in the schedule
S32	The second Cutter number for the main entry, Scher
1997	The date of publication

Neither is the Biography Table used for collective biography classed in "General works" numbers. Such works are cuttered in the same manner as other general works.

A combined biography of two closely related people, for example, siblings and spouses, is treated as an individual biography. A biography of the members of one family is also classed as an individual biography, unless special provision has been made for individual families in the schedules, for example:

Patton, Samuel Ellsworth. *Ten decades of the Sam Pattons : Macon, Georgia, 1900-1995 : Samuel Emory Patton, Mary Thomas Patton.* c1996

CT	Subclass: Biography
274	Individual families from the United States
.P384	The first Cutter number for the name of the family, Patton
P39	The second Cutter number for the main entry, Patton
1996	The date of publication

Individual Biography

Finding the appropriate placement in the classification is the first problem with individual biography. When the life of a biographee has a predominant topical focus, and the topic is one that is easily located in the schedules, the matter is straightforward. In general, biographical works are classed with the topic with which the biographee is mostly closely identified.

Many biographees, however, have multifaceted careers; others have worked in a given discipline but in different areas of the field. If an individual biography emphasizes a single facet of someone's career, even if that person is better known for other aspects of his or her life, the work is classed under the emphasized topic. A work on Albert Schweitzer as a musician is classed in ML; a work on Leonardo da Vinci as a scientist is classed in Q; a work on Theodore Roosevelt as a naturalist is classed in QH. If a biography discusses several careers of a person with no one of them given particular emphasis, it is classed with the field with which the biographee is most closely associated: da Vinci with art, Roosevelt with United States history, and so on. If none of the careers is emphasized and the biographee is not generally associated with any one field, the biography is classed in CT, as in the case of Schweitzer. Biographies of persons not associated with particular fields are also classed in CT.

Placement in subclass CT is generally by country, but there is special provision for biography of women. The most common pattern for subarrangement for individual biography is to use one Cutter number based on the name of the biographee and a second based on the main entry. Often, further differentiation is called for, and the means of doing this are discussed in the next section. The following examples show the general pattern for both classification and Cutter number assignment:

Fisseler, Brenda Lincke. *The forgotten son : a historical narrative of Charles Ferdinand Lincke.* c1996

CT	Subclass: Biography
275	Individual persons from the United States
.L457	The first Cutter number for the biographee, Lincke
F57	The second Cutter number for the main entry, Fisseler
1996	The date of publication

Frenkel, Cornelia. *Raoul Hausmann : Kunstler, Forscher, Philosoph.* 1996

N	Subclass: Visual arts
6888	German artists (388, Special artists from Germany, added to the base number 6500, History of art in special countries)
.H35	The first Cutter number for the artist, Hausmann
F74	The second Cutter number for the main entry, Frenkel
1996	The date of publication

Smith, Marshall. *Memories of Mickey Mantle : my very best friend.* 1996

GV	Subclass: Recreation and leisure
865	Biography in the field of baseball
.M33	The first Cutter number for the biographee, Mantle
S55	The second Cutter number for the main entry, Smith
1996	The date of publication

Bowler, Peter J. *Charles Darwin : the man and his influence.* [1996]

QH	Subclass: Natural history (general)
31	Individual biography
.D2	The first Cutter number for the biographee, Darwin
B743	The second Cutter number for the main entry, Bowler
1996	The date of publication

The Library of Congress has provided the following instructions on assigning Cutter numbers for individual biographies.[3] Biography may be classed in a number specifically designated for biographical works, or in a "general" number (that is, a number not designated as biography) when no biography number is provided. Subarrangement and cuttering of works by and about an individual differ in these situations as shown in the following table and explained in the sections below.

Works Classed in Biography Numbers
Collected works
Selected works
(No provisions for separate works)
Autobiography
Letters
Speeches
Biography/criticism

Works Classed in General Numbers
Collected works
Selected works
Separate works (alphabetical order)
Autobiography
Letters by title proper
Speeches by title proper
Biography/criticism

Biography Classed in Biography Numbers

For individual biography, special numbers for biography are provided under many topics whose class numbers have been developed to any extent in the LC schedules. These numbers are used for more than strictly biographical works. They are also used for any work intended to relate an individual or group of individuals to a topic. Such a work may contain personal details, or it may simply discuss the individual's activities, contributions, views, etc., relating to the topic in question.[4] It may include a collection of an individual's letters or a compilation of a person's speeches. To works about individual persons classed in "biography" numbers, double Cutter numbers are assigned according to the following procedures:

1. Biographee represented by the first Cutter number. When the first Cutter number represents the biographee, a second Cutter number is assigned according to the Biography Table. Different types of biographical writings about a person, such as autobiography, letters, speeches, or biography and criticism, are assigned the same class number (usually containing a Cutter number based on the name of the biographee) and are differentiated by means of successive Cutter numbers. A table has been devised for this purpose and is used for subarranging biographical works classed in "Individual biography" numbers in all classes except those, such as Classes N and P, that have their own special biography tables. For ease of reference in the following discussion and examples, the Biography Table is reproduced below:[5]

BIOGRAPHY TABLE

.x	Cutter for the individual
.xA2	Collected works. By date
.xA25	Selected works. Selections. By date Including quotations
.xA3	Autobiography, diaries, etc. By date
.xA4	Letters. By date

.xA5   Speeches, essays, and lectures.   By date
                 Including interviews
.xA6-Z   Individual biography, interviews, and
                 criticism.   By main entry
                 Including criticism of selected works,
                 autobiography, quotations, letters,
                 speeches, interviews, etc.

For example:

Baiul, Oksana.   *Oksana : my own story.*   c1997
GV   Subclass: Recreation and leisure
850   Biography in the field of ice skating
.B35   The first Cutter number for the biographee, Baiul
A3   The second Cutter number meaning autobiography,
                 according to the Biography Table
1997   The date of publication

Lowenstein, Roger.   *Buffett : the making of an American capitalist.*
c1995
HG   Subclass: Finance
172   Individual biography
.B84   The first Cutter number for the biographee, Buffett
L69   The second Cutter number for the main entry, Lowenstein
1995   The date of publication

Kerans, Marion Douglas.   *Muriel Duckworth, a very active pacifist : a
biography.*   c1996
JZ   Subclass: International relations
5540.2   Individual biography of people involved with the
                 promotion of peace
.D83   The first Cutter number for the biographee, Duckworth
K47   The second Cutter number for the main entry, Kerans
1996   The date of publication

Selected works, including quotations, are assigned A25 as the second Cutter
number, subarranged further by date. If there is more than one work by the
same author, a letter beginning with "b" is added to the date, for example:

Einstein, Albert. *The quotable Einstein.* 1996

QC	Subclass: Physics
16	Individual biography
.E5	The first Cutter number for the biographee, Einstein
A25	The second Cutter number (from the Biography Table) meaning selected works including quotations
1996	The date of publication

Einstein, Albert. *Bite-size Einstein : quotations on just about everything from the greatest mind of the twentieth century.* 1996

QC16.E5 A25 1996b

Folsing, Albrecht. *Albert Einstein : a biography.* 1997

QC16.E5 F5913 1997 [F5913 = Cutter number F59 for the main entry, Folsing, and the successive element (13 from the Translation Table) for an English translation]

Goldman, Robert N. *Einstein's God : Albert Einstein's quest as a scientist and as a Jew to replace a forsaken God.* 1997

QC16.E5 G67 1997 [G67 = Cutter number for the main entry, Goldman]

Table C30, Table for Biography (1 Cutter No.), in Class C is the same as the Biography Table, for example:

Hayes, Thelma Thomas. *A Tennessee daughter : me & my family.* 1996

CT	Subclass: Biography
275	Individual persons from the United States
.H4838	The first Cutter number for the biographee, Hayes
A3	The second Cutter number (based on Table C30) meaning Autobiography
1996	The date of publication

2. Biographee represented by the second Cutter number. When the first Cutter number represents a topical or geographical aspect and the biographee's name is represented by the second Cutter number, the Biography Table is not applied. Instead, a series of successive Cutter numbers is used to interfile works by and about the person according to the main entry, disregarding autobiography or other subdivisions shown in the Biography Table,

as illustrated in the following examples. The previous practice of filing auto-biographical works before other works about the person has been discontinued.

> Boyd, Aaron. *Smart money : the story of Bill Gates.* 1995

HD	Subclass: Economic history and conditions
9696	Electronic industries
.C62	The first Cutter number (.C6) for computers with the successive element (2) meaning General works and history, including biography (according to Table H21)
G333	The second Cutter number (G33) for the *biographee*, Gates, and the successive element (3) for the *author*, Boyd
1995	The date of publication

> Wallace, James. *Overdrive : Bill Gates and the race to control cyber-space.* 1997

HD	Subclass: Economic history and conditions
9696	Electronic industries
.C62	The first Cutter number (.C6) for computers with the successive element (2) meaning General works and history, including biography (according to Table H21)
G3379	The second Cutter number (G33) for the *biographee*, Gates and the successive element (79) for the *author*, Wallace
1997	The date of publication

In the two examples above, since the biographee is represented by the second Cutter number G33, the successive elements (3 and 79) are assigned in such a way so that the work by Boyd precedes the one by Wallace.

 3. Personal Narratives. A personal narrative classed in a biography number is treated as an autobiography, for example:

> Fennell, Desmond. *Dreams of oranges : an eyewitness account of the fall of communist East Germany.* 1996

DD	Subclass: History of Germany
287.7	Individual biography during the period after 1961-
.F46	The first Cutter number for the biographee, Fennell
A3	The second Cutter number for an autobiography
1996	The date of publication

If the class number is specified for personal narratives only, Cutter numbers are assigned as they would be for a work classed in a general class number (see explanation and examples in the next section).

In some schedules, for example, in Classes D-F, biography numbers have been established under specific subtopics. In other cases, for example, in Class Q, the biography numbers are generally established under disciplines or broad topics and occasionally under specific subtopics. In general, the biography numbers under the subdisciplines, if available, are assigned to biographies of persons associated with the subdisciplines. For example, the biography of a nuclear physicist is classed in the biography number established under Nuclear physics:

A gift of prophecy : essays in celebration of the life of Robert Eugene Marshak. 1994

QC	Subclass: Physics
774	Nuclear and particle physics, Atomic energy, Radioactivity: Individual biography, A-Z
.M37	The first Cutter number for the biographee, Marshak
G54	The second Cutter number for the main entry under the title, *gift of* . . .
1994	The date of publication

On the other hand, if biography numbers have not been established under subdisciplines, the biography number under the broad discipline is used, as shown in the following example:

Hermes, Matthew E. *Enough for one lifetime : Wallace Carothers, inventor of nylon.* c1996

QD	Subclass: Chemistry
22	Individual biography
.C35	The first Cutter number for the biographee, Carothers
H47	The second Cutter number for the main entry, Hermes
1996	The date of publication

Biography Classed in "General" Numbers

Biographies about individual persons closely associated with a special topic under which "biography numbers" are not specifically provided are classed in "general numbers" (i.e., numbers not designated as biography). In such cases, double Cutter numbers are assigned, the first for the biographee and the second for the main entry, for example:

Kilpatrick, Andrew. *Of permanent value : the story of Warren Buffett.* c1994

HG	Subclass: Finance
4928.5	Stock brokerage, Security dealers, and Investment advisors in the United States
.B84	The first Cutter number for the biographee, Buffett
K538	The second Cutter number for the main entry, Kilpatrick
1994	The date of publication

Lapomarda, Vincent A. *The Boston mayor who became Truman's Secretary of Labor : Maurice J. Tobin and the Democratic Party.* c1995

F	Subclass: United States local history
73.5	Boston, 1865-1950
.T63	The first Cutter number for the biographee, Tobin
L37	The second Cutter number for the main entry, Lapomarda
1995	The date of publication

When works by and about a person are classed in the same number, all works about the person are filed immediately after all works by that person according to the Preferred Shelflist Order (see discussion in chapter 3). A single Cutter number is assigned to all works except biography and criticism, for which the same first Cutter number is assigned to all biographies about a particular individual, with a second Cutter based on the main entry as shown in the examples above.

Special Cases

Works About Rulers and Chiefs of State

Biography numbers in the history schedules are assigned to the following types of works relating to heads of state and governors: biographies, unofficial speeches, and the texts of the archives and papers.[6] Individual and collected speeches delivered in their official capacity without a topical focus are classed in numbers for legislative and executive papers in Class J. Speeches on specific topics are classed with the appropriate topical numbers.

Some class numbers in the history schedules D-F are divided by period according to the reigns of individual rulers or administrations of chiefs of state. In such cases, no distinction is made between biographies of the ruler or chief of state and general works about the period. For works classed in these numbers, including those written by the ruler or chief of state, Cutter numbers are assigned according to the main entry, for example:

Patterson, W. B. *King James VI and I and the reunion of Christendom.* 1997

DA	History of Great Britain
391	General works on life and reign of James I
.P38	The Cutter number for the main entry, Patterson
1997	The date of publication

Stevenson, David. *Scotland's last royal wedding : the marriage of James VI and Anne of Denmark.* c1997

DA	History of Great Britain
391	General works on life and reign of James I
.S78	The Cutter number for the main entry, Stevenson
1997	The date of publication

In some cases, separate numbers are provided in the schedules for general works of a reign or administration and for biography of the ruler or chief of state. For example:

President Reagan and the world. 1997

E	History of the United States
876	General works on Reagan's administration
.P743	The Cutter number for the main entry under the title, *President . . .*
1997	The date of publication

Pemberton, William E. *Exit with honor : the life and presidency of Ronald Reagan.* 1997

E	History of the United States
877	A general biography of Ronald Reagan
.P46	The Cutter number for the main entry, Pemberton
1997	The date of publication

As shown in the examples above, under a number designated as the biography number for a ruler or chief of state, only one Cutter number is assigned, based on the main entry.

Works About Statesmen, Public Figures, Etc.

Works about statesmen, politicians, other public figures, and persons identified with specific historical events or movements are also classed in the history classes, D and E-F. Normally, the local history number is chosen unless the person is more prominent on the national than on the local level, in which case the number for biography under a particular monarch's reign, a particular president's administration, etc., or under a particular historical period, is chosen.

Powell, Colin L. *My American journey.* 1995

E	Subclass: History of the United States
840.5	Later 20th-century military biography, A-Z
.P68	The first Cutter number for the biographee, Powell
A3	The second Cutter number for an autobiography (Table E1)
1995	The date of publication

If the person is more prominent on the local level and the locality is further subdivided by periods, the number for the appropriate period is used. Double Cutter numbers—that is, the first for the biographee and the second for the main entry—are used even when the class number is not designated specifically for biography.

Sanford, William R. *Daniel Boone : wilderness pioneer.* 1997

F	Subclass: United States local history
454	Early history of Kentucky
.B66	The first Cutter number for the biographee, Boone
S26	The second Cutter number for the main entry, Sanford
1997	The date of publication

Memoirs of persons associated with particular companies are classed with the numbers for the companies in H or T, if possible, or with the activity in which the companies are engaged, for example:

Middleton, Haydn. *Henry Ford : the people's carmaker.* c1997

HD	Subclass: Economic history and conditions
9710	Automobile industry
.U52	The first Cutter number (.U5) for the United States and the successive element (2) for general works including biography

F6655   The second Cutter number (F66) for the biographee,
Ford, with the successive element (55) for subarrangement
for different works about Ford, based on the relative
position of the main entry, Middleton, in the alphabetical
sequence
1997   The date of publication

SERIAL PUBLICATIONS

A serial is defined according to *Anglo-American Cataloguing Rules,*
Second Edition 1998 revision (AACR2R) as a "publication in any medium
issued in successive parts bearing numeric or chronological designations
and intended to be continued indefinitely. Serials include periodicals;
newspapers; annuals (reports, yearbooks, etc.); the journals, memoirs, proceedings, transactions, etc., of societies; and numbered monographic series."[7]
    Serial publications not limited to a particular subject are classed in
the appropriate subclasses in Class A, General works. Serial publications on
specific subjects are classed in Classes B-Z. Normally a serial publication is
classified in one of three ways: (1) in a special form number for periodicals,
etc., under the appropriate subject; (2) by means of an "A" Cutter number;
or (3) in the "General works" number under the appropriate subject.
    Reprint editions and translations of periodicals are assigned the
same class numbers as the originals with successive Cutter numbers in order
of receipt. The Translation Table is not used with periodicals. Dates are not
added to the call numbers for periodicals.[8]

Special Form Numbers for Serials

In the schedules, at the head of each important topic, there is normally
a class number or a group of class numbers designated for serial publications
on that topic, generally with the caption "Periodicals, societies, congresses,
serial collections, yearbooks" or "Periodicals and societies."[9] Unless there
are specific provisions to the contrary, this number is used for all serial publications, including periodicals, yearbooks, numbered monographic series,
and topical serial society publications. This number is not used for congresses
or nonserial collections or collected works unless these are specifically provided for in the caption. Previously, special numbers for yearbooks were
established under certain class numbers. These numbers are defunct and
are being removed as the schedules are revised.

The following examples illustrate specially assigned form numbers:

Proceedings. Mathematical, physical, and engineering sciences. 1996-
Vol. 452, no. 1944 (8 Jan. 1996)- Monthly

QA	Subclass: Mathematics
1	Periodicals, societies, congresses, serial collections, yearbooks
.P783	The Cutter number for the main entry under the title, *Proceedings* . . .

What's on (Port Louis, Mauritius) *What's on.* 1994- No. 1 (June 1994)- Monthly

QA	Subclass: Mathematics
75.5	Periodicals, societies, congresses, serial collections, yearbooks on electronic computers
.W4855	The Cutter number for the main entry, What's on (Port Louis, Mauritius)

Early Music America : the magazine of historical performance. 1995-
Vol. 1, no. 1 (fall 1995)- Quarterly

ML	Subclass: Literature on music
1	Periodicals, serials
.E15	The Cutter number for the main entry under the title, *Early* . . .

Studies in the decorative arts. 1993- Vol. 1, no. 1 (fall 1993)-
Semiannual

NK	Subclass: Decorative arts, Applied arts, Decoration and ornament
1	American and English periodicals
.S78	The Cutter number for the main entry under the title, *Studies* . . .

World affairs (New Delhi, India : 1997) *World affairs : the journal of international issues.* 1997- Vol. 1, issue 1 (Jan.-Mar. 1997)- Quarterly

AP	Subclass: Periodicals
8	English publications from Asia
.W642	The Cutter number for the main entry, *World affairs* (New Delhi, India: 1997)

Note that for serial publications, the date of publication is not included in the call number.

"A" Cutter Numbers for Periodicals or Serial Publications

In the past, LC shelflisters were instructed to assign "A" Cutter numbers to periodicals or serial publications[10] if the schedule for the topic did not provide individual classification numbers for them. These "A" Cutter numbers were not generally recorded in the printed schedules, however, but only in the LC shelflist. The practice of assigning unpublished "A" Cutter numbers was discontinued some years ago. Currently, all "A" Cutter numbers for periodicals are published in the schedules, and only those "A" Cutter numbers included in the schedules are being used now. An example of an "A" Cutter number for periodicals that appears in the schedule is shown below:

QA	MATHEMATICS
	Probabilities
273.A1	Periodicals, societies, congresses, serial collections, yearbooks
273.A3	Dictionaries and encyclopedias

★★★★★

	Mathematical statistics
276.A1	Periodicals, societies, congresses, serial collections, yearbooks

Probability measures on groups and related structures : proceedings Ober-wolfach. 1995- 11 (23-29 Oct. 1994)- Irregular

QA	Subclass: Mathematics
273	Probabilities
.A1	The "A" Cutter number for Periodicals, societies, etc.
P765	The second Cutter number for the main entry under the title, *Probability* . . .

American Statistical Association. *ASA organizational rosters.* Annual

QA	Subclass: Mathematics
276	Mathematical statistics
.A1	The "A" Cutter number for Periodicals, societies, etc.
A47b	The second Cutter number for the main entry, American Statistical Association

"A" Cutter numbers are no longer established when new numbers for a major topic are being developed for the first time; a whole number or a decimal number is used instead.

"General Works" Numbers Used for Periodicals

At the Library of Congress, periodicals are classed in "General works" numbers and cuttered by author or title in the manner of monographs, if no special number or Cutter number exists for periodicals under the topic.

An example of a periodical classed in a "General works" number is:

QA	MATHEMATICS
	Geometry
	Algebraic geometry
564	General works, treatises, and textbooks
	Higher algebraic curves
565	General works, treatises, and textbooks

Algebraic geometry. 1994- 1-

QA	Subclass: Mathematics
564	General works on algebraic geometry
.A354	The Cutter number for the main entry under the title, *Algebraic* . . .

Other examples include:

Automation in archives. 1993- [1993]-

CD	Subclass: Diplomatics, Archives, Seals
973	Archives: special methods and techniques, A-Z
.D3	The first Cutter number for the topic, Data processing
A88	The second Cutter number for the main entry under the title, *Automation* . . .

NetGuide : the guide to online services and the internet. 1994- Vol. 1, no. 1 (Dec. 1994)-

TK	Subclass: Electrical engineering, Electronics, Nuclear engineering
5105.875	Wide area networks
.I57	The first Cutter number for the topic, Internet
N48	The second Cutter number for the main entry under the title, *NetGuide*

In cases where a topic is assigned only one number in the schedule, it is used for both monographs and serials, for example:

Geosynthetics international.   1994-   Vol. 1, no. 1-   Bimonthly

TA	Subclass: Engineering (General)
455	Nonmetallic materials
.G44	The first Cutter number for the topic, Geosynthetics
G4425	The second Cutter number for the main entry under the title, *Geosynthetics international*

Koerner, Robert M.   *Designing with geosynthetics.*   c1998

TA	Subclass: Engineering (General)
455	Nonmetallic materials
.G44	The first Cutter number for the topic, Geosynthetics
K64	The second Cutter number for the main entry, Koerner
1998	The date of publication

Certain types of serial publications are given special treatment. These are discussed below.

Yearbooks

Before 1986, separate numbers for yearbooks were established under major disciplines and topics. But early in 1986, the distinction between yearbooks and other types of periodicals was dropped for classification and subject headings both, and specially designated numbers for yearbooks are no longer being used. Yearbooks are now classed in numbers for periodicals. The one exception is that a new serial title that is a continuation of a serial already classed in a yearbooks number is assigned the same number as the earlier title providing that the numbering of the serial continues.[11]

Discussions and examples of serial publications issued by corporate bodies appear in later sections of this chapter, where "Society Publications" and "Government Publications" are also addressed.

Monographic Series

A monographic series is defined according to *Anglo-American Cataloguing Rules* as "a group of separate items related to one another by the fact that each item bears, in addition to its own title proper, a collective title applying to the group as a whole. The individual items may or may not be numbered."[12]

Individual titles in a monographic series or a set may be cataloged as separate monographs or as a collected item (analyzed in part or in full, or not analyzed).[13] The call numbers are assigned according to the treatment selected for the particular series.

When cataloged as separate items, each item is assigned the class number appropriate to the content of that item, according to established procedures for monographs.

When cataloged as a collected item, a class number appropriate for the entire series or set is assigned. When classifying a collected item on the basis of one volume, the classifier should be careful not to assign a number appropriate for that volume only (i.e., a number appropriate for the analytic rather than for the entire set).

For a monographic series classified as a collected item, the number designated for periodicals is used if there is one. Otherwise, the "General works" number is used, for example:

Studies in the history of music. 1983-

ML	Subclass: Literature on music
1	The integral number meaning a periodical or serial published in the United States
.S899	The Cutter number for the main entry under the title, *Studies . . .*

Nineteenth century. 1975-1984

N	Subclass: Visual arts
6450	The integral number meaning a general work on 19th-century art
.N53	The Cutter number for the main entry under the title, *Nineteenth century*

Subseries

Subseries of serial publications, when cataloged as separate publications, are assigned the same call number as the main series with the addition of the word "subser." For example:

American Academy of Arts and Letters. *Proceedings of the American Academy of Arts and Letters.* 1994- 2nd ser., no. 44 (1993)- Annual
AS36 .A473 subser.

If there is more than one subseries, the same call number is assigned to all. For example:

Studies in the history of art. c1972-   1971, 1972-
N386.U5 S78

Studies in the history of art. Symposium papers.   1987-
N386.U5 S78 subser.

Studies in the history of art.   Monograph series.   1985-
N386.U5 S78 subser.

Studies in the history of art.   Symposium series.   1982-
N386.U5 S78 subser.

Serial Continuations

When there are changes in the title of a serial publication, the issuing corporate body, or the name of the corporate body under which the serial publication is entered, a new cataloging record is created according to *Anglo-American Cataloguing Rules.* The Library of Congress normally assigns the same call number with the same Cutter number to a "true continuation."[14] Whether a periodical is a "true continuation" of another is determined by: (1) the presence of two linking notes, "Continued by [new title]" and "Continues [former title]"; and (2) either the fact that the numbering continues, or that the continuation is an annual, semiannual, or other such publication. For example:

Journal of garden history. c1981-c1997. Vol. 1, no. 1 (Jan.-Mar. 1981)-v. 17, no. 4 (Oct.-Dec. 1997). Quarterly
Continued by: *Studies in the history of gardens & designed landscapes*
LC call number: SB451 .J76

Studies in the history of gardens & designed landscapes. c1998- Vol. 18, no. 1 (Jan.-Mar. 1998)- Quarterly
Continues: *Journal of garden history*
LC call number: SB451 .J76

Studies in the history of art (Washington, D.C.). Symposium series. 1982-1986. 5 v.
Continued by: *Studies in the history of art (Washington, D.C.). Symposium papers*
LC call number: N386.U5 S78 subser.

Studies in the history of art (Washington, D.C.). Symposium papers.
1987- v.
Continues: *Studies in the history of art (Washington, D.C.). Symposium series*
LC call number: N386.U5 S78 subser.

Acta polytechnica Scandinavica. Mathematics and computer science series.
1975-1993. No. 26-no. 63
Continued in 1994 by: *Acta polytechnica Scandinavica. Mathematics and computing in engineering series*
LC call number: QA3 .A25

Acta polytechnica Scandinavica. Mathematics and computing in engineering series. 1994-1995. No. 64-no. 76
Continues: *Acta polytechnica Scandinavica. Mathematics and computer science series*
Continued in 1996 by: *Acta polytechnica Scandinavica. Mathematics, computing, and management in engineering series*
LC call number: QA3 .A25

Acta polytechnica Scandinavica. Mathematics, computing, and management in engineering series. 1996- No. 77-
Continues: *Acta polytechnica Scandinavica. Mathematics and computing in engineering series*
LC call number: QA3 .A25

NONSERIAL COLLECTIONS, COLLECTED SETS, AND COLLECTED WORKS

Nonserial Collections or Collected Works

Class numbers with the caption *Collected works (Nonserial)* found at the head of major topics in the schedules are used with the following types of publications:[15]

1. Multipart items or multivolume monographic works by two or more authors. This category comprises groups of monographs issued in the form of collected sets, such as the *Harvard Classics*. It includes multivolume monographs that the Library of Congress has classed as a set with full analytics. Multivolume monographs that are not analyzed are classed with "General works."

2. Collected works of one author, such as the complete works of an author on a topic, including monographs, essays, etc. For example:

Tiago de Oliveira, J. *Collected works = Obras.* 1994-

QA	Subclass: Mathematics
3	Collected works (nonserial)
.T482	The Cutter number for the main entry, Tiago de Oliveira
1994	The date of publication

Cramer, Harald. *Harald Cramer : collected works.* 1994

QA	Subclass: Mathematics
3	Collected works (nonserial)
.C497925	The Cutter number for the main entry, Cramer
1994	The date of publication

3. Collections of abstracts if there is no special number for abstracts under the particular topic. See also the discussion on pages 496-97.

When there is no special number provided for nonserial collections or collected works, the "General works" number is used. The class number designated for periodicals is not used for the collected works of one author or multivolume sets of more than one author, for single volumes of miscellaneous works by one or more authors, or for anthologies, unless the caption of the number specifically provides for these types of works.

Selected Works

The selected works of a monographic nature by one author are treated in the same manner as general works on the particular topic.

Gurlik, Philip. *Selected works.* 1996

N	Subclass: Visual arts
6537	Special artists from the United States (37 from Table N5 added to the base number 6500)
.G86	The first Cutter number for the artist, Gurlik
A4	The second Cutter number for Reproductions (Collections) (Table N6)
1996	The date of publication

Galen. *Selected works*. 1997

B	Subclass: Philosophy (General)
577	Ancient Greco-Roman philosophy
.G22	The first Cutter number .G2 for the philosopher, Galenus, and the successive element (2 from Table 5) for translations
E5	The second Cutter number for English language
1997	The date of publication

Asian Art Museum of San Francisco. *Selected works*. 1994

N	Subclass: Visual arts
7262	Collections of Asian art (762 from Table N5 added to base number 6500)
.A882	The Cutter number for the main entry, Asian Art Museum
1994	The date of publication

In Class P, literary authors often have special numbers for their collected works and selected works designated in the schedules or tables. For example:

Blake, William, 1757-1827. *Selected works* / edited by David Stevens. 1995

PR	Subclass: English literature
4142	Selected works by William Blake (2 in Table P-PZ33 added to base number 4140)
.S73	The Cutter number for the editor, Stevens
1995	The date of publication

ANALYSIS OF MONOGRAPHIC SERIES AND SETS

A monographic series or multipart item classed as a "collected set" (i.e., all volumes or parts being assigned the same call number and shelved together) may be analyzed in full, in part, or not analyzed. A separate cataloging record is created for each item in an analyzed series or set, and the call number for each analytic consists of the call number for the collected set with the addition of the series number and volume designation based on the series tracing in the description for English and foreign (except Asian) language publications. For Asian language publications, the prefixes *vol.*, *no.*, and *pt.* in hierarchical order are used regardless of what appears in the series tracing. This practice also applies to cases where the volume designation is not supplied in the series tracing.[16]

An alternate class number appropriate for the content of the individual title is assigned in addition to the collected call number except when the collected number and the alternate number are the same or when the alternate number is in Class K, Law. The author Cutter numbers are omitted from the alternate number, because it does not represent a valid LC call number, but the alternate class number is carried out as far as needed to cover topical elements, including names of persons, places, or institutions as subjects.[17] For example:

> *Having our way : women rewriting tradition in twentieth-century America.*
> 1995
> [Series title: *Bucknell review* ; v. 39, no. 1]
> LC call number: AP2 .B887 vol. 39 no. 1
> Alternate class number: PS151

> Coleridge, Samuel Taylor. *Shorter works and fragments.* 1995
> [Series title: *The collected works of Samuel Taylor Coleridge ; 11*]
> [Series title: *Bollingen series* ; 75]
> LC call number: PR4470 .F69 vol. 11
> Alternate class number: PR4472

> Ambers, Clifford P. *The role of carbonate bedrock in the formation of Indianaite halloysitic clays.* 1995
> LC call number: QE109 .A32 no. 65
> [Series title: *Indiana Geological Survey bulletin* ; 65]
> Alternate class number: QE391.I53

Analytics containing multiple parts, each of which carries a different main series number, are called "open analytics." The call number for an open analytic includes the main series number of the first volume cataloged. An example is shown below:

> *Arthropod natural enemies in arable land.* 1995-1997. v. 1-3
> [Series title: *Acta Jutlandica* ; 70:2-72:2]
> [Subseries title: *Acta Jutlandica* ; 70:2-72:2]. *Natural science series* ;
> 9-11
> LC call number: AS281 .A34 vol. 70, pt. 2, etc.

In LC cataloging records, when a series containing subseries is classed as a "collected set," the call number for the subseries consists of the call number for the collected set with the addition of the word **subser**.

If the individual pieces of the subseries are analyzed, an alternate number is assigned to each piece and no alternate number is assigned to the subseries, for example:

> *The interpretation of architectural sculpture in Greece and Rome.*   c1997
> [Series title: *Studies in the history of art* ; v. 49]
> [Subseries title: *Symposium papers* ; 29]
> LC call number for the main series: N386.U5 S78
> LC call number for the subseries: N386.U5 S78 subser
> LC call number for the issue: N386.U5 S78 vol. 49
> Alternate class number for the individual issue: [NA3340]
> No alternate number is assigned to the subseries.

If the analytic is a subseries that is not analyzed, an alternate number is assigned to the subseries unless the subseries is a periodical. Alternate monographic class numbers are also provided for occasional numbers of periodicals or other series for which analytic records are provided.

MATERIALS CATALOGED UNDER CORPORATE HEADINGS

Classification

A corporate body is defined according to *Anglo-American Cataloguing Rules*, as

> an organization or group of persons that is identified by a particular name and that acts, or may act, as an entity. Typical examples of corporate bodies are associations, institutions, business firms, nonprofit enterprises, governments, government agencies, religious bodies, local churches, and conferences.[18]

Not all material issued by a corporate body is entered under a corporate body name; much of it is entered under title, and some of it under a personal name. This section confines itself primarily to discussion of how to handle items with main entry under a corporate heading. The few exceptions are noted below.

Works entered under corporate bodies are classed in the appropriate subject numbers according to their content. In assigning Cutter numbers, however, special procedures have been established by the Library of Congress.[19]

Shelflisting Procedures

The following procedures for shelflisting monographs and serials apply to many works with main entry under corporate body. There are, however, some major exceptions. These are, first, works classed under society numbers in Classes B-Z (see pages 476-77); second, conferences and congresses (see pages 481-86); and third, works classed in K, Law. In Class K, corporate bodies are cuttered alphabetically by main entry and title, unless otherwise specified in the schedules.

Monographs

The date of publication is used in the call number for a monographic work entered under a corporate body.[20] The date of a later printing given in a note is ignored.

In some cases, special provisions or tables are included in the schedules for works by and about corporate bodies, whether or not they are entered under the corporate bodies in question. These provisions are followed in assigning Cutter numbers. One example is Table L7 for institutions of higher education in Class L:

L7 TABLES OF SUBDIVISIONS: INSTITUTIONS WITH
ONE NUMBER OR CUTTER NUMBER IN AMERICAS,
GREAT BRITAIN
Official publications
.A1-4   Serial
.A5-7   Nonserial
.A8-Z   Other works.   By author
                     Including student yearbooks, etc.

In this case, official publications with main entry under an institution's name are assigned the Cutter numbers .A1-A7 under the appropriate class number.

When there is no special provision in the schedules, the following procedures for shelflisting are followed.[21]

1. All publications entered under a corporate name heading and classified under the same number, including translations, selections, editions, etc., are assigned the same Cutter number, based on the first element of the main entry and disregarding the title.

2. The date of publication is added to make each call number unique. For example:

American Library Association. Subcommittee to Revise the
Guide for Written Collection Policy Statements. *Guide for
written collection policy statements.* 1996

Z	Subclass: Libraries
687	A general work on library collections
.A518	The Cutter number for the main entry, American Library Association . . .
1996	The date of publication

Art Institute of Chicago. *Italian drawings before 1600 in the Art
Institute of Chicago : a catalogue of the collection.* 1997

NC	Subclass: Drawing, Design, Illustration
255	Italy (General works) (155 from Table N3 added to the base number 100)
.A72	The Cutter number for the main entry, Art Institute of Chicago
1997	The date of publication

California. Bureau of State Audits. *Department of Alcohol and
Drug Programs : a review of the processes used to allocate and dis-
burse alcohol and drug funds to counties.* [1997]

HV	Subclass: Social pathology
5297	Alcoholism in the United States, by region or state, A-Z
.C2	The first Cutter number for the state of California
C334	The second Cutter number for the main entry, California. Bureau of State Audits
1997	The date of publication

Smithsonian Institution. Libraries. *Rare books and special collections in the Smithsonian Institution Libraries.* 1995

Z	Subclass: Libraries
733	Bibliography of publications of individual libraries in the United States, A-Z
.S67	The first Cutter number based on the name of the library, Smithsonian Institution Libraries
S64	The second Cutter number for the main entry, Smithsonian . . .
1995	The date of publication

In some cases, the second Cutter number represents a topic or place.

New York (State). Energy Planning Board. *New York State energy plan.* [1994]

HD	Subclass: Economic history and conditions
9502	A general work on energy policy
.U53	The first Cutter number U5 for the United States with the successive element (3 according to Table H20) for local subdivision
N5243	The second Cutter number for New York State
1994	The date of publication

3. If there is more than one publication issued by the same corporate body in a given year, a work letter, beginning with the letter "a" and continuing through the alphabet, is added to the date. The letter "z" is not used to represent an unknown date as it is in most other cases, since the letters are assigned in order of receipt. If the exact date of publication is not known, an approximate date is used, with zeroes in place of dashes, for example, 1970 in place of 197- and 1900 in place of 19--.

   Examples of two or more publications in the same year are shown below:

Archives nationales du Québec. *Catalogue des fonds et collections d'archives d'origine privée.* c1992
LC call number: CD3645.Q27 A75 1992a

Archives nationales du Québec. *Archives écrites d'origine gouvernementale conservées au Centre d'archives de Québec et de Chaudière-Appalaches.* c1992
LC call number: CD3645.Q27 A75 1992b

Archives nationales du Québec. *Archives d'origine privée conservées au Centre d'archives de l'Estrie : guide.* c1992
LC call number: CD3645.Q27 A75 1992c

Archives nationales du Québec. *Etat général des petits fonds et collections d'archives manuscrites d'origine privée conservés au Centre d'archives de Montréal, de Laval, de Lanaudière, des Laurentides et de la Montérégie.* c1992
LC call number: CD3645.Q27 A75 1992d

4. In formulating a Cutter number for a corporate heading, all subheadings are ignored. For example, the same Cutter number is used to shelflist publications cataloged under the following headings:

American Library Association
American Library Association.   Library Administration
   Division
American Library Association.   Reference Services
   Division

5. Two or more corporate bodies having the same name but different qualifiers are treated as different corporate bodies, and each is assigned a different Cutter number, for example:

LB2335
.7   Loyola University of Chicago.
.L68   *Faculty tenure . . .*   1982.
1982

LB2335
.7   Loyola University (New Orleans, La.).
.L69   *Faculty tenure . . .*   1983.
1983

6. If the corporate body's name consists of the name of a country or other jurisdiction followed by a division or agency of the government, the Cutter number is based on the main heading under the jurisdictional name (see exception noted in 7 below) and the first subheading, disregarding all further subheadings. The "A" Cutter numbers are assigned to documents only when specifically called for in the schedules.

7. If the entire class number is for the official documents of a specific country or state, the Cutter numbers are based on the names of the particular divisions or agencies. If the name of the country appears at the beginning of the entry, it is disregarded. As stated in the preceding paragraph, further subheadings that appear in the heading are also disregarded. For example, the same Cutter number, D46, is used to shelflist all publications cataloged under the following headings:

Oregon.   Dept. of Forestry.   *Marketing Oregon Produced Poles . . .* 1980.
SD12.O7 D46 1980

Oregon.   Dept. of Forestry.   East Central Oregon
District.   *Statistical Data . . .*   1981.
SD12.O7 D46 1981

Oregon.   Dept. of Forestry.   *Annual Report.*
Statistical Data Supplement.   19--
SD12.O7 D46a

Oregon.   Dept. of Forestry.   East Central Oregon
District.   *Annual Report.*   19--
SD12.O7 D46b

Oregon.   Dept. of Forestry.   *Coos District annual*
report.   19--
SD12.O7 D46c

Oregon.   Dept. of Forestry.   Western Lane District.
Annual Report.   19--
SD12.O7 D46e

Oregon. Dept. of Forestry. Central Oregon District.
Central Oregon District . . . annual report.   [1986-   ]
1986-   Annual
SD12.O7 D46h

Oregon. Dept. of Forestry.   *Fiscal financial report.*
[-1992]   -1992.   Annual
SD12.O7 D46i

Oregon. Dept. of Forestry.   *Proprietary funds financial*
report. [1993-   ]   1993-   Annual
SD12.O7 D46j

Works About Corporate Bodies

Double Cutter numbers are assigned to a work about a corporate
body: the first Cutter number is the same one for works entered under the
corporate heading classed in the same number, and the second Cutter
number is taken from the main entry. For example:

Blaauw, Adriaan. *History of the IAU : the birth and first half-century of the International Astronomical Union.* c1994

QB	Subclass: Astronomy
1	Periodicals, societies, congresses, serial collections, yearbooks
.I627	The first Cutter number for the society, International Astronomical Union
B53	The second Cutter number for the main entry, Blaauw
1994	The date of publication

Schaffer, Alan. *Visions : Clemson's yesteryears, 1880s-1960s.* 1990

LD	Subclass: Colleges and universities in the United States
1061	An institution with a name beginning with the letter C
.C3	The first Cutter number for the name of the institution, Clemson University
S33	The second Cutter number based on the main entry, Schaffer and, according to Table L7, meaning an un-official publication
1990	The date of publication

Commentaries and Supplements

A commentary on or a supplement to the works of a specific corporate body is assigned the call number of the original work with the addition of *Suppl.*

Indexes

For an index to a work entered under a corporate body, the call number for the original work plus *Index* is assigned.

Serials

Dates of publication are not added to the call numbers for serials. To formulate distinctive call numbers for serials (e.g., periodicals or monographic series) entered under a corporate heading, successive work letters, beginning with "a" for the first serial, are added to the Cutter number for the corporate heading in order of receipt of the publications. Following is an example of a serial cataloged under a corporate heading:

American Library Association. Reference and Adult Services Division. *RASD update*. 1980-1996. Quarterly

Z	Subclass: Libraries
711	Reference work
.A388a	The Cutter number (.A388) for the main entry, American Library Association, and the work letter (a) for a serial publication

Changes of Name

When a corporate body changes its name, a separate entry is established under the new name in accordance with *Anglo-American Cataloguing Rules*. In classification, the same Cutter number is used for a corporate heading with a minor or insignificant change,[22] for example:

LB2328	
.M32	Maryland. State Board for Community Colleges.
1976	*Statewide Master Plan for Community . . .* 1976

LB2328	
.M32	Maryland State Board for Community Colleges.
1984	*State Plan for Community Colleges . . .* 1984

However, a different Cutter number is assigned for the new heading if the change is significant, for example,

CD2097	
.R34S72	State Archives of Rajasthan.
1976	*Rajasthan State Archives . . .* [1976?]

CD2097	
.R34R34	Rajasthan State Archives.
1980	*A List of the English . . .* [1980?]

MATERIALS FROM SPECIAL SOURCES

Society Publications

A society is defined as "a group of persons joined together for a common interest,"[23] including a club, a fraternity, a lodge, or an association. Form captions at the head of each major discipline in the classification schedules normally provide both for serials (including periodicals) and for societies. The caption usually includes both forms, for example, "*Periodicals. Societies. Serials*," or some variation thereof. Sometimes, however, these forms are on separate lines, each with its own class number(s):

```
R                     MEDICINE (GENERAL)
       Medicine (General)
          Periodicals.  Societies.  Serials
             America
                English
                   United States.   Canada
11                      Periodicals.   Serials
15                      Societies
```

Unless there are explicit provisions to the contrary, separate class numbers for societies are reserved for both monographs and serials *about* particular societies, including official business publications, membership lists, constitutions, histories, reports of business meetings, and so on. For example:

> Wolinsky, Howard. *The serpent on the staff : the unhealthy politics of the American Medical Association.*   c1994

R	Subclass: Medicine (General)
15	Societies in the United States and Canada
.A55	The first Cutter number for the name of the society, American Medical Association
W58	The second Cutter number for the main entry, Wolinsky
1994	The date of publication

If no separate number is designated for societies under the particular topic, both monographs and serials are classed in the number with the caption "*Periodicals. Societies. Serials.*"

Publications issued by a society on topics of interest to the society, or on both topical matters and matters about the society itself, are classed in numbers appropriate to the particular topic and form of the publication.[24] For example, an official guide on collection development issued by the American Library Association is classed with the topic, not with the number for library societies.

> American Library Association. Subcommittee on Guide for Training Collection Development Librarians. *Guide for training collection development librarians.* 1996

Z	Subclass: Libraries
687.2	The collections, by region or country, A-Z
.U6	The first Cutter number for the United States
A48	The second Cutter number for the main entry, American Library Association
1996	The date of publication

Previously, the Library of Congress used a Three-Number Table and a Nine-Number Table[25] for assigning Cutter numbers to publications of societies classed in numbers in Classes B-Z that carry the following captions:

> Periodicals, etc.
>
> Periodicals, societies, congresses, serials,
>
> > collections, yearbooks
>
> Societies

These tables continue to be used for societies for which there are already established patterns in the shelflist. For societies being classified for the first time in Class A, Cutter numbers are assigned according to procedures described in chapter 6 under Class A. For societies being classified for the first time in Classes B-Z, Cutter numbers are assigned according to procedures outlined in the section "Materials Cataloged under Corporate Bodies" in this chapter.

Government Publications Classed in Documents Numbers

Government documents[26] are no longer handled as a distinct category of material unless the schedule in which the document is classed contains a separate provision for documents. Below is an indication of which publications are to be classed as documents when the schedule expressly provides for documents.

Monographs. Monographic documents are not classed in document numbers unless the schedule includes separate numbers for monographic documents. Only works entered under a corporate heading consisting of a jurisdictional name plus an agency name as a subheading, for example, **United States. Dept. of State**, are treated as documents. Furthermore, unless monographs are explicitly mentioned, it is assumed that the provision is only for serial documents, and that monographic documents are to be classed as any other monographic publication.

Corporate Entries. Document numbers are not used unless the corporate main entry heading in question consists of a jurisdictional name with the agency name as a subheading. If the main entry heading has been established in any other manner, as in the case of a government body entered under its own name, such as **Naval Research Laboratory**, the work is treated as a non-document publication.

Examples of government documents classed in "documents" numbers:

United States. Forest Service. Pacific Northwest Region. *Annual monitoring report. Mt. Baker-Snoqualmie National Forest.* [1992] Fiscal year 1991.   Annual

SD	Subclass: Forestry
11	U.S. federal documents
.U55d	The first Cutter number for the main entry, United States, with the letter "d" for a serial publication

Minnesota. Forestry Heritage Resources Program. *Annual report.* 1995-   Annual

SD	Subclass: Forestry
12	U.S. state documents
.M68	The first Cutter number for the state of Minnesota
M55a	The second Cutter number for the main entry, Minnesota, with the letter "a" for a serial publication

British Columbia. Forest Practices Board. *Annual report.* 1996-1995-   Annual

SD	Subclass: Forestry
14	Canadian local documents
.B7	The first Cutter number for the local place, British Columbia
B75a	The second Cutter number for the main entry, British Columbia, with the letter "a" for a serial publication

Examples of government documents classed in "General works" numbers:

Philippines. Dept. of Energy. *Philippine energy plan, 1994-2010.* 1993

HD	Subclass: Economic history and conditions
9502	Energy industries
.P62	The Cutter number (.P6) for the Philippines with the successive element (2) meaning a general work, according to Table H20
P47	The second Cutter number for the main entry, Philippines
1993	The date of publication

United States. Dept. of Energy. *Information architecture.* 1997

T	Subclass: Technology (General)
58.5	General works on Information systems
.U537	The Cutter number for the main entry, United States …
1997	The date of publication

Victoria. Dept. of Agriculture, Energy, and Minerals. *Annual report.* 19-- SERIAL

HD	Subclass: Economic history and conditions
2155	The number (1780+375) meaning Agriculture in a local place in Australia
.V5	The first Cutter number for Victoria
.V52a	The Cutter number for the main entry, Victoria …, and the letter "a" for a serial publication

Congressional and State Legislative Hearings and Reports

U.S. Congressional hearings and reports of U.S. state legislatures are classed in subclass KF.[27] Hearings and reports of committees of the U.S. Congress are classed in KF25-32.5.

United States. Congress. House. Committee on Rules. *Congressional gift reform : hearings before the Committee on Rules, House of Representatives, One Hundred Fourth Congress, first session on H. Res. 250 … November 2 and 7, 1995.* 1996

KF	Subclass: Law of the United States
27	House committee hearings

.R8   The Committee on Rules
1995   The date of the hearings

United States. Congress. Senate. Committee on Appropriations. Subcommittee on Agencies. *HUD management and budget crisis : hearings before a Subcommittee of the Committee on Appropriations, United States Senate, One Hundred Fourth Congress, first session : special hearings--Congressional Budget Office, Department of Housing and Urban Development, General Accounting Office, nondepartmental witnesses.* 1996

KF   Subclass: Law of the United States
26   Senate committee hearings
.A666   The Committee on Appropriations
1996c   The date of the hearings

United States. Congress. House. Committee on the Budget. *Balanced Budget Act of 1997 : report of the Committee on the Budget, House of Representatives, to accompany H.R. 2015, a bill to provide for reconciliation pursuant to subsections (b)(1) and (c) of section 105 of the concurrent resolution on the budget for fiscal year 1998, together with additional and minority views.* 1997

KF   Subclass: Law of the United States
32   House standing committee reports
.B8   The Committee on the Budget
1997   The date of original publication

However, U. S. Congressional committee prints are classed with the appropriate topics in Classes B-Z.

Hearings and reports of U.S. state legislative committees are classed in the appropriate form numbers in subclasses KFA-KFW. Such reports include only those issued by a legislative committee to accompany a specific bill when it is reported out of the committee to its parent legislative body after hearings have been held and/or the committee has considered and made its recommendations on the bill in question. Reports that do not meet these criteria are classed in the appropriate topical numbers in subclasses KFA-KFW, if legal. Nonlegal reports are classed with their appropriate topics in Classes B-Z. Following is an example of state legislative reports:

California. Legislature. Assembly. Committee on Utilities and Commerce. *A joint report of legislative action, 1995/96 legislative session, interim report.* [1996?]

KFC   Subclass: Law of California

10.62	Joint legislative reports
.U75	The Committee on Utilities ...
1996	The date of publication

Publications of other countries that are the equivalent of U.S. Congressional or state hearings, reports, or committee prints are classed with the appropriate topics in Classes B-Z, or in J, if general.

Conferences, Congresses, Etc.

Classifying Conferences, Congresses, Etc.

At the head of major topics in the schedules, there is usually a special form number for congresses. This number is assigned to (1) collected papers delivered at, or published for, one or more named or unnamed congresses, symposia, conferences, meetings, etc.; (2) condensations of these papers; (3) reports of the proceedings and discussions, program statements, lists of delegates, etc., of congresses; or (4) combinations of the above. The main entry for such material may be the name of a congress, the name of a corporate body, or a title.[28]

International Conference on Software for Electrical Engineering Analysis and Design (3rd : 1996 : Pisa, Italy) *Software for electrical engineering analysis and design.*   c1996

TK	Subclass: Electrical engineering, Electronics, Nuclear engineering
5	Congresses
.I59	The Cutter number for the main entry, International ...
1996	The date of conference

International Symposium on Theory and Practice in Transport Economics (13th : 1995 : Luxembourg, Luxembourg) *Transport : new problems, new solutions : introductory reports and summary of discussions : Luxembourg, 9-11 May 1995.*   c1996

HE	Subclass: Transportation and communications
11	Congresses
.I6	The Cutter number for the main entry, International ...
1995	The date of conference

Hazardous air pollutants : the London Workshop. c1995

TD	Subclass: Environmental technology, Sanitary engineering
881	Periodicals, societies, congresses, etc., on air pollution and its control
.H39	The Cutter number for the main entry under the title, *Hazardous . . .*
1995	The date of publication

LC guidelines for classifying congresses are outlined below.

1. If a congress number exists under the topic, it is used for all congresses, including serial congresses. Congress publications, either monographic or serial, are not classed with periodicals unless congresses are explicitly stated in the periodicals caption, as in Class Q.

2. If a congress number does not exist under the topic, congresses are classed in the "General works" number. The periodicals number, if provided, is used for congresses cataloged as serials.

3. Publications related to the proceedings of business meetings of organizations with little or no substantive material on a topic are not classed as congresses but are treated as society publications. See discussion on pages 476-77.

4. If the subject matter of a particular named congress varies from one meeting to another and separate bibliographic records have been created for each meeting, each is classed in the appropriate number with no attempt to keep them together.

5. When two or more serial records represent continuations of the same congress, the general rules for serial continuations are followed, that is, they are classed in the same number if the numbering continues. Otherwise, they are treated as independent works.

6. Works about a congress are classed in the same number that would be assigned to the congress itself.

Shelflisting Conferences, Congresses, Etc.

The following shelflisting procedures[29] are applied by the Library of Congress to all publications of conferences, congresses, meetings, etc., except when the conference, etc., is classed in a society number, in which case the provisions outlined on pages 476-77 are followed.

1. Conference publications

    (a) When the main entry is under the heading of a conference or similar entity, the same Cutter number is assigned to all publications (including proceedings, papers, abstracts, translations, selections, editions, etc.) of the conference classed in the same number, differentiated by the addition of the *date of the conference* appearing in the main entry heading,[30] or the date of publication if the heading does not include the date of the conference. If the date of the conference covers more than one year, the later date is used in the call number. The following examples show publications with main entry under conference headings:

Museums for the New Millennium Symposium (1996 : Washington, D.C.) *Museums for the new millennium : a symposium for the museum community September 5-7, 1996.* 1997

AM	Subclass: Museums, Collectors and collecting
2	Congresses
.M88	The Cutter number for the main entry, Museums for ...
1996	The date of conference

Israel Symposium on the Theory of Computing and Systems (5th : 1997 : Ramat-Gan, Israel) *Proceedings of the Fifth Israeli Symposium on Theory of Computing and Systems, June 17-19, 1997, Ramat-Gan, Israel.* c1997

QA	Subclass: Mathematics
75.5	Periodicals, societies, congresses, serial collections, yearbooks on computer science
.I77	The Cutter number for the main entry, Israel Symposium ...
1997	The date of conference

If there is more than one publication in a given year, work letters a, b, c, ... x, y, aa, bb, cc, etc. (in order of receipt of the publication) are added to the date for differentiation. The work letter z is not used for this purpose; it is reserved for commentaries on specific conferences.

(b) When the main entry is under the title, the Cutter number is based on the title rather than the name of the conference. In this case, the date of publication rather than the date of the conference is used to complete the call number. For example:

The gift as material culture : report of a Yale-Smithsonian seminar held at the Smithsonian Institution, Washington, D.C., April 28-30, 1991. 1995

GT   Subclass: Manners and customs

3040   General works on exchange of gifts

.G53   The Cutter number for the main entry under the title, *The gift as* . . .

1995   The date of publication

Jordan algebras : proceedings of the conference held in Ober-wolfach, Germany, August 9-15, 1992. 1994

QA   Subclass: Mathematics

252.5   Jordan algebras

.J67   The Cutter number for the main entry under the title, *Jordan algebras*

1994   The date of publication

(c) When the conference heading lacks numbering, date, and place, the date of publication is used.

(d) When the headings for a series of conferences are the same, except that some of the headings contain the number, year, etc., while others do not, successive Cutter numbers are used to differentiate the two groups, for example, A75, A76, and so on.

(e) When a conference publishes both monographic and serial works, successive Cutter numbers are assigned. For serial publications, since no date is included in the call number, the work letter is added to the Cutter number, following the procedures outlined above.

IEEE-IMS Workshop on Information Theory and Statistics. *Proceedings* . . . *IEEE-IMS Workshop on Information Theory and Statistics.* 1995-   1994-

QA   Subclass: Mathematics

276   Mathematical statistics

.A1   Periodicals, societies, congresses, serial collec-
        tions, yearbooks
I34a   The Cutter number for the main entry under
        the title, *IEEE-IMS* . . .

2. Works About Conferences, Congresses, Etc.

    (a) The same class number, Cutter number, and the date of
        conference is assigned to a commentary on a specific con-
        ference. A work letter beginning with z, za, zb, etc., is
        added to the date to represent a commentary.

    (b) If the work is about a named conference with no specific
        year given, double Cutter numbers, the first representing
        the conference and the second the main entry of the com-
        mentary, are assigned. In this case, the date of publica-
        tion is used to complete the call number. In cases where
        the second Cutter number represents the conference, it is
        expanded by adding a digit or digits to represent the
        main entry of the commentary.

    (c) If the conference has been entered under the title, the
        Cutter number for a work about it consists of the Cutter
        number for the original plus a second Cutter number for
        the main entry.

    (d) For a work about several conferences, the Cutter number
        is based on the main entry of the commentary, for example:

        Truth without facts : selected papers from the first three inter-
        national conferences on adult education and the arts.   c1995
        LC   Subclass: Special aspects of education
        5209   Congresses and conferences on adult education
        .T78   The Cutter number for the main entry under
                the title, *Truth* . . .
        1995   The date of publication

3. Supplements and Indexes
    Conference entries that are designated as supplements or indexes
    to serials entered under a conference heading are assigned the
    call number of the original work plus **Suppl.** or **Index**.

Following are additional examples of classifying and shelflisting
congresses, conferences, etc.:

1. Monographs classed in a combined (Periodicals, societies, congresses, etc.) number with main entry under the conference:

   FCT '97 (1997 : Krakow, Poland) *Fundamentals of computation theory : 11th International Symposium, FCT '97, Krakow, Poland, September 1-3, 1997 : proceedings.* c1997

QA	Subclass: Mathematics
75.5	Periodicals, societies, congresses, serial collections, yearbooks on computer science
.F367	The Cutter number for the main entry, FCT '97
1997	The date of conference

2. Monographs classed in "General works" numbers or regular numbers designated for the subject:

   Large facilities in physics : 5th EPS international conference, University of Lausanne, Dorigny, Switzerland, 12-14 September 1994. c1995

QC	Subclass: Physics
51	Laboratories
.A1	The first Cutter number for general works
L37	The second Cutter number for the main entry under the title, *Large facilities . . .*
1995	The date of publication

   Conference on "Managing fare collection" (1994 : Bologna, Italy) *Managing fare collection : state of the art : cases and evaluations = Gérer la billettique : état de l'art : études de cas et évaluation.* [1994]

HE	Subclass: Transportation and communications
4341	General works on fares for subways
.C66	The Cutter number for the main entry, Conference on . . .
1994	The date of conference

   Conference on the Course of Social and Economic Change in Québec (1996 : Québec, Québec) *A society based on responsibility and solidarity : making choices together.* 1996

HN	Subclass: Social history and conditions
110	Local places in Canada
.Q4	The first Cutter number for Québec (Province)
C64	The second Cutter number for the main entry, Conference on . . .
1996	The date of conference

WORKS RELATED TO OTHER WORKS

A work related to another work or group of works, such as an edition, a translation, a parallel text, an abridgment, a commentary, or a supplement, is normally classed with the original work. The call number is often that of the original plus an additional element. At the Library of Congress, if the original work is not yet in the collection, a call number would be constructed for the original work with the additional element for the related work.

Editions

See discussion on pages 142-43 in chapter 5.

Translations

In many places in the schedules, special numbers are assigned to translations. If there is no such number under a particular discipline or topic, a translation is assigned the same call number as the item translated, with a successive Cutter element attached to the book number. The successive Cutter element, based on the language of the translation, is attached to the last Cutter number in the call number. Cutter numbers for translation are discussed in chapter 3, pages 86-87.

The general pattern for subarranging translations in different languages is presented in the Table for Translations on page 86. Following are examples of classifying translations of individual works:

Piaget, Jean. *Sociological studies.* 1995

HM	Subclass: Sociology
55	French treatises
.P613	The Cutter number (.P6) for the main entry, Piaget, and the successive element (13) meaning an English translation
1995	The date of publication

Freud, Sigmund. *Totem and taboo : resemblances between the psychic lives of savages and neurotics.* c1998

RC	Subclass: Internal medicine
530	General works on Neuroses
.F74313	The Cutter number (.F743) for the main entry, Freud, and the successive element (13) meaning an English translation
1998	The date of publication

Freud, Sigmund. *Wit and its relation to the unconscious.*   1993

PN	Subclass: Collections of general literature
6149	Special topics of wit and humor
.P5	The first Cutter number for the topic, Philosophy and theory
F6813	The second Cutter number (.F68) for the main entry, Freud, and the successive element (13) meaning an English translation
1993	The date of publication

Parallel Texts

As a general rule, a publication that contains an original text as well as a translation of the text is treated as a translation and assigned a translation number.[31] This is because users of this type of publication are normally more interested in the translation and the critical matter that is in the language of the translation than in the text of the original. This is especially true if the title page and/or the introductory material and notes are in the language of the translation.

Josephus, Flavius. *Antiquitates Judaicae*
DS116 .J74

Josephus, Flavius. *Les antiquités juives.*   1995-   [French and Greek on opposite pages]
DS116 .J7414 1995

Sepulveda, Juan Gines de. *Democrates secundus*
F1411 .S43

Sepúlveda, Juan Ginés de. *Democrates segundo ; Apología en favor del libro sobre las justas causas de la guerra.*   1997   [Latin text and Spanish translation on facing pages]
F1411 .S4318 1997

Abridgments

An abridgment is defined as "a reduced form of a work produced by condensation and omission, but retaining the general sense and unity of the original."[32] Summaries, synopses, and epitomes are considered abridgments. However, an adaptation (i.e., a work rendered in a different literary form) or a simplified work for juvenile readers is not considered an abridgment.

Some schedules provide special numbers for abridgments. An example is BS418, Epitomes, summaries of the Bible. If there are no special provisions, the abridgment is assigned the same number as the original work expanded by the digit "2" and the date of publication of the abridgment, for example:

Original work:
Drinker, Elizabeth Sandwith. *The diary of Elizabeth Drinker.* c1991

F	Subclass: United States local history
158.9	Individual elements in the population of Philadelphia, Pennsylvania
.F89	The first Cutter number meaning Friends, Society of Friends, Quakers
D75	The second Cutter number for the main entry, Drinker
1991	The date of publication

Abridgment:
Drinker, Elizabeth Sandwith. *The diary of Elizabeth Drinker : the life cycle of an eighteenth-century woman* / edited and abridged by Elaine Forman Crane. c1994
LC call number: F158.9.F89 D752 1994

Original work:
Biography and genealogy master index : a consolidated index to more than 3,200,000 biographical sketches in over 350 current and retrospective biographical dictionaries. c1980

Z	Subclass: Subject bibliography
5305	Biography, genealogy, heraldry, by region or country, A-Z
.U5	The first Cutter number for the United States
B57	The second Cutter number for the main entry under the title, *Biography* . . .
1980	The date of publication

Abridgment:
Abridged biography and genealogy master index : a consolidated index to more than 2,150,000 biographical sketches from over 260 selected current and retrospective biographical dictionaries indexed in Biography and genealogy master index through 1994. c1995
LC call number: Z5305.U5 B572 1995

Adaptations

Adaptations of existing works are classed as independent works without regard to the original. For example:

Napoli, Tony. *Moby Dick.* c1996

PS	Subclass: American literature
3564	Late 20th-century authors whose names begin with "N"
.A57	The first Cutter number for the author Napoli
M63	The second Cutter number for the title, *Moby Dick*
1996	The date of publication

Harnetiaux, Bryan Patrick. *The snows of Kilimanjaro : a full-length play.* c1995

PS	Subclass: American literature
3558	Late 20th-century authors whose names begin with "H"
.A624763	The first Cutter number for the author Harnetiaux
S66	The second Cutter number for the title, *snows of . . .*
1995	The date of publication

Commentaries on Individual Works

Unless there are specific provisions in the schedules or practices that have been developed in specific areas in the past, a commentary[33] on an individual work is assigned the call number for the original work in the original language with the following additions:

1. If the call number for the original work contains a single Cutter number, the digit "3" is added to it; and a second Cutter number is assigned for the commentator. An exception is made for a commentary on the works of a corporate body, which is treated as a supplementary work (see page 474).

2. If the call number for the original work contains double Cutter numbers, the digit "3" is added to the second Cutter with additional digit or digits representing the main entry.

For example, the call number for Alfred North Whitehead's *Process and reality* is B1674.W353 P76, and commentaries on this work were classed in B1674.W353 P7632 and B1674.W353 P7636:

Cooper, Ron L. *Heidegger and Whitehead : a phenomenological examination into the intelligibility of experience.* c1993

B	Subclass: Philosophy (General)
1674	Late 19th- and 20th-century philosophers
.W353	The first Cutter number (.W35) for Whitehead and the successive element (3) for a separate work, according to Table B-BJ5
P7632	The second Cutter number (P76) for the title of the original work, *Process* . . . , with the successive element (3) for a commentary, and the element (2) based on the main entry, Cooper
1993	The date of publication

Materialien zu Whiteheads "Prozess und Realität". 1991
B1674.W353 P7636 1991

In some cases, special numbers for criticism or commentaries are provided in the schedules, for example:

Darwin, Charles. *The origin of species.* 1996

QH	Subclass: Biology (General)
365	Works of Darwin
.O2	Editions of *On the origin of species*
1996	The date of publication

Charles Darwin's the origin of species : new interdisciplinary essays. c1995

QH	Subclass: Biology (General)
365	Works of Darwin
.O8	The first Cutter number for criticism and reviews of *On the origin of species*
C48	The second Cutter number for the main entry under the title, *Charles* . . .
1995	The date of publication

Supplementary Works

A supplementary work is defined as "a separately issued *subordinate* work which continues or complements a previously issued work."[34] Such works include supplements, appendices, indexes, addenda, etc.[35] Indexes not issued as *subordinate* works are discussed in the next section.

Supplements Cataloged Separately

A separately cataloged supplement to an individual monographic work is classified with the main work. The call number for the main work with the addition of the designation **Suppl.** is assigned to the supplement. If the call number of the main work does not include a date, as in the case of works cataloged according to previous practice, no date is shown in the call number for the supplement. The date of the supplement is not included in the call number. For example:

Main work:
Nobel prize winners : an H.W. Wilson biographical dictionary. 1987

AS	Subclass: Yearbooks
911	Associations, "funds," foundations
.N9	The first Cutter number for Nobel Prizes
N59	The second Cutter number for the main entry under the title, *Nobel* . . .
1987	Date of publication

Supplement:
Nobel Prize winners. Supplement, 1987-1991 : an H.W. Wilson biographical dictionary. 1992
LC call number: AS911.N9 N59 1987 Suppl.

If there is more than one supplement to a particular work, successive numbers, beginning with the number 2, are added to the designation, for example, **Suppl., Suppl. 2, Suppl. 3**, etc.

Clements, Richard Barrett. *Quality manager's complete guide to ISO 9000. 1998 cumulative supplement.* c1998

TS	Subclass: Manufactures
156	General works on quality control
.C6	The Cutter number for the main entry of the original work, Clements
1993	The date of publication of the original work
Suppl. 4	The fourth supplement

Cameron, Kenneth Walter. *The Emerson tertiary bibliography with researcher's index. Supplement two.* 1997

Z	Subclass: Personal bibliography
8265	Emerson, R.W.
.C36	The Cutter number for the main entry of the original work, Cameron
1986	The date of publication of the original work
Suppl. 2	The second supplement

A monograph or serial (except indexes) issued as a supplementary work to a serial is not treated as a supplement in classification. The supplement and the original work are treated as two distinct titles and classed in numbers appropriate to their subject matter, for example:

Aktuelle Probleme der Meeresumwelt : (Deutsche Hydrographische Zeitschrift. Supplement ; 1) 1994

GC	Subclass: Oceanography
1291	North Sea
.A39	The Cutter number for the main entry under the title, *Aktuelle . . .*
1994	The date of publication

However, a serial issued as a supplementary work to a monograph is treated as a supplement according to the procedures outlined above.

Supplements Covered by a Statement in the Physical Description Area or a Note

When a supplementary work such as a volume of tables or maps is cataloged as part of the original work with a statement in the physical description area, the appropriate label, for example, **Tables, Maps**, etc., is added to the call number on the physical item. The designation **Suppl.** is used when there is no specific identifying label. The label is not added to the call number on the bibliographic record.

Indexes

The following summarizes LC policies regarding the treatment of indexes to individual works or groups of works.[36]

1. An index to an individual publication, including a serial, is classed with the work being indexed. In general, the call number for the work being indexed is assigned, with the label **Index** added.

    Original work:
    Afro-American Historical and Genealogical Society (Washington, D.C.) *Journal of the Afro-American Historical and Genealogical Society.* Summer 1980-
    LC call number: E185.96 .A46a

    Index:
    Walker, Barbara D. *Index to the Journal of the Afro-American Historical and Genealogical Society quarterly issues of 1980-1990.* 1991

E	Subclass: History of the United States
185.96	Genealogy of Afro-Americans
.A46a	The Cutter number for the main entry, Afro-American Historical . . .
Index	An index

Successive numbers beginning with the number 2 are added to the designation for additional indexes to the same work.

Oliver, Bill. *Index to Roster of Ohio soldiers in the War of 1812, published under authority of law by the Adjutant General of Ohio, 1916.* 1997

E	Subclass: History of the United States
359.5	The American Army in the War of 1812
.O2	The first Cutter number for Ohio
O3	The second Cutter number for the main entry of the original work, Ohio. Adjutant General's Dept.
1968	The date of publication of the original work
Index 2	A second index

Further example:

Finkelstein, David. *An index to Blackwood's magazine, 1901-1980.* 1995

AP	Subclass: Periodicals
4	British periodicals, 1801-

.B6   The Cutter number for the main entry of *Blackwood's magazine*

Index   An index

2. An index to the publications of an individual author is classed in the biography and criticism number for that author or in a more specific number for indexes under the author, if provided.

Delrieu, Alain. *Sigmund Freud : index general.* c1997
BF   Subclass: Psychology
109   Individual biography
.F74   The first Cutter number for Freud
D45   The second Cutter number for the main entry, Delrieu
1997   The date of publication

3. An index to the publications of an individual society, organization, etc., is classified in Z1201-7999 with bibliographies on the topic in which the organization specializes.

4. A comprehensive index to a list of two or more monographs or serials on a single topic is classified as a bibliography on the topic in Z1201-7999, K, or M.

Science fiction and fantasy reference index, 1992-1995 : an international subject and author index to history and criticism. 1997
Z   Subclass: Bibliography
5917   Subject bibliography on fiction, by special topics, A-Z
.S36   The first Cutter number for the special topic, Science fiction
S2974   The second Cutter number for the main entry under the title, *Science . . .*
1997   The date of publication

Sprug, Joseph W. *Index to fairy tales, 1987-1992 : including 310 collections of fairy tales, folktales, myths, and legends : with significant pre-1987 titles not previously indexed.* 1994
Z   Subclass: Bibliography
5983   Subject bibliography on folklore, by special topics, A-Z
.F17   The first Cutter number for the special topic, Fairy tales
S67   The second Cutter number for the main entry, Sprug
1994   The date of publication

WORKS REQUIRING SPECIAL TREATMENT

Abstracts and Annotated Bibliographies

For classification purposes, a collection of abstracts is regarded as a collection of miscellaneous works.[37] Abstracts, therefore, should normally be classed with a "Collected works" number under the topic in the topical classes, unless a specific number for abstracts has been provided. On the other hand, annotated bibliographies, which also list publications with comments, seldom critical in nature, are classed in Z. The difference is that abstracts summarize works in a way that includes substantive (evaluative and critical) information on the topic, whereas most annotated bibliographies offer only descriptive comments about the works.

LC guidelines for classifying abstracts are summarized below:

1. Abstracts are classed with the subjects in the topical classes rather than in Class Z. Numbers designated for abstracts, if the schedule provides specifically for them, are used; however, such numbers are rare.

2. If no special number exists, a work containing abstracts is classed with the "Collected works (Nonserial)" number, if such a number or its equivalent exists.

3. If the work being cataloged is a serial, it is classed with the number for periodicals.

4. If no special form captions are provided, the abstracts are classed in the "General works" number.

The Library of Congress will normally establish a number for "Collected works (Nonserial)" or for periodicals, as required, if the topic in the schedule already provides for other forms, such as dictionaries, congresses, addresses, essays, lectures, etc.

Classification of abstracts is illustrated in the following examples:

Nicklas, Linda. *Abstracts of early East Texas newspapers, 1839-1856.* c1994

F	Subclass: United States local history
385	Texas genealogy
.N53	The Cutter number for the main entry, Nicklas
1994	The date of publication

Wells, Carol.   *Abstracts of Giles County, Tennessee : county court minutes, 1813-1816, and circuit court minutes, 1810-1816.*   1995

F	Subclass: United States local history
443	Tennessee: Regions, counties, etc., A-Z
.G4	Giles County
W38	The Cutter number for the main entry, Wells
1995	The date of publication

Mathews, Nathan.   *Abstracts of Georgia land plat books A & B, 1779-1785.*   c1995

F	Subclass: United States local history
285	Genealogy of Georgia
.M38	The Cutter number for the main entry, Mathews
1995	The date of publication

Classification of annotated bibliography is illustrated in the following examples:

Crawford, Walter Byron.   *A supplement to Samuel Taylor Coleridge : an annotated bibliography of criticism and scholarship, volumes I-III.*   1996

Z	Subclass: Personal bibliography
8182	Coleridge, S.T.
.C73	The Cutter number for the main entry, Crawford
1996	The date of publication

Roth, Barry.   *An annotated bibliography of Jane Austen studies, 1984-94.*   1996

Z	Subclass: Personal bibliography
8048	Austen, Jane
.R69	The Cutter number for the main entry, Roth
1996	The date of publication

Albert, Richard N.   *An annotated bibliography of jazz fiction and jazz fiction criticism.*   1996

Z	Subclass: Subject bibliography
5917	Special topics in fiction, A-Z
.S5	The first Cutter number for the topic, Short stories
A43	The second Cutter number for the main entry, Albert
1996	The date of publication

Incunabula

At the Library of Congress, incunabula, that is, books printed before 1501, are housed in the Rare Book Division, except those assigned to special collections such as the Law Library. Materials assigned to the incunabula collection in the Rare Book Division receive one of two broad classifications: "Incun. [date]" (used for entries that have definite imprint dates) or "Incun.X" (used when the precise date of publication is uncertain). A Cutter number based on the main entry is added to complete the call number. For example:

Isidore, of Seville, Saint, d. 636. *Isidorus de summo bono.* 1499
LC call number: Incun. 1499 .I85 <Batchelder Coll>

Nanni, Giovanni, 1432?-1502. *Tractatus de futuris Christianoru[m] triumphis in Sarcenos Magistri Johannis Viterbiensis.* ca. 1485
LC call number: Incun. 1485 .N46 <Rare Bk Coll>

Chanca, Diego Alvarez. *Libro del ojo.* 1499
LC call number: Incun. 1499 .C43 <Rare Bk Coll>

Ars moriendi. ca. 1500
LC call number: Incun. 1500 .A77 <Rare Bk Coll>

Niccolo, de' Tudeschi, Archbishop. *Lectura domini abbatis super rubrica de translatione episcoporu[m].* [ca. 1478]
LC call number: Incun. X .N5 <LL RBR>

Thomas, Aquinas, Saint. De periculis contingentibus circa eucharistiam. [1470]
LC call number: Incun. X .T451

The previous practice of assigning alternate numbers has been discontinued.

Facsimiles of individual incunabula or excerpts from such facsimiles are treated as normal works and classed by subject. The class number Z241 is assigned only when it is clear that the publisher intends the work to serve as a specimen of early printing.

"Bound-With" Books

As a general rule, a volume of two or more bibliographically independent works bound together after publication is classed with the first work of the volume.[38] If the book contains only two titles, it is classed with the larger work. A book bound in the "upside-down" manner is classed with the topic listed first in the classification scheme. For example, if one work belongs in PS, and the other in PR, the volume is classed in PR.

The same call number is assigned to the cataloging record of each work in the volume.

Jons, John A. R. *Studies of the French dog sports (Ring, Campagne, IPO, Tracking) "Championships of France" (1982-1989) ; and, The Belgian shepherd dog breeds (Malinois, Tervuren, Groenendael and Laekenois) in Schutzhund competition in the U.S.A. (1979-1988).* 1995

SF	Subclass: Animal culture
425.18	Dog shows and competitive events, by region or country, A-Z
.F8	France
J66	The Cutter number for the main entry, Jons
1995	The date of publication

Comic Books

Comic books are classed in PN6700-PN6790 if they possess all of the following characteristics:[39]

1. The characters and action are portrayed in a succession of panel drawings;

2. A series of panels advances a fictional narrative line; and

3. The dialogue, if present, is generally presented in "balloons" or their equivalent, or at the bottom of the panels.

A comic book may contain a single continuous narrative or a collection of separate narratives. "Photo novels" (i.e., novels that consist almost entirely of photographs, with or without balloon dialogue) and comic strip adaptations from other media, such as motion pictures, dramas, or novels, are treated like comic books.

Examples of comic books classed in PN6700-6790 are shown below.

Simpsons comics : Wingding. c1997

PN	Subclass: Collections of general literature
6728	Individual comic books, strips, etc., from the United States, arranged by title, A-Z
.S49	The first Cutter number for the title of the comic, Simpsons
S56	The second Cutter number for the main entry, *Simpsons comics*
1997	The date of publication

Schulz, Charles M.   *Have another cookie (it'll make you feel better).*   1996

PN	Subclass: Collections of general literature
6728	Individual comic books, strips, etc., from the United States, arranged by title of comic strip, A-Z
.P4	The first Cutter number for the title of the comic strip, *Peanuts*
S3117	The second Cutter number for the main entry, Schulz
1996	The date of publication

Schulz, Charles M.   *Snoopy, not your average dog.*   1996

PN	Subclass: Collections of general literature
6728	Individual comic books, strips, etc., from the United States, arranged by title of comic strip, A-Z
.P4	The first Cutter number for the title of the comic strip, *Peanuts*
S327517	The second Cutter number for the main entry, Schulz
1996	The date of publication

Trudeau, G. B.   *Virtual Doonesbury, virtual Doonesbury.*   1996

PN	Subclass: Collections of general literature
6728	Individual comic books, strips, etc., from the United States, arranged by title, A-Z
.D65	The first Cutter number for the title of the comic strip, *Doonesbury*
T7823	The second Cutter number for the main entry, Trudeau
1996	The date of publication

Trudeau, G. B.   *Washed out bridges and other disasters.*   c1994

PN	Subclass: Collections of general literature
6728	Individual comic books, strips, etc., from the United States, arranged by title, A-Z
.D65	The first Cutter number for the title of the comic strip, *Doonesbury*
T7825	The second Cutter number for the main entry, Trudeau
1994	The date of publication

Note that the second Cutter number in the call numbers for the works by Schulz and Trudeau above are adjusted to accommodate different works of these authors classed in the same number with identical first Cutter numbers.

Books that contain certain comic book elements but do not meet all the criteria stated above are classed as follows:

1. Collections of single panel cartoons, single photographs with balloon captions, and similar presentations are classed in NC1300-1763, if they do not contain a continuing narrative line. For example:

Rowlandson, Thomas. *Thomas Rowlandson's Doctor Syntax drawings : an introduction and guide for collectors.* 1997

NC	Subclass: Drawing, Design, Illustration
1479	Special artists of Caricature, pictorial humor and satire from Great Britain
.R8	The Cutter number for the artist, Rowlandson
A4	Reproductions (Collections)
1997	The date of publication

2. Fictional narratives that consist essentially of text written in book style with occasional illustrations employing comic characters (with or without balloon dialogue) are classed as literary works in Class P.

3. Works that are primarily intended for juvenile readers and picture books presented in cartoon or comic strip format are classed in PZ as juvenile belles lettres. Juvenile materials are discussed in the last section of this chapter.

Schulz, Charles M. *Kick the ball, Marcie.* 1996

PZ	Subclass: Juvenile belles lettres
7	American and English, 1870-
.S38877	The Cutter number for the main entry, Schulz
Ki	Work mark for the title, *Kick . . .*
1996	The date of publication

4. Nonfiction works written in comic book style are classed in the appropriate subject numbers in Classes A-Z.

Green, Martin I. *Voodoo child : the illustrated legend of Jimi Hendrix.* 1995

ML	Subclass: Literature on music
410	Individual biography of composers
.H476	The first Cutter number for Hendrix
G74	The second Cutter number for the main entry, Green
1995	The date of publication

Audiovisual Media and Their Catalogs

The Library of Congress does not use class numbers for shelving audiovisual media and special instructional materials. Publisher names followed by accession numbers and symbols for special collection/custodial assignments (e.g., <M/B/RS> for the Motion Picture/Broadcasting/Recorded Sound Division, <MRC> for Machine Readable Collection, etc.) are used instead. For example:

> Strauss, Johann. *Tales from the Vienna woods* [sound recording] : *featured in M-G-M film The great waltz* / words by Oscar Hammerstein, II ; music by Johann Strauss, II ; adaptation by Dimitri Tiomkin. 193-?
> Victor 4410 (RDI 0008/0441) <Rec Sound>

> Wright, Robert Craig. *Song of Norway* [sound recording]. p1997
> Jay CDJAY2 1253 <Rec Sound>

> *Burlando la ley* / Dirsol, S.A. de C.V. presents ; director, story, Valentin TTrujillo ; adaptation, Valentin Trujillo and Francisco Perez Nieto. 1995.
> VAE 3611 (viewing copy) <M/B/RS>

> *Battling Butler* / Buster Keaton Productions ; director, Buster Keaton ; presenter, Joseph M. Schenck ; screen adaptation, Paul Gerard Smith, Al Boasberg, Charles Smith, Lex Neal.   1995
> VAE 2905 (viewing copy) <M/B/RS>

The previous practice of assigning alternate numbers to sound recordings has been discontinued.

Discographies

General (nontopical) discographies of music sound recordings are classed in ML156+.[40] For example:

> Garrod, Charles. *Capitol transcription listing.*   1995
>
> ML   Subclass: Literature on music
> 156.2   Catalogs of individual record companies, etc.
> .G314   The Cutter number for the main entry, Garrod
> 1995   The date of publication

Topical musical discographies are classed in ML156.4.

Harvard College Library. Judaica Division. *Judaica sound record-ings in the Harvard College Library : a catalog.* 1996

ML	Subclass: Literature on music
156.4	Topical lists of sound recordings
.J4	The first Cutter number for the topic, Jewish music
H37	The second Cutter number for the main entry, Harvard...
1996	The date of publication

Snow, Barbara. *Index of songs on children's recordings.* 1993

ML	Subclass: Literature on music
156.4	Topical lists of sound recordings
.C5	The first Cutter number for the topic, Children's music
S6	The second Cutter number for the main entry, Snow
1993	The date of publication

For further examples, see chapter 6, pages 332-33.

Topical nonmusic discographies are classed with the appropriate topics in Classes B-L and N-Z. Discographies of nonmusic sound record-ings not limited to a topic are classed in ZA4750, for example:

Garrod, Charles. *Columbia 78 RPM master number listing, New York 20000-22999, October 5, 1936 thru March 24, 1938.* 1995

ZA	Subclass: Information resources (General)
4750	Discography
.G37	The Cutter number for the main entry, Garrod
1995	The date of publication

Catalogs of Films

Catalogs of films, including motion pictures and videorecordings, are classed with the appropriate subject. General catalogs of films are classed in PN1998.

The Time out film guide. 1997

PN	Subclass: Literature: General
1998	Motion pictures (miscellaneous works)
.T46	The Cutter number for the main entry under the title, *Time out . . .*
1997	The date of publication

Taussig, H. Arthur. *Film values/family values : a parents' guide.* 1997

PN	Subclass: Literature: General
1998	Motion pictures (miscellaneous works)
.T38	The Cutter number for the main entry, Taussig
1997	The date of publication

Mayo, Mike. *Videohound's video premieres : the only guide to video originals and limited releases.* 1997

PN	Subclass: Literature: General
1998	Motion pictures (miscellaneous works)
.M32	The Cutter number for the main entry, Mayo
1997	The date of publication

Microforms

At the Library of Congress, microfilms and microfiche are arranged by accession numbers. Most of them receive minimal level cataloging. Important microform items are given full cataloging.[41] The call number assigned to a microfilm consists of the following elements.

Microfilm	
[control number]	(a sequential number)
([class or subclass letter(s)])	(based on the class or subclass)
<[symbols for special collection/ custodial assignments]>	(e.g., <So Asia> for South Asian Section of the Asian Reading Room, <MicRR> for Microform Reading Room, etc.)

For full cataloging, a class number, including topical, form, and geographic Cutter numbers but without the item number, is included. For minimal level cataloging, a main-class letter is usually assigned. For example:

> *Princeton University Latin American pamphlet collection. Socioeconomic conditions in Cuba [microform].   1986-1992.*   [no date]
> LC call number: Microfilm 97/264 (H)

> Jog, Narayan Gopal.   *Churchill's blind-spot, India* [microform].   1944
> LC call number: Microfilm BUL-ENG-379 (D)   <So Asia>

> Das, Rashvihari.   *A handbook to Kant's critique of pure reason* [microform].   1949
> LC call number: Microfilm ECL-ENG-501 (B)   <So Asia>

> Das, Rashvihari.   *The philosophy of Whitehead* [microform].   [1937]
> LC call number: Microfilm BUL-ENG-046 (B)   <So Asia>

> *Electronics now.* [microform].   1992-   Vol. 63, no. 7 (July 1992)-
> Monthly
> LC call number: Microfilm 06211   <MicRR>

Microfiche are classed in the same way as microfilms except for the label. A call number for a microfiche consists of the following elements:

> Microfiche
> [control number]
> ([class or subclass letter(s)])
> <[symbols for special collection/custodial assignments]>

For example:

> Josyer, G. R., 1891-   *Winston Churchill [microform] : some sidelights.*
> [1942]
> LC call number: Microfiche 97/61001 (D)   <So Asia>

> *American biographical archive. II* [microform].   [1995?]
> LC call number: Microfiche 97/15 (C)

> *Index, Jewish applicants for emergency U.S. passports, 1915-1924* [microform].   [1991?]
> LC call number: Microfiche 97/31 (E)   ALSO   Hebr Fiche 58
> <Hebr Ref>

The importance of Japanese trading in the countries of Southern Asia
[microform].   1946
LC call number: Microfiche 96/61196 (H)   <So Asia>

Computer Files and Software

Computer files are assigned class numbers appropriate for the topics
represented. Software is classed in the same number in which a book about
that software would be placed.[42] The number for "Data processing" under
the appropriate topic is chosen, unless a provision of the type "Special programs,
A-Z" exists in the schedules. The Library of Congress does not provide item
numbers for computer files or software because such materials are not
shelflisted at the Library. For example:

Physicians' SilverPlatter. *Cardiology* [computer file].   Quarterly
LC class number: RC666 <MRCRR>

Digizine [computer file].   1995-   Vol. 1, no. 1 (fall 1995)-
Quarterly
LC class number: AP2   <1997, 01042> <MRC>

*The nineteenth century on CD-ROM [computer file] : bibliographic records,
the general collection & the specialist collections.*   Began in 1991.   Annual
LC class number: AP4   <MRCRR>

In the examples above, <MRC> and <MRCRR> refer to the Machine
Readable Collection, formerly called the Machine Readable Collection
Reading Room.

JUVENILE MATERIALS

Juvenile nonfiction was mentioned briefly in the Class P section of
chapter 6, in the discussion of subclass PZ (page 362). This section covers the
classification of a wide range of juvenile materials.

Whether or not material is considered juvenile depends on the per-
ceived intent of the author. In general, at the Library of Congress, all works
meant for children in the age group from preschool through fifteen or the
ninth grade are treated as juvenile materials. Thus, works designated by the
publisher as "10 up," "14+," or "suitable for senior high school students"
are treated as juvenile, since the lower end of the designated span includes at

least one year of the 0 through 15 range. Generally, works with the notation "for all ages" may also be considered juvenile.

Library of Congress call numbers are supplied for all juvenile titles added to the Library's classified collection.

Juvenile Belles Lettres

Class numbers PZ5-90 are used for the following types of juvenile works in all languages:[43] juvenile and young adult fiction, general (multi-genre) collections of juvenile belles lettres, picture storybooks, alphabet and counting books with a story line, stories in rhyme, individual song texts illustrated for children, juvenile folk tales, and traditional nursery rhymes. Juvenile poetry, drama, humor, and comic books, on the other hand, are classed with literature in subclasses P-PT.

For works written in the English language classed in PZ5-10.3, unique Cutter numbers are assigned to individual authors, and work letters are used to distinguish different works by the same author. The work letters, based on the title (disregarding initial articles), consist of a capital letter followed by one or more letters in lowercase. Variant editions of the same work are differentiated by date, for example, variant editions of Collodi's *Pinocchio* carry the numbers PZ8.C7 Ph 1986, PZ8.C7 Ph 1987, PZ8.C7 Ph 1988, etc.

Examples of the classification of juvenile materials are shown below:

Henderson, Kathy.   *Disney's Pooh's grand adventure : the search for Christopher Robin.*   1997

PZ	Subclass: Juvenile belles lettres
7	American and English juvenile belles lettres, 1870-
.H3805	The Cutter number for the main entry, Henderson
Dp	The work letters based on the title, *Disney's Pooh's* . . .
1997	The date of publication

Henry, O.   *The gift of the magi.*   1996

PZ	Subclass: Juvenile belles lettres
7	American and English juvenile belles lettres, 1870-
.H3964	The Cutter number for the main entry, Henry
Gi	The work letters based on the title, *gift* . . .
1996	The date of publication

Ziefert, Harriet. *Henny-Penny.* 1997

PZ	Subclass: Juvenile belles lettres
8.1	Folklore, legends, romance
.Z55	The Cutter number for the main entry, Ziefert
He	The work letters based on the title, *Henny-Penny*
1997b	The date of publication

Mattern, Joanne. *The adventures of Robin Hood.* 1996

PZ	Subclass: Juvenile belles lettres
8.1	Folklore, legends, romance
.M427	The Cutter number for the main entry, Mattern
Ad	The work letters based on the title, *adventures* . . .
1996	The date of publication

Barrett, Peter, *A day in the life of a puppy.* 1997

PZ	Subclass: Juvenile belles lettres
10.3	Animal stories
.B2705	The Cutter number for the main entry, Barrett
Dp	The work letters based on the title, *day* . . . *puppy*
1997	The date of publication

For works with main entry under the title, the Cutter number is based on the title, and the work letters are then unnecessary.

Stories from the sea. 1996

PZ	Subclass: Juvenile belles lettres
8.1	Folklore, legends, romance
.S8667	The Cutter number for the main entry under the title, *Stories* . . .
1996	The date of publication

Disney's Bambi. 1996

PZ	Subclass: Juvenile belles lettres
10.3	Animal stories
.D6325	The Cutter number for the main entry under the title, *Disney's* . . .
1996	The date of publication

Work letters are not used with juvenile belle lettres in languages other than English.

> Pavan, Luisa. *Le fiabe magiche.* [1995]
>
> | | |
> |---|---|
> | PZ | Subclass: Juvenile belles lettres |
> | 44.9 | Miscellaneous stories in Italian |
> | .P38 | The Cutter number for the main entry, Pavan |
> | 1995 | The date of publication |

> Abdel-Qadir, Ghazi. *Schamsi und Ali Baba.* 1995
>
> | | |
> |---|---|
> | PZ | Subclass: Juvenile belles lettres |
> | 36.3 | Animal stories in German |
> | .A15 | The Cutter number for the main entry, Abdel-Qadir |
> | 1995 | The date of publication |

Picture Books for Children

A work intended by its publisher to be a picture story book for young children with little or no accompanying text is classed with juvenile belles lettres in the PZ juvenile area. Even when the work is entered under the artist, it is not regarded as a work of art to be classed in N but is treated as a story book. For example:

> Waite, Michael P. *Butterflies for two : my first sharing book.* c1995
>
> | | |
> |---|---|
> | PZ | Subclass: Juvenile belles lettres |
> | 8.3 | Stories in rhyme |
> | .W136 | The first Cutter number for the main entry, Waite |
> | Br | The work letters based on the title, *Butterflies* . . . |
> | 1995 | The date of publication |

> *1, 2 buckle my shoe.* c1997
>
> | | |
> |---|---|
> | PZ | Subclass: Juvenile belles lettres |
> | 8.3 | Stories in rhyme |
> | .A10025 | The Cutter number for the main entry under the title, *1, 2* . . . |
> | 1997 | The date of publication |

In the example above, the Cutter number .A10025 is assigned on the principle of numerals preceding letters in the alphabetical arrangement.

Topical Juvenile Materials

The former practice of classing certain topical juvenile materials in PZ9-10 and PZ15-16 has been discontinued. All topical juvenile materials are now classed with the subjects in the regular subject classes. If there is a number for "Juvenile works" under the appropriate subject, that number is chosen. For example:

The American heritage children's dictionary. 1997

PE	Subclass: English philology and languages
1628.5	Juvenile school dictionaries
.A44	The Cutter number for the main entry under the title, *American* . . .
1997	The date of publication

My favorite animals. c1997

QL	Subclass: Zoology
49	Juvenile works
.M89	The Cutter number for the main entry under the title, *My* . . .
1997	The date of publication

Kain, Kathleen. *Inspector McQ presents All about pets.* 1995

SF	Subclass: Animal culture
416.2	Juvenile works on pets
.K43	The Cutter number for the main entry, Kain
1995	The date of publication

Petty, Kate. *You can jump higher on the moon.* 1997

TL	Subclass: Motor vehicles, Aeronautics, Astronautics
793	Juvenile works
.P463	The Cutter number for the main entry, Petty
1997	The date of publication

If no "Juvenile works" number is available under the particular topic, the "General works" number or the regular number for adult works is used, as follows:

Micklethwait, Lucy.   *A child's book of art : great pictures : first words.*
1993

N	Subclass: Visual arts
7477	Popular works on art appreciation
.M53	The Cutter number for the main entry, Micklethwait
1993	The date of publication

Jackson, Carol A.   *Jesus and me : [a study of the life of Christ : 52 lessons for ages 6 to 9].*   1993

BT	Subclass: Doctrinal theology
207	Study and teaching of Christology
.J33	The Cutter number for the main entry, Jackson
1993	The date of publication

Glavich, Mary Kathleen.   *A child's book of miracles.*   1994

BT	Subclass: Doctrinal theology
366	Miracles in the life of Jesus Christ: General works, 1951-
.G63	The Cutter number for the main entry, Glavich
1994	The date of publication

School Textbooks

School textbooks for children up through the age of fifteen or ninth grade are classed with the subject in the regular subject classes, just as are textbooks for students older than fifteen. Under the topic in question, the class number for textbooks is assigned.[44]

Berg, Linda R.   *Introductory botany : plants, people, and the environment.*   c1997

QK	Subclass: Botany
47	Textbooks
.B48	The Cutter number for the main entry, Berg
1997	The date of publication

If there is no textbook number in the schedules, the number for "Juvenile works" is used if the textbook is for children sixteen or younger.

Lambert, David. *The living world.* 1997
QH   Subclass: Natural history (General)
48   Juvenile works
.L24   The Cutter number for the main entry, Lambert
1997   The date of publication

If neither number is available, a school textbook is classed with the "General works" number, never under the "Study and teaching" number.

School textbooks and works on teaching methods in special subjects are also discussed in the section on Class L, Education, in chapter 6 (pages 317-19).

NOTES

1. "Biography," in Library of Congress, Office for Subject Cataloging Policy, *Subject Cataloging Manual: Classification*, 1st ed. (Washington, DC: Cataloging Distribution Service, Library of Congress, 1992), F275; and "Biography," in Library of Congress, Cataloging Policy and Support Office, *Subject Cataloging Manual: Shelflisting*, 2nd ed. (Washington, DC: Library of Congress, 1995), G320.

2. "Biography," Library of Congress, *Subject Cataloging Manual: Classification*, F275, p. 2.

3. "Biography," Library of Congress, *Subject Cataloging Manual: Shelflisting*, G320.

4. "Biography," Library of Congress, *Subject Cataloging Manual: Classification*, F275, p. 1.

5. Ibid., 5.

6. "Government Officials' Biographies, Speeches, and Papers," in Library of Congress, *Subject Cataloging Manual: Classification*, F605.

7. *Anglo-American Cataloguing Rules*, 2nd ed., 1998 revision, prepared under the direction of the Joint Steering Committee for Revision of AACR, a committee of: the American Library Association, the Australian Committee on Cataloguing, the British Library, the Canadian Committee on Cataloguing, the Library Association, the Library of Congress; ed. Michael Gorman and Paul W. Winkler (Chicago: American Library Association, 1998), 622.

8. "Serials," Library of Congress, *Subject Cataloging Manual: Shelflisting*, G820, p. 2.

9. "Periodicals," Library of Congress, *Subject Cataloging Manual: Classification*, F210.

10. "Periodicals: 'A' Cutters," Library of Congress, *Subject Cataloging Manual: Classification*, F220.

11. "Yearbooks," Library of Congress, *Subject Cataloging Manual: Classification*, F230.

12. *Anglo-American Cataloguing Rules*, 622.

13. "Series: Monographic Series," Library of Congress, *Subject Cataloging Manual: Shelflisting*, G840.

14. "Serials," Library of Congress, *Subject Cataloging Manual: Shelflisting*, G820, p. 1.

15. "Collected Works (Nonserial)," Library of Congress, *Subject Cataloging Manual: Classification*, F250.

16. "Series: Monographic Series," Library of Congress, *Subject Cataloging Manual: Shelflisting*, G840.

17. "Alternate Class Numbers: Analytics in Collected Sets," Library of Congress, *Subject Cataloging Manual: Classification*, F130.

18. *Anglo-American Cataloguing Rules*, 617.

19. "Corporate Bodies," Library of Congress, *Subject Cataloging Manual: Shelflisting*, G220.

20. "Dates," Library of Congress, *Subject Cataloging Manual: Shelflisting*, G140, p. 3.

21. "Corporate Bodies," Library of Congress, *Subject Cataloging Manual: Shelflisting*, G220.

22. Ibid., 8-9.

23. "Societies," Library of Congress, *Subject Cataloging Manual: Shelflisting*, G240.

24. "Societies," Library of Congress, *Subject Cataloging Manual: Classification*, F225.

25. "Societies," Library of Congress, *Subject Cataloging Manual: Shelflisting*, G240.

26. "Government Documents," Library of Congress, *Subject Cataloging Manual: Classification*, F603.

27. "Legislative Hearings and Reports," Library of Congress, *Subject Cataloging Manual: Classification*, F618.

28. "Congresses," Library of Congress, *Subject Cataloging Manual: Classification*, F240.

29. "Conferences, Congresses, Meetings, Etc.," Library of Congress, *Subject Cataloging Manual: Shelflisting*, G230.

30. "Dates," Library of Congress, *Subject Cataloging Manual: Shelflisting*, G140, p. 2.

31. "Parallel Texts," *Cataloging Service* 114 (Summer 1975):11.

32. "Abridgements of Individual Works," Library of Congress, *Subject Cataloging Manual: Classification*, F475.

33. "Commentaries on Individual Works," Library of Congress, *Subject Cataloging Manual: Classification*, F570; and "Criticism/Commentaries," Library of Congress, *Subject Cataloging Manual: Shelflisting*, G340.

34. "Supplementary Works," Library of Congress, *Subject Cataloging Manual: Shelflisting*, G850.

35. "Supplementary Works," Library of Congress, *Subject Cataloging Manual: Classification*, F720.

36. "Indexes," Library of Congress, *Subject Cataloging Manual: Classification*, F610; and "Supplementary Works," Library of Congress, *Subject Cataloging Manual: Shelflisting*, G850, p. 5.

37. "Abstracts," Library of Congress, *Subject Cataloging Manual: Classification*, F480.

38. "Bound-with Books," Library of Congress, *Subject Cataloging Manual: Classification*, F520.

39. "Comic Books," Library of Congress, *Subject Cataloging Manual: Classification*, F565.

40. "Discographies," Library of Congress, *Subject Cataloging Manual: Classification*, F582.

41. "Microforms," Library of Congress, *Subject Cataloging Manual: Classification*, F650.

42. "Software," Library of Congress, *Subject Cataloging Manual: Classification*, F710.

43. "Juvenile Materials," Library of Congress, *Subject Cataloging Manual: Classification*, F615.

44. Ibid.

Appendix A: General Tables

Cutter Table

After initial vowels

	b	d	l-m	n	p	r	s-t	u-y
for the second letter:	b	d	l-m	n	p	r	s-t	u-y
use number:	2	3	4	5	6	7	8	9

After initial letter S

	a	ch	e	h-i	m-p	t	u	w-z
for the second letter:	a	ch	e	h-i	m-p	t	u	w-z
use number:	2	3	4	5	6	7	8	9

After initial letters Qu

	a	e	i	o	r	t	y
for the second letter:	a	e	i	o	r	t	y
use number:	3	4	5	6	7	8	9

For initial letters Qa-Qt
use numbers: 2-29

After other initial consonants

	a	e	i	o	r	u	y
for the second letter:	a	e	i	o	r	u	y
use number:	3	4	5	6	7	8	9

For expansion

	a-d	e-h	i-l	m-o	p-s	t-v	w-z
for the letter:	a-d	e-h	i-l	m-o	p-s	t-v	w-z
use number:	3	4	5	6	7	8	9

Source: Library of Congress, *Subject Cataloging Manual: Shelflisting*, G60, p. 14.

Regions and Countries Table

Abyssinia *see* Ethiopia

Afghanistan A3

Africa A35
  Africa, Central A352
  Africa, East A353
  Africa, Eastern A354
  Africa, French-Speaking West . . A3545
  Africa, North A355
  Africa, Northeast A3553
  Africa, Northwest A3554
  Africa, South *see* South Africa
  Africa, Southern A356
  Africa, Sub-Saharan A357
  Africa, West A358

Albania A38

Algeria A4

Alps A43

America A45

American Samoa A46

Andorra A48

Angola A5

Anguilla A54

Antarctica A6

Antigua *see* Antigua and Barbuda

Antigua and Barbuda A63

Arab countries A65

Arctic regions A68

Argentina A7

Armenia A75

Armenia (Republic) A76

Aruba A77

Asia A78
  Asia, Central A783
  Asia, East *see* East Asia
  Asia, South *see* South Asia
  Asia, Southeastern A785
  Asia, Southwestern *see* Middle East

Australasia A788

Australia A8

Austria A9

Azerbaijan A98

Bahamas B24

Bahrain B26

Balkan Peninsula B28

Baltic States B29

Bangladesh B3

Barbados B35

Barbuda *see* Antigua and Barbuda

Belarus B38

Belgium B4

Belize B42

Benelux Countries B425

Bengal B43

Benin B45

Bermuda B46

Bhutan B47

Bolivia B5

Bonaire B52

Bosnia and Hercegovina B54

Botswana B55

Brazil B6

British Guiana *see* Guyana

British Honduras *see* Belize

British Isles B65

Brunei B7

Bulgaria B9

Burkina Faso B92

Burma B93

Burundi B94

Byzantine Empire B97

Cambodia C16

Cameroon C17

Canada C2

Canary Islands C23

Cape Verde C25

Source: Library of Congress, *Subject Cataloging Manual: Shelflisting*, G300.

Greece G8

Greenland. G83

Grenada. G84

Guadeloupe G845

Guam G85

Guatemala G9

Guiana. G915

Guinea G92

Guinea-Bissau G93

Guyana G95

Haiti H2

Hispaniola H55

Holland *see* Netherlands

Honduras H8

Hong Kong. H85

Hungary H9

Iceland I2

India. I4

Indochina I48

Indonesia I5

Inner Mongolia *see* China

Iran I7

Iraq. I72

Ireland I73

Islamic countries I74

Islamic Empire. I742

Islands of the India Ocean I743

Israel I75

Italy I8

Ivory Coast *see* Côte d'Ivoire

Jamaica. J25

Japan J3

Java *see* Indonesia

Jerusalem J4

Jordan J6

Jugoslavia *see* Yugoslavia

Jutland *see* Denmark

Kampuchea *see* Cambodia

Kazakhstan K3

Kenya K4

Kerguelen Islands K43

Kiribati K5

Korea. K6

Korea (Democratic People's Republic) *see*
    Korea (North)

Korea (North) K7

Korea (Republic) *see* Korea

Korea (South) *see* Korea

Kuwait. K9

Kyrgyzstan K98

Laos. L28

Latin America L29

Latvia. L35

Lebanon L4

Lesotho. L5

Liberia L7

Libya L75

Liechtenstein. L76

Lithuania L78

Luxembourg. L9

Macao. M25

Macaronesia M26

Macedonia M27

Macedonia (Republic) M275

Madagascar. M28

Malagasy Republic *see* Madagascar

Malawi. M3

Malay Archipelago. M35

Malaya *see* Malaysia

Malaysia M4

Maldives M415

Mali. M42

Malta M43

Marshall Islands M433

Martinique M435

Mauritania M44

Mauritius. M45

Melanesia M5

United States

Alabama	A2	Montana	M9
Alaska	A4	Nebraska	N2
Arizona	A6	Nevada	N3
Arkansas	A8	New Hampshire	N4
California	C2	New Jersey	N5
Colorado	C6	New Mexico	N6
Connecticut	C8	New York	N7
Delaware	D3	North Carolina	N8
District of Columbia *see* Washington (D.C.)		North Dakota	N9
		Ohio	O3
Florida	F6	Oklahoma	O5
Georgia	G4	Oregon	O7
Hawaii	H3	Pennsylvania	P4
Idaho	I2	Rhode Island	R4
Illinois	I3	South Carolina	S6
Indiana	I6	South Dakota	S8
Iowa	I8	Tennessee	T2
Kansas	K2	Texas	T4
Kentucky	K4	Utah	U8
Louisiana	L8	Vermont	V5
Maine	M2	Virginia	V8
Maryland	M3	Washington (D.C.)	W18
Massachusetts	M4	Washington (State)	W2
Michigan	M5	West Virginia	W4
Minnesota	M6	Wisconsin	W6
Mississippi	M7	Wyoming	W8
Missouri	M8		

Canadian Provinces

Alberta	A3	Nova Scotia	N8
British Columbia	B8	Ontario	O6
Manitoba	M3	Prince Edward Island	P8
New Brunswick	N5	Quebec (Province)	Q3
Newfoundland	N6	Saskatchewan	S2
Northwest Territories	N7	Yukon (Territory)	Y8

Source: Library of Congress, *Subject Cataloging Manual: Shelflisting*, G302.

Biography Table

.x	Cutter for the biographee
.xA2	Collected works. By date
.xA25	Selected works. Selections. By date
	Including quotations
.xA3	Autobiography, diaries, etc. By date
.xA4	Letters. By date
.xA5	Speeches, essays, and lectures. By date
	Including interviews
.xA6-Z★	Individual biography, interviews, and criticism.
	By main entry
	Including criticism of selected works, autobiography,
	quotations, letters, speeches, interviews, etc.

★Main entries of biography/criticism that begin with A (only in biography classes). Biography and criticism in the Biography Table are limited to the range .xA6-Z. If the main entry of a biographical or critical work begins with A and the work is classed in a biography class, do not Cutter lower than A6. The suggested Cutter numbers for entries beginning with A are:

Aa-Af	A6-699
Ag-Al	A7-799
Am-Ar	A8-899
As-Az	A9-999

Note: The Translation Table can be applied to the .xA6-Z of the Biography Table. Do not use the Translation Table with the .xA2-.xA5 area of the Biography Table.

Source: Library of Congress, *Subject Cataloging Manual: Shelflisting*, G320.

Preferred Shelflist Order - Individual Authors

When the works of an individual author are filed in a single
class number, they are arranged in the following order.

Example

Collected works	By date	.L54 1966
Translations	By date	.L5412-5419 1986
Selected works	By date	.L542 1986
Translations	By date	.L54212-54219 1986
Separate works	By title	
Original work	Cutter and date	.L55 1952
Facsimile or photocopy of original work	Cutter and date with *a*	.L55 1952a (.L55 1952aa, ab, etc.)
Edition or reprint	Cutter and date	.L55 1967
Facsimile or photocopy of edition	Cutter and date of edition with *a*	.L55 1967a (.L55 1967aa, ab, etc.)
Translation	Cutter expanded by 12 - 19 and date	.L5513 1963 *[English translation]*
Selection, abridgement, or condensed version	Cutter expanded by 2 and date	.L552 1981 .S6L552 1981
Translation of selection, abridgement, or condensed version	Cutter expanded by 212 - 219 and date	.L55213 1982 *[English translation]*
Adaptations	By adapter, A-Z *[used only for works cataloged prior to AACR 2. Adaptations are now classed with works of adapter]*	
Criticism	Cutter expanded by 3 or 3 - 39 and date	.L553T5 1976 .S6L5537 1976
Biography and criticism	By author, A-Z	.L56B78 1986

Source: Library of Congress, *Subject Cataloging Manual: Shelflisting,* G60.

Translation Table

.x	Original work
.x12	Polyglot★
.x13	English translation
.x14	French translation
.x15	German translation
.x16	Italian translation
.x17	Russian translation
.x18	Spanish translation

★The Cutter for polyglot is assigned when a work is written in several languages.

Music Translation Table

.x	=	Original work
.x15	=	Polyglot
.x2	=	English
.x3	=	French
.x4	=	German
.x5	=	Italian, Latin
.x6	=	Portuguese
.x7	=	Russian
.x8	=	Spanish
.x9	=	Swedish, etc.

Source: Library of Congress, *Subject Cataloging Manual: Shelflisting*, G800.

Appendix B:
Models for Subarrangement
Within Disciplines

Model for the D Schedule
(not to be used for development in E and F)

Part 1—General

Periodicals.   Societies.   Serials
Museums, exhibitions, etc.
   Individual.   By place, A-Z
Congresses
Sources and documents
Gazetteers.   Dictionaries, etc.
Place names (General)
Directories
Guidebooks
General works
Pictorial works
Historic monuments, landmarks, etc. (General)
      For local, *see* [...]
   Preservation
Historical geography
Geography
Description and travel
   History of travel
   Early through [...]
   [*individual periods*]
Antiquities
      For local antiquities, *see* [*number for local history and description*]
Social life and customs.   Civilization.   Intellectual life
   By period, *see* the specific period or reign
Ethnography
   National characteristics
   Individual elements in the population, A-Z
   [...] in foreign countries (General)
      For [...] in a particular country, *see* the country

Source: Library of Congress, *Subject Cataloging Manual: Classification*, F195.

History
  Periodicals.   Societies.   Serials, *see [number for periodicals above]*
  Dictionaries.   Chronological tables, outlines, etc.
  Biography (Collective)
      For individual biography, *see* the specific period, reign, or place
    Rulers, kings, etc.
    Houses, noble families, etc.
      Individual, A-Z
  Historiography
    Biography of historians, area studies specialists, archaeologists, etc.
      Collective
      Individual, A-Z
  Study and teaching
    Local, A-Z
  General works
    Through 1800
    1801-
  Pictorial works
  Philosophy of [...] history
  Military history
      For individual campaigns and engagements, *see* the period or reign
  Naval history
      For individual campaigns and engagements, *see* the period or reign
  Political history
    Sources and documents
    General works
    By period, *see* the specific period or reign
  Foreign and general relations
      Class general works on the diplomatic history of a period with the
        period, e.g. [...].   For works on relations with a specific country
        regardless of period, *see [number below for relations with individual*
        countries].
    Sources and documents
    General works
    Relations with individual countries, A-Z
      For list of countries, *see* pp. [...]
  By period

Part 2 —Major periods or centuries

Periodicals.   Societies.   Serials
Congresses
Sources and documents
Dictionaries
Historiography
General works
Social life and customs.   Civilization.   Intellectual life
Military history

Naval history
Political history
Foreign and general relations
Biography and memoirs
    Collective
    Individual, A-Z
[individual periods or reigns]

Part 3—Major cities

Periodicals.   Societies.   Serials
Museums, exhibitions, etc.
      Subarranged by author
Sources and documents
Directories.   Dictionaries.   Gazetteers
Guidebooks
General works
Description.   Geography
   Early and medieval
   [other individual periods]
Pictorial works
Antiquities
Social life and customs.   Civilization.   Intellectual life
Ethnography
   Individual elements in the population, A-Z
History
   Biography (Collective)
      For individual biography, *see* the specific period
   General works
   By period
     Early and medieval
     [other individual periods]
Sections, districts, suburbs, etc.
   Individual, A-Z
Monuments, statues, etc.
   Individual, A-Z
Parks, squares, cemeteries, etc.
   Individual, A-Z
Streets, bridges, gates, etc.
   Individual, A-Z
Buildings
   Individual, A-Z
Other cities, towns, etc., A-Z

Model for the H Schedule

Periodicals.   Societies.   Serials
Congresses
Dictionaries.   Encyclopedias
Terminology.   Abbreviations.   Notation
Directories
Theory.   Method.   Relations to other subjects
   Classification
   Relation to [*individual named subjects*]
Communication of information
   Information services
Study and teaching.   Research
   Audiovisual aids
   Problems, exercises, examinations
   By region or country
      United States
      Other regions or countries, A-Z
Museums.   Exhibitions
   By region or country, A-Z
      Under each country:
      .x   General works
      .x2   Individual, by name, A-Z
History
   By period
   Special schools
   By region or country, A-Z
Biography
   Collective
   Individual, A-Z [*if individual biography classes with the country, omit this line and create only one line: Biography (Collective)*]
General works, treatises, and advanced textbooks
Pictorial works
Juvenile works
Policy (General)
Statistics
   Collections of statistics
   Theory
Handbooks, manuals, etc.
Charts, diagrams, etc.
Forms
[*subtopics*]
By region or country, A-Z

Model for the Q Schedule

Periodicals, societies, congresses, serial publications
Voyages and expeditions
Dictionaries and encyclopedias
Communication of [...] information
    Information services
    [...] literature
    Abstracting and indexing
    Language.   Authorship
    Translating.   Translating services
Philosophy
Nomenclature, terminology, notation, abbreviations
Classification
History
    By region or country, A-Z
Biography
    Collective
    Individual, A-Z
Directories
Early works [...]
General works, treatises, and advanced textbooks
Elementary textbooks
Pictorial works and atlases
[...] illustration
Popular works
Juvenile works
Recreations
[...] as a profession.   Vocational guidance
Study and teaching.   Research
    Outlines, syllabi
    Problems, exercises, examinations
    Experiments
    Laboratory manuals
Laboratories
    Individual laboratories, A-Z
Technique
Instruments and apparatus
Collecting and preservation
Museums.   Exhibitions
Handbooks, tables, formulas, etc.
Miscellany and curiosa

Model for the R Schedule

Periodicals. Societies. Serials
Hospitals, clinics, etc.
   By region or country, A-Z
Congresses
Nomenclature. Terminology. Abbreviations
Dictionaries and encyclopedias
Communication in [...]
   Information centers
   [...] archives
   [...] literature
Directories
Laboratories, institutes, etc.
   Individual. By city, A-Z
Museums. Exhibitions
   By region or country, A-Z
      Under each country:
         .x   General works
         .x2   Special. By city, A-Z
History
   By region or country, A-Z
Biography
   Collective
   Individual, A-Z
General works
Handbooks, manuals, etc.
Problems, exercises, examinations
Outlines, syllabi, etc.
Popular works
Juvenile works
Atlases. Pictorial works
[...] as a profession
Study and teaching
   Audiovisual aids
   By region or country, A-Z
Research. Experimentation
Clinical cases
Statistics and surveys
   By region or country, A-Z
Practice of [...]. [...] economics
     Including business methods and employment surveys
Instruments, apparatus and appliances
Pathology
Examination. Diagnosis
Therapeutics
[*special subtopics*]

Bibliography

Aldred, Thomas. "The Expansive Classification." *Library Association Record* 7 (1905):207-19.

Angell, Richard S. "Development of Class K at the Library of Congress." *Law Library Journal* 57 (November 1964):352-76.

Angell, Richard S. "On the Future of the Library of Congress Classification." In *Classification Research: Proceedings of the Second International Study Conference Held at Hotel Prins Hamlet, Elsinore, Denmark, 14th to 18th September 1964*, edited by Pauline Atherton, 101-12. Copenhagen: Munksgaard, 1965.

Anglo-American Cataloguing Rules. 2nd ed., 1998 revision. Prepared under the direction of the Joint Steering Committee for Revision of AACR, a committee of: the American Library Association, the Australian Committee on Cataloguing, the British Library, the Canadian Committee on Cataloguing, the Library Association, the Library of Congress, edited by Michael Gorman and Paul W. Winkler. Chicago: American Library Association, 1998.

Bead, Charles C. "The Library of Congress Classification: Development, Characteristics, and Structure." In *The Use of the Library of Congress Classification: Proceedings of the Institute on the Use of the Library of Congress Classification*, edited by Richard H. Schimmelpfeng and C. Donald Cook, 18-32. Chicago: American Library Association, 1968.

Bindman, Fred. "Classification of Musical Materials." In *Proceedings of the Institute on Library of Congress Music Cataloging Policies and Procedures, January 26-27, 1971, Coolidge Auditorium, Library of Congress, Washington, D.C.*, transcribed and compiled with editorial comments by David Sommerfield, 63-72. Musical Library Association Technical Reports, No. 3. Ann Arbor, MI: Music Library Association, 1975.

Cataloging Service 1-125 (June 1945-Spring 1978). Washington, DC: Library of Congress, Processing Department.

Cataloging Service Bulletin 1-   (Summer 1978-   ). Washington, DC: Library of Congress, Processing Services.

Chan, Lois Mai. "Classification, Present and Future." *Cataloging & Classification Quarterly* 21, no. 2 (1995):5-17.

Chan, Lois Mai. "Library of Congress Class Numbers in Online Catalog Searching." *RQ* 28 (Summer 1989):530-36.

Chan, Lois Mai. "Library of Congress Classification: Alternative Provisions." *Cataloging & Classification Quarterly* 19, nos. 3-4 (1995):67-87.

Chan, Lois Mai. "Subject Analysis Tools Online: The Challenge Ahead." *Information Technology and Libraries* 9 (September 1990):258-62.

Childs, J. B. "Genesis of the Library of Congress Classification." *Herald of Library Science* 15 (July/October 1976):330-34.

Chressanthis, June D. "The Reclassification Decision: Dewey or Library of Congress? (Experience of Mississippi State University)." *Cataloging & Classification Quarterly* 19, nos. 3-4 (1995):169-82.

Clemons, H. "D.C. vs. L.C." *Libraries* 35 (January 1930):1-4.

Cutter, Charles Ammi. *Charles Ammi Cutter: Library Systematizer*, edited by Francis L. Miksa. Littleton, CO: Libraries Unlimited, 1977.

Cutter, Charles Ammi. *Cutter-Sanborn Three-Figure Author Table*. Swanson-Swift revision. Chicopee, MA: distributed by H. R. Huntting Company, 1969.

Cutter, Charles Ammi. "The Expansive Classification." In *Transactions and Proceedings of the Second International Library Conference, London, July 13-16, 1897*, 84-88. London: Printed for Members of the Conference by Morrison & Giblex of Edinburgh, 1898.

Cutter, Charles Ammi. *Expansive Classification. Part 1: The First Six Classifications*. Boston: C. A. Cutter, 1891-1893.

Cutter, Charles Ammi. *Expansive Classification. Part 2: Seventh Classification*, edited by W. P. Cutter. Boston; n.p., 1896-1911. 2 vols. with suppl. pages.
    [Much of the seventh expansion was completed by Cutter's nephew, William P. Cutter, after the elder Cutter's death. This work was issued in parts and is difficult to describe bibliographically.]

Dewey, Melvil. *Decimal Classification and Relativ Index for Libraries, Clippings, Notes, Etc*. 5th ed. Boston: Library Bureau, 1894.
    [This is the edition of Dewey's *Decimal Classification* that was available for consideration by Hanson and Martel.]

Drabenstott, Karen Markey, Leslie C. Riester, and Bonnie Aileen Dede. "Shelflisting Using Expert Systems." In International Study Conference on Classification Research (5th: 1991: Toronto, Ont.). *Classification Research for Knowledge Representation and Organization*, 199-208. Amsterdam; New York: Elsevier, 1992.

Edmands, John. *New System of Classification and Scheme for Numbering Books, Applied to the Mercantile Library of Philadelphia*. Philadelphia: Grant, Faires & Rodgers, Printers, 1883.

Ensor, Pat L. "Web Organization: Use of the Library of Congress Classification," *Technicalities* 16 (March 1996):11-12.

Fellows, Dorcas. "Library of Congress Classification vs. Decimal Classification." *Library Journal* 50 (April 1, 1925):291-95.

Foskett, A. C. "The Library of Congress Classification." In *The Subject Approach to Information*, 409-18. 4th ed. Hamden, CT: Linnet Books, 1982.

Goldberg, Jolande E. *Library of Congress Classes JZ and KZ: Historical Notes and Introduction to Application*. Washington, DC: Cataloging Distribution Service, Library of Congress, 1997.

Goldberg, Jolande E. "Library of Congress Law Classification: The Regional Schedules." *Law Library Journal* 79 (Winter 1987):67-91.

Guenther, Rebecca S. "Automating the Library of Congress Classification Scheme: Implementation of the USMARC Format for Classification Data." *Cataloging & Classification Quarterly* 21, nos. 3-4 (1996):177-203.

Guenther, Rebecca S. "The Development and Implementation of the USMARC Format for Classification Data (Presented at the Fifth International Study Conference on Classification Research)." *Information Technology and Libraries* 11 (June 1992):120-31.

Guenther, Rebecca S. "The Library of Congress Classification in the USMARC Format." *Knowledge Organization* 21, no. 4 (1994):199-202.

Halle. Universität. Bibliothek. *Schema des Realkatalogs der königlichen Universitätbibliothek au Halle a. S.* Beihefte zum Zentralblatt für Bibliothekswesen; 3, edited by Otto Hartwig. Leipzig: O. Harrassowitz, 1888.

Hanson, J. C. M. "The Library of Congress and Its New Catalogue: Some Unwritten History." In *Essays Offered to Herbert Putnam by His Colleagues and Friends on His Thirtieth Anniversary As Librarian of Congress: 5 April 1929*, edited by William Warner Bishop and Andrew Keogh, 178-94. New Haven, CT: Yale University Press, 1929.

Hanson, J. C. M. "Library of Congress Classification for College Libraries." *Library Journal* 46 (February 15, 1921):151-54.

High, Walter M. "Library of Congress Classification Numbers as Subject Access Points in Computer-Based Retrieval." *Cataloging & Classification Quarterly* 11, no. 1 (1990):37-43.

Hulme, E. Wyndham. "Principles of Book Classification." In *Library Association Record* 13 (1911):354-58, 389-94, 444-49; 14 (1912):39-46, 174-81, 216-21.

Immroth, John Phillip. *Analysis of Vocabulary Control in Library of Congress Classification and Subject Headings*. Research Studies in Library Science, No. 3. Littleton, CO: Libraries Unlimited, 1971.

Immroth, John Phillip. "Expansive Classification." *Encyclopedia of Library and Information Science* 8 (1972):297-316.

Immroth, John Phillip. "Library of Congress Classification." In *Classification in the 1970s: A Second Look*, edited by Arthur Maltby. Rev. ed. London: Clive Bingley/Hamden, CT: Linnet Books, 1976.

Institute on Library of Congress Music Cataloging Policies and Procedures. *Proceedings of the Institute on Library of Congress Music Cataloging Policies and Procedures, January 26-27, 1971, Coolidge Auditorium, Library of Congress, Washington,*

D.C., transcribed and compiled with editorial comments by David Sommerfield. Musical Library Association Technical Reports, No. 3. Ann Arbor, MI: Music Library Association, 1975.

Institute on the Use of the Library of Congress Classification. *The Use of the Library of Congress Classification: Proceedings of the Institute on the Use of the Library of Congress Classification*, edited by Richard H. Schimmelpfeng and C. Donald Cook. Chicago: American Library Association, 1968.

Jaakkola, Helvi S. "Shelflisting of Musical Materials." In *Proceedings of the Institute on Library of Congress Music Cataloging Policies and Procedures, January 26-27, 1971, Coolidge Auditorium, Library of Congress, Washington, D.C.*, transcribed and compiled with editorial comments by David Sommerfield, 73-80. Musical Library Association Technical Reports, No. 3. Ann Arbor, MI: Music Library Association, 1975.

Johnston, George F. "The Literature of Classical Antiquity and the PA Schedule." *Cataloging & Classification Quarterly* 17, nos. 1-2 (1993):69-85.

Johnston, William Dawson. *History of the Library of Congress, 1800-1864*. Washington, DC: Government Printing Office, 1904.

LaMontagne, Leo E. *American Library Classification with Special Reference to the Library of Congress*. Hamden, CT: Shoe String Press, 1961.

Larsgaard, Mary Lynette. *Map Librarianship: An Introduction*. 3rd ed. Englewood, CO: Libraries Unlimited, 1998.

Larson, Ray R. "Experiments in Automatic Library of Congress Classification." *Journal of the American Society for Information Science* 43 (March 1992):130-48.

Library of Congress. *Annual Report of the Librarian of Congress*. Washington, DC: Government Printing Office, 1901- .

Library of Congress. *The Library of Congress and Its Activities*. Washington, DC: Government Printing Office, 1926.

Library of Congress. *The Library of Congress and Its Work*. Washington, DC: Government Printing Office, 1907.

Library of Congress. *Library of Congress Filing Rules*. Washington, DC: Library of Congress, 1980.

Library of Congress. *The Library of Congress Shelflist*. Microfiche ed. Ann Arbor, MI: University Microfilms International, [1978-79].

Library of Congress. *Report of the Librarian of Congress and Report of the Superintendent of Library Grounds for the Fiscal Year Ending June 30, 1916*. Washington, DC: Government Printing Office, 1916.

Library of Congress. Catalog Division. Card Section. "An Account of the Catalogs, Classifications, and Card Distribution Work of the Library of Congress." *Bulletin* No. 7 (June 15, 1904).

Library of Congress. Geography and Map Division. *Geographic Cutters*. 2nd microfiche ed. Washington, DC: Library of Congress, 1989.

Library of Congress. Jefferson Collection. *Catalogue of the Library of Thomas Jefferson,* compiled with annotations by E. Millicent Sowerby. Washington, DC: Library of Congress, 1952-59. 5 vols.

Library of Congress. Subject Cataloging Division. *Classification.* Washington, DC: Library of Congress, 1901-   .

Library of Congress. Subject Cataloging Division. *LC Classification Outline.* 6th ed. Washington, DC: Library of Congress, 1990.

Library of Congress. Subject Cataloging Division. *Library of Congress Subject Headings.* Washington, DC: Library of Congress, 1914-   .

Library of Congress. Office for Subject Cataloging Policy. *Subject Cataloging Manual: Classification,* 1st ed. Washington, DC: Library of Congress, 1992.

Library of Congress. Cataloging Policy and Support Office. *Subject Cataloging Manual: Shelflisting.* 2nd ed. Washington, DC: Library of Congress, 1995.

Mann, Thomas. *Library Research Models: A Guide to Classification, Cataloging, and Computers.* New York: Oxford University Press, 1993.

Mann, Thomas. *Cataloging and Classification Quality at the Library of Congress.* Washington, DC: Cataloging Forum, Library of Congress, 1994.

Martel, Charles. "Classification." In *Report of the Librarian of Congress and Report of the Superintendent of the Library Buildings and Grounds for the Fiscal Year Ending June 30, 1911,* 58-64. Washington, DC: Government Printing Office, 1911.

Martel, Charles. "Classification: A Brief Conspectus of Present Day Library Practice." *Library Journal* 36 (August 1911):410-16.

Martel, Charles. "Classification: Present Tendencies." *Library Journal* 29 (December 1904):C132-34.

Martel, Charles. "Library of Congress Classification." *Bulletin of the American Library Association* 5 (July 1911):230-32.

Martel, Charles. "The Library of Congress Classification: Some Considerations Regarding the Relation of Book or Library Classification to the 'Order of the Sciences'." In *Essays Offered to Herbert Putnam by His Colleagues and Friends on His Thirtieth Anniversary As Librarian of Congress: 5 April 1929,* edited by William Warner Bishop and Andrew Keogh, 327-32. New Haven, CT: Yale University Press, 1929.

Mearns, David Chambers. *The Story Up to Now, The Library of Congress, 1800-1946.* Washington, DC: Government Printing Office, 1947.

Micco, H. Mary. "Report on Linking Subject Headings to LC Classification Numbers and Suggestions for Automating the Classification Schedules for the Explicit Purpose of Improving Subject Access in Online Public Access Catalogs." In *Advances in Classification Research: Proceedings of the 1st ASIS SIG/CR Classification Research Workshop Held at the 53rd ASIS Annual Meeting, Toronto, Ontario, Canada, November 4, 1990,* edited by Susanne M. Humphrey and Barbara H. Kwasnik, 107-18. Learned Information, Inc., 1990.

Micco, H. Mary. "Suggestions for Automating the Library of Congress Classification Schedules." In International Study Conference on Classification Research (5th: 1991: Toronto, Ont.). *Classification Research for Knowledge Representation and Organization*, 285-94. Amsterdam; New York: Elsevier, 1992.

Miksa, Francis L. *The Development of Classification at the Library of Congress*. Occasional Papers, No. 164. Urbana: University of Illinois, Graduate School of Library and Information Science, August 1984.

National Library of Medicine (U.S.). *Medical Subject Headings*. Bethesda, MD: National Library of Medicine, 1975- .

National Library of Medicine (U.S.). *National Library of Medicine Classification: A Scheme for the Shelf Arrangement of Books in the Field of Medicine and Its Related Sciences*. Bethesda, MD: National Library of Medicine, 1951- .

Pattie, Ling-yuh W. "Reclassification Revisited: An Automated Approach." *Cataloging & Classification Quarterly* 19, nos. 3-4 (1995):183-93.

Perreault, Jean M. "The Classification of Philosophy." *Libri* 14, no. 1 (1964):32-39.

Perreault, Jean M. "Lois Mai Chan's New Edition of Immroth's Manual on the Library of Congress Classification." *International Classification* 7, no. 3 (1980):126-30.

Putnam, Herbert. "Manual: Constitution, Organization, Methods, Etc." In *Report of the Librarian of Congress for the Fiscal Year Ending June 30, 1901*. Washington, DC: Government Printing Office, 1901.

Scott, Edith. "J. C. M. Hanson and His Contribution to Twentieth Century Cataloging." Ph.D. diss., University of Chicago, 1970, 177-228.

Scott, Mona L., and Christine E. Alvey. *Conversion Tables: LC-Dewey, Dewey-LC*. Englewood, CO: Libraries Unlimited, 1993.

Smither, Reginald Ernest. "Library of Congress Classification." *Library World* 16 (November 1913):130-36.

Spofford, Ainsworth Rand. *A Book for All Readers: Designed As an Aid to the Collection, Use and Preservation of Books and the Formulation of Public and Private Libraries*. 3rd ed., rev. New York: Putnam, 1909, 362-72.

Studwell, William E. "What's the Number? An Unofficial and Unabashed Guide to the Library of Congress Classification for the Social Sciences." *Behavioral & Social Sciences Librarian* 13, no. 1 (1994):39-48.

United States Armed Forces Medical Library. *Classification: Medicine. Preclinical Sciences: QS-QZ, Medicine and Related Subjects: W*. 1st ed. Washington, DC: Government Printing Office, 1951.

USMARC Format for Bibliographic Data, Including Guidelines for Content Designation. Prepared by Network Development and MARC Standards Office. 1994 ed. Washington, DC: Cataloging Distribution Service, Library of Congress, 1994- .

USMARC Format for Classification Data, Including Guidelines for Content Designation. Prepared by Network Development and MARC Standards Office. Washington, DC: Cataloging Distribution Service, Library of Congress, 1991.

Williamson, Nancy J. "The Library of Congress Classification: Problems and Prospects in Online Retrieval." *International Cataloguing* 15 (October 1986):45-48.

Williamson, Nancy J. "The Library of Congress Classification and the Computer: Research in Progress." *International Cataloguing and Bibliographic Control* 18 (January 1989):8-12.

Wynar, Bohdan S. *Introduction to Cataloging and Classification.* 8th ed. Prepared by Arlene Taylor. Englewood, CO: Libraries Unlimited, 1992.

Index